T0342574

THE MONEY DOCTORS FROM JAPAN

Finance,
Imperialism,
and the Building of
the Yen Bloc,
1895–1937

Harvard East Asian Monographs 339

THE MONEY DOCTORS FROM JAPAN

Finance, Imperialism, and the Building of the Yen Bloc, 1895–1937

Michael Schiltz

Published by the Harvard University Asia Center
and distributed by Harvard University Press
Cambridge (Massachusetts) and London, 2012

Printed in the United States of America

The Harvard University Asia Center publishes a monograph series and, in coordination with the Fairbank Center for Chinese Studies, the Korea Institute, the Reischauer Institute of Japanese Studies, and other faculties and institutes, administers research projects designed to further scholarly understanding of China, Japan, Vietnam, Korea, and other Asian countries. The Center also sponsors projects addressing multidisciplinary and regional issues in Asia.

Library of Congress Cataloging-in-Publication Data

Schiltz, Michael, 1972–
    The money doctors from Japan : finance, imperialism, and the building of the yen bloc, 1895–1937 / Michael Schiltz.
        p. cm. -- (Harvard East Asian monographs ; 339)
    Includes bibliographical references and index.
    ISBN 978-0-674-06249-8 (hbk. : alk. paper) 1. Finance--Japan--History--20th century. 2. Monetary policy--Japan--History--20th century. 3. Foreign exchange--Political aspects--Japan--History--20th century. 4. Yen, Japanese--History--20th century. 5. Japan--Territorial expansion--History--20th century. I. Title.
    HG187.J3S35 2012
    332'.042095209041--dc23

                                                                                    2012010745

Index by David De Cooman

♾ Printed on acid-free paper

Last figure below indicates year of this printing

22 21 20 19 18 17 16 15 14 13 12

To Mikiko,

and our son, Yukinari

Acknowledgments

I remember very well the circumstances in which this project was conceived. I was in Vienna with my wife to attend the 2004 conference of the European Association of Japanese Studies (EAJS). Those were exciting days, if one may say so, for the small group of international researchers in Japanese financial history. My good friend Simon James Bytheway had just published his research on the role of foreign capital in Japan's development before World War II; another good friend and a marvelous colleague, Mark Metzler, had almost completed his monograph on the crisis of liberalism in prewar Japan. There was more to come: John Sagers's book about the construction of a modern market economy in nineteenth-century Japan was about to be published; and I knew that Richard Smethurst, unfortunately not with us in Vienna, would soon finish a study of the life and times of Takahashi Korekiyo, "Japan's Keynes."

Still in the process of exploring the field of Japanese financial history, and especially interested in colonialism and empire, I inquired what the little group—already a close-knit group of dear friends, completely unaffected by competition or greed (a rare thing in academia, I am inclined to believe)—would think of a larger work documenting Japanese colonial finance, more specifically attempts at monetary and financial reform at the early stage of establishing gold-exchange standards in several countries or regions in Northeast Asia. The reaction was enthusiastic and encouraging. Simon, friendly as always, urged me to take this project forward. Mark told me he had wanted to start a similar project himself, but then had abandoned the idea for a host of reasons. The energetic Katalin Ferber never tired of insisting on the importance of my research, and the need to "persist" (*ganbaru*) until it would be finished. If this book is in any way considered successful, it is as much to their credit as it is to mine.

There have been many people along the road who contributed more than a little to the book's completion. In Japan, I especially thank Nishibe Makoto and his great group of students at Hokkaido University. Discussions with Makoto always produced insights that added to my argument. I greatly thank him for the time he took to examine the book's theoretical foundations, the theoretical implications of much historiographical fact-finding, and, of course, the friendship that is the most pleasant result of our collaboration, be it face-to-face or online. At Kansai University, Takaya Sadayoshi was always ready to discuss the larger macroeconomic issues confronting Japanese policy makers at the time, and to speculate on how contemporary policy makers would deal with the same challenges. Wakatabe Masazumi of Waseda University, whom I met later, gave very important feedback on the chapter on Korea; I am forever grateful for the time he took for discussions, including about my obstinate interest in Japan during the Great Depression. I thank Yasutomi Ayumu, for sharing his intricate knowledge of Manchurian finance; and Ishii Kanji, for being willing to read some of my earlier papers. At the Bank of Japan, Ōmiya Hitoshi must be given due credit for his assistance when consulting the bank's rich archives.

In North America, too, many people tirelessly assisted me in pursuing my research goals. Of particular importance to the project was a longer research stay at the Kluge Center of the Library of Congress, generously sponsored by Mr. John Kluge. Dr. Carolyn Brown, Mary-Lou Reker, and JoAnne Kitching created circumstances that would make any other researcher envious. The staff of the Library's Asian Division was equally supportive. Itō Eiichi deserves special mention. He did much more than ensure I saw the materials I asked for; on several occasions, he provided resources or information that I had not thought of, sometimes of great importance to my research. Eiichi, you are definitely the reference librarian who made this book into what it finally became. Thank you, also, for ongoing communication and collaboration on Zotero. I benefited from sharing thoughts with several colleagues at the Kluge Center: Stephen Stathis, Suk-Young Kim, Tobie Meyer-Fong, Fabrizio De Francesco, and especially Herman and Monique Van der Wee. Dan "the man" Chudnov of the Library's Office of Strategic Initiatives was a great partner for discussing "things Japanese" and for enjoying good Japanese food and *sake*. Ed Miller challenged many of my ideas about the nature of the prewar U.S.-Japan conflict of interests, for which I am very grateful. I hope he will enjoy reading this book as much as I enjoyed reading his. Eric Helleiner showed his support for this project and urged me to rethink several of my earlier findings about monetary reforms in Korea; it was refreshing to receive such advanced remarks and criticisms. My stay in Washington, DC, was important for more than just this project: I thank Dan Cohen and his colleagues at George Mason University's Center for History and New Media for their refreshing ideas about scholarship in the digital era and their dedication to sharing knowledge online.

Back home in Belgium, I found the freedom to concentrate on studying my sources and turning them into a monograph, thanks to a Starting Grant of the European Research Council; its generous funding made it possible to develop a research question that is at once multifaceted and complex. I have gratefully used the opportunity to develop my project at its own pace. In Leuven, Willy Vande Walle never complained about the time I dedicated to this project. Kim Oosterlinck of the University of Brussels proved a great networker for the study of financial history in Belgium, and a good friend for discussions. Hans Coppens and Fred Truyen always gave friendly and professional assistance when it came to questions regarding carrying out research online or sharing research results digitally. Their insight into how digital tools can transform the nature of scholarship have considerably shaped the way I chose to approach my source material and compose the story in the following chapters. As any researcher knows, there are many people along the road who lay important bricks for a smooth research infrastructure. Christian Loos is thanked for the unsurpassable logo-design for my current ERC Starting Grant project, and Stijn Delauré and Patricia Pardon for figuring out the management of European research projects. The University of Leuven's friendly interlibrary loan staff generously helped find much needed resources. Paul Arblaster, my copyeditor, greatly enhanced the readability of my book manuscript and made important contributions to the final version of the book. At the Harvard University Asia Center, William Hammell deserves credit for friendly advice with regard to manuscript preparation. Obviously, responsibility for all remaining errors is my own.

Contents

Map, Tables, and Figures

Map

Tables

Figures
(gallery follows page 120)

Preface

Permit me to issue and control the money of a nation, and I care not who makes its laws.
—Attributed to Meyer Anselm Rothschild

Whoever controls the volume of money in any country is absolute master of all industry
and commerce.   —James A. Garfield

A well-known passage from John Maynard Keynes contains many useful indicators for students of economic history:

Lenin is said to have declared that the best way to destroy the capitalist system was to debauch the currency. By a continuing process of inflation, governments can confiscate, secretly and unobserved, an important part of the wealth of their citizens. By this method they not only confiscate, but they confiscate *arbitrarily*; and, while the process impoverishes many, it actually enriches some. The sight of this arbitrary rearrangement of riches strikes not only at security but [also] at confidence in the equity of the existing distribution of wealth. [. . .] Lenin was certainly right. There is no subtler, no surer means of overturning the existing basis of society than to debauch the currency. The process engages all the hidden forces of economic law on the side of destruction, and does it in a manner which not one man in a million is able to diagnose.[1]

Although Lenin is now known never to have made such a statement,[2] Keynes here correctly indicates the profoundly political nature

---

1. Keynes, *Economic Consequences of the Peace*, 134; italics in the original.
2. Fetter, "Lenin, Keynes, and Inflation."

of money and currency (its relationship with "political space," in the words of Eric Helleiner) and the sociopolitical consequences of controlling money issuance. In a subtle and poignant way, he interprets the latter as no less than the precarious difference between discipline and destruction. As a means of creating stability, currencies and monetary policies have been powerful tools for maintaining social order in capitalist society. Conversely, their equal potential to destabilize has made them important ingredients in the recipes of leftist revolutionaries and saboteurs—as in the infamous Operation Bernhard, for instance, but also in American efforts, from the outset of the Pacific War, to circulate counterfeit Japanese war notes.[3]

This book, although not interested in the problem of inflation per se, shares Keynes's conviction. It explores the degree to which Japanese policy makers in the pre–World War II period not only were aware of both the disciplinary and the destructive characteristics of national currencies, but also actively sought to employ those insights when establishing gold-exchange standards in Japan's colonies (Taiwan and Korea) and, later, a yen bloc in regions and countries in Japan's sphere of influence (such as Manchuria). It addresses what I at several points have dubbed "currency wars," or the use of currency in the context of expansionist endeavor. Much has been written about the military aspects of Japanese expansionism. Students of prewar Japanese history are furthermore acquainted with more informal elements in Japanese empire building, such as the South-Manchurian Railway Company, colonial education, and propaganda. Yet the role of monetary and financial matters in the project of "total empire" remains conspicuously unexamined. This omission may have to do with the technicalities of finance and money, but it remains that contemporary Japanese insistence on monetary reforms sharply contrasts with the minimal scholarly attention the matter has received.

I am aware that databases rarely make it into footnotes, but in this book I want to make an exception, and even insert a few of them into

---

3. Operation Bernhard was a German plan devised during World War II to destabilize the British economy by flooding the country with forged Bank of England £5, £10, £20, and £50 notes. It has recently become more widely known through fictionalization in the Oscar-winning Austrian movie *Die Fälscher* (The Counterfeiters; 2007).

this preface. The findings as they are presented here would not have been possible were it not for some Japanese databases that can be found online and that can be accessed without cumbersome login procedures. I particularly profited from the excellent "Prewar Days Newspaper Economic Article Database" in the Kobe University Digital Archive (www.lib.kobe-u.ac.jp/sinbun/index.html), which contains the full text of numerous newspaper articles published between the late Meiji period and 1945. I learned that this database makes it possible to reconstruct the lively macroeconomic debates in the prewar period; any project attempting to do so without having a comparable database available would be an extremely time-consuming effort. The Japan Center for Asian Historical Records (JACAR, www.jacar.go.jp) proved extremely useful when reconstructing political and economic circumstances in the colonies. I am convinced other researchers too have found these databases among their most accessed websites, and I therefore gratefully acknowledge both.

This being said, I also feel compelled to insert a disclaimer: throughout the whole project that lies at the heart of this book, I have often been humbled by the advanced state of the field of financial history within Japan proper. Although still a very new field in the West, it is not uncommon to find financial history as part of the undergraduate curriculum in Japanese economics departments. Consequently, there are more professorships, more secondary publications, and more documentation of the field (official banking histories, biographies of core policy makers, and so on) than one finds in the United States or Europe. In preparing this manuscript, I have attempted to be as complete as possible, but I realize that it is hard to convey to the non-Japanese reader the richness and complexity of the field as it exists in Japan. Nevertheless, I hope to spur further interest in and research into the financial history of a country that still has a remarkable standing in the twenty-first century.

A Note on Sources and Conventions

The focus of this book is a number of Japanese attempts to establish gold-exchange standards and later a "yen bloc" in several countries in its immediate sphere of influence, reconstructed mostly from primary and secondary sources in Japanese. Among my preferred sources are the historical data, published in bilingual tables, of the Japan Statistical Association or Nihon tōkei kyōkai; the *Economic Statistics of Japan's Former Colonies: Estimates and Analysis*, published by Mizoguchi Toshiyuki and Umemura Mataji in 1988; the detailed and largely reliable surveys of the colonies (especially Korea); and the many autobiographies, memoirs, and diaries written or published by key policy makers in colonial finance. Among secondary works, the books (and papers) of both Namikata Shōichi and Shibata Yoshimasa were invaluable aids when trying to look beyond easy explanations of the statistics at hand.

As indicated above, I consider it useful to make explicit reference to those Japanese databases that are freely available online. Items in the database of the Japan Center for Asian Historical Records are marked as JACAR, together with the relevant reference code. Newspaper clippings found in the "Prewar Days Newspaper Economic Article Database" at Kobe University are marked as KUDA, together with the identification code of the clipping in the database. Newspaper titles are abbreviated as in the table below; the date of publication is taken in the format used by KUDA, i.e., yyyy/mm/dd. I encourage interested readers to take a look at these primary materials. Names of newspapers are abbreviated as follows:

Chūgai shōgyō shinpō	CSS
Fukuoka Nichinichi shinbun	FNN
Jiji shinpō	JJS
Keijō nippō	KJN
Kokumin shinbun	KMS
Kōbe shinbun	KSB
Kōbe yūshin nippō	KYN
Manshū Nichinichi shinbun	MNNS
Manshū nippō	MNP
Ōsaka Asahi shinbun	OAS
Ōsaka Jiji shinpō	OJJS
Ōsaka Mainichi shinbun	OMS
Taiwan Nichinichi shinpō	TNN
Tōkyō Asahi shinbun	TAS

Monetary figures are mostly presented in Japanese yen, as this was—to state the obvious—the most important currency within the prewar Japanese empire. In the text, Japanese yen are indicated by the symbol

¥; \$ stands for US dollars; £ for pounds sterling. When it is necessary to refer to amounts of note issue, exchange rates, and the like, I sometimes refer to the indigenous currency. With regard to the value of the yen, we can be brief: under the gold standard, that is, when "pegged to gold," it was worth 49 to 50 cents in the period between 1899 and 1931 (thus, as a rule of thumb, \$1 = ¥2; for convenience, one may also reckon £1 = ¥10). When Finance Minister Takahashi Korekiyo took Japan off gold in 1931, the value of the yen plummeted: it fell as low as 20 cents in 1932–1933, then climbed to an average of 25.2 cents (late 1933) and 29.5 cents (1934), and stabilized at 28.3 cents until 1939; after that it was devalued to 23.437 cents.[4] It is difficult to estimate the yen's value after July 1941, when there was no longer an organized exchange market, but it is beyond doubt that its value stood very low, possibly around 11 or 12 cents or less, by Ed Miller's estimate. The values of the indigenous currencies of those countries in which Japan established gold-exchange standards are given in the respective chapters. In order to grasp the relative significance of yen amounts given in the text, the reader may multiply the amount by a factor of one thousand.

A last issue concerns linguistic conventions. For romanization of Japanese terms, I have used the revised Hepburn system: this mainly means that I have not rendered *n* into *m* before labial consonants, but stuck to *n* instead (thus *Asahi shinbun* rather than *Asahi shimbun*). Names familiar to English-speaking readers are presented "as known"; so "Tokyo" is used, rather than the linguistically more correct "Tōkyō." Names of Japanese people are given in the Japanese order (family name followed by given name, e.g.: Megata Tanetarō), unless bibliographic references are being given to works in the English language in which the name appears in the Western order.

Sometimes the readings of Japanese names are various: Megata Tanetarō, for example, is sometimes referred to as Mekata Tanetarō or Megata Jutarō. I chose to include the reading that is most common in Japanese sources. Korean terms and names are transcribed according to the McCune-Reischauer system of romanization; Chinese terms and names are transcribed using *pinyin*, but with tonal marks omitted. In both cases, however, I again make an exception for bibliographic ref-

---

4. Compare Nihon ginkō tōkeikyoku, ed., *Meiji ikō honpō shuyō keizai tōkei*, 318ff.

erences to works in the English language in which names appear differently, or when the author himself prefers a different transcription. Thus I refer to 涂照彦 as Twu Jaw-Yann.

Names of banks and institutions are abbreviated as follows:

Chōsen ginkō (Bank of Chosen)	BOC
Minami Manshū tetsudō (South Manchurian Railway Company)	SMRC
Nihon ginkō (Bank of Japan)	BOJ
Nihon kōgyō ginkō (Japan Industrial Bank)	JIB
Taiwan ginkō (Bank of Taiwan)	BOT
Yokohama shōkin ginkō (Yokohama Specie Bank)	YSB

THE MONEY DOCTORS FROM JAPAN

Finance,
Imperialism,
and the Building of
the Yen Bloc,
1895–1937

INTRODUCTION

The War of the Words

[Ishii Kikujirō] made . . . a suggestion that there should be a Monroe doctrine for the Far East. And I told him that there seemed to be a misconception as to the underlying principle of the Monroe doctrine; that it was not an expression of primacy or paramount interest by the United States in its relation to other American republics; that its purpose was to prevent foreign powers from interfering with the separate rights of any nation in this hemisphere, and that the whole aim was to preserve to each republic the power of self-development.

—Robert Lansing

Viscount Ishii seems to have been essentially correct when in 1917, in his efforts to secure American recognition for Japan's special position in Manchuria, he pointed out the analogy of the situation in the Far East to the relationship between America and Mexico, and made the first more or less official mention of an "Asiatic Monroe Doctrine."

—Takagi Yasaka

In our own time, foreign financial consultants negotiating debt services for countries that rely on wealth from abroad continue to define those countries' economic outlooks and trajectories of development. In an East Asian example, South Korea's spectacular strategy of economic growth since World War II cannot be seen apart from Federal Reserve advisory missions,[1] guidance by the International Monetary Fund (IMF),

---

EPIGRAPHS. Secretary of State Robert Lansing, testifying before the Senate Committee in Foreign Relations in 1919, cited in C. W. Young, *Japan's Special Position in Manchuria*, 338–39; Takagi, "World Peace Machinery and the Asia Monroe Doctrine," 948–49.

1. For a rare case study, see Alacevich and Asso, "Money Doctoring after World War II."

and almost continual IMF standby program support after 1965. Unfortunately, monetary advice can be much less successful. In an attempt to lessen the effects of the Asian crisis of 1997—itself often explained as the result of U.S. resistance to the establishment of an Asian Monetary Fund, or AMF—the IMF again provided guidance, this time for measures aimed at South Korea's financial liberalization. This effort largely failed, partly because of the rapidity with which the IMF sought to push its agenda.[2] Supervisory agencies, established at the IMF's request, were institutionally constrained from carrying out proper supervision, and the country became embroiled in a costly bout of financial instability.[3] In such times of crisis, the high risks and high stakes associated with lending and corollary financial reform bring a second and even more important observation to the fore.

Today as in the past, the role and activities of foreign financial consultants remain contentious, as such consultants rarely manage to provide advice free from political interests. Why should financial advisors, administrators, or "money doctors" invest resources and expertise in crisis-ridden foreign nations? The answer is that crisis lending and "money doctoring" may be profitable. The unequal distribution of money, ideas, and economic problems among nations translates into an unequal distribution of possible gains and losses. In the examples mentioned, both the (Japanese) initiative in favor of an AMF and the American rebuttal were fundamentally political events.[4] Foreign financial advice is not by any means a disinterested business—after all, "one cannot stay rich when one's debtor gets poor."[5] International financial advising is fundamentally *interested*, even though its claims and aspirations

---

2. For assessments of this case, see Stiglitz, *Globalization and Its Discontents*, 89ff.; Chung and Eichengreen, *Korean Economy Beyond the Crisis*; Cho, "The Role of Poorly Phased Financial Liberalization in Korea's Financial Crisis."

3. Demetriades, Fattouh, and Shields, "Financial Liberalization and the Evolution of Banking and Financial Risks"; Amess and Demetriades, "Financial Liberalisation and the South Korean Financial Crisis"; Kim and Lee, "Post-Crisis Financial Reform in Korea."

4. Amyx, "Moving Beyond Bilateralism?"; Katada, "Japan and Asian Monetary Regularisation."

5. Flandreau, *Money Doctors*, 5.

may suggest otherwise. One is thus hardly surprised to find that the countries chosen in IMF programs are highly affected by geopolitics.[6]

Marc Flandreau makes this tension between the claim of neutrality and the political surroundings of foreign financial advice the locus of his history of money doctoring: "We [. . .] reach a conclusion which might appear obvious to some: namely that at the very heart of money doctoring is an inseparable combination of economics and politics. The economic dimension defines the structural constraints faced by the various players involved in financial turmoil (range of opportunities, set of eligible policies). The political dimension, on the other hand, shapes the incentives of ailing countries, markets and international lenders."[7] Informed by Flandreau's and others' insights, this book concentrates on a temporally and geographically well-defined case of foreign financial advising: the activities of Japanese government officials, mostly from the Ministry of Finance, in different countries and regions in Northeast Asia between 1895 and 1937. More specifically, it investigates the role of the following financial advisors or money doctors: Gotō Shinpei (in Taiwan), Megata Tanetarō (in Korea), Nishihara Kamezō (in China), and Nangō Tatsune (in Manchuria).

I feel it important to stress that these cases are in some ways sui generis, as they concern monetary advice to countries under Japanese dominion, or at least in Japan's direct sphere of influence. Tokyo was deeply politically invested and made no secret of its political interests. Prewar attempts to establish a "yen bloc" and a more or less self-sufficient Asian economic zone contrast sharply with the internationalist agenda of previous and later money doctors; in many ways, yen diplomacy was a reaction *against* internationalism. The differences between the Japanese case and more traditional money doctoring efforts may aid us in understanding the complex relationships between political aims and economic profitability, because, in the Japanese case, the two were so bound up with one another. Historical research has yet to uncover another instance of money doctoring that was so patently politically or so strategically designed and articulated.

---

6. Barro and Lee, "IMF Programs."
7. Flandreau, *Money Doctors*, 5.

The History of Money Doctoring

Who or what are money doctors? Nowadays the term refers, more often than not, to institutions rather than to individual persons; and these bodies do not perform exclusively technocratic roles and missions, even if they prefer to portray themselves as such actors. Throughout the history of international financial advising, money doctors hung and still hang their respective hats in many agencies, public and private.[8]

The proverbial forefather of money doctoring is the French economist Jean-Gustave Courcelle-Seneuil, who fled France after the coup of Napoleon III for South America, where he held the professorship of political economy at the National Institute of Santiago, Chile, from 1853 to 1863. His career ran counter to a central pattern of later money doctors: whereas they all came from (relatively) stable countries to the aid of countries in turmoil, he went from a disrupted France to a country in relative tranquility—and returned to France in 1863, when the political situation there seemed to have calmed down. Later he was made a councilor of state, and in 1882 he was elected a member of the Académie des Sciences Morales et Politiques. Courcelle-Seneuil had, however, blazed trails for Western European advisors (central bankers, government officials, and academics) who in the decades to come would operate in the crisis-ridden countries on the periphery of late nineteenth- and twentieth-century industrialization and the gold-exchange standard. Among them would be Charles Rist, the famous interwar French money doctor; Jean Monnet; Montagu Norman of the Bank of England; and the highly controversial Hjalmar Schacht, governor of the Reichsbank in Hitler's Germany, and later economic and financial advisor to several developing countries.[9]

The heyday of money doctoring coincided with the early twentieth-century shift of geopolitical paramountcy from Great Britain to the United States and the ascendancy of New York as the world's international financial hub. In the United States, this shift was regarded as not just another transformation of the international power structure but as a watershed, a paradigmatic event. Sources at the time—scholars, journalists, economists, and policy makers—were inclined to character-

---

8. With a tip of the hat to Schuker, "Money Doctors between the Wars," 52.
9. For an overview of their relationships, see ibid.

ize this period as a break with the power-dominated discourses of a European-led world order and the inauguration of an era defined by the possibilities of free trade and international cooperation.

It is illuminating to consider these claims in the wider context of the history of technology and communications. For the United States, the beginning of the twentieth century was marked by a bureaucratic revolution in the organization of the state and corporations; the rise of the vocabulary of professionalism; and the snowballing effects of new means of transportation and communication. Amid these changes, the growth of global commerce begun in the 1870s and the rising importance of international financial transactions defined the rhetorical parameters within which U.S. officials would develop the country's foreign policy.

As Emily Rosenberg has demonstrated, the development of this foreign policy raised two hotly contested and related questions that also dominated domestic politics at the time: which monetary standard to adopt (gold versus bimetallism), and how assertive the United States should be in the international arena.[10] During the elections of 1896, these controversies reached their boiling point.[11] On one side were the proponents of bimetallism. Finding their support mainly in the ethical-religious discourses of Christianity or socialist radicalism, they were deeply distrustful of money and of the newly developing semantics of capitalism and professionalism. For them, money was a destructive force of greed, especially when it developed into professions such as lending at interest (usury). They regarded with abhorrence liberalism's view that the search for private gain was a building block of the social order, charging instead that it threatened social cohesion. They (correctly) feared that the gold standard would mainly benefit the moneylenders and international financiers and therefore advocated the coinage of silver under a bimetallist standard in order to create an adequate circulating medium for the common people.[12] Internationally, they argued, it would be a

---

10. Rosenberg, *Financial Missionaries to the World*, 4.

11. For a contemporary overview of the debate, see White, *Silver and Gold*.

12. This echoes a concern plaguing all metallic currency systems—namely the problem of supplying enough coins of small denomination, something inherently difficult due to the costs of metal and of striking coins—coupled with the problems of regular

grave mistake to abandon silver, as the nation's main trading partners were eventually to be found in the developing silver-standard countries of Latin America and Asia. It was therefore in the United States' interest to remain content with its current nondominant mercantile role in international matters.

On the other side, the advocates of the gold standard defined policy realities very differently. In their discourse, which Rosenberg identifies as "professional-managerial,"[13] the international dimension of a monetary standard was of primary importance. Economists and financiers looked at the industrialized powers of Western Europe and felt that the United States should emulate them, joining their ranks and playing a leading role in administering international finance. By their reasoning, domestic concerns for the common people were exaggerated by the Silverites with their "Free Silver" ideology; instead, a centralized yet flexible international order, run by experts, was fundamental to an efficient and scientific modern society.[14] They too perceived a fundamentally moral dimension to money and commerce. Silver, they stressed, was typically the metal of countries that were backward and uncivilized, characterized by social and economic disorder. Gold was the metal of the strong and advanced nations, and the gold standard would instill discipline and responsibility. Symbolizing self-restraint, it guaranteed the accumulation of wealth through thrift and delayed gratification, and thus combated the "feminine" traits of profligacy and weakness.

The proponents of gold saw in this effect a missionary importance and gold's true international appeal. If the developing countries of Latin America and Asia were to be America's main trading partners, the United States had to reform them and teach them the virtues of regularity and sound debt servicing, if only because the latter, coupled with the stability of the gold price at the time, would guarantee a return on investments by American creditors (inflationary silver, on the other hand, would scare investors away). The developing world could earn its

---

shortages and depreciation. Eventually, economists solved the problem by introducing fiat money. See, in this context, Sargent and Velde, *The Big Problem of Small Change*.

13. Rosenberg, *Financial Missionaries to the World*, 6.

14. This echoes the often difficult relationship of the money doctors to democracy. Rist's famous saying that "democracy killed the gold standard" is emblematic. See also Pauly, *Who Elected the Bankers?*

share in prosperity and progress, provided it was converted to the principles of market capitalism and a corollary ethics of responsibility and self-determination. The contemporary observer will be struck by a definitional tension between democracy and entrepreneurialism on the one hand, and capitalism and imperialism on the other. Yet this vision of a global world governed by market discipline and free exchange united late nineteenth-century American economists, technocrats, government officials, and business managers alike.

The Birth of a Financial Elite and the Gold-Exchange Standard

Emerging victorious from the 1896 elections, the technocrats at once seized the opportunity to turn their vision into reality. Under the McKinley and Theodore Roosevelt administrations, American policy makers embarked on a political and ideological journey that would not only be of formidable importance for the countries that were to be reformed but would also be meticulously reflected in the policies of its later rival, Japan, who would turn the struggle for monetary and financial gain into a military conflict, with disastrous consequences. Rosenberg sums up the objectives of the American professional elite: "The policies devised and implemented by this first generation of experts in foreign currency reform sought to bring small nations in which the United States had an interest onto a gold-standard, run by a central bank, with gold funds deposited in New York and coinage denominated in U.S. money. The goal behind spreading this Americanized gold-exchange standard was not only to simplify international transactions, thereby facilitating trade and investment, but to create a gold-backed dollar bloc, centered in New York, to rival the gold-backed pound sterling that dominated international trade."[15] This practice formally consolidated the practice of international financial advising and turned it into a profession of its own. From roughly 1896 until well into the first half of the twentieth century, the United States sought to establish an army of bankers, officials, and academics who were to be invited abroad in order to assist in currency reform, oversee the establishment of institutions (not least a central bank) crucial to their vision

---

15. Rosenberg, *Financial Missionaries to the World*, 5.

of gold and free exchange,[16] and provide legitimacy for policies that would otherwise be hard to enforce. These advisors were in the very forefront of "dollar diplomacy"—a doctrine of international relations that echoed the ideals of the Open Door policy of President Monroe and that sought to avoid costly military intervention and even the outward appearance of direct political pressure, yet nonetheless intended to bind the fate of other countries to that of the United States by monetary and financial means, particularly through the extension of loans and the granting of economic agreements. (This did not preclude the dispatching of marines in "times of emergency.")[17]

The tool used to achieve the aim described was the establishment of so-called gold-exchange standards.[18] Gold-exchange standards differed essentially from classic gold standards in that the currency of a country was not expressed in (quantities of) gold, but in foreign exchange, for instance in pounds sterling, French francs, U.S. dollars or another stable currency that was based directly on a gold reserve. Backing currency with a foreign-exchange reserve has implications that far exceed that of a multi-level international gold-standard system.[19] The gold-exchange standard re-imports the concept of national boundaries and territoriality through its concern with the demand and supply of national currencies (instead of bullion, which is obviously devoid of territorial conno-

---

16. Characteristically, Charles Conant, one of the crucial figures in formulating policy in the early days of dollar diplomacy, wrote the influential *History of Banks of Issue.*

17. For an excellent overview of money doctoring activities in Latin America, see Drake, *Money Doctors, Foreign Debts, and Economic Reforms;* on dollar diplomacy, see Rosenberg, *Financial Missionaries to the World.*

18. For a good discussion, see Conant, "The Gold Exchange Standard in the Light of Experience." Interestingly, this was also the topic of J. M. Keynes's first study, *Indian Currency and Finance.*

19. Metzler, *Lever of Empire,* 36. Compare also: "What we could call first-order money in this system—gold—was leveraged into a larger supply of gold-based national monies, such as the British pound—'second-order' money. This second-order money in turn constituted the monetary base for banks who leveraged it into a much greater volume of money by making loans and creating bank deposits—'third-order' money. In a like way, gold-exchange standards in peripheral countries pyramided gold-based foreign exchange money such as the British pound into third-order or fourth-order money. While such a description is too simple and schematic to capture the complexity of many actual monetary arrangements, it suggests the leveraged, multi-layered structure of the international gold-standard system" (37).

tations). As Feliks Mlynarski noted in the context of the gold-exchange standard of the 1920s, the accumulation of foreign-exchange reserves instead of gold turned liquidity into an immediate concern of the financial authorities of the center countries. Ultimately, the volume of claims on the reserve-currency country (Great-Britain, the United States, and the like) was proportional to doubts about that country's central bank's ability to convert its currency into the "hard metal" gold: "The banks which have adopted the gold exchange standard will become more and more dependent on foreign reserves, and the banks which play the part of gold centers will grow more and more dependent on deposits belonging to foreign banks. Should this system last for a considerable time the gold centers may fall into the danger of an excessive dependence on the banks which accumulate foreign exchange reserves and vice versa the banks which apply the gold exchange standard may fall into an excessive dependence on the gold centers. The latter may be threatened with difficulties in exercising their rights to receive gold, whilst the former may incur the risk of great disturbances in their credit structure in the case of a sudden outflow of reserve deposits."[20] Although the "Mlynarski dilemma" did never pose itself as such in the pre–World War I era (not least because the peripheral countries did not have the political sway to demand the conversion of their foreign-exchange reserves), it is nevertheless a remarkable characteristic of the gold-exchange standard. It upsets the idea of an indiscriminate (apolitical) mechanism restoring international trade imbalances by means of "anonymous gold," as in the idealized view of the traditional gold standard. It is unfortunate that quite a few authors have regarded the gold-exchange standard as an anomaly, or at best a transitory situation not qualifying as a standard in its own right.[21]

---

20. Mlynarski, *Gold and Central Banks*, 89.

21. Vissering, *The Netherlands East Indies and the Gold-Exchange Standard*; this view is also adopted by Laughlin, "The Gold-Exchange Standard," esp. 663. In line with the geopolitical situation at the time, a host of French authors viewed the gold-exchange standard as a specifically British institution, and tended to think of it as a device for maintaining and extending London's international financial power. Japanese views of their experience with the gold-exchange standard have been influenced by these French authors. See in particular Matsuoka, *Kin kawase hon'isei no kenkyū*.

So, how were gold-exchange standards set up? The prerequisite to the system is the creation of an exchange fund held abroad. In essence, colonies or semi-sovereign countries were provided with a gold fund (basically a loan), that was kept in one of the world's financial centers, partly in the currency of that nation, and partly in money denominated in the currency of the country given the fund. This device produces a more complicated version of the "hydraulic gold-standard machine" we know as Hume's price-specie-flow mechanism. In order to keep the currency at a certain rate against, say, the pound or dollar, the host country first agreed to use this fund to sell *without limit* demand drafts on London (or New York, as the case might be) on the domestic market at a price slightly under the exchange rate, and coinciding with what was perceived to be the supposed gold export point in the host country. As a result, a possible further lowering of the exchange rate beyond the supposed gold export point would be offset through a contraction of the currency supply: these demand drafts would be paid in the borrower's currency, thereby contracting its supply and raising its value. At the same time, fears of a fall in the exchange rate were offset by the very provision to sell without limit. Second, the lending government would sell, again *without limit*, demand drafts on the borrowing country at a price slightly higher than the exchange rate. Thus, the tendency for a possible further increase in the price of the borrower's currency would be reversed by expanding its supply, thereby making it cheaper vis-à-vis domestic commodities.[22]

This is only one example of the possible technical organization of monetary leverage. There was also an unmistakably political-economical dimension, which goes much further than simply acknowledging the centrality of the lending country's position in the world's monetary geography. It did that too, but, as such, transformed and enhanced the political and economic role of the lending country. As we will see, such policies did so directly, for instance by virtually wiping out exchange costs between the borrowing and lending country.

------

22. Following Laughlin, "The Gold-Exchange Standard," 648–49. Again, this is the working of the gold-exchange standard in theory; in practice, countries deviated from provisions such as that requiring them to sell demand drafts without limit, as legislation regarding the Indian case makes clear. In general, the gold-exchange standard is thought to have existed in its purest form in the Philippines (650ff.).

But these policies also operated indirectly (in ways more difficult to measure and to assess), through the principle of money creation. By endorsing the center-periphery distinction offered by (Japanese) authorities, borrowing countries also enabled the (Japanese) state to leverage its own money and credit creating power, and to buffer its home (*naichi*) system from shocks originating in the surrounding world market. Equally important but often overlooked were the seigniorage benefits accruing to Japanese private and semi-official banks by means of accounts held in colonial currency and foreign exchange in the many overseas (colonial) branches. What was at work here was thus, in Ben Bernanke's words, a "financial accelerator": money held in the accounts administered by Japanese banks could be put to use for further colonial investment and saving, or eventually employed for the continuing appropriation of foreign land, workforces, and other resources. The endorsement of the Japanese yen as the dominant currency in a sphere of wider East Asian economic interdependencies basically amounted to a zero-interest loan *extended by the peripheral countries to the central country* within the yen's sphere of influence. The "peripheral" countries were, in that case, paying for their own subordination and colonization— a remarkable outcome of monetary and financial internationalization.

Early House Calls of American Money Doctors

Puerto Rico was the U.S. money doctors' first patient. It was firmly on the silver standard, so policy makers were immediately confronted with the problems of implementing the "cure" of establishing a gold-exchange standard in a silver-standard area. That the gold-exchange standard was to be the cure appeared obvious to the U.S. administration. According to the prophets of gold, such a currency system would attract foreign capital and stimulate material progress; and it would inevitably bring with it an ethos of thrift and sound debt servicing, needed to sustain development. Yet policy makers wondered: Would currency reform invite instability? And would economic dislocation lead to popular resistance to American policies? As it happened, the policy met with little resistance, and in a matter of months the former Spanish coinage had disappeared from circulation.

Money doctors were now convinced that their diagnoses and remedies would also work in other, sometimes very different, parts of the world. The Philippines, the second Spanish colony to be taken over by the United States, would also become the blueprint for later U.S. monetary and financial interventionism. Its case posed the problem, similar to Puerto Rico's, of moving a country from a silver standard onto a gold-exchange standard, and thus U.S. reformers did not question the validity of their diagnosis. But the Philippines' economic connections, unlike those of Puerto Rico, were mainly with the silver-standard countries of Asia. Would abandoning silver result in a deteriorating commercial position because the country would no longer be able to use falling silver prices to its advantage? Charles Conant, an ardent defender of gold, was called upon to provide his expertise. Drawing heavily on the British-led initiative to bring India onto the gold standard, Conant went ahead with his reforms (which Keynes would later refer to as an "almost slavish" imitation, "unworthy of study"),[23] and thus became the founder of the profession of international financial advising in the United States. Later, he would also oversee reform in Panama, where America's commercial interest in the Panama Canal suggested an obvious parallel to British interest in the Suez Canal and Britain's subsequent economic annexation of Egypt.[24]

This episode led to the reorganization of financial advising through the establishment of several formal and informal institutions. Among them, the most important was the three-person Commission on International Exchange convened at the instigation of President Theodore Roosevelt, consisting of Charles Conant, Jeremiah Jenks, and Hugh Hanna. They were entrusted with the task of overseeing the installment of a gold-exchange standard in Mexico. The Mexican dollar was one of the world's main currencies, used for instance in the West's dealings with Asia, so its reform gave rise to even more substantial policy choices.[25] Yet China, where all the Western nations were competing for concessions and access to the markets of East Asia, became the Com-

---

23. Keynes, *Indian Currency and Finance*, 19.

24. For a detailed description of Conant's work in the Philippines and Panama, see Kemmerer, "The Establishment of the Gold Exchange Standard in the Philippines"; Commission on International Exchange, *Report on the Introduction of the Gold-Exchange Standard*, 313–33.

25. Andrew, "The End of the Mexican Dollar." For the Japanese case, see the authoritative Ono, *Kindai Nihon heisei to higashi Ajia ginkaken*.

mission's first test case—and the first time that American and Japanese interests came into conflict.

After the Boxer Rebellion of 1900, an armed popular uprising in reaction to foreign encroachments on Chinese territory, the United States laid down the law. China was forced into signing a treaty with all the major international powers in which it agreed to pay an indemnity for damages incurred during the rebellion. Yet, as had been the case in the negotiations following the first Sino-Japanese War (1894–95), the treaty did not stipulate in which currency the indemnity was to be paid, nor did it indicate whether it was to be paid in gold or in silver. The Chinese had begun to pay the indemnity in silver, but were rebuked for this by the European powers. The United States then attempted to befriend the Chinese government by not joining with the European powers in this matter, but later feared that the Europeans would use the issue as a precedent for declaring China in default and starting military action. Thus Secretary of State John Hay proposed that China, by accepting U.S. financial advisors, had obliged itself to move to gold. Jeremiah Jenks of the Commission on International Exchange was to lead the Americans' visit to China in 1903. Typical of the American approach, Jenks solicited the advice and opinion of his international colleagues; those he met with included the Japanese Minister of Finance, Sakatani Yoshirō (Yoshio), who would later pursue his own agenda for the financial penetration of China.[26] Yet despite careful preparation, the mission was a complete failure. Silver prices were finally rising again after decades of dramatic depreciation, relieving the Qing government of the former pressure of gold payments. Consequently, it lost interest in Jenks's visit, which was seen as simply another foreign plot to extend influence over what was essentially a Chinese policy matter. In the aftermath of the mission, it appeared that Jenks had met only low-level Chinese officials with no substantial authority.[27] In 1905, China would indeed enact a currency reform, but one that was, in effect, a nationalistic reaction to the U.S. proposal.

Although the Commission's adventure in China all but marked the end of government-funded advisors spreading the gold-exchange stan-

---

26. The report of this meeting can be found in Hanna, Conant, and Jenks, *Gold Standard in International Trade*, 30–32.

27. Rosenberg, *Financial Missionaries to the World*, 23.

dard abroad, U.S. interest in financial and economic diplomacy was undiminished. It reached its zenith a decade later, when Edwin Kemmerer, a student of Conant's, would give the profession of foreign financial advice the name by which it is still known.[28] Professor of Economics at Princeton University from 1917 to 1930, Kemmerer is known as the money doctor par excellence, the man who directed many financial reform missions in a large number of developing countries. After receiving his Ph.D. in 1903, he served as financial advisor to the U.S. Philippines commission and as chief of the division of currency of the treasury of the Philippine Islands; he also headed financial commissions to South Africa (1924–25), Poland (1926), and China (1929); served as consultant to the Dawes commission (1925); and co-chaired an economic survey of Turkey (1934). But he was most active in South America, serving as economic advisor or heading financial missions to seven Latin American countries.[29] Famous for staunch commitment to his assignments, he must also be credited for the profession's rather unfortunate inclination to assert its detachment from politics.[30] During an informal address to the American Economic Association (over which he presided) in St. Louis, Missouri, on December 29, 1926, he emphasized "the well founded belief, in many countries, that the United States is not looking for political aggrandizement and is less likely than most great powers to exploit the services of her nationals, who advise other governments, as a means of extending her political power. This consideration is particularly applicable in cases of European countries and the Orient."[31]

Had the United States indeed acted in good faith? And was Kemmerer really unaware of the political dynamics of financial advising? Perhaps the anti-imperialist spirit of his times obliged him to depict American economic diplomacy in these noble terms. Approximately three decades earlier, in 1898, Charles Conant had described what was

---

28. Think, for instance, of the nickname "Dr. Debt" under which Jeffrey Sachs would supervise monetary reform at the end of the twentieth century.

29. Eichengreen, "House Calls of the Money Doctor."

30. For a contemporary example, compare Jeffrey Sachs's remarks about his work in Bolivia: "Much of my work is just sitting quietly in a backroom analyzing data with members of the government." "The Harvard Debt Doctor's Controversial Cure."

31. Kemmerer, "Economic Advisory Work for Governments," 2.

at stake in a more accurate, albeit cynical manner. His essay "The Economic Basis of Imperialism" actually celebrated what would later become known as Lenin and Hobson's critique of imperialism.[32] The advanced nations, so Conant's argument ran, had a "superabundance of loanable capital" that, in an age of growing internationalization, would seek to invest in those nations that had not yet sufficiently industrialized, in its quest for profitable rates of interest.[33] This "is not a matter of sentiment. It is the result of a natural law of economic and race development. The great civilized nations have to-day at their command the means of developing the decadent nations of the world."[34] The United States should not regard this mission as a burden, because it would also be in its own interest. It should embark on "a broad national policy" of conquest for economic profit, which was anyway inevitable. At the heart of this policy was the law of diminishing returns, as expressed by Conant: "capital becomes less productive in earning power [. . .] because less productive use can be found for the excess above a certain limit."[35]

This danger was real: the United States had already started to experience overproduction and consequent declining profits, although not to the degree of the European nations. Abandoning saving, in Conant's view a "socialist" measure, was not something that the "civilized nations" would easily be brought to consider; nor would it be sufficient to create new demands at home for the absorption of capital. So what solution was left? "Aside from the waste of capital in war, which is only one form of consumption, there remains, therefore, as the final resource, the equipment of new countries with the means of production and exchange."[36]

---

32. Conant, "The Economic Basis of Imperialism." For an appreciation of Conant's theories, see also Rosenberg, *Financial Missionaries to the World*, 16.

33. Conant, "The Economic Basis of Imperialism," 334.

34. Ibid., 326. Compare: "The writer is not an advocate of 'imperialism' from sentiment, but does not fear the name if it means only that the United States shall assert their right to free markets in all the old countries which are being opened to the surplus resources of the capitalist countries and thereby given the benefits of modern civilization" (339).

35. Ibid., 334.

36. Ibid., 337.

The Rise of Japan as a Regional Power

At the time Conant wrote this chillingly accurate description of the basis for American economic assertiveness, a country on the far side of the Pacific was reassessing its own role in the dynamics of "economic and race development." After the first Sino-Japanese War, Japan managed to acquire the financial means to move onto the gold standard and stand alongside the great Western powers of the time. In Conant's words, "Japan has already made her entry, almost like Athene full-armed from the brain of Zeus, into the modern industrial world."[37] The surprise expressed by his words reflects just how steep Japan's rise had been.

This well-rehearsed story begins around 1850, with the brusque "opening up" of the country after two-and-a-half centuries of political, economic, and cultural isolation. Internationalization, and more specifically confrontation with the realities of the world economy, turned out to be profoundly destabilizing. This confrontation particularly eroded Japan's monetary system, which despite some remarkably modern traits was built on the premise of the country's closure.[38] Political friction with the Great Powers, revolving around questions of free trade, was followed by creeping inflation and an even more destructive speculation.[39] The most visible result was a large-scale export of Japan's gold reserves. Ill-conceived attempts at financial and monetary reform further deepened the crisis, which would end in the demise of Japan's feudal order and one of the most impressive efforts by a non-Western nation to join the ranks of the modern, militarized, and imperialist West.

For our discussion, the ideological or semantic context of the crisis and consequent reform carries particular relevance. Nowhere else were forced globalization and the traumas consequent on foreign depen-

---

37. Ibid., 338.

38. Metzler, *Lever of Empire*, 15ff.; for an analysis of Japan's gold standard *avant la lettre*, see Nishikawa, "Edo-ki sanka seido no hōga" and "Edo-ki sanka seido."

39. As an intermediate measure, the Meiji government sought to differentiate domestic from international trade by introducing a "trade dollar" or *bōeki-gin* in February 1875. The government failed to have it widely adopted in Asian trade, and the system was discontinued within three years of its inception. Matsukata refers to the Imperial Ordinances instigating the minting of the trade dollar and its suspension in his *Report*, 10–12.

dence as striking as in nineteenth-century Japan. The opening up to the West and the frustrating negotiations about foreign trade had led to the financial and political impasse in the first place. The *bakufu* or shogunate had enjoyed a strictly enforced monopoly on silver and gold mines.[40] Both the *bakufu* and the Meiji government that superseded it were abhorred by the foreign banks opening for business in the port of Yokohama (which the *bakufu* had chosen as the location for dealings with foreign merchants and the business of foreign exchange), rightly regarding foreign banks as a threat to the government's grip on financial matters.[41]

The intrusion of foreign banking institutions had begun in 1863, when the Central Bank of Western India set up in Yokohama, with Charles Rickerby as acting manager. The Chartered Mercantile Bank of India, London and China followed it a month later. Five other banks soon joined their ranks: the Commercial Bank of India (1863); the Bank of Hindustan, China, and Japan (1864); the powerful Oriental Bank Corporation (1864); the Hongkong and Shanghai Banking Corporation (1866); and the French Comptoir d'Escompte de Paris (1867). In terms of assets, these banks represented the epitome of grand modern banking. The Comptoir d'Escompte de Paris alone accounted for approximately 90 million *ryō* 両 (the standard of the Edo trimetallic system). This eclipsed even the mighty merchant houses of Mitsui and Konoike, and the sheer size of the foreign banks contributed to later debates about domestic financial and monetary reform.

The Meiji government also discovered other reasons for fearing foreign encroachment. Experiences with treacherous Western intermediaries had instilled a deep distrust of internationalism; to put it anachronistically, liberalism and openness were perceived as an imperialist threat.[42] The infamous Lay Affair (1870), in which Horatio Nelson Lay, a former member of the British consulate, had deceived the Meiji government about the interest rate on a government loan on the London capi-

---

40. Kobata, *Kahei to kōzan*.
41. Tamaki, *Japanese Banking*, 17–18; Tatewaki, *Zainichi gaikoku ginkōshi*.
42. Gallagher and Robinson, "The Imperialism of Free Trade," 1–15.

tal market, reminded policy makers of the ultimate danger of foreign loans and foreign dependence: economic colonization.[43]

Currency Imperialism

In a cynical twist, Japan's policy makers concluded that the best way to deal with the situation just outlined was by seizing the lash whose strokes they feared. They too would embark on the road of expansionism, seeking to be the equal of the Western powers that had threatened their nation's independence. Military intervention was to be only one pillar of the Japanese colonial empire. Indeed, it was often only the prelude to more pervasive forms of influence and dominion affecting politics, culture, and the economy.

As both the political and cultural dimensions of Japanese imperialism have received considerable attention, and as some issues of economic imperialism have been tackled in other studies,[44] this book turns to a selective set of tactics that have rarely, if ever, been given attention in the West. It concerns a particular case of experimentation with money doctoring that made no attempt to disguise the profoundly political nature of its ambitions. This set of tactics will be referred to as "currency imperialism," as defined by Shibata Yoshimasa:

Currency imperialism is a [set of] policies by means of which a nation uses its own currency for circulation outside its borders or links it [to another currency] in some form; through which it employs such linkage in the settlement of its balance of payments, and through which it economizes with regard to

---

43. Suzuki, *Japanese Government Loan Issues on the London Capital Market.* Lay had signed a loan contract of 1 million pounds sterling for the Japanese government at an annual interest rate of 12 percent and a 10-year term of payment. However, he began selling railway bonds in London at an annual rate of 9 percent with an issue price of 98 percent of the face value. In other words, Lay intended to earn a 3 percent margin from every bond he sold. The Japanese government, becoming mistrustful, consulted the head of the Yokohama branch of the Oriental Bank (a British bank), with the result that the government terminated the contract with Lay and appointed the bank as its representative in London. For a more extensive treatment of the Lay scandal, see Kaida, *Meiji zenki ni okeru Nihon no kokusai hakkō to kokusaishisō,* 91–139. On Lay's activities in China, see Gerson, *Horatio Nelson Lay and Sino-British Relations.*

44. In particular the Japanese version of "railway imperialism" through the South-Manchurian Railway Company. For a very thorough account in English, see Matsusaka, *The Making of Japanese Manchuria.*

the holdings of its own foreign exchange; and by means of which it furthers the investments of its enterprises [in another country], while at all times avoiding risks associated with foreign exchange. Currency imperialism is a powerful means of introducing informal empire and, especially in the case of occupied territories, a tool for enhancing linkages with the mainland. [. . .] It is a means of grasping empire from the perspective of monetary and financial policy.[45]

Like all definitions, this one leaves some ambiguity. It does not, for instance, list all the possible tools that may be applied to achieve currency-imperialist objectives. It does not describe the role of currency imperialism among other means of projecting influence and power abroad. It does not define degrees of currency imperialism, if such exist. Yet definitional shortcomings should not constitute a reason for dismissing every attempt at analysis. Whether the agenda behind U.S. dollar diplomacy, for instance, should be treated as an instance of currency imperialism is left unanswered (and while there are strong arguments in favor of doing so, there are also many differences in the Japanese example, primarily regarding public presentation). However, these issues are not strictly relevant.

Methodologically, it suffices to look at the historical-systemic nature of international politics and the making of foreign policy. Imperialist tactics do not exist in a social and temporal vacuum. They originate in and operate through the specific dynamics of geopolitical perceptions, partaking in these dynamics and transforming them. In other words, they are both causes and outcomes of these very specific perceptions, and need not be confined to an immutable set of actions. Moving the discussion to focusing on observations spares us many thorny questions about the "essence" of currency imperialism. Japanese currency imperialism can be discussed as an empirically observable set of perceptions, strategic objectives, and tactical tools; and it should also and always be examined in its historically contingent context—in reference to and interaction with its identified object, namely American policies in East Asia and American descriptions of East Asian events at the time.

This methodological shift entails some important consequences. First, it underlines the necessary ambiguity of all claims of disinterested political activity: American money doctoring in Asia cannot be dis-

---

45. Shibata, *Senryōchi tsūka kin'yū seisaku no tenkai*, 4.

cussed apart from the context of Pacific rivalry (in Flandreau's words, interests invite themselves). Even more important, it demonstrates the centrality of primary materials, including documents regarding policy formation and political and economic theories of the time. Such an approach makes it possible to avoid the risks and fallacies of ex post facto reconstruction and, in turn, to highlight the relative importance Japan's imperialists themselves ascribed to money and finance, something that has not gone unnoticed by Japanese observers.[46]

Indeed, definitional differences in this very respect between the American and the Japanese side were construed, if not always intentionally, so as to become a mainstay of the ensuing U.S.-Japan conflict. American and Japanese efforts to acquire monetary and/or financial influence in Asia (through loans, assistance in currency reform, and so on) simply endorsed and amplified their meaning as measures of international competition, indeed as "aggressions" toward the countries to which these efforts were extended. The "war of the words" thus necessarily translated into a "war of the worlds," or a relentless race—and, at least for the Japanese side, an unavoidable and all-consuming battle—for superiority in the Pacific.

This evolution is quite clear from contemporary descriptions of the Japanese project in Asia or, as it became known, "Japan's Monroe Doctrine." Even the liberal-minded Takagi Yasaka, the professor of American history quoted in the epigraph, explains Japan's position in China "by an analogy with the history of 'Manifest Destiny' in America." This doctrine, he argues, represented no more than "the inevitable process of the so-called biological necessity of American expansion," hence its acquisition of "Florida, Texas, and California, and perhaps Cuba." Similarities with the Japanese case, he insists, are clear: Japanese demands with regard to the peace and security of Manchuria "may be said also to be an expression of the irrepressible need for the biological development of the Japanese nation, and be called the pent-up cry of 'Manifest Destiny' on the part of the late comer in the circle of the society of nations." Consequently, "Americans would probably be the first to understand Japan's position,"[47] especially because that position was by

---

46. Shibata Yoshimasa himself draws attention to Japan's strong investment in the monetary and financial elements of empire (*Senryōchi tsūka kin'yū seisaku no tenkai*, 4).

47. Takagi, "World Peace Machinery and the Asia Monroe Doctrine," 942, 944, 946.

no means an example of nineteenth-century European-style aggression, but instead a manifestation of progress through peaceful means.[48] In the case of Manchuria, for instance, this progress required "the economic penetration of Manchuria by Japanese capitalism as the unavoidable requisite of the industrialization of her own country."[49]

Another recurrent, and related, theme of this book, is the contentious nature of all policy making related to prewar Japanese (financial) expansionism. It appears that Benjamin Schwartz and his colleagues, when working as army officers in signal intelligence monitoring Japanese radio traffic during World War II, were constantly struck by the discord between the many representatives of Japanese interests in China, both military and civilian.[50] If anything, this book endorses their firsthand experience. Both prewar and wartime Japanese imperialism were anything but a monolithic entity, contrary to popular versions of pre-1945 history. At the same time, I add to Schwartz's observation that, in all their contentiousness, conflicting perceptions and beliefs about the Japanese cause were nevertheless structured into bipolar opposition. Such bipolarization is to a certain extent self-explanatory. As we know from the sociology of Niklas Luhmann and others, it is in the nature of social order that artifacts, social systems, and so on are constructed along the lines of a primal difference, an originating distinction.[51] Mark Metzler gives an example from budgetary policy: "'austerity,' as a policy, is a relative term—it means less—and one cannot logically have an 'austerity policy' unless it is in reaction to more (whether conceptualized as 'luxury' or 'excessive spending,' etc.)"[52] Yet why perceptions and beliefs about Japanese economic policy polarized in the way they did is fundamentally revealing about the "problem" they constructed and addressed.

The polarity of beliefs is directly related to the perceived Hobbesian nature of the international geopolitical order, and especially to the role

---

48. For a similar and ingenious argument, see Tsurumi Yūsuke, "The Difficulties and Hopes of Japan."

49. Takagi, "World Peace Machinery and the Asia Monroe Doctrine," 944.

50. This is briefly discussed in Coble, *Chinese Capitalists in Japan's New Order*, xii.

51. See, for the introduction of some core concepts, Niklas Luhmann, *Social Systems*; George Spencer-Brown, *Laws of Form*. For an exploration of similar notions in the field of financial history, see Metzler, "Policy Space, Polarities, and Regimes."

52. Metzler, "Policy Space, Polarities, and Regimes," 130.

of the United States within it. Indeed, there was minimal discussion of whether Japan was a vulnerable player; everybody in Tokyo was convinced that it was. Cleavages in the policy-making constituency did not, therefore, develop along the lines of imperialist versus anti-imperialist. For instance, even the liberalist politician Inoue Junnosuke did not resent the Nishihara loans to China because they were imperialistic; he condemned them because they were never repaid. This is an important difference. As an ultimate policy goal, expansion was not contested. Instead, the discussion concentrated on the means of securing real political and economic influence in East Asia, and on the political styles and tactics that would best secure a degree of autonomy and independence in an environment that was, in fact, defined as fundamentally adverse to both prospects. Nowhere does this become as clear as in Japan's convoluted dealing with the ambiguous (from the Japanese perspective) agenda of the Open Door Policy. Was Tokyo to follow the lead of the formidable, because potentially self-sufficient, United States, constrain its own advance into Asia, and thus jeopardize what it construed as a step toward hard-won autonomy? Or was it to condemn the U.S.-led order and, after the German example, replace it with a new order of a world divided into several economic blocs—at the risk of antagonizing the most powerful country in the world?

Perceptions of this core dilemma united certain policy makers against others; created alliances between policy makers and bankers against other, similar alliances; and gave rise to improbable marriages between army factions and (semi-)governmental organizations, always defined in opposition to other factions and cliques. Remarkably, this dilemma also mobilized support for monetary standards, with gold the metal of the pro-autarky group and silver the metal of the more pragmatic-minded imperialists. In the end, these complex policy stances and their consequences contributed to the disaster of the Japanese Empire.

◆

In this book I tell the story of how Manifest Destiny of the kind described by Takagi came into being, developed over time, and ended in the "manifest destitution" of the Great Japanese Empire and its yen bloc. I limit the discussion to the financial and monetary aspects of Japanese expansionism, but refer to the related phenomena of military interventionism, railway imperialism, and so forth.

The journey of the Japanese money doctors starts in 1895, with a house call on Taiwan. This first experiment with colonial finance is at the same time the most ambivalent one, at least in strategic terms. It had none of the "urgency" that characterized later examples of Japanese money doctoring. As explored in Chapter 1, a host of reasons, geographical remoteness not least among them, made Taiwan more of a liability than an asset to policy makers in Tokyo, hampering a swift and thorough reform effort. Instead, Taiwan (or Formosa, as it was then known) became a test kitchen for policy recipes: control versus limited local initiative, assimilation versus independence, and so forth. Taiwan's lack of strategic appeal also produced an unfortunate second-order effect for the twenty-first-century historian: minutely detailed reports and statistics are lacking, and one has to rely on the reformers' own relatively sparse and possibly self-congratulatory assessments of their ventures. Journalistic reports are even harder to trace and in any case do not provide a sufficient window onto topics such as the monetary effects of reforms on the Taiwanese economy or the redistributory effects on the island's agricultural organization and development. Nevertheless, the case of Taiwan is important for understanding Japanese colonial finance, as it became an important tactical exemplar for later imperialist schemes. It was in Taiwan that the versatile and visionary Gotō Shinpei pioneered the centralist, hands-on, and comprehensive reforms (including far-reaching institutional and cultural initiatives) that cast their shadow on all later colonialist policy.

The reports and assessments that we lack for a fuller reconstruction of monetary events in Taiwan abound for the reform efforts in Korea, taken up in Chapter 2. Again the explanation is strategic value: extensive reporting was required to guarantee a smooth follow-up of Tokyo's many plans for Korea, on its immediate periphery—a "dagger pointing at the heart of Japan." What is more, the so-called Megata reform was quite successful. It was not a loosely knit fabric of ad hoc measures, but a single consistently premeditated reform plan, including preset benchmarks and alternative measures geared to the well-defined objective of monetary subjugation. As I will make clear with data gathered from the extant (often superbly published) primary sources, authorities at the time made no secret of the planned thoroughgoing impact of monetary and financial reforms. This was an era still captivated by the missionary rhetoric of uplifting premodern societies toward thrift and prosperity, rather than by talk of notions such as sovereignty, which was later considered a more fundamental national right. It is thus no surprise that the Japanese authorities deemed Megata's authoritarianism legitimate and even desirable. However hard the reform may have been on Korean commoners, the wealth of documentary material it produced makes it possible to write an extensive case study, detailing several aspects and phases of the reform program, and describing their effect on the Korean populace.

From there, we travel further into the Asian interior, and discuss in Chapter 3 the very different but highly illuminating Nishihara loans to China. They were negotiated only a decade after the Megata reform, but by then the geopolitical climate and Japan's domestic constituency had been profoundly transformed. The shift of the international balance of power, the United States' adoption of a multilateralist agenda, and its push for the universalist vocabulary of the Open Door gave momentum to a counter-ideology that had been accorded marginal status only a few years earlier. Until around 1915, Pan-Asianism, or the view that Asia's destiny was not to be decided by the Western imperialist powers, was not substantially represented in the ranks of the political classes occupying Japan's early democracy. In 1916, however, this ideology energized the bureaucratic activity and foreign policy of the Terauchi cabinet. It was clear from this administration's penchant for secrecy—several of the most substantial loans in the portfolio were pushed through on the administration's last day in office and without further clarification—that its plans were audacious indeed. The financially risky Nishihara loans were sure to offend the United States, and had the predictable consequence of leading to Japan's international humiliation. In this chapter, I trace the origins of Pan-Asianism as a specific brand of Japanese expansionism, highlight its relationship with events in China, and identify the very unlikely alliances it engendered. The chapter discusses the involvement of naive idealists, cynical imperialists, and bankers and businessmen riding on the coattails of imperialism; and it explains how this explosive mix illustrates the dilemmas that were to confront policy makers in later phases of the Greater Japanese Empire.

Even if its lofty visions were superseded in the 1910s, Pan-Asianism was not necessarily rejected by later administrations. It remained latent, often because of a realist element in foreign policy making (as in the immediate aftermath of the Nishihara loans) or because of economic factors (the postwar bust, the Great Kantō Earthquake, and financial problems in the late 1920s). But at the beginning of the 1930s, in the wake of the worldwide Great Depression, Takahashi Korekiyo's successful countercyclical economic policies restored Japan's national self-confidence. Although far from Takahashi's own aspirations, his success translated into further assertiveness in Northern China and, indirectly, into Japan's disregard of internationalist values as embodied in the League of Nations and related institutions. Unexpectedly, money doctoring in Manchuria, recounted in Chapter 4, also took on a chimerical twist. The monetary reformers behaved in a thoroughly technocratic and professional manner; but contrary to—or should one say, because of?—their self-referential professionalism, their efforts became one building block of an impossible Utopia, a country with multinational and multicultural claims yet with an imperialist core.

In the epilogue, I briefly review money-doctoring activities after the outbreak of the second Sino-Japanese War in 1937. Although primary sources are rather scarce and statistics often unreliable, these episodes are still exemplary of the later nature of Japanese militarism. Taking into account price evolutions in different regions, it becomes possible to reconstruct the Greater East-Asia Co-Prosperity Sphere as a set of concentric circles. As reflected in the semantic distinction between *naichi* and *gaichi*, or "inner sphere" and "outer sphere," outer rings were set up as buffers for the core (the Japanese mainland). This very structure must be understood not as an enhancement of Japan's security, but as its exact opposite. Like the Nazi *Großraumwirtschaft*, it was the endorsement of Japan's vulnerability, evidence of the country's incapacity to take on the role of a stabilizing factor or "hegemon" in its own economic bloc. The book concludes by reviewing the difficult discussion of continuities and discontinuities with the postwar period.

ONE

The First Patient and His Cure:
The Bank of Taiwan and Early Attempts
at Monetary and Financial Reform, 1897–1906

From now on, international conflict will not consist of invading countries and their peoples by means of military might [*wanryoku*], but of occupying [them] by means of financial power [*kinryoku*]. In other words, it is a fact that we will have to wage conflict not [according to the principles of] military tactics [*senryaku*], but [of] business strategy [*shōryaku*].
—Gotō Shinpei

The annexation of the island of Taiwan in 1895 heralded Japan's decades-long experiment with expansion into the whole of East Asia.[1] But Taiwan was not the prototypical candidate for inclusion in the political, economic, and cultural *Großraum* that later developed into the Greater East Asia Co-Prosperity Sphere. Unlike Korea and Manchuria, Taiwan could not justifiably be described as of paramount strategic concern for the defense of the Japanese mainland. Nor could Japanese

---

EPIGRAPH. Gotō, quoted in Tsurumi Yūsuke, *Taiwan jidai*, 513.

1. Approximately twenty years before, in 1874, Tokyo had launched an expedition to Taiwan at the suggestion of General Charles LeGendre. See Thomson, "Filibustering to Formosa"; Presseisen, "Roots of Japanese Imperialism."

policy makers claim "inalienable rights" to or a "special position" for Taiwan, as they would later do repeatedly with Northern China.[2]

This lack of strategic importance is explained by the geography of the island: Formosa, as it was known at the time, lay more than 2,200 kilometers away from Tokyo. Only very rudimentarily developed, and populated in part by what Japanese reports described as *banjin* ("savages"), it did not promise an immediate and easy return on the costly investment of cracking down on guerrilla resistance and, later, installing a full colonial administration.[3] Neither was the state of Japan's own economy such as to encourage "surplus capital" to venture into overseas territory. As a matter of fact, the country was struggling with a severe postwar recession. The cost of war, Matsukata Masayoshi's expansionist programs aimed at establishing an economy geared toward military production, and preparations for moving Japan onto the gold standard were a heavy burden on state finances.[4] What did convince Japan to consider annexing Taiwan was probably its aspiration to the standing of the Western powers.[5]

The adoption of Western colonial practices and the related discourse of appealing to the beneficial effects of modernity and industrialization also entailed a colonial administration and a host of reforms in the fields of politics, law, and education, as well as commerce and the economy.[6] We do not need to discuss in detail whether this initiative translated into a historically unique and uniquely ambiguous relationship between colonizer and colonized.[7] Instead, a more traditional look at financial reform

---

2. See Quo, "British Diplomacy and the Cession of Formosa, 1894–95."

3. "Political conditions on the island had not been favorable to economic expansion. The administration was in the hands of Peking officials who paid little attention to the local interests and who conducted affairs in mandarin which was unintelligible to the local population speaking Fukienese and Cantonese dialects. Land relations were feudal, and marked by frequent agrarian and clan riots." Grajdanzev, "Formosa (Taiwan) under Japanese Rule," 313.

4. See Matsukata, *Report on the Post-Bellum Administration of Japan.* For an explanation of the postwar crisis, see Schiltz, "Money on the Road to Empire."

5. Eskildsen, "Of Civilization and Savages"; Ching, "Savage Construction and Civility Making."

6. See, for example, E. P. Tsurumi, "Colonial Education in Korea and Taiwan"; Tai, "Kokugo and Colonial Education in Taiwan."

7. Recently, several authors have explored the importance of the concurrence (rather than consecutiveness) of Japanese colonialism with Japan's own modernizing efforts for

efforts must suffice, for a simple methodological reason: analyses of co-lonial Taiwanese currency and finance are still too scarce to include a larger discussion about center-periphery dynamics. The following analy-sis will therefore pay no attention to the self-referential qualities of colo-nialist policy, but instead be confined to the policy's design, objectives, means of implementation, and achievements. Specifically, who were the actors in the policy-making constituency? What were their motives? And how did they approach the obstacles they encountered, for instance the magnitude of the surrounding Asian silver sphere?

Even more than in later cases of financial policy making in colonies and occupied territories, the reforms in Taiwan were tightly bound up with the thoroughly developmentalist programs of the colonizers, and especially with their commitment to molding the island's agriculture to the needs of the Japanese mainland. "Industrial Japan, agricultural Taiwan" (*kōgyō Nihon / nōgyō Taiwan*) was not a hollow slogan. And in-deed, this phrase indicates linkages between Taiwanese agriculture and the still developing character of Japanese capitalism itself—including the dislocation of Japan's economic composition by increased diversion from agriculture to industry. More important was the significance of Taiwan as a laboratory for the experiments of Japan's reform-minded colonizers. It furnished a political, cultural, and economic tabula rasa. There was not a single institutional remnant of earlier attempts at colo-nization (as there were in Korea); no rich premodern legacy that re-formers felt to be at the core of their own identity (as in the case of the Chinese "cultural sphere"); no modern infrastructure echoing the mod-ern designs of rationalization and progress (as, for instance, in the city of Harbin in Manchuria). Thus Taiwan was a natural starting point for the hands-on policies and the "steady sense of imperial purpose"[8] for which Japanese expansionism became famous. Even so, a narrow yet important fissure developed in Japan's decision-making constituency. The strategy of assimilationism for which the Taiwanese case has be-come known was not rigorously adhered to in the "hard" field of fi-nance and fiscal matters. In this sense, Taiwan was Japan's first encoun-ter with the limits of expansionism and empire.

---

the definition and direction of Japanese modern identity. See, for example, Schmid, "Co-lonialism and the 'Korea Problem' in the Historiography of Modern Japan."

8. Kerr, "Formosa: Colonial Laboratory," 52.

Taiwan's Late Nineteenth-Century Economy

Finance turned out to be a very rich field for experimentation with colonial designs. As is often the case with late-feudal or premodern economies, Taiwan's financial infrastructure and mechanisms of introducing credit were underdeveloped. Typically, the largest institutions were in the hands of Western businesses or Chinese traders. Based in the commercial centers, they operated in an upper layer of the island's economy and had very little contact with local producers in Taiwan's demographically still strongly differentiated *Hinterland*.

Pivotal to the island's economy was a layer of middlemen: the *mazhenguan*—*mazhen* being a sinicization of the English word "merchant"—specialized in the tea trade.[9] These trading operations were mostly located in the region around Taipei, the island's hub for tea production, and they were administered as a sort of cooperative (called *chabang*) by affluent tea-trading families from cities such as Xiamen (Amoy), Canton, and Shantou.[10] Merchants in the original meaning of the word, *mazhenguan* organized the movement of goods. Yet, unlike conventional tea merchants, they also served as financiers for a sector which was both

---

9. For more on the largely unknown role of these middlemen, see "Taiwan no kin'yū jōtai: (1) ryōtaimae no kin'yū kikan; (2) Taiwan ginkō shutsugen; (3) tsūka no tōitsu; (4) minkan ginkō no hattatsu; (5) yokin oyobi kashidashi; (6) ginkōgyō irai no kin'yū kikan; (7) tōmen no mondai; (8) kakuginkō no gaikyō" 台湾の金融状態: (1) 領台前の金融機関; (2) 台湾銀行出現; (3) 通貨の統一; (4) 民間銀行の発達; (5) 預金及貸出; (6) 銀行業以来の金融機関; (7) 当面の問題; (8)各銀行の概況 (The financial state of Taiwan: [1] financial institutions before Taiwan's occupation; [2] the appearance of the Bank of Taiwan; [3] unification of the currency; [4] development of public banks; [5] deposits and loans; [6] other financial institutions; [7] today's problems; [8] outline of each bank), JJS 1923.4.30, KUDA-ID: 00473870. See also remarks by Esaki Masumi, at the time director of the Bank of Taiwan ("Taiwan kin'yūkai no kaiko: Taiwan ginkō o chūshin ni shite" 台湾金融界の回顧:台湾銀行を中心として [Reminiscences of Taiwan's financial world: with a focus on the Bank of Taiwan], parts 1–3b, TNN 1923.5.3–1923.5.6 KUDA-ID 00473873): "The term '*mazhenguan*' is derived from the English 'merchant'; it is an eminent institution [acting] among tea producers, but rather than a tea merchant in the pure sense of the word or a tea middleman, it is [an institution] engaging in the consignment sale [*itaku hanbai*] of tea, while at the same time functioning so as to channel funds [to the tea producers] by using tea as collateral."

10. The importance of the tea trade in Taiwan's economy also explains the island's economic orientation toward South China.

capital-intensive and naturally prone to seasonal fluctuations, and thus highly credit-dependent.[11]

Although quite a number of these *mazhenguan* boasted about their capital base and behaved as veritable nabobs within their respective domains, it would be a mistake to regard them as an autonomous class of credit institutions. Indeed, chronic capital shortages typical of pre-modern economies hardly made them a credit institution in the modern sense of the word. Because they were capital-dependent on the Western banks and, to a lesser degree, the traditional micro-banks (*qianzhuang*), it would be more accurate to describe them as links in the credit chain with the function of channeling funds from the Western banks in the upper strata toward producers in the real economy. In this respect, they were not unlike the *liangzhan* or "crop-dealers" operating in North China. This "levered" pyramid of lending (with interest charged at several levels) had dire consequences for economic growth. Exceptionally high interest rates, sometimes reaching 20 or 30 percent per annum, hampered wealth accumulation, investment opportunities, and the possibility of techno-logical innovation.[12] Namikata Shōichi proposes that in the sugar sector things may have been even worse. Characterized by a comparable credit pyramid, this sector furthermore clung to a strict business hierarchy. Other bank-like institutions, such as the exchange houses (*huiduiguan*) or mail-order offices (*xinji*, comparable to the *hikyakuya* of Japan's Edo period) were unable to alleviate the pressures of tight credit.

Monetary conditions were probably even more problematic than the island's banking infrastructure. Japanese reports of the time unequivo-cally identify the Taiwanese monetary system as a state of utter con-fusion: terms such as "chaos" (*bunran*) and "extreme disarray" (*kiwamete ranmyaku*) are commonplace. Such characterizations were, to be fair, not entirely correct. In economies with regional and stratificatory differentia-tion, currencies are arguably complementary—that is to say, their con-

---

11. See Anderton and Barrett, "Demographic Seasonality and Development."

12. Namikata, "Taiwan ginkō no setsuritsu to heiseikaikaku," 37, esp. n. 6. In the following paragraphs, I follow Namikata's discussion closely and rely on leads provided in his footnotes, e.g., to the *Japan Bankers' Magazine* (*Ginkō tsūshinroku*). Namikata him-self follows the outline of his 1974 paper in *Nihon shokuminchi kin'yū seisakushi no kenkyū*, 60ff. The bank does have an official short history: *Taiwan ginkō enkaku ryaku* 台湾銀行沿革略, JACAR Ref. A08071700500.

currence might be functional rather than incidental. Different currency circuits can coexist without integration, first because they account for different demands for (and velocities of) monies within upper-level and lower-level markets, and second because they are thereby hindered from developing synchronization.[13] For reformers planning uniformity and synchronization of currencies within a unified market, however, such a situation must have been both an enigma and a source of headaches.

In an effort to measure the seriousness of the problem, the well-known Japanese Ministry of Finance report on the implementation of the 1897 Currency Law[14] (by dint of which Japan adopted the gold standard) compares it to a state in which "the merchants from Taipei do not know the measures [used by] the merchants in Tainan."[15] More than a hundred different types of currency circulated, many of which also differed in kind: within a single region people used both weight and token currencies, resulting in widely varying transaction costs. In addition, there was not just one standard of value, but two—one for the silver currency system and one for the copper currency system. *Yuan* (元) was taken as the unit of account for silver coins and *wen* as the unit for copper coins, with 1 *yuan* [1 *yuan* = 1 Japanese yen] = 10 *diao* (角) = 100 *dian* (点) [1 *dian* = 1 Japanese *sen* (銭)] = 1000 *wen* (文) [1 *wen* = 1 Japanese *rin* (厘)].

To make matters worse, the meaning of the *yuan* differed according to locality. This was especially so when it was calculated in terms of the (imaginary) "treasury standard" or *kuping tael*, the measure of weight by means of which late imperial China attempted to maintain a degree of control over coins in circulation. In the northern region of Taiwan, for instance, one *yuan* was treated as 0.72 *tael*, as it was in mainland China;

---

13. Differences in demand may be caused, for instance, by seasonality in agriculture or transport (as in the case of harbors that are ice-bound during winter months). For an illuminating discussion in the Chinese context, see Kuroda, "What is the Complementarity among Monies?" and "Concurrent but Non-integrable Currency Circuits."

14. *Kaheihō seitei oyobi jisshi hōkoku* 貨幣法制定及実施報告 (Report on the design and implementation of the currency law); see Nihon ginkō chōsakyoku, ed., *Nihon kin'yū-shi shiryō: Meiji Taishō hen*, vol. 17, 1–289, esp. 258ff.

15. Namikata, "Taiwan ginkō no setsuritsu to heiseikaikaku," 40.

in the middle region, it was treated as 0.7 *tael*, whereas, in the south, its value was yet lower, corresponding to a mere 0.68 *tael*.[16]

With respect to silver coins—the medium par excellence for international trade at the time—Taiwan must be considered a showcase. Like other countries in the region, it had been flooded with silver pieces competing with the Mexican dollar for dominance as the medium of exchange.[17] Although figures do not exist for the numbers of currencies in circulation, the "Report on the Design and Implementation of the Currency Law" lists the most important (non-Japanese) coins and their rate against the Japanese yen (see Table 1.1). Apart from those listed in the table, the coins in circulation also included some privately issued silver coins, Japanese one-yen pieces, and several types of so-called trade dollars (*bōeki gin*). Even the age-old and variously shaped *sycee* ingots, such as the famous "horseshoe-silver pieces" (*ma ti yin*), were still in use (although probably not in circulation because of their high value).

The many different varieties of coins, and the coexistence of weight and token currency, gave rise to a variety of mechanisms for checking these coins' relative purity. Taiwan had a complicated and exotic naming system that extended to grading a coin's quality; its exchange houses often resorted to "chopping" as a means of approving the acceptance of a silver coin of a certain quality at a certain rate.[18] In effect, some (originally token) currencies were thus also treated as a sort of bullion.

---

16. In the Western vocabulary of the time, one *yuan* was considered equal to 0.72 *tael*, or 7 *mace* and 2 *candereens*. Namikata, "Taiwan ginkō no setsuritsu to heiseikaikaku," 39–40.

17. For a thorough discussion of currency competition in the Asian silver sphere, see Ono, *Kindai Nihon heisei to higashi Ajia ginkaken*. Hong Kong silver pieces had been minted between 1866 and 1868 and were the expression of a British effort to dethrone the Mexican dollar. This "Hong Kong dollar," bearing the effigy of Queen Victoria, was not popular with the Chinese, who preferred the more familiar Mexican dollar. As a result, the mint closed after only two years in operation, and its machinery was dismantled and sold to Japan, where it was installed at the mint in Osaka. See Pond, "The Spanish Dollar: The World's Most Famous Silver Coin"; Garnett, "The History of the Trade Dollar"; "Imperial Canton Mint; Clever Moves of the Chinese with their Coinage," *The New York Times*, July 3, 1892.

18. Compare "Taiwan kin'yūkai no kaiko: Taiwan ginkō o chūshin toshite" 台湾金融界の回顧：台湾銀行を中心として (Reminiscences of Taiwan's financial world: with a focus on the Bank of Taiwan), TNN 1923.5.3–1923.5.6 KUDA-ID 00473873, esp. part 1, "History of the Currency."

Table 1.1: Main silver currencies (including subsidiary currencies) circulating in Taiwan, with rate of exchange against Japanese yen

Name	Weight (*tael* 両)	Exchange rate (1:x yen)
Spanish silver piece (dollar)	0.72	1:1
Mexican silver piece (dollar)	0.58	1:0.812
	0.6	1:0.84
	0.64	1:0.896
Hong Kong 20 *qian* silver piece	n/a	1:0.18
Canton 1.44 *qian* silver piece	n/a	1:0.20
Taiwan 1.44 *qian* silver piece	n/a	1:0.20
Hong Kong 10 *qian* silver piece	n/a	1:0.09
Taiwan 0.72 *qian* silver piece	n/a	1:0.10
Canton 10 *qian* silver piece	n/a	1:0.10
Hong Kong 5 *qian* silver piece	n/a	1:0.05
Canton 0.36 *qian* silver piece	n/a	1:0.05
Taiwan 0.36 *qian* silver piece	n/a	1:0.05

NOTE: There were three types of denominations of subsidiary coins: 2 *diao*, 1 *diao*, and 5 *dian*.
SOURCE: "Kaheihō seitei oyobi jisshi hōkoku," in Nihon ginkō chōsakyoku, ed., *Nihon kin'yūshi shiryō Meiji Taishō hen*, vol. 17, 259.

The basket of copper coins was even more varied. According to several sources, more than a hundred types circulated.[19] Because they were less important for international trade, we will not treat them in detail. It suffices to note that they included provincial as well as private issues, and that even the late-feudal Japanese *Kan'ei tsūhō* was not uncommon.[20]

Preparations for the Establishment of a Central Bank

In addition to this intrinsic turmoil, extrinsic stumbling blocks in the form of botched decision making and lack of unanimity with regard to the future of Taiwan hampered a swift reform effort. Minister of Finance Matsukata Masayoshi had been quick to order legislation ena-

---

19. See, for instance, "Ryōtai tōji no Taiwan heisei: tsūka 100-shu 10-shu, kōsaku o kiwamu" 領台当時の台湾幣制／通貨百数十種、交錯を極む (The currency system at the time of Taiwan's occupation / hundreds of coins in ten varieties, taking confusion to the extreme) TNN 1935.6.17 KUDA-ID 00474844.

20. Apparently, *Kan'ei tsūhō* coins for the Taiwanese market had been commissioned from the Nagasaki domain by Zheng Chenggong (known as Koxinga). Li, "Jūkyū seiki no tōa ginkaken to Taiwan no heisei kaikaku," 143.

bling the establishment of a colonial bank, as we can infer from a few issues of the *Ginkō tsūshinroku* (*Japan Bankers' Magazine*) and some personal memoirs. Matsukata, as always a headstrong leader, apparently expressed his intention to embark on large-scale development of Taiwan, for which he deemed the establishment of a central bank to be of the utmost importance.[21] Imperial Ordinance No. 9, promulgated by Matsukata on February 1, 1897, therefore stipulated that "the currency and banking administration of Formosa shall be placed in charge of the Minister of State for Finance. In all matters concerning the said administration the Governor-General of Formosa shall act under the supervision of the Minister of State for Finance."[22] After this first frenzy of bureaucratic activity, the Ministry drew up a draft of a Bank of Taiwan Act, which was presented to the Diet in March 1897. A month later, on April 1, the act was officially proclaimed.[23] Its main provisions were:

Art. 4:   The capital of the Bank of Taiwan is set at 5 million yen

Art. 5:   The Bank of Taiwan has the following tasks:

        1. Discounting bills of exchange and other types of commercial bills

        2. exchange and documentary bills (*nigawase*)

        [. . .]

        4. lending against secure real estate or movables

        5. deposits or overdrafts

---

21. Taiwan ginkō, *Taiwan ginkō nijūnen-shi*, 14; for a similar statement, see "Kinka hon'i jisshi man nijūnen kinenkai kiji" 金貨本位実施満二十年紀念会記事 (An article on the occasion of the twentieth anniversary of the implementation of the gold currency standard); compiled by Soeda Juichi 添田壽一, in Nihon ginkō chōsakyoku, ed., *Nihon kin'yūshi shiryō: Meiji Taishō hen*, vol. 17, 662. The *Japan Bankers' Magazine*, however, suggests that the plan was first conceived within the Bank of Japan. See *Ginkō tsūshinroku* 133 (December 1896). The Bank of Japan had opened an exchange office in Taipei and had been appointed to act as Taiwan's treasury, engage in the business of foreign exchange, and so on, but in the event fulfilled these duties only halfheartedly and may therefore have prepared a proposal for a colonial bank of issue. On its opening of an exchange office in Taipei, see Nihon ginkō chōsakyoku, ed., *Nihon kin'yūshi shiryō: Meiji Taishō hen*, vol. 17, 261.

22. "Taiwan ni okeru kahei oyobi ginkō ni kansuru jimu shukan no ken" 台湾ニ於ケル貨幣及銀行ニ関スル事務主管ノ件 (On the supervision of administering Taiwan's currency and banks), JACAR Ref. A03020275100. The English translation is taken from Matsukata, *Report on the Adoption of the Gold Standard in Japan*, 382.

23. For the law's full text, see "Taiwan ginkōhō" 台湾銀行法 (Bank of Taiwan Act); JACAR Ref. A03020272900.

6. the safe deposit of gold and silver coins, precious metals and securities (*shōken*)
7. the purchase and selling of gold and silver specie
8. acting as representative for the business of other banks

Art. 8:   The Bank of Taiwan has the right to issue bearer notes of a value of five yen or more [. . .]

Art. 9:   The Bank of Taiwan is obliged to hold, with respect the amount of bearer notes issued, an equivalent amount of gold and silver coins or specie as a reserve. Should it wish to issue bearer notes above the amount of this reserve, it is [bound by] the limit of 5 million yen. It has the right to use government paper money, convertible notes or other sound securities and commercial papers as guarantee; yet, the amount [of bearer notes to be issued] is not to exceed the amount of issue used as reserve. If, as a result of market conditions, [the Bank of Taiwan] deems necessary the issuance of bearer notes above [the amount specified in] the preceding paragraphs, it is obliged to obtain approval from the cabinet minister responsible. It has the right to use government paper money, convertible notes or other sound securities and commercial papers as guarantee [for this extra amount]. In that case, [the bank] is obliged, according to rules specified by government decision, to pay a tax not to be less than 5 percent per annum.

From this moment on, however, preparations leading up to the establishment of a colonial central bank fizzle out. First, it was unexpectedly difficult to find people willing to sit on a founding committee (*sōritsu iinkai*). When solicited, many of the newly formed Meiji elite politely demurred. One issue of the *Japan Bankers' Magazine* reports that even the influential Masuda Takashi, then managing director of the Mitsui Trading Company and one of the key figures of Japan's rising business class, had "decided to decline a role as a founding member."[24] Such reluctance was understandable: although in the immediate aftermath of the Sino-Japanese War investment in Taiwan increased, returns on these investments were far from certain and they were therefore considered risky by Japan's vested business interests and indeed in wider public opinion at the time. Because the cost of the war had been much higher than anticipated, the territory came to be considered a liability (*yakkai-*

---

24. See *Ginkō tsūshinroku* 141 (August 1897).

mono) to the Japanese mainland;[25] there was even talk of selling the island to France.

Second, a series of cabinet breakups in the politically tumultuous 1890s stood in the way of effective decision making. Although drafts of the bank's charter circulated at a fairly early stage, the economic crisis following the Sino-Japanese War hung over the committee's deliberations.[26] Crisis-ridden Japanese companies were not inclined to take up stocks of a bank with an uncertain future. With the formation of the third Itō cabinet on January 12, 1898, the project appeared to be moving forward; yet the parliamentary crisis over the raising of the land tax forced Itō to resign and once more brought the decision making process back to the bureaucrats' desks. In fact, the land tax crisis proved so severe that committee meetings were temporarily suspended.[27] Meetings resumed in May 1898, but this time it looked impossible to secure sufficient government guarantees for raising the bank's capital. Difficult discussions ensued, and yet again, frictions between party factions, in the succeeding Ōkuma cabinet (June 30, 1898–November 8, 1898), closed the door on a solution of remaining issues.

Worst of all was the uninterested or even hostile attitude of Japan's entrepreneurial class toward the prospect of a Bank of Taiwan. Interested in quick profit, they resisted long-term strategies of investing in the island's development. The reluctance of industrialists to join the founding committee of its central bank became more pronounced, as even members of the bank's founding committee presented the idea of a Bank of Taiwan in a very different light: in the autumn of 1898,

---

25. Tsurumi Yūsuke, *Taiwan jidai*, 513, 232ff.

26. See Nagaoka, "Nisshin sensō go no kyōkō to menshihōsekigyō (1)" and "Nisshin sensō go no kyōkō to menshihōsekigyō (2)." For an English report on financial difficulties at the time, see Matsukata, *Report on the Post-Bellum Administration of Japan*. For the original version in Japanese, see *Sengo zaisei shimatsu hōkoku* 戦後財政始末報告 (Report on the financial administration after the war), JACAR Ref. A04017267000.

27. Again, the *Ginkō tsūshinroku* proves a sound guide: "Taiwan ginkō setsuritsu iinkai to sono setsuritsu" 台湾銀行創立委員会と其設立 (The founding committee of the Bank of Taiwan and its establishment), *Ginkō tsūshinroku* 146 (January 1898); "Taiwan ginkō setsuritsu no miawase" 台湾銀行創立の見合せ (The postponing of the establishing of the Bank of Taiwan), *Ginkō tsūshinroku* 147 (February 1898); "Taiwan ginkō setsuritsu ni kessu" 台湾銀行創立に決す (Deciding the establishment of the Bank of Taiwan), *Ginkō tsūshinroku* 156 (November 1898).

Yasuda Zenjirō, a highly influential industrialist, proposed to drop the concept of a bank of issue and, instead, to transform the Bank of Taiwan into a Sino-Japanese Bank (Nisshin ginkō).[28] This was a radical departure indeed. Not only was the Sino-Japanese Bank to have a capital of ten million yen; its main office was to be in Tokyo, with a strong branch office in Taiwan. From the industrialists' perspective, it need not even be a bank of issue. Instead, "as financial institutions specializing in the trade with China and Korea are still insufficient, it should establish branch offices both in China and Korea" in order to "further Sino-Japanese trade relations."[29] Contemporary Japanese industrialists and financiers—unlike their Western counterparts at the time—were not yet ready to embrace the lofty visions of concession imperialism: "they focused on penetration of the Chinese market and did not perceive the significance of the Bank of Taiwan as a colonial bank. [Members of] Japan's bourgeoisie at the time did not clearly recognize the modern character of Western imperialist competition vis-à-vis China; they did in other words [not yet recognize] the Bank of Taiwan in the context of a stage in the history of capitalism associated with the dawn of the twentieth century. And consequently, the establishment of the Bank of Taiwan was *not* a response to a demand innate to industrial capital."[30]

Gotō Shinpei and the Birth of Japanese Money Doctoring

The eventual establishment of the Bank of Taiwan was the fruit of the visionary schemes and the energetic leadership of two civilian bureaucrats: Governor-General Kodama Gentarō and, even more importantly, Gotō Shinpei.[31] The latter, at that time the head of civilian affairs in

---

28. Although this plan eventually went nowhere, the idea of a Sino-Japanese Bank died hard. See Namikata, "Nisshin ginkō Manshū ginkō setsuritsu undō no tenkai katei: Meijiki ni gentei shite"; Mamiya, "Nihon shihonshugi to keizai dantai: Nisshin ginkō setsuritsu keikaku o megutte" and "Nihon shihon shugi to Nisshin ginkō setsuritsu keikaku."

29. Quoted in Namikata, "Taiwan ginkō no setsuritsu to heisei kaikaku," 47. Compare *Ginkō tsūshinroku* 155 (October 1898); "Nisshin ginkō" (Sino-Japanese Bank), *Ginkō tsūshinroku* 159 (February 1899).

30. Namikata, "Taiwan ginkō no setsuritsu to heisei kaikaku," 48 (italics added).

31. There is abundant biographical material on Gotō. See the multivolume biography by Tsurumi Yūsuke and the "Gotō Shinpei no Kai," at http://goto-shimpei.org/.

Kodama's government, was a brilliant career civil servant with an impressive background. Born in Isawa (in present-day Iwate prefecture), he had entered Sukagawa Medical School in Fukushima at the age of seventeen. After graduation, he became a doctor in Nagoya, but it soon became clear that his ambitions lay elsewhere. After serving as a medic for the government forces during the Satsuma Rebellion when only 25 years old, he became president of the Nagoya Medical School. In 1882, he entered the Home Ministry. Recognizing his talents, the Japanese government sent him to Germany in 1890 for further studies. After returning, he became, in 1892, the head of the Department of Health (Eiseikyoku) in the Home Ministry. A few years later, he moved to Taiwan, after being chosen by Kodama for his experience on the quarantining of soldiers returning from the Sino-Japanese War. Ironically, Japan's first money doctor was a medical doctor by training. Gotō adopted a scientific vision of colonial policy, which he thought should be ruled according to "biological principles" (*seibutsugaku no gensoku*). He emulated the positivist attitude of the doctor who studies the patient's medical history in order to determine treatment, as in his creation of the Provisional Council for the Investigation of Old Habits of Taiwan (Rinji Taiwan kyūkan chōsakai).[32]

The Bank of Taiwan (BOT) was central to Gotō's interest in the long-term development of the island and especially its integration with Japan's modernity while avoiding enforcement through military force.[33] Before taking part in discussions about the bank's structure and mission, he had written several proposals for raising a giant loan to pay for large-scale infrastructural modernization, although they had not come to anything. A central bank, he calculated, might further his plan. In two letters, one to Soeda Juichi of Japan's Ministry of Finance and one to the vice-minister of the Home Ministry,[34] Gotō attributed Taiwan's lack of appeal to

---

32. Suzuki, "Gotō Shinpei to Okamatsu Santarō ni yoru kyūkan chōsa (1): Taiwan no baai."

33. Contemporary commentators spoke of an "organic" theory of the state or *kokka yūkitai-setsu*, in which the direction of the (socialist) state's future was shaped by a combination of "carrot and stick"—in Japanese *"ame to muchi*," a calque of the German "Zuckerbrot und Peitsche," itself coined by Franz Mehring in the context of Otto von Bismarck's *Eisen und Blut* policies.

34. Tsurumi Yūsuke, *Gotō Shinpei*, vol. 3, 252–55, 258–59.

Japanese investors to the combination of tight credit conditions in Japan proper and the absence of a powerful bank in Taiwan. The Japanese government should take the lead, he stressed, with finance as the government's most effective tool: "Financial institutions are [by their very nature] the lifeblood of the capitalist economy [*shihonshugi keizai no dōmyaku*]. *Just as trade follows the flag, industrial development follows financial institutions.* And the one institution that should function as the pivot [*sūjiku*] of the financial institutions of the new territory is the Bank of Taiwan."[35] This statement makes it clear that there was something in this project for the expansionist elements in Tokyo. An emphasis on finance and trade did not exclude ambitions for further conquest, as can be seen in the epigraph to this chapter. In attempts to legitimate his civilian and anti-military stance, Gotō stressed the missionary importance of the BOT's "modernist" cure and its potential to gain influence for Japan farther south. His plea fell upon receptive ears in Tokyo. In June 1897, the BOT opened its doors in Taipei; its capital was 5 million yen, of which one-fourth was paid up. The foundations of Japan's southward economic advance were laid.[36]

Japan's Gold Standard and Taiwanese Monetary Reform

To understand the effect of these events on Taiwan's monetary development, we should briefly consider the situation in Japan proper at the time. The establishment of the BOT more or less coincides with the adoption of the gold standard in Japan, the passing of related currency laws, and preparations for the redemption of the old silver yen circu-

---

35. Ibid., 251 (italics added).

36. The strongest impulse for extending the bank's leverage in Southeast Asia came under the tenure of the Bank of Taiwan's second governor, Yagyū Kazuyoshi. See Yokoi, "Yagyū Kazuyoshi to Taiwan ginkō no 'Nanshi Nan'yō' chōsa." For later newspaper references to the southward mission of the Bank of Taiwan, see "Nan'yō hatten no undō ga giron o sugite jikkō no jidai to natte kita" 南洋発展の運動が議論の時代を過ぎて実行の時代となって来た (The movement for the southward advance is beyond the stage of discussion and reaches an era of realization), nos. 1–5, TNN 1917.10.18–1917.10.22 KUDA-ID 00501260; "'Shin hokushu nanshinron' o toku wakawakashii kakki" 「新北守南進論」を説く若々しい活気！ (Explaining the new idea of safeguarding the north and advancing south: new vitality!), CSS 1936.2.4 KUDA-ID 00485100.

lating in Japan and some regions in East Asia.[37] Perhaps unwillingly, Japanese leaders had to address two crucial questions that would henceforth confront colonial policy making: whether newly acquired territory should be left to self-develop or should be assimilated (*dōka*) into the Japanese empire, and whether assimilation was feasible in the first place. Assimilationist thought soon gained currency in Tokyo and would (at least rhetorically) dominate later debates about the management of newly acquired territory—eventually leading to the notion of "imperializing" (*kōminka*) peoples, that is, educating them to become loyal subjects ruled by a benevolent Japanese emperor. It falls outside the scope of this chapter to discuss how assimilation came to be defined in the context of Taiwan,[38] but it is worth noting that the majority of colonial policy makers in a wide variety of fields employed the term or at least tacitly adopted the stance it implied.[39]

Matsukata Masayoshi's Imperial Ordinance No. 9 (see above), for instance, adopted the assimilationist stance by clearly articulating the idea that Taiwan's financial and monetary administration was ultimately subordinate to the Minister of State for Finance (Matsukata himself). Accordingly, the BOT was not granted the privilege of note-issue, as would have been the case for an independent central bank, but had only the right to issue bearer notes (Bank of Taiwan Law, Article 8).[40]

The consequences of an assimilationist policy reached beyond terminology to raise the question of whether Taiwan was to be brought onto the gold standard simultaneously with Japan, and what this would mean for monetary reform. Would the island need a currency law separate from the one that had taken effect on Japanese shores? What was

---

37. For a contemporary official report in English, see Matsukata, *Report on the Adoption of the Gold Standard in Japan*. A very good academic discussion is to be found in Ono, *Kindai Nihon heisei to higashi Ajia ginkaken.*

38. For a good discussion on the origination and growth of assimilationism, see Yamamoto, "Shokuminchi tōji ni okeru 'dōkashugi' no kōzō: Yamanaka moderu no hihanteki kentō."

39. See discussions in the Imperial Diet with regard to the Bank of Taiwan: Nihon ginkō chōsakyoku, ed., *Nihon kin'yūshi shiryō Meiji Taishō hen*, vol. 15, 1169–1352.

40. The privilege of note issue would have required amendment of the Bank of Japan Law. Stipulations with regard to the issuing of bearer notes, limitations of issue, and amounts of specie reserve and security reserve to be held are contained in Article 8 and 9. See also "[. . .] Taiwan ginkōhō," JACAR Ref. A03020272900.

to be done with remaining Japanese and other foreign silver coins? What would the adoption of the gold standard mean for Taiwan's macro-economic future? These were contentious issues. Matsukata's aides understood that the specie- and capital-poor Japanese government would have grave difficulties upholding the gold standard in Japan proper, let alone being able to fully absorb other territories in its frail gold-standard zone.[41] Even so, the assimilationist strand in their thinking was strong and, probably on Matsukata's personal instructions, they defended the case for having Taiwan—eventually—adopt the gold standard as well. With regard to any separate currency law, officials of the Finance Ministry curtly declared that it was rendered "unnecessary"[42] by the way the relationship between the currency systems had been defined. But did this mean that they envisaged the practicalities of making Japanese and Taiwanese currency uniform?

It did not. Embarrassed by its limited scope for more policy maneuvering, the Ministry of Finance was forced to push through a hybrid solution to Taiwan's currency problems. In a memorandum to the cabinet presented on September 22, 1898, its delegate Soeda Juichi proposed: "While it shall be our aim to make in some future time the currency system of Formosa uniform with that at home, it is believed to be advisable, in view of present conditions, to leave for the time being the currency system unchanged from what it has been in the past. For this reason, it is now proposed to put into circulation in Formosa the 1-yen silver coin, which will be retired after October 1 of this year, by stamping it with a government mark and allowing its use at a current valuation in all public payments to the Government, and at the same time prohibiting the use of foreign coins, and other coins with private

---

41. For Japan's difficulties in maintaining the gold standard, see Metzler, *Lever of Empire*, 67ff., esp. 69: "The gold standard had been instituted to enable borrowing, but its maintenance seemed to require further borrowing. As chief of general affairs [*eigyō kyokuchō*] at the Bank of Japan, Fukai Eigo confronted the problem directly: 'Because the gold raised by overseas bond issues became [Japan's] overseas gold funds, one could even say that we floated overseas bonds in order to maintain the gold standard.'"

42. Nihon ginkō chōsakyoku, ed. *Nihon kin'yūshi shiryō: Meiji Taishō hen*, vol. 15, 1180, 1204.

stamp marks on them, which have been hitherto permitted to be used in public payments to the Government."[43]

By dint of Imperial Ordinance 374 (October 22, 1897),[44] the proposal became law. Its directives remained ambiguous, for the silver coins that were to be put into circulation were not defined as mere subsidiary coinage (that is, as token coins whose value did not correspond to their bullion value but was defined as a certain quantity of gold). Instead, the current valuation at which the stamped one-yen silver coins were circulated was based on the market rate of exchange in Hong Kong.

What kind of standard was this? It is obvious from discussions at the time that Ministry of Finance officials were bothered by what looked liked a half measure. In an attempt to explain that Taiwan's monetary standard was not different from, yet also not the same as, the one in Japan proper, Soeda somewhat cautiously—and incorrectly—called it a "nominal gold coin standard" (*meigiteki kinka hon'i*),[45] balancing on differences between two separate metallic standards. Stipulations with regard to reserve holdings had already made clear that this was a gold-*exchange* standard at best.[46] However, by maintaining references to the

---

43. Quoted in Matsukata, *Report on the Adoption of the Gold Standard in Japan*, 383. For similar statements, see Nihon ginkō chōsakyoku, ed., *Nihon kin'yūshi shiryō: Meiji Taishō hen*, vol. 15, 1178.

44. See "Taiwan ni oite seifu gokuin tsuki ichien ginkahei kōnō shiyō no ken" 台湾ニ於テ政府極印附一円銀貨幣公納使用ノ件 (About the use of the one-yen government stamped silver coin for public payments), JACAR Ref. A03020311600. Matsukata's *Report on the Adoption of the Gold Standard in Japan* gives the following English translation: "Art. 1: The one-*yen* silver coin, with a Government stamp mark on it, may be used in Formosa for payment either to or by the Government. The payment of the Government shall only be made with the consent of the payee. Art. 2: The government stamp mark mentioned in the preceding article shall be placed on the face of the retired one-*yen* silver coin, in the form as shown below [. . .] Art. 3: All foreign coins or the coins with private stamp marks on them, shall not be used hereafter in public payments. This article shall not apply to the cases of payments to the Government, where a special arrangement has already been made for making those payments in foreign coins" (383). The government in Tokyo also circulated a note explaining this stipulation: "Taiwan ni oite seifu gokuin tsuki ichien kinkahei o kōnō ni shiyō su" 台湾ニ於テ政府極印附一円銀貨幣ヲ公納ニ使用ス (Using the one-yen government stamped silver coin for public payments in Taiwan), JACAR Ref. A01200863700.

45. Nihon ginkō chōsakyoku, *Nihon kin'yūshi shiryō: Meiji Taishō hen*, vol. 17, 266.

46. See Matsuoka, "The Expansion and Consolidation of the Japanese Gold Exchange Standard."

market rate of the one-yen silver piece, the compromise worked out between the Ministry of Finance and the Residency General also did not render the silver standard obsolete. Cleverly designed policy statements only underlined the system's profound ambivalence. In Taiwan, silver was "not to be circulated as silver" (*gin o gin toshite*), but to be "circulated as silver that had been counted as gold" (*gin o kin toshite keisan shite ryūtsū*)[47]—an "extremely peculiar" (*kiwamete hensokuteki*) system, as Namikata has pointed out.[48]

Japan's weakness can be interpreted as a missed opportunity. While focusing on Japan's (and other countries') motivations for adopting the gold standard, one often loses sight of where all the silver went. At the time, fear of large amounts of exported silver yen coming back for redemption was one of the objections to the plan for bringing Japan onto gold.[49] By offsetting the effects of the inflow of re-imported coins through putting silver to use in newly acquired territories, the Ministry of Finance probably thought it had found a key solution to alleviating at least a part of the pressure inherent in a monetary reform on the scale of adopting the gold standard.[50] Unfortunately, Japan chose to leave key aspects of the island's silver standard intact, thus imposing transaction costs between the mainland and Taiwan, which its ideological stance of treating the island as an integral part of its territory should have prohibited.

In any case, the Taiwan Office of the Governor-General decided to take forward the hybrid proposal. As the mainland officially adopted the gold standard on October 1, 1897, it moved to issue Notification 67 (November 14), thereby fixing the value of one-yen silver coins for the time being at the rate of 1,037 pieces of the silver one yen for 1,000 gold yen.[51] On January 27, 1898, the Taiwan Office issued Notification

---

47. Nihon ginkō chōsakyoku, ed., *Nihon kin'yūshi shiryō: Meiji Taishō hen*, vol. 15, 1229.

48. Namikata, "Taiwan ginkō no setsuritsu to heiseikaikaku," 56.

49. Compare, for instance, Soyeda, "Letter From Japan," esp. 472.

50. This is a key argument in Ono Kazuichirō, *Kindai Nihon heisei to higashi Ajia ginkaken*. In the context of Taiwan's monetary reform only, see Li, "Jūkyū seiki no tōa ginkaken to Taiwan no heisei kaikaku." Li relies heavily on Ono's discussion.

51. This notification is reproduced in Namikata, "Taiwan ginkō no setsuritsu to heiseikaikaku," 63. Later, it was amended by introducing Notification 70, which reformulated the above value of one-yen silver coins "at the rate of 96 *sen* and 4 *rin* apiece." This was apparently done because it was "soon considered inconvenient in making cal-

6, which indicated that "persons desirous of getting the convertible banknotes exchanged for one-yen silver coins having the Government Stamp mark may apply for exchange at the Government Treasury. The Treasury may, however, decline to make exchange if the sufficient amount of the said one-yen silver coin is not at hand."[52] According to this plan, monetary reform would fit within a narrow time window harmonized with the course of events on the mainland: after April 1, 1898 (the date silver coins would officially cease to circulate in Japan proper), unstamped silver coins would not be accepted for payments of taxes and other public dues, making them principally and factually unfit as a medium of exchange.

Monetary Independence?

This procedure was, however, prone to further difficulties. One reason was that because stamped one-yen silver coins were legal tender, using them for payment required consent of the payee. This made it was almost impossible to guarantee their wide circulation. Furthermore, as a large number of "uninjured" one-yen silver pieces (*mukizu ichi'en ginka*) were circulating in the Taiwanese hinterland, it was impractical to prohibit the use of those pieces for paying taxes. Finally, Taiwan's macroeconomic environment was hard to ignore. How to manage the use of stamped one-yen coins in dealings with merchants from, Hong Kong and Amoy, for instance, where regulations governing the circulation of these coins did not apply? The authorities had apparently been too optimistic about the feasibility of their scheme and were soon forced to alter the terms and conditions for the withdrawal of unstamped one-yen pieces. Inoue Kaoru, then Minister of Finance, indicates the need for a policy reversal in a memorandum to the Tokyo government:

While it has been the aim of the Government in the currency administration of Formosa to make the same system in vogue in Formosa at some future time as at home: and while as a step toward that object it was decided to allow the use of the stamped one-yen silver coin in all transactions [. . .], it has been ascertained that the stamped one-yen coin was disliked not only by the people

----

culations to fix the valuation of the stamped one-yen silver coin in terms of number of pieces." Matsukata, *Report*, 384.

52. Ibid., 385.

of Formosa, but also by people in Amoy, Hongkong, &c., whose commercial relations with the people of Formosa are naturally very close [. . .]. Owing to this circumstance, a great inconvenience is being now experienced in commercial transactions. [. . .]

I beg therefore to present to the Cabinet Council the following scheme concerning the currency of Formosa:

I.   To allow for the time being the unlimited circulation of the uninjured one-yen silver coin.

II. The ratio between the one-yen silver coin mentioned in the preceding paragraph and the gold coin shall be officially determined, being based on the current ratio between silver and gold.
     [. . .]

IV. The uninjured one-yen silver coins shall be allowed to circulate with the expiration of the period allowed for their exchange [. . .]. So long as the period lasts the existing policy shall be pursued.

V.   The one-yen silver coin with the Government stamp mark shall not be paid out by the Government, after the uninjured one-yen silver coin is allowed to circulate; though it will be accepted by the Government at the current rate of valuation for payments made to it.[53]

Apart from a minor revision of the ratio of the silver yen coin relative to the gold yen coin, Inoue's proposal was adopted and turned into Ordinance 19, issued by the Governor-General on July 30, 1898. Shedding Taiwan's "silver fetters" turned out to be more difficult than anticipated.

Around the same time, Taiwan's monetary predicament also began to appear on the radar of public opinion in Japan. Because the public had been led to believe—erroneously—that Taiwan would join Japan in adopting the gold standard, the Finance Ministry's questionable decision to define Taiwan's monetary standard as a nominal gold coin standard and the consequent move to allow one-yen silver coins to circulate struck many opinion makers and even several officials, among them no less a figure than Takahashi Korekiyo, as deeply inconsistent. In a series of articles in leading liberalist journals such as *Jiji shinpō*, *Tōyō keizai shinpō* (*The Oriental Economist*), and *Tōkyō keizai zasshi* (*The Tokyo Economist*), they launched sharp critiques of government policy.[54] Four arguments can be distinguished:

---

53. Ibid., 386–87.
54. For an overview, see Namikata, *Nihon shokuminchi kin'yū seisakushi no kenkyū*, 88.

1. Shifts in the rate between silver and gold were harmful for trade between Taiwan and the mainland.
2. These shifts were especially prohibitive for attracting Japanese investments and thus contradictory to the plan of developing Taiwan's economy.
3. They gave rise to a host of difficulties with regard to procedures for the exchange of money.
4. Using silver yen in the name of Taiwanese monetary reform was an "indecent" policy [*kokka no tokugi-jō futokusaku*].

Namikata indicates, correctly, that the strength of their arguments was to be found in their ideological appeal.[55] He makes clear that the *Oriental Economist*, home to some of the most vocal critics, pushed for clarification on the relationship between Japan and the newly acquired territory of Taiwan. If Taiwan was indeed incorporated into the Japanese empire, the journal's authors stressed, why would it have to be content with a different monetary system? Although not quite irredentist, such allegations evoking nationalist-imperialist sentiment may have been used because their authors were aware that they were hard to ignore.

A few months later, the authorities were indeed forced to clarify their position on what could formerly be left shrouded in ambiguity. Late in 1898 the Japanese government suddenly reversed its policy of assigning the right of issuing banknotes solely to the Bank of Japan (BOJ). It first decided to amend Article 23 of the original Bank of Taiwan Act and to strengthen the right of oversight of the minister of finance with regard to the issuing of bearer notes;[56] but almost simultaneously, by dint of Law 38 (March 1, 1899), it amended Article 8 of the same act to grant the Bank of Taiwan the right to "issue banknotes to the amount of one yen and more."[57] Official reports were apologetic about this change and cited numerous impracticalities. They argued, for instance, that issues of five-yen bearer notes were not fit for use in the Taiwanese economy, which was capital-poor in the first place; or they indicated that, with the adoption of the gold standard on the Japanese mainland, the provision of converting these bearer notes into gold coin had been rendered obsolete.

---

55. Namikata, *Nihon shokuminchi kin'yū seisakushi no kenkyū*, 89.
56. See "Taiwan ginkōhō dai 23-jō kaisei" 台湾銀行法第二十三条改正 (Amendment of Article 23 of the Bank of Taiwan Act), JACAR Ref. A03020328300.
57. See ibid., JACAR Ref. A03020372900.

Yet if we look at the fiscal history of Taiwan's administration, it is clear that budgetary matters rather than these issues played an over-arching role in this decision. Costs associated with Taiwan's early ad-ministration had originally been included in the "Extraordinary War Expenditures Special Account" (*rinji gunjihi tokubetsu kaikei*) of the Sino-Japanese War.[58] Yet, starting with fiscal year 1896 (beginning in April 1896),[59] this special account was eliminated, and the costs of Taiwan's administration were included in the General Account (*ippan kaikei*). It was also around this time that policy makers became aware of the extra-ordinary costs of the administration of the newly acquired territory—the expense of suppressing the anti-Japanese movement proved particularly unexpected[60]—leading to the difficult debate about Japan's capability to administer the island in the first place.

Although this is not very well known, the government at that time unofficially departed from its original ambition to assimilate Taiwan into Japanese territory and promulgated the "Law with Respect to the Special Account of the Taiwan Governor-General" (Taiwan sōtokufu tokubetsu kaikei hō).[61] This law once more separated expenditures for Taiwan from the General Account and adopted, again unofficially, a policy line presupposing a certain degree of Taiwanese independence, more or less as a colony. In a typical phrasing, the law projected "the growth of the territory's revenue, in order to attain a status of inde-pendence" (*sainyū no zōka o hakari owari ni dokuritsu no mokuteki o tassei shimuru*).[62] In a different formulation, the rationale of this law was "to cover Taiwan's expenditures by means of its receipts" (*Taiwan no sai-*

---

58. For an overview, see Nihon ginkō tōkeikyoku, ed., *Meiji ikō honpō shuyō keizai tō-kei*, 143.

59. Japanese statistics are given for fiscal years starting on April 1.

60. See Morris, "The Taiwan Republic of 1895 and the Failure of the Qing Mod-ernizing Project."

61. See "Taiwan sōtokufu tokubetsu kaikeihō" 台湾総督府特別会計法 (Law with respect to the special account of the Taiwan government-general), JACAR Ref. A03020269300. For an official explanation concerning its adoption: "Taiwan sōtokufu tokubetsu kaikeihō o sadamu" 台湾総督府特別会計法ヲ定ム (On deciding the law with respect to the special account of the Taiwan government-general), JACAR Ref. A01200861700.

62. Ibid.

shutsu wa sono sainyū o motte shiben suru o gensoku to shi).[63] In relation to the new policy direction, Gotō Shinpei had drawn up the scheme to float an enormous loan mentioned above, again in an effort to secure the island's "fiscal independence."[64]

But it is one thing to have a plan, and another to accomplish it. At least at the very early stages of Taiwan's development, its financial status was far from self-sufficiency. In fiscal year 1896, for instance, the island's revenues stood at ¥2.7 million, whereas its expenditures amounted to ¥9.65 million. The difference of ¥6.94 million, or roughly 250 percent of the island's revenue was to come from the mainland's treasury, which already found it difficult to cope with the postwar financial administration.[65] Once Japan went onto the gold standard, budgetary stringency was only reinforced. It is thus no surprise that the Japanese government first imposed higher taxes on the Taiwanese population and then abolished the BOJ's monopoly on note issue by granting the BOT the right to issue notes of 1 yen and higher. Whether or not this was demanded by public opinion, the government had at least been forced to take a stance.

The Predicament of the International Price of Silver

Beginning around the turn of the century, the Japanese government had a rude awakening to the reality that it was not solely in control of Taiwan's monetary future. With the formation of the international gold standard system coming to a close, there also came an end—at least temporarily—to the fall of the price of silver (see Table 1.2), and with it

---

63. Ōkurashō, *Meiji Taishō zaiseishi*, vol. 19 (1958), 12. Also mentioned in Namikata, *Nihon shokuminchi kin'yū seisakushi no kenkyū*, 70.

64. The plan to raise a loan of ¥35 million was ratified (but never put into effect) after 1899, by dint of the Act for the Raising of Loans with Regard to Taiwan's Public Works: "Taiwan jigyō kōsaihō" 台湾事業公債法, JACAR Ref. A03020377000. The idea of raising a loan for Taiwan's development is briefly discussed by Namikata, *Nihon shokuminchi kin'yū seisakushi no kenkyū*, 71ff. Assimilationist thought persisted unabated in the fields of culture and language education; see, for example, E. P. Tsurumi, "Education and Assimilation in Taiwan under Japanese Rule"; Ching, *Becoming Japanese*.

65. Matsukata, *Report on the Adoption of the Gold Standard in Japan*. For a scholarly treatment of problems of public finance at the time, see Nochi, "Nisshin-Nichiro sengo keiei to taigai zaisei 1896–1913."

Table 1.2: Silver price in the London market and gold-silver parity, 1870–1909

Year	Silver price (pence)	Gold-silver parity	Year	Silver price (pence)	Gold-silver parity
1870	60 9/16	15.57	1890	47 11/16	19.77
1871	60 1/2	15.57	1891	45 1/16	20.92
1872	60 5/16	15.65	1892	39 13/16	23.68
1873	59 1/4	15.92	1893	35 5/8	26.70
1874	58 5/16	16.17	1894	28 15/16	32.57
1875	56 7/8	16.62	1895	29 7/8	31.57
1876	54 3/4	17.77	1896	30 3/4	30.59
1877	54 13/16	17.22	1897	27 9/16	34.20
1878	52 9/16	17.92	1898	26 15/16	35.36
1879	51 1/4	18.39	1899	27 7/16	34.36
1880	52 1/4	18.06	1900	28 1/4	33.33
1881	51 11/16	18.24	1901	27 3/16	34.68
1882	51 5/8	18.27	1902	24 1/16	39.15
1883	50 9/16	18.64	1903	24 3/4	38.10
1884	50 5/8	18.58	1904	26 3/8	35.70
1885	48 5/8	19.39	1905	27 13/16	33.87
1886	45 3/8	20.78	1906	30 7/8	30.54
1887	44 5/8	21.11	1907	30 3/16	31.24
1888	42 7/8	21.99	1908	24 3/8	38.64
1889	42 11/16	22.10	1909	23 11/16	39.74

NOTE: The price is given in pence per ounce of silver 925 fine.
SOURCE: Laughlin, *A New Exposition of Money, Credit, and Prices*, vol. 2, Appendix 2. For a schematic view of price variations between 1903 and 1908, see Kemmerer, "The Recent Rise in the Price of Silver and Some of Its Monetary Consequences," 217.

a necessary redefinition of the linkages between the Japanese mainland and its Taiwanese satellite.[66] This development posed several challenges to the monetary authorities. They had decided to leave the use of silver coins in place, not as a subsidiary coinage of the nominally adopted gold coin standard, but as silver coins whose price was determined on the basis of the market price of silver in Hong Kong. Importantly, this market price was to be updated not every day but rather through "snapshots" at intervals of several months. In Inoue's memorandum, for instance, the "current ratio shall be made out every six months, by

66. See Kemmerer, "The Recent Rise in the Price of Silver and Some of Its Monetary Consequences." For a discussion of the effect of the price of silver on British money doctoring in East Asia, see Ono Kazuichirō, *Kindai Nihon heisei to higashi Ajia ginkaken*, 151ff.

taking the average of the prevailing price of silver in Shanghai, Hong-kong, Formosa, &c., for the past six months"; the final revision narrowed the intervals to four months.[67]

Already by 1902, this method of regularly redefining the price of the one-yen silver piece had become a source of annoyance to the Office of the Governor-General.[68] Still, in a period in which the price of silver continued to fall (it had fallen by more than 50 percent from 1870 to 1902), silver holders from all over the world expected further losses and looked for ways to recoup them preemptively. Such expectations embodied in collective action became self-reinforcing, partly explaining the pronounced fall in the price of silver between 1900 and 1902. But, importantly for our discussion, this fall also underlines that the one-yen silver coin had been continuously overvalued relative to the swiftly changing world price and that its value was lagging behind further price decreases.[69] Taiwan thus became an attractive haven for the silver supply in the contracting world silver market. The practical effect on the island's money supply must have been substantial: foreign silver coins and bullion flooded the country, with an unavoidable contraction (or, rather, a series of sharp reductions) in the amount of (undervalued) BOT silver notes.

Even more troubling for the island's economy, however, was the volatility of the world price of silver after 1902. As shown in Table 1.2, the price of silver rallied in early 1903 and continued to climb until 1907, albeit not without frequent interruptions. For the years 1903 and 1904 alone, for instance, the average price of silver (per ounce) reached almost 28 pence in October 1903 and then fell below 26 pence in December of the same year; it climbed again to over 26 ½ pence in February 1904, only to fall back to 25 pence in April; after that its increase became slightly more continuous.[70] The straightforward arbitrage

---

67. Matsukata, *Report on the Adoption of the Gold Standard in Japan*, 387.

68. In this period, the right to determine the official price of the silver yen had been transferred from the Minister of Finance to the Office of the Governor-General of Taiwan, coinciding with the decision to have the BOT issue banknotes.

69. For example, the price was adjusted on July 30, 1898 (to 92 *sen*); on November 26, 1898 (to 94 *sen*); and so on. Matsukata, *Report on the Adoption of the Gold Standard in Japan*, 388–89.

70. Data taken from Kemmerer, "The Recent Rise in the Price of Silver and Some of Its Monetary Consequences," 217.

described above gave way to waves of more speculative actions: silver holders did not simply attempt to prevent further losses, but pro-actively sought to exploit and manipulate the price differences through the aggressive making and withdrawing of deposits and exchanges.[71] For the BOT, it must have been a frustrating process. Witnessing shifts in the world price of silver but with no direct control over the flow of silver into or out of Taiwan, the only step it could take was to adjust the official price of the one-yen silver piece, often only to see speculation intensify. Namikata describes what happened:

When the official price [of the one-yen silver piece] appeared to be overvalued, for instance, then [the monetary authorities would see an increase] in bank de-posit withdrawals, or receive [an increased number of] applications for loans; if, on the other hand [the one-yen silver piece appeared to be undervalued], one saw an increase in bank deposits and an increase in repayments of loans. In this way, the in- and outflow of capital, which was originally dissociated from economic activity, caused pervasive troubles for the Bank of Taiwan. This also detrimentally affected foreign exchange. When the official price was relatively low, money flowed from the [Japanese] mainland into Taiwan in or-der to be exchanged for silver coin, which was then transferred to Hong Kong or Amoy, where the market price of silver was higher. [. . .] And inversely, when the official price was relatively high, [people] exported silver coins from the Chinese coastal areas into Taiwan [. . .], exchanged them into silver notes, presented them for redemption into gold in Japan, and thus made a handsome profit on the difference in the price of gold and silver.[72]

Taiwan's money supply was not only inversely proportionate to the world price of silver; worse, that price had now become highly un-predictable. During this period, the BOT suffered considerable losses, whereas in the days when the price of silver could safely be predicted to fall further, the bank most certainly took its own share in the profits of arbitrage as well. The *Japan Bankers' Magazine* at the time estimated the BOT's losses due to swings in the price of silver in 1903 alone at

---

71. Compare "Taiwan ginkō: jigyō to kaisha" 台湾銀行：事業と会社 (The Bank of Taiwan: its activities and the institution), nos. 1–5, KMS 1924.8.14, KUDA-ID 10033215. The author of the article speaks of *kingin hika tōki* (arbitrage with respect to differences in the prices of gold and silver).

72. Namikata, *Nihon shokuminchi kin'yū seisakushi no kenkyū*, 251; italics added.

¥160,000.[73] In the same publication, Yagyū Kazuyoshi (then governor of the bank, and beyond question one of the bank's strong leaders in this early period) described the situation as one in which the BOT "could not duly perform its tasks as a credit institution."[74] From a convenient and briefly profitable tool for putting Japan's silver yen holdings to use and escaping massive demands for redemption, silver had become a liability both to the macroeconomic future of Taiwan within the Japanese empire and, more fundamentally, to attempts to uphold the gold standard in Japan proper. When its perceived advantages turned out to be elusive and temporary, it was accordingly cast aside. Borrowing a metaphor from Kemmerer, one may say that, before 1903, silver had been to Taiwanese and Japanese authorities "like the proverbial dog which licked the hand of the master who was about to beat it."[75]

Taiwan Joins the Gold Standard

In 1903, the BOT's governor, Yagyū, made up his mind: the time had come to beat the dog and discard the unstable metal. The reason to do so was not only silver's sudden and unpredictable price rise but also the steep increase in Taiwan's trade with gold-standard countries, especially with Japan proper. Whereas the share of trade with gold-standard countries was 39 percent in 1898, it reached 62 percent in 1902.[76] "Blocist" ideology in Tokyo and Taipei wanted only to boost this share further. In a series of pamphlets and memoranda, Yagyū and officials of the Taiwanese Office of the Governor-General demanded that the Ministry

---

73. "Taiwan engin tsūyō haishi" 台湾円銀通用廃止 (The prohibition of the use of the Taiwanese silver *yen*), *Ginkō tsūshinroku* 224 (June 1904), 30. Also mentioned in Namikata, *Nihon shokuminchi kin'yū seisakushi no kenkyū*, 252.

74. Taiwan ni okeru kinken no ryūtsū oyobi kangyō shikin kashidashi" 台湾に於ける金券の流通及勧業資金貸出 (The circulation of gold notes in Taiwan and the lending of funds for industrial development), *Ginkō tsūshinroku* 227 (September 1904), 21. For more information on Yagyū Kazuyoshi, see Yamazaki, *Yagyū Kazuyoshi*; on his legacy at the Bank of Taiwan, see Hekiyōkai, *Yagyū tōdori no hen'ei*.

75. Kemmerer, "The Recent Rise in the Price of Silver and Some of Its Monetary Consequences," 216.

76. Percentages taken from Namikata, *Nihon shokuminchi kin'yū seisakushi no kenkyū*, 252. Namikata regards this period as formative for the consolidation of Taiwan as a nominally sovereign state (*meigiteki na sōshukoku*)—with obvious allusion to the aforementioned policy of a "nominal gold coin standard."

of Finance consider further monetary reform in order to gain more sway in steering Taiwan's macroeconomic destiny.

The Ministry of Finance had received a request for implementation of the gold standard in Taiwan in 1902, but the Ministry deemed it "rather premature [*jiki naho hayashi to shi*] and therefore rather difficult to implement."[77] The BOT continued to put pressure on the Ministry, but to no avail despite the gravity of its situation. Although the Ministry would eventually organize a monetary council (*kahei kaigi*) in which Yagyū was also invited to take part, frantic military preparations in the lead-up to the Russo-Japanese War made monetary difficulties in Japan's periphery a less pressing issue. Initially there was not even a response to the urgent demand to pay out silver yen to the BOT so it could, in the event of jumps in the price of silver and consequent demands for conversion of silver notes, at least counteract the acute dearth of silver reserves.[78] Only once, and after strong and repeated pressure from Yagyū, would it deviate from its policy of non-interventionism and pay out silver yen.

Yagyū therefore undertook a range of measures that furthered the original Ministry strategy of granting Taiwan relative monetary and fiscal independence. Importantly, he chose to adopt the notion of "self-help measures" (*jieisaku*)[79] and used this as a means to bring the Ministry of Finance to consider further action. He proposed these possible policy lines in a pamphlet of August 1904:

1. Have Taiwan adopt a full silver coin standard [*junzen taru ginka seido*] and abolish the official price of silver system.
2. If (1) is impossible, have the Japanese government guarantee any loss the Bank of Taiwan would incur due to the volatile price of silver.
3. If both (1) and (2) should prove impossible, have the Japanese government pay out silver yen coins in its possession if the occasion calls for it [*zuiji haraisage*]; with regard to demands for the conversion of silver notes into

---

77. "Senji zaisei to taigin" 戦時財政と台銀 (Wartime finance and the Bank of Taiwan), in TNN 1908.04.19 [not included in KUDA].

78. In this respect, see "Gaichi zaisei no sōsetsu, Taiwan zaisei" 外地財政の創設・台湾財政, in *Ōkurashōshi*, vol. 1, 405–9.

79. Taiwan ginkōshi hensanshitsu, ed., *Taiwan ginkōshi*, 33.

silver coins or bullion, and the conversion of silver coins into silver notes, allow for a system of charging a premium [*uchibu*].[80]

In their brazenness, these proposals leave nothing to the imagination. Unless the Ministry and the Government were prepared to lose face and forgo the ideology that claimed Taiwan as part of Japan's territory, these options were nonstarters. These proposals were a clever way to convince Tokyo that it made no sense to put off the adoption of the gold standard.

Perhaps Yagyū was also aware that his proposals would alarm key constituencies in Taiwan, and could thus be used to mobilize them to put pressure on Tokyo. The Taipei Forum for Commerce and Industry (Taipei shōkō danwakai) was particularly wary of option 3, the suggestion of a premium, which would lead to isolation of the Taiwanese market from the Japanese mainland. As its members were highly dependent on credit from the BOT and were looking forward to expanding their foreign trade portfolio, this isolation would harm their commercial activities considerably. Whether their response to Yagyū's proposal was more or less directed by Yagyū and BOT officials is unknown, but the reaction was decisive, and without doubt to Yagyū's liking. After convening an emergency meeting in September 1903 (less than one month after the announcement of Yagyū's proposals), the Taipei Forum submitted a position statement to Gotō Shinpei and Shimosaka Fujitarō, then managing director of the BOT. The statement summed up earlier opposition to a separate Taiwanese monetary standard and also strongly condemned the premium system on grounds that were implied in Yagyū's proposals: it would disturb the island's commerce, shake its fiscal foundations, and be detrimental to trade relations with Japan proper. In a joint communiqué with the BOT, the Forum went on to publish "Opinions with Regard to Taiwan's Monetary Reform" (Taiwan heisei kaikaku ni kansuru iken) in November 1903, repeating the need for the adoption of the gold standard in the very near future. It was only one of many such pamphlets circulating at the time.

---

80. This proposal provided for receiving bank deposits at a lower rate than the officially determined price of silver and, conversely, paying out deposits at a rate higher than the official price. Cited in Namikata, *Nihon shokuminchi kin'yū seisakushi no kenkyū*, 253.

In September 1903, the Office of the Governor-General had set out its own proposal in a draft presented to the Minister of Finance. More practical in nature, it hinted at a gradual adoption of the gold standard, and included benchmarks and strategies with regard to currency redemption. In rough outline it looked like this:

1. Amend the Bank of Taiwan act, allow the issue of gold notes [*kinken*], and call back the former silver notes for redemption.
2. Silver yen coins should not be redeemed by the Government, but could be allowed for public payment to the Government at an official exchange rate, as in the case of the silver notes; [apart from that], they may furthermore be considered legal tender.
3. Silver yen coins and silver notes received by the Government will not be paid out again.
4. Prohibit the importation of silver coins for as long as necessary.
5. Depending on the circulation of gold coins, prohibit the use of silver yen coins and silver notes for public payments to the Government.
6. [Thereafter] have the acceptance of silver coins be dependent on mutual consent of the Taiwanese people, excluding official interference [with regard to the determination of their value].[81]

The Government was eventually convinced of the need to carry Taiwanese monetary reform forward. It decided to discuss the issue and amend the Bank of Taiwan Act at the upcoming Nineteenth Diet Session. In preparation for the coming reform, the importation of "crude silver" (*sogin*) and privately issued—and impure or damaged—copper coins (referred to as *daiqian* or *aiqian*, literally "perished coins" or "dumb coins") was prohibited.[82] After October 1903, the BOT furthermore strictly limited the amounts of deposits and demands for exchange, in an effort to counter speculation; postal orders too were limited to the amount of ¥500 per person per draft.[83]

Even then, the Russo-Japanese War was still too high on Tokyo's agenda for it to follow up with monetary events in Taiwan. Only in May 1904, and after the price of silver had continued to damage the

---

81. Ibid., 254.
82. "Taiwan ginkō: jigyō to kaisha," nos. 1–5, KUDA-ID 10033215; see also Tsutsumi, "Shinmatsu Taiwan ni okeru hosen no ryūtsū to Beikoku torihiki."
83. "Taiwan ginkō: jigyō to kaisha," nos. 1–5, KUDA-ID 10033215.

BOT, in part as a result of the Russo-Japanese War itself,[84] did the Government allow the Office of the Governor-General to draw up administrative orders (*ritsurei*) for the issue of gold notes.[85] These were promulgated one month later. Although this procedure did not amend the Bank of Taiwan Act, and thus allowed the parallel circulation of both silver notes and gold notes as legal tender, the introduction of the gold notes was a success.[86] Its timing was particularly fortunate. Coinciding with another surge in the international price of silver, gold notes filled the demand for cash at a time when silver was once more being drawn away from Taiwanese shores. Understandably, Yagyū himself spoke of "an extraordinarily positive outcome" (*igai no kōkekka*);[87] the *Taiwan Daily Newspaper* announced that "silver notes have virtually disappeared from the market; silver yen coins, of which one may assume that large amounts would be in circulation on the island, have pretty much vanished as well."[88]

In 1906, the Japanese Government acknowledged that Taiwan was in practice incorporated within Japan's gold standard system. It amended the Bank of Taiwan Act and allowed more flexibility in the bank's reserve holdings. Around the same time, the island embarked on a spectacular economic stimulus and reform program.[89] Adhering to Gotō's

---

84. See Kemmerer, "The Recent Rise in the Price of Silver and Some of Its Monetary Consequences," 236: "The price level of one silver standard country may of course be temporarily out of equilibrium with that of other silver standard countries, because of some sudden alteration in the demand for (or supply of) silver in that country, as was the case of Manchuria at the time of the Russo-Japanese War, when military operations in that country created an exceptionally large demand for silver and drained off large quantities of the white metal from nearby silver standard countries."

85. See "Taiwan ginkōken hakkōhō" 台湾銀行券発行方 (On the issuing of gold notes by the Bank of Taiwan), JACAR Ref. A01200962000.

86. The Bank of Taiwan Act was eventually amended in February 1906: "Taiwan ginkōhō chūkaisei kajo" 台湾銀行法中改正加除 (Additions to and deletions from the Bank of Taiwan Act), JACAR Ref. A03020654700.

87. Yagyū Kazuyoshi, "Taiwan ni okeru kinken ryūtsū oyobi keizaikai no kinjō" 台湾に於ける金券流通及経済界の近状 (The circulation of gold notes in Taiwan and the recent state of the business world), *Ginkō tsūshinroku* 239 (September 1905), 15.

88. "Kahei ryūtsū no genjō" 貨幣流通の現状 (The current state of the circulation of monies), TNN 1905.06.08 (not in KUDA).

89. This economic growth was also well covered by newspapers at the time. See "Taiwan no keizai jōtai" 台湾の経済状態 (Taiwan's economic situation), nos. 1–29, OAS 1913.10.17–1913.11.24, KUDA-ID00472134; "Taiwan dai-hatten-ron" 台湾大発

credo of scientific colonialism, Japanese reformers were extremely thorough in transforming Taiwan's agriculture to meet the needs of the Japanese mainland.[90] And as in later examples of Japanese imperialism, money and finance were at the root of the reformers' success.[91] Before and during World War I, the BOT would open numerous branch offices in Southeast Asia, becoming a financial player for competitors to reckon with. Only late in the 1920s, when the bank overextended into risky lending schemes with the Suzuki Trading Company, did its influence start to wane.[92]

展論 (The idea of Taiwan's great development), nos. 1–17, TNN 1920.4.27–1920.5.23, KUDA-ID00472462.

90. Taiwanese agricultural transformation has attracted scholarly attention outside the context of the island's monetary and financial history. An authoritative account is provided by Twu, *Nihon teikokushugi ka no Taiwan*; on the role of the Bank of Taiwan in the island's development, see pp. 271ff. In English, see S. Ho, "Agricultural Transformation Under Colonialism"; Y. M. Ho, *Agricultural Development of Taiwan*; Anderton and Barrett, "Demographic Seasonality and Development."

91. On the role of credit institutions, see Namikata, *Nihon shokuminchi kin'yū seisaku-shi no kenkyū*, 259ff.

92. See Lynn and Rao, "Failures of Intermediate Forms"; Imada, "Taiwan ginkō no ichidanmen."

Table 1.3: Principal accounts of the Bank of Taiwan, 1899–1919 (in thousands of yen)

Year	Lending					Deposits					Paid-in capital
	Total	Public[a]	Private[b]	Loans[c]	Overdrafts[d]	Total	Public[a]	Private[b]	Time[e]	Current[f]	
1899	3,374	2,500	874	100	145	965	—	965	103	682	1,250
1900	7,672	6,200	1,472	204	188	4,974	—	4,974	2,863	1,584	1,250
1901	6,988	5,200	1,788	256	242	4,539	—	4,539	1,969	1,772	1,250
1902	9,987	6,850	3,137	435	479	6,470	—	6,470	2,607	1,979	2,500
1903	8,873	3,978	4,895	579	486	5,563	—	5,563	2,359	1,839	2,500
1904	9,686	3,551	6,134	921	598	6,017	—	6,017	2,290	2,141	2,500
1905	10,443	1,609	8,834	1,480	492	6,835	—	6,835	2,419	2,119	2,500
1906	14,012	—	14,012	2,515	865	10,171	—	10,171	3,685	3,020	2,500
1907	17,948	—	17,948	2,741	1,283	11,862	—	11,862	5,387	3,111	3,750
1908	18,995	796	18,198	2,563	1,193	11,188	—	11,188	4,262	3,421	5,000
1909	25,822	5,046	20,757	2,410	1,664	17,436	—	17,436	9,399	3,790	5,000
1910	27,403	5,641	21,761	4,115	1,189	18,860	—	18,860	9,057	4,491	6,250
1911	35,086	4,749	30,337	4,710	3,373	23,869	—	23,869	9,685	7,715	6,250
1912	45,157	5,095	40,061	4,012	3,619	34,029	—	34,029	15,226	8,894	6,250
1913	52,708	5,339	47,368	6,492	3,219	43,286	—	43,286	15,237	15,200	7,500
1914	56,055	5,767	50,288	7,481	2,856	54,187	—	54,187	19,519	11,859	8,750
1915	75,321	6,148	69,173	6,036	5,167	74,580	—	74,580	33,212	16,814	12,500
1916	102,300	5,911	96,389	9,520	8,378	111,019	—	111,019	58,845	19,930	15,000
1917	222,139	4,350	217,789	25,992	15,428	240,264	—	240,264	151,947	46,489	20,000
1918	328,052	3,105	324,946	61,641	34,222	389,201	—	389,201	220,736	40,519	25,000
1919	380,101	2,378	377,722	59,928	35,675	286,528	—	286,528	136,699	35,786	37,500

NOTES: (a) refers to government and public agencies; (b) refers to private corporations and individuals; (c) and (d) figures are included in private lending; (e) and (f) refer to deposit types, figures are included in private deposits.
SOURCE: Nihon ginkō tōkeikyoku, *Hundred Year Statistics of the Japanese Economy*, 212.

TWO

"As Close as Lips and Teeth":
The First Bank and Megata Tanetarō in Korea

Japan has only done what a good surgeon would have done to a patient in order to save
his life.

—*Seoul Press*, 1910

Unlike other imperial states Japan has never been accused of having neglected her colonies; on the contrary, if any charge may be made, it is that Korea [. . .] suffered from excessive attention.

—Hyman Kublin

The acquisition of Taiwan was an example of the susceptibility of Japanese policy makers to the lure of imperialist prestige rather than political
strategy. In contrast, the decision to engage with the "Korea problem"
was from the outset a matter of paramount strategic concern rather than
economic profit. Yet sociopolitical and military explanations of this instance of Japanese imperialism are not wholly satisfying, because they
do not pay attention to the role of a series of monetary and financial reforms that both the Japanese government and the Government-General
in Korea sought to implement immediately after the peninsula had been
turned into a protectorate. If these reforms were insignificant, why were
they pushed through with such force and at such high cost? Why had

EPIGRAPHS. Quotation from an article published in the *Seoul Press* (1910) and cited in
Bank of Chosen, *Economic History of Chosen*, 27; Kublin, "The Evolution of Japanese Colonialism," 80.

financial and monetary matters figured so prominently in the agreement pertaining to the creation of the protectorate? And more important, why did the monetary advisers stress the importance these reforms and corollary surveys of the country's developmental potential? In the words of one official history, because financial disorganization was "one of the chief causes which led Korea to ruin," it "was from the fiscal side that [Japan] first undertook [. . .] reform."[1]

In this chapter, I review the prehistory of Korea's annexation and reiterate the importance of considerations of Japan's national security. I also draw particular attention to a number of inconsistencies at the core of Japanese policies concerning Korea. These inconsistencies lead to the conclusion that Japan's aspiration to achieve the status of a Western power in its dealings with its immediate neighbor was ultimately self-defeating. Financial and economic considerations, indeed the very alliance between politicians and high financiers, eroded the strategy of establishing Korea as Japan's "line of interest." In the immediate aftermath of the Russo-Japanese War, the tide seemed to turn to Japan's economic and political advantage. However, the enormous burden of foreign loans made Korea a breeding ground for the growing ideology of national mobilization and economic autarky, an attempt to integrate political and economic objectives. Although such integration was impossible to achieve in the social and political diversity of the Japanese mainland, Korea's thoroughly militarized government aggressively pursued just such an agenda. Korea thus became an experiment with the type of mass mobilization that would come to characterize Japan only in the 1930s.

Finance and monetary matters were a major instrument for facilitating Korea's societal transformation. What came to be known as the "Megata reform" turned Korea into a subsidiary of the Japanese economy, intended to relegate the peninsula to the position of Japanese *lebensraum*—what later generations of politicians would refer to as the Greater East-Asia Co-Prosperity Sphere (*dai tōa kyōeiken*). The Megata reform was thus not an economic answer to an economic problem; rather, it was developed in reaction to a strategic need.

---

1. Bank of Chosen, *Economic History of Chosen*, 37.

Early Contacts with the "Hermit Nation"

In order to understand Japanese financial and monetary meddling in Korea, it is helpful to go back to early Meiji days. During this well-documented phase in Japanese history, the nation, shaken by a brutal "opening up" (*kaikoku*), chose to emulate the Western imperialist example. Only a few years after the country had been forced into signing the so-called unequal treaties with the Western powers (1866), Japanese reformers tapped into the discourse of the Western-led framework of "international law" and sought to apply its principles through the conclusion of a similar unequal treaty with China.[2] Its first experiment with imperialism was not a success—China, in the person of Li Hongzhang, forcefully rejected Japanese demands—but the event nevertheless revealed a Japan prepared to dismiss the Sinocentrist Asian constituency, dissociating itself from other Asian nations and treating them in the same way that the Western powers did.

By contrast, Korea, or the "Hermit Nation,"[3] as it came to be called, remained firmly embedded in the pre-imperialist Sinocentric system and continued to send tributary envoys to its much larger neighbor. It was not a Western country but Japan that would end Korea's politico-cultural isolation and "improve its conditions," as one British commentator phrased it at the time.[4] Japan did so as part of a remarkable effort to join the ranks of the "Western barbarians" that had subdued it; such an initiative required the adoption of the vocabulary and institu-

---

2. For a contemporary critical assessment of Western values, notions of international law, and free trade, see Pyle, *Japan Rising*, 69ff. For a description of the mercantilist view that free trade was no more than self-serving semantics of the imperialist victors, see Metzler, "The Cosmopolitanism of National Economics." For an assessment of international law from a Japanese perspective, consider the entry in the diary of Kido Kōin (Kido Takahashi) for December 21, 1868: "One cannot depend on international law without having a well-prepared military force. Many countries use the cloak of international law to seek their own interest in dealing with weaker nations. This is one of the reasons that I call international law a mere tool for depriving a weak nation of its rights." Brown and Hirota, trans., *Diary of Kido Takayoshi*, 148; also quoted in Miyoshi, *As We Saw Them*, 143.

3. Griffith, *Corea, the Hermit Nation*.

4. Maxey, "The Reconstruction of Korea."

tions of the nation-state and industrialization, as well as the acquisition of (semi-)colonies.[5]

Early disputes between Japan and Korea concerned whether Korea would choose to cling to the old ways or would adopt the modern customs of the Western conquerors. The fall of the Tokugawa provided a litmus test. Japan's reformers had been consistent in recognizing political changes that had taken place right after 1868 and employed a terminology avoiding references to China's role in the new order. Korea rejected the Japanese stance, for it would imply recognizing the Chinese and Japanese emperors as equals, which, in turn, would place Korea in the difficult and possibly irreconcilable position of being the underdog in two different political systems.

Japan originally declared Korea's refusal to recognize the legitimacy of the Meiji emperor as head of state of the Japanese empire a casus belli, in 1873. The ensuing debate, which came to be known as the *seikanron* (literally, the "punish Korea debate"), centered on whether Korea should be penalized for its "insulting behavior."[6] In many ways, this conflict constitutes a case study for those who perceive the origins of imperialism in domestic conflicts and efforts to divert attention from them by means of conquest of foreign territory.[7] Indeed, this debate exposed schisms among the Meiji modernizers, and it even led to the estrangement of several leading figures from the reform movement.[8] Yet these differences should not be overstated: there was near unanimity at the time about Korea's eventual position in the world of Japan's making. Tensions arose about the tactical question of *when* Japan was to intervene in Korean affairs. With Japan still in the process of reforming its own institutions, a foreign expedition could have compromised Japan's modernization, as several Meiji leaders recognized.

---

5. For Western accounts of Japanese efforts to bring Korea within its sphere of influence, see Duus, *The Abacus and the Sword*; Conroy, *The Japanese Seizure of Korea*.

6. For a detailed overview of domestic events at the time, see Mayo, "The Korean Crisis of 1873 and Early Meiji Foreign Policy."

7. See, for instance, Wehler, "Industrial Growth and Early German Imperialism."

8. Most notably, it caused the "last samurai" Saigō Takamori to turn away from the restoration movement and eventually launch a rebellion, which was forcefully repressed. See Ravina, *The Last Samurai*.

As a first step, Japan resorted to a sort of gunboat diplomacy to intimidate the Korean government into concluding the Kanghwa treaty of 1876.[9] This Japanese-Korean Friendship Treaty (Nitchō shūkō jōki), as it came to be known, officially recognized Korea's independence. Completely in line with the objectives of the unequal treaties forced upon Japan, however, it was designed to open up two Korean ports other than Pusan for trade (Wŏnsan and Inch'ŏn); it permitted the continuation of Japanese coastal surveys (which had been the source of hostilities in the first place); and it granted Japanese subjects the right of extraterritoriality and other rights whose restriction had been regarded as an affront to "national dignity" at home.[10] From the Japanese perspective, the treaty's conclusion marked a radically new beginning for Japan-Korea relations. It ended the ceremonial exchanges through the Sō family on Tsushima, instead stipulating intercourse between the two countries on the basis of the "law of nations." Although the treaty did not mention tariffs or other trade regulations, it nonetheless clearly was an unequal treaty.

If Japan's intentions were not already evident from this first agreement, the supplementary treaty and trade regulations negotiated through the summer of 1876 left no room for doubt. In many ways, these placed Korea in a worse position than Japan's when it fell victim to Western gunboat diplomacy.[11] Japanese nationals were exempted from all tariffs on imports and exports, and Japan agreed not to impose levies on any products coming from or going to Korea. Most important for the discussion here, Korean merchants were required to accept Japanese currency at face value in exchange for their products; in other words, the exchange of Japanese yen and Korean copper coins was regulated on the basis of pure equality of type and weight (*dōshu dōryō kōkan*).[12]

---

9. The Japanese military probably stage-managed an incident by sending a gunboat, the *Un'yō*, into Korean waters. Korean batteries at Kangwha Island opened fire, but were silenced by the *Un'yō*'s guns. Later, the military sent a fleet led by Special Envoy Kuroda Kiyotaka, demanding an apology from the Joseon government and conclusion of a commercial treaty between the two nations.

10. Deuchler, *Confucian Gentlemen and Barbarian Envoys.*

11. Duus, *The Abacus and the Sword*, 48.

12. For the original text of this stipulation, see "Shūkō jōki furoku narabi bōeiki shōtei fukoku no ken" 修好条規附録並貿易章程布告ノ件 (About the promulgation

Without tariffs, however modest, and without even a premium for converting Japanese currency into Korean currency, Japanese merchants gained a considerable advantage over their foreign counterparts—a prime example of "free-market imperialism." The establishment of a branch of Shibusawa Eiichi's First National Bank (Daiichi kokuritsu ginkō) in Pusan in 1878 gave Japan a powerful instrument for gaining influence on the peninsula. This action assisted policy makers in the establishment of a Korean pro-Japan faction, by making clear beyond all doubt that Japan had real interests on the peninsula. If judged in terms of its objectives, early policy thus seemed successful. The yen had gained a toehold on the Asian continent and seemed bound to earn Tokyo political sway on the peninsula, without a costly intervention.[13] It remained to be seen whether it could consolidate that position and become a tool powerful enough to gain Japan political leverage.

Incompatible Objectives

Unfortunately for the Meiji leaders, there was much more at stake than political motives. From the very outset, commercial interests had been engraved in the treaties and their appendices, prepared and negotiated by the very same politicians. Because the older merchant houses such as Mitsui, Ono, and Shimada took little interest in trade with the peninsula, the government decided to take the lead. It did so by turning to a new generation of successful Japanese businessmen: people such as

----

of the supplement to the Friendship Treaty and the trade regulations), JACAR Ref. B06150027600.

13. The debate about Tokyo's motives toward Korea is a thorny one. Korean historians have stressed the cynicism of the Japanese government's use of the rhetoric of national sovereignty and have accused Meiji leaders of indifference to the needs of the Korean populace and its desire to achieve true independence and progress. Yet Japanese concern for Korea's independence may have been genuine. Peter Duus, probably following Hilary Conroy, has pointed out that the "Japanese insistence on reform was too persistent, and in execution often too politically inept" to support alternative interpretations. Duus, *The Abacus and the Sword*, 71; compare 51ff. Without applauding Japan's objectives, or attributing idealism to its leading individuals, one cannot deny a genuine concern with Korea's autonomy. This concern was not inspired by the ideals of internationalism, but it did not have to be. Japanese insistence on Korean independence rather pointed toward its ability to be a strong element in Japan's "line of interest," as Yamagata put it in his famous memorial on foreign policy.

Iwasaki Yatarō, Ōkura Kihachirō, and Shibusawa Eiichi, all doyens of Meiji entrepreneurialism. What distinguished them was their involvement in promoting foreign trade. Politicians like Ōkubo Toshimichi and Ōkuma Shigenobu, who had vested working relationships with the business world, were particularly favorable to them.

Consecutive leaders would continue to endorse the rationale of Korea's economic penetration. In 1894, at the heat of the Sino-Japanese War, Matsukata Masayoshi spoke of "obtaining real interests and real rights" (*jitsuri jikken*) there, and thus enhancing the interest of the Japanese state, without directly intervening politically.[14] He proposed furthering the Japanese presence in other treaty ports, obtaining mining concessions, building a railroad between Seoul and Pusan, and obtaining permission to lay telegraph lines. Knowingly or not, he and others were contributing to a policy framework that would hamper, and in the end undermine, the widely shared political objective of Korean independence. It is important to realize that this contradiction was born from the early policy framework itself. Assessing its relative preeminence over or subordination to exogenous factors is therefore only a matter of detail. The point is that once combined with these factors, the inconsistencies inherent in Japanese policy triggered a dynamic that made an increasingly interventionist attitude toward Korean affairs more likely.

The nub of the problem was the treaty's stipulation that Korean merchants were to accept Japanese currency at face value in exchange for their products and that Japanese nationals were to be allowed to use and transport Korean copper coins. This created a situation that was not unlike the currency crisis Japan itself had faced when forced to internationalize. The influx of foreign currency distorted the exchange rate of indigenous copper coins. Since the early seventeenth century, this coin had been the *Sangp'yŏng t'ongbo* (in Japanese, *Jōhei tsūhō*), so called after the four characters inscribed upon it. Originally minted by a kind of famine relief office, this coin had been important in Korean monetary history, as it symbolized the establishment of cash money as the medium of the economy. It was followed by the issue of other

---

14. Tokutomi, *Kōshaku Matsukata Masayoshi den*, vol. 2, 499.

coins, minted in several forms and in different pretexts, all referred to as *yŏpchŏn*, "[copper] cash."[15]

The problem with the clause stipulating "exchange on the basis of equality of type and weight" was that Korean copper coins could be exchanged not directly for silver yen, Japan's de facto standard at the time, but instead for Japanese copper coins of the same weight. As the latter were themselves subsidiary coins on Japanese shores, the yen-*chŏn* 錢 exchange rate was thus determined indirectly.[16] Takashima Masaaki has explained that this resulted in a rate that, in comparison with the earlier *bakumatsu* rate, was not only disadvantageous to Korean merchants (1 yen = 660 *chŏn*), but was also dangerously close to the bullion price of copper. Fluctuations in the supply of copper *chŏn* at times caused the bullion price for copper to be higher than the face value of the coins; the laws of economics would then do their work, making it attractive for Japanese merchants to melt down Korean coins and ship them to Japan as bullion. Although the merchants might have chosen to make a profit by selling the bullion and turning the proceeds into gold, they were most likely to use the obtained capital to repeat the process and close the exchange circle.[17]

The possibility of such arbitrage naturally invited the interest of Japanese bankers. As early as March 1878, Shibusawa Eiichi's First National Bank opened an exchange office—in the parlance of the day, *kōkansho*—in the port of Pusan, with the self-proclaimed mission of "smoothing and facilitating commerce between Korea and Japan."[18] Its mandate unambiguously sought to provide all kinds of financial services to Japanese

---

15. For a monetary history of Korea before 1910, see Yi, *Kankoku kahei kin'yūshi*.

16. In practice, 1 silver yen = 1 *kanmon* of Japanese copper *sen* (*Kan'ei tsūhō*) = 660 Korean copper *chŏn* (*kansen*).

17. Takashima, *Chōsen ni okeru shokuminchi kin'yūshi no kenkyū*, 34ff. In *bakufu* times, the exchange rate used for trade between the daimyo of Tsushima and Korean merchants was much more favorable, with 1 yen = 500 *chŏn*.

18. The exchange office also came to be known as the First National Bank Pusan Branch Office. Shibusawa had originally planned the establishment of an exchange office to be jointly owned with Ōkura; the office would operate with paid-in capital of 50,000 yen, half provided by Shibusawa and half by Ōkura; they also sought to obtain a government loan of 100,000 yen. However, the Japanese Ministry of Finance at the time did not allow banks to engage in commercial activities other than banking and, due to high expenditures caused by the Seinan rebellion, was not keen on extending a loan. Compare Daiichi ginkō 80-nenshi hensanshitsu, ed., *Daiichi ginkōshi*, 414–16.

nationals—foreign exchange, the acceptance of deposits, secured loans, handling bills of exchange, documentary bills (*nigawase*), remittance bills ("money orders," *namigawase*), and the like. As the only financial institution in town, it soon saw its business flourish. The official history of the First Bank takes pride in mentioning that the Japanese consular office in Pusan used it for the disbursement of its funds, and that it acted as the agent for the Tokyo Marine Insurance Company. Its business records too speak of formidable progress. In the first half of 1879, only one year after opening its doors, its number of customers had risen to more than 700 and its revenue had doubled.[19] Shibusawa was too shrewd to allow an opportunity with such strong political support to slip through his fingers and dreamed of more profit. When two new treaty ports, Wŏnsan and Inch'ŏn, were opened (in 1880 and 1883 respectively), he immediately set up new offices there. The branch in Inch'ŏn was to handle the finances of the consular office there and in Seoul.

In 1882, the establishment of the Bank of Japan (BOJ) brought the era of national banks to a close and deprived them of the privilege of issuing banknotes. The First National Bank had no choice but to adapt and reinvent itself as a private bank. It drastically cut back the number of domestic branches; within Japan, only its abbreviated name (First Bank) indicated its once illustrious origin. In Korea, however, the First Bank stepped up its presence on the peninsula. Paul Georg von Möllendorf, the German-born superintendent of the newly established Korean Maritime Customs Office, concluded with Inoue Kaoru the so-called Tariff Agreement (1883), stipulating that the First Bank could handle the custom revenues (*kaikanzei*), a privilege indeed; the 8 percent tariff rate and a most-favored-nation clause made it a reasonably favorable deal for Japanese traders.[20]

The bank's activities continued to receive direct and indirect support from the government in Tokyo and it effectively operated as a semi-governmental institution. Buying up gold dust (*sakin*) in Korea and silver *tael* in Shanghai to supply the newly established BOJ with specie to back its convertible notes now became one of its main sources of

19. Ibid., 415–16.
20. On the Tariff Agreement, see Lee, *West Goes East*, esp. 49–59; correspondence preceding the agreement is reproduced in *Daiichi ginkōshi*, 527ff.

revenue.[21] After concluding an agreement with the BOJ in 1886, this activity took up a large part of the First Bank's portfolio. In the period between 1886 and 1889, the total of gold and silver bullion remitted to the BOJ amounted to no less than ¥2.6 million.[22] The Japanese economic presence in Korea now seemed to have entered a new stage in its development.

The impact on the Korean monetary system was immediate and considerable. The dramatically accelerated, almost overnight, inflow of Japanese yen (mainly paper currency) into Korea effectively disrupted the economy of a country that had long insisted on its own traditional ways (see Table 2.1). Takashima estimates that the influx of yen relegated to a subsidiary role the Korean copper *chŏn*, the value of which was entirely dependent on the actions of exchange offices and Japanese merchants.[23] This effectively drove the value of copper *coins* to fall further still, adding to the distress of Korea's currency system by causing ever more copper coins to flow out of the country. In turn, monetary and financial questions would now become an issue in negotiations between Japanese and Korean officials. More important, they would become crucial in determining Japanese attitudes toward the peninsula.

Shibusawa's ambitions were even more far-reaching. With the prospect of such an exchange bonanza, he envisioned a role for his First National Bank that may have seemed farfetched at the time, but that foreshadowed much of Japan's increasing interference in Korean affairs. In an 1883 letter to Ōhashi Hanshichirō (who was to manage the Pusan branch) he spoke of the issuance of bills of exchange that "may eventually be used as banknotes."[24] He was apparently toying with the idea of his bank's eventually becoming Korea's national bank. Needless to say, this aspiration was beyond anything attainable by any Japanese business, even the wealthy and respected First Bank. But it underscores how political ambitions and economic interests were, in the end, incompatible.

---

21. The Bank of Japan did not print banknotes until 1884; for a short description of the business of buying bullion, see Daiichi ginkō 80-nenshi hensanshitsu, ed., *Daiichi ginkōshi*, 537–38.

22. Ibid., 538.

23. Takashima, *Chōsen ni okeru shokuminchi kin'yūshi no kenkyū*, 39.

24. Mentioned in Tatai, *Chōsen ginkō*, 31.

Table 2.1: Estimates of inflow/outflow of Japanese paper notes into/out of Korea (in thousands of yen)

Year	Japan to Korea	Korea to Japan
1872	43,275	–
1873	–	–
1874	–	–
1875	60,482	37,990
1876	13,488	6,116
1877	13,500	5,965
1878	7,369	–
1879	12,367	565
1880	2,620	–
1881	9,200	–
1882	–	102
1883	25,000	100
TOTAL	187,302	50,840

NOTE: Some figures have been rounded.
SOURCE: Takashima, *Chōsen ni okeru shokuminchi kin'yūshi no kenkyū*, 38.

The Start of the Currency Wars

Japanese action had not gone unnoticed in neighboring countries. Aware of Tokyo's penchant for predatory monetary action in Korea, both China and, later, Russia, would engage Japan in what can only be described as "currency wars" on Korean soil. The outcome of these wars was, at least throughout the 1880s, far from clear. Politically, Japan's position in Korea remained bleak. The few reforms that were implemented—"gas lights for the palace, a postal system, the establishment of a national mint [the so-called Chŏnhwan'guk, or in Japanese Ten'enkyoku], and the like"[25]—did nothing to enhance Korean independence or national strength. Furthermore, China had been monitoring Japanese activity on the peninsula closely and had sought to have Korea conclude equal trade arrangements with several Western countries. It also resorted to imperial tactics to reassert dominance over its former vassal state. It managed, for instance, to conclude a set of Regulations of Sino-Korean Maritime and Continental Trade (Seikan suiriku bōeiki shōtei, 1882), according to which Chinese merchants were allowed to settle and trade

25. Duus, *The Abacus and the Sword*, 59.

beyond the treaty ports in the Korean hinterland—a provision not available to their Japanese counterparts.

Japanese officials were aware that they were losing ground, and their commitment to Korean independence, once believed to be a viable and noble objective, suddenly wavered. Official reactions were characterized by vacillation. Most of the proposals to issue a loan to the Korean pro-Japan faction came to naught. The loans that did materialize were too small to have an impact on reform, and were little more than sweeteners for the pro-Japan faction.[26]

Why this caution? For one thing, Japanese businessmen like Shibusawa and Gotō Shōjirō were not eager to invest in a venture whose outcome was not sure to bring them a safe and profitable return.[27] Statesmen, meanwhile, believed it unwise to offer substantial financial support, especially after a failed coup d'état in 1884 appeared to have been orchestrated by Tokyo.[28] This coup attempt probably sealed the fate of the pro-Japan faction. Around 1884, the Japanese government seemed to realize that its future in Korea did not lie with the reform movement. Equally important, the young Meiji state was unable to commit itself substantially to lending to Korea.

But what was the impact of China's renewed assertiveness on Korea's monetary and financial constituency? Contrary to what one might expect, the inflow of Mexican silver dollars (*yōgin* or *kokugin*) into Korea was never sufficient to topple the newly established yen-led monetary constituency.[29] Monetary differentiation between port towns and the Korean hinterland remained great. Around 1890, Japan had managed to fortify its position largely through the trustworthiness and soundness of the First Bank. Statistics on the circulation of Japanese yen in Pusan in the period between 1889 and 1891 show leaps of 337 percent for Japanese silver coins and of 239 percent for silver-denominated Japanese

---

26. Ibid., 55ff.

27. The proposals of some businessmen in this respect did not reflect political sensibilities. Ōkura Kihachirō, for instance, proposed in 1882 a loan secured against part of the production of Korea's gold mines. See *Nihon gaikō bunsho*, vol. 15, 156–57. On Gotō Shōjirō, see Ōhashi, *Gotō Shōjirō to kindai Nihon*.

28. For a full account in English, see Cook, *Korea's 1884 Incident*.

29. See Andrew, "The End of the Mexican Dollar."

paper currency, amounting respectively to ¥414,265 and ¥291,735.[30] The explanation therefore must be sought in the nature of the silver dollar itself. Often stamped or chopped by endorsers beyond all recognition, these coins were of notoriously low quality. The Japanese silver yen, in contrast, not only was of higher quality but also had gained credibility as a stable currency. Its reputation was so good that Korean merchants in the port cities would often change their copper *chŏn* into Japanese silver yen for saving (Gresham's law); Chinese merchants often shipped them to China.[31] These diversions of silver coins in turn enhanced the importance of paper currency and convertible notes of the Bank of Japan (*Nichigin dakanken*).

Seen in this light, Japan's monetary takeover of Korea was already complete more than a decade before the protectorate was established. But monetary dominion did not necessarily produce price stability. Seasonal fluctuations in the volume of trade produced sharp swings in the exchange rate of Korean copper, the minting of which rarely responded to relative increases or decreases in monetary demand.[32] Apparently, Japanese merchants in Korea tried to restore the stability of Korean currency by issuing *chŏn*-convertible bills of exchange (*kansen tegata*); the First Bank added to the effort by printing tax bills of exchange (*zeikan tegata*). By 1891, the Korean economy thus found itself in an impossible situation. On the one hand, it faced strong political pressure from its large Chinese neighbor, whose merchants represented the lion's share of Korea's foreign trade. But on the other hand, Japanese monetary presence loomed larger than ever. The need for reform was pressing.

Financial reform had first presented itself through heavy-handed Chinese pressure. Wary of Japan's ambitions on the peninsula, Li Hongzhang had been lobbying insistently for the appointment of von Möllendorf as adviser to the Korean government in 1882, with the sole aim of "spiting the Japanese."[33] Reportedly a dedicated and loyal individual, von

---

30. *Nihon gaikō bunsho*, vol. 24, 176. This investigation was part of a larger project supervised by Matsukata Masayoshi, aimed at documenting the circulation of Japanese currency in a variety of Asian countries; the investigation's aim was closely connected to the preparation of the adoption of the gold standard.

31. Takashima, *Chōsen ni okeru shokuminchi kin'yūshi no kenkyū*, 43–44.

32. For statistics, see ibid., 51.

33. See Chien, *The Opening of Korea*, 42–44.

Möllendorf was truly committed to his employer and to restoring Korea's monetary independence.[34] But while his aspirations were sincere, the implementation and outcome of his reform were disastrous. Under his direction, the Chŏnhwan'guk would mint large quantities of low-quality copper coins. Apparently von Möllendorf had not given thought to the question of the standard to be adopted by Korea; with Korean copper coins de facto subsidiary currency to the Japanese yen, the mere minting of extra copper coins would not benefit Korea's monetary independence, let alone the country's wealth.[35] It was soon obvious that this ill-defined plan had opened Pandora's box. Commodity prices soared and, throughout the country, rebellious soldiers from Korea's traditional army units launched a campaign against Japanese interventionism.

It was to be another eight years before the Korean government would once more ponder the possibility of monetary reform. In 1891 it promulgated the Regulations with Regard to the Currency of Great Korea (Dai Chōsenkoku kahei jōrei). Related to an earlier plan to solicit foreign loans in order to establish a banking system and build a railroad between Seoul and Inch'ŏn,[36] this time two Japanese businessmen were approached to assist in the attempt at monetary reform. In a letter to members of the Korean pro-international faction, Ōmiwa Chōbei, the founder of the Fifty-Eighth National Bank, stressed that he and Masuda Nobuyuki of the Ōsaka Copper Company (Ōsaka seidō kaisha) had a great interest in "ameliorating and modernizing" Korea's currency, and aspired to strive for the "orderly organization of your country's finances."[37] Their reform effort likewise ended in failure. Although the proposal had considerable financial backing and may have had a chance of succeeding—it sought to regulate foreign exchange by establishing a silver standard after Japan's example—it was no match for strong nationalist sentiment within Korea, nor for Chinese maneuvering against any reform effort that involved Japanese consultants. Soon after several coinage proofs had been minted, the project was aborted. As a result, the state of Korea's currency system deteriorated even fur-

---

34. Lee, *West Goes East*, 45–49.
35. These criticisms were also voiced in the immediate aftermath of the incident.
36. Takashima, *Chōsen ni okeru shokuminchi kin'yūshi no kenkyū*, 48–49.
37. Ibid., 49. This invitation of Japanese financiers also attracted attention in the *Tōkyō keizai zasshi* at the time. Compare Taguchi, "Chōsen no shin kahei chūzō jigyō."

ther. The exchange rate of the yen with the copper *chŏn* dropped every day, reaching record lows in 1893 and 1894.[38]

The Sino-Japanese War and Mounting Japanese Assertiveness

The Sino-Japanese War (1894–95) marked a sea change in the relationship between Tokyo and Seoul, and provided the framework within which Japan sought to expand its monetary and financial grip.[39] The desire to acquire commercial interests on the peninsula was in fact incompatible with the original plan of establishing Korea's independence as a means of defending Japan's "line of interest." Sooner or later, Japanese statesmen would have to make different and difficult strategic choices. This happened in 1894, when the insurgence of the so-called Tonghak rebels (a religious sect promising fundamental social reform) made it clear to policy makers that Korean independence was not an option and that reform would have to be imposed from outside. The chronology of events and the course of hostilities is outside the scope of this chapter, but we cannot forgo a discussion of the monetary and financial experimentation that accompanied them.[40]

First and foremost is Japan's shift from "free-trade imperialism" and a corollary "hands-off" approach to a more interventionist policy, including thorough institutional reform and the establishment of economic interests, most directly through railroad concessions.[41] For Itō

---

38. For statistics, see *Nikkan tsūshō kyōkai hōkoku* 日韓通商協会報告 (Report of the organization for trade between Japan and Korea), vol. 28 (December 1897).

39. W. G. Beasley perceives a change as early as 1885 (Beasley, *Japanese Imperialism*, 45): "Before 1882 some 76 per cent of [exports] had [. . .] consisted of Western textiles, bought in Shanghai and transshipped in Japan for Korean destinations. As Japan's own textile industry grew, however, re-exported Western goods were replaced by Japanese products, which amounted to 87 per cent of the total by 1892." Beasley cautions that the effect should not be overestimated: "Most scholars have concluded that economic interests on this limited scale did not constitute a sufficient reason for hostilities." This is reinforced by the figures we have: exports to Korea in 1893 did not exceed 1.7 million yen. In this respect compare Peng, *Meiji shoki Nichi-Kan-Shin kankei no kenkyū*, 279–330.

40. There are several comprehensive accounts: Chaïkin, *The Sino-Japanese War, 1894–1895*; White, *The War in the East*; Shinobu, *Nisshin sensō*; Konishi, *Nisshin sensō*; Ichikawa, *Nisshin sensō*; Kyū sanbō honbu, ed., *Nisshin sensō*.

41. On Japanese "railroad imperialism" in Korea, see Hunter, "Japanese Government Policy, Business Opinion and the Seoul-Pusan Railway, 1894–1906"; Duus, *The*

Hirobumi, political reform had been paramount. Matsukata Masayoshi was, as we have seen, the champion when it came to gaining Japan "real rights and real interests"; he showed himself rather concerned about direct political assistance.[42] Inoue Kaoru, Japan's most experienced man in Korean affairs, maneuvered between these visions.[43] He realized that reform, especially of the financial mismanagement of the Korean court, would fit very well with Japanese interests. And he was right: reform and Japanese interests did not necessarily contradict one another. Let us therefore consider the issues of trade and commerce.

By the outbreak of Sino-Japanese hostilities, it had come to the Korea-based Japanese merchants' attention that swings in the yen-*chŏn* exchange rate were, in the last analysis, contrary to Japanese commercial interests. (There had been several instances of speculation against copper *chŏn*, but the profits of these had been temporary, and had done nothing to sustain a commercial relationship.) Responding to calls for currency reform emanating from Korean bureaucrats, and to their aspiration to establish a national bank, Japan now found it reasonable to aid with the restructuring of the financial system and stabilizing of commodity prices. Japanese reform efforts would be directed at the establishment of sound national finance, buttressed by all the aspects that would later be central to the Megata reform: a balanced budget with clear accounting of revenues and expenditures, a reformed tax system, and the uniformization of currency. The means to those ends included several instrumental and profitable functions for Japanese financiers. They could assist in furthering the presence of BOJ convertible notes, and thus relieve the longstanding problem of capital shortage; and they could bind Korea's monetary and financial future to Japan's, for instance by extending loans. The politician Inoue Kaoru expressed this most frankly: "How was it that the British had an excuse for interven-

---

Abacus and the Sword, esp. 103–68. An official history in Japanese is Chōsen sōtokufu, *Chōsen tetsudōshi*.

42. Tokutomi, *Kōshaku Matsukata Masayoshi den*, vol. 2, 499.

43. Inoue had accompanied Kuroda Kiyotaka to Seoul as vice-plenipotentiary for the negotiation of the Kangwha treaty; later, as Foreign Minister, he presided over the negotiations of the Treaty of Chemulpo (1882); in 1885 he served as plenipotentiary in the negotiations of the Treaty of Seoul. For a firsthand description of his career, see Inoue Kaoru kō denki hensankai, ed. *Segai Inoue kō den*, esp. vol. 3.

ing in Egypt? Was it not in the fact that England had obtained its position of interest by providing Egypt with capital? [. . .] If we wish to solidify our position in Korea and to provide a basis for intervention in its internal affairs, it is most urgent that we strengthen our position in terms of real rights, whether railroads or financial loans, and prepare the way from financial interventions to other relations."[44]

Opportunities for financial intervention arose as soon as the Sino-Japanese War broke out. There was the First Bank loan to the Korean pro-reform faction, amounting to ¥130,000, at 8 percent. But there also was the failure of the giant ¥5 million loan in specie. Its story is an interesting one that once again reveals contradictions in Japan's policy-making constituency. The loan had actually been strongly supported by several elder statesmen, because its magnitude offered the possibility of a genuine impact on the Korean reform process. The Japanese government had engaged in careful preparations, with reports describing which conditions the Korean government had to meet.[45] These conditions not only included the provision that the loan would be secured against Korean tax revenues but also demanded that the Korean government employ a Japanese financial adviser to "supervise the whole system of national finance, and send envoys to the provinces in order to monitor the collection of taxes."[46] This last provision, it was explained, did "not diminish the profit of Korea, nor the profit of Japan; instead, it wishes to further the benefit and profit of both"—an interesting change in attitude for somebody who had once envisioned the Egyptianization of the country.[47] But then again—businessmen were, understandably, interested only in a secure and profitable return on their investments.[48] Uncertain that the reform of the country would in

---

44. Quoted in Cho, *Kindai Kankoku keizaishi*, 193–94, translation by Duus, *The Abacus and the Sword*, 134–35; and Metzler, *Lever of Empire*, 41. Compare the letter to Itō Hirobumi explaining to Inoue Kaoru the need of a ¥1 million loan: Inoue Kaoru kō denki hensankai, ed., *Segai Inoue kō den*, vol. 4, 440–41. For Inoue's activities in Korea, see Inoue Kaoru kō denki hensankai, ed., *Segai Inoue kō den*, vol. 4, 381–539.

45. For the full story, see Inoue Kaoru kō denki hensankai, ed., *Segai Inoue kō den*, vol. 4, 451ff.

46. Ibid., 452.

47. Ibid., 453.

48. Duus has rightfully remarked that "big capital was less prepared for the 'Egyptianization' of Korea than Inoue was" (*The Abacus and the Sword*, 94).

any way succeed, the Mitsui Bank was willing to consider a loan only at the high rate of 10 percent. Inoue recalls this event as at odds with Japan's political attitude: "Just think how inconsistent it is to charge such high interest considering that this government is practically in our hands."[49] Ultimately, Mitsui suggested putting up the loan, but on conditions that would have entailed total financial control over the peninsula. The bank would print gold-backed paper currency for circulation and tie it to the Japanese yen. If this plan had been realized, it would have been a very early example of a gold-exchange standard maintained by an East Asian country.

However, the time was not yet ripe. Inoue had to settle for a ¥3 million BOJ loan, only half of which was to be paid in silver coins (the other half in paper currency).[50] The BOJ's agenda was unambiguously different from those of Shibusawa and other entrepreneurs: as a semigovernmental institution with the explicit mandate of strengthening Japan's commerce, it was prepared to finance Korea's financial penetration. Yet, in the end, even this modified loan plan did not materialize.[51] Japanese domestic political sentiment had grown bitter about what was perceived as a soft and inept approach to Korea. According to Duus, the debate was dominated by "ebullient patriotism" in the wake of the victory over China; Diet members called for a proactive hawkish approach and pondered an official protest against the Triple Intervention (*sangoku kanshō*) by Russia, Germany, and France on April 23, 1895 (less than a week after the signing of the peace treaty with China).[52] These were hard times for proponents of the conciliatory and cooperative loan plan. In such circumstances, the newly formed Itō cabinet regarded a ¥3 million "contribution" to political reform inopportune.

---

49. *Nihon gaikō bunsho*, vol. 28.1, 139.

50. This was the result of painstaking rounds of negotiations. Inoue had first proposed to use 5 or 6 million yen from the Chinese indemnity to make a contribution to Korea; 3 million yen would be used for the repayment of Korea's debts to Japan, 1 or 1.5 million would be a gift to the Korean court, and an equivalent amount would be invested in profitable enterprises such as railways, telegraphs, and so forth. His second proposal was basically an attempt to appease Koreans' resentment caused by earlier loan negotiations (Inoue Kaoru kō denki hensankai, ed., *Segai Inoue kō den*, vol. 4; Duus, *The Abacus and the Sword*, 106).

51. Inoue Kaoru kō denki hensankai, ed., *Segai Inoue kō den*, vol. 4, esp. 484ff.

52. Duus, *The Abacus and the Sword*, 107.

Whether or not this decision was justified, the BOJ's perception of opportunity was not at odds with the realities of the Korean market. Not only had the Japanese yen gained in importance as trade currency, but it was also declared to be legal tender by Article 7 of the Regulations with Regard to the Issuing of New Money (Shinshiki kahei hakkō shōtei), which the Korean government promulgated in July 1894. This situation was unprecedented. Transaction costs between the Japanese mainland and the Korean peninsula were now officially at a zero rate. Consider furthermore the economic aspects of the battlefield. Japanese military forces were already paying for provisions with paper money, and thus created a temporary yen bloc in a country that was already replete with Japanese money.[53] Although it is impossible to estimate total military spending during this first China campaign, the *Tōkyō keizai zasshi* at the time argued that it increased the circulation of yen in Korea to somewhere between ¥1.3 million and ¥1.5 million (from the prewar ¥1 million).[54] Admittedly, the benefits were spread unevenly: whereas Japanese merchants were now able to make great profits, the Korean commercial class was confronted with ever more complicated exchange procedures (Japanese paper yen into Japanese silver yen into Korean copper *chŏn*) and consequent losses. Such losses were another source of strong anti-Japanese sentiment, and certainly contributed to the rejection of reform efforts. But the promoters of a Japanese economic presence in Korea must have seen the strong presence of the yen in Korea as a dream come true.

---

53. Compare Moriyama, "Kōgo kaikaku ni okeru shakkan mondai: Inoue Kaoru no kanyo shita dainiji kaikaku to Chōsen shidōshasō taiō o chūshin ni shite," esp. 119–26. The First Bank had already in 1891 taken up a scheme of issuing "*kansen* substitute securities" (*kansen daiyō shōken*), a kind of military scrip (*gunpyō*), as their objective (presumably) was to prevent Japanese currency from being further drawn into markets on the Asian mainland. As a reserve for this currency, it planned to use Japanese silver yen, bank notes, and Japanese subsidiary coinage. The plan was never approved by Japanese government authorities. Takashima, *Chōsen ni okeru shokuminchi kin'yūshi no kenkyū*, 56–57. Duus adds that the unwillingness of the Korean populace in the hinterland to accept "foreign" currency forced the Japanese army to exchange their coins into Korean copper *chŏn*, thus creating a temporary rise in their value. Duus, *The Abacus and the Sword*, 160.

54. "Nikkan bōeki-ron hoi," 428.

The Russian Episode

Perhaps we should say that they saw their dream come true only for a while. An unintended consequence of Japan's overwhelming economic leverage was to weaken its political position. Although Japan had won the war, the European powers won the peace. The Triple Intervention by Russia, Germany, and France in April 1895 forced Japan to return the Liaodong peninsula and greatly damaged its international prestige.[55] Japanese leaders became aware that, from now on, they had to proceed with caution, as the Western powers had now discovered their own "real rights and real interests" in East Asia.[56] Although Western governments framed their objections to Japan's activities in the vocabulary of international law, they were themselves involved in a scramble for concessions in the Far East and sought to head off Japanese attempts to monopolize the peninsula.[57] This attitude was especially strong in Russia, which found itself contained on the western border of its empire, and thus tried to project influence over its less powerful southern and eastern neighbors.[58] These developments signaled a new phase in Korea's monetary and socioeconomic history.

The shift toward Russian predominance was triggered not so much by external factors as by a change of course in Japan's policy making regarding Korea. The assassination of Queen Min in the Eulmi Incident in October 1895, largely caused by the clumsy diplomacy of Miura Gorō, who succeeded Inoue as the Japanese Minister to Korea, "cultivated enmity, not friendship."[59] Although Gorō was immediately replaced by Komura Jutarō, a young and ambitious bureaucrat with a great deal of foreign experience, Tokyo found it increasingly difficult to cultivate allies among Korean leaders, let alone to establish credibility

---

55. See Kajima, *The Diplomacy of Japan 1894–1922*, vol. 1; Iklé, "The Triple Intervention." Takashima considers it an instance of Western rejection of Japanese sovereignty. Takashima, *Chōsen ni okeru shokuminchi kin'yūshi no kenkyū*, 62.

56. Apparently, Mutsu Munemitsu, plenipotentiary negotiator of the treaty, warned Inoue in the wake of the negotiations to use "extreme caution" in his negotiations with the Koreans. See Kim C. M., *Nikkan gaikō shiryō shūsei*, vol. 4, 365.

57. See Duus, *The Abacus and the Sword*, 143–68.

58. For a general overview of events, see Seung, *The Russo-Japanese Rivalry over Korea*, esp. 153ff.

59. Duus, *The Abacus and the Sword*, 108ff. See Suzuki Kōichi, *Nisshin sensō, Minbi ansatsu, kyōaku satsujin no jidai*; Tsunoda, *Minbi ansatsu*.

with Western diplomats.[60] The specter of losing Korea's independence and thus Japanese sovereignty loomed larger than ever.

Anti-Japanese sentiment was especially strong in the early days of Russo-Korean rapprochement.[61] This is not to say that many members of the Korean elite preferred Russian influence to Japanese influence. However, Russia's foreign minister, Aleksey Lobanov-Rostovsky, and Sergey Witte, the architect of much of Russia's East Asia policy, used anti-Japanese opinion to quickly expand their grip on the political class and hasten the acquisition of concessions.[62] Witte, who had become dissatisfied with similar efforts to obtain railroad concessions in China and other interests through the Russo-Chinese Bank (a heavily subsidized bank operating with French and Belgian money),[63] found Korea a less contested target for his expansionist plans.

At the outset, the new Korean government was eager to help. It not only dismissed all Japanese advisers who had been appointed to the ministries in 1895, it also gave in to Russian pressure to appoint, among others, Dmitri Dimitrievich Pokotilov (head of the Russo-Chinese Bank) as a financial adviser.[64] In 1897 he was replaced by Kiril A. Alexeev, an official of the Russian customs service, who was in turn placed under McLeavy Brown, an Englishman who had been in charge of the national finances since 1893 (his job being to see to it that Korea's foreign creditors were properly repaid) and now refused to leave his post as customs director.[65] Russia also came up with the idea of a Russo-Korean Bank, which was to take over the deposit of custom duties from the First Bank

---

60. On Komura, see Nakayama, *Komura Jutarō den*; Okamoto, "A Phase of Meiji Japan's Attitude toward China"; Okazaki, *Komura Jutarō to sono jidai*.

61. See Crist, "Russia's Far Eastern Policy in the Making"; Malozamoff, *Russian Far Eastern Policy 1881–1904*.

62. A detailed account is Seung, *The Russo-Japanese Rivalry over Korea*, esp. 224ff.; see also Conroy, *The Japanese Seizure of Korea*, 326–27; Crist, "Russia's Far Eastern Policy in the Making."

63. See Quested, *The Russo-Chinese Bank*.

64. Subsequent Russian intervention in Korea's monetary and political affairs is documented in Seung, *The Russo-Japanese Rivalry over Korea*, 234ff.

65. See Metzler, *Lever of Empire*, 52; Duus, *The Abacus and the Sword*, 123; Seung, *The Russo-Japanese Rivalry over Korea*, 250–53.

(although this never happened; by the time the bank opened its doors in 1898, Russian interest in Korea had largely faded away).[66]

In the meantime, the Korean government moved to eradicate other symbols of Japanese influence in Korean society. Most forcefully, it resorted to a scheme of issuing large amounts of nickel currency (*paekt'ong*, Jp. *hakudōka*) of low denomination, partly in an attempt to drive Japanese currency out of the market. Nickel coins of 2.5 *chŏn*, introduced by the Regulations with Regard to the Issuing of New Money, occupied a place between the standard money (5 silver *yang* 両) and the still circulating copper *chŏn* (see Table 2.2).[67] This ill-conceived measure was to have detrimental consequences for Korea's monetary constituency.

Japan's Adoption of the Gold Standard

This attempt to drive Japanese currency out of Korea was at least in part the result of a sharp shift in Japan's own monetary geography: the decision in 1897 to adopt the gold standard. Before that, conditions for the yen on the peninsula had actually been promising. Merchants in the port cities, with the exception of Pusan, treated it as a most stable currency.[68] Because it could be expected that silver coins would return to Japan for redemption, financial policy makers were to pay extraordinary attention to the challenges posed by circulation of silver yen convertible paper money. The fall of the price of silver, a natural con-

---

66. Seung, *The Russo-Japanese Rivalry over Korea*, 259–60.

67. Its exchange rate versus the latter was defined as 1:25, i.e., one *paekt'ong* coin of 2.5 *chŏn* was exchanged for 25 pieces of old coin. These regulations were a flawed effort to establish a wholly new monetary system on the peninsula. They recognized coins made of 4 metals: silver, nickel, cuprite (red copper), and brass. Monetary units and their relations were as follows: 1 *yang* 両 = 10 *chŏn* 錢 = 100 *fun* 分 (instead of the earlier unit of 文). The mint issued coins of 1 *fun* (brass), 5 *fun* (cuprite), 2.5 *chŏn* (nickel), and respectively 1 and 5 *yang* (silver). The New Regulations also recognized foreign coins of similar weight and denomination as legal tender: 1 Chinese *tael* coin and 1 Japanese yen coin were considered equal to one piece of 5 *yang*. In order to measure amounts of money, the government used the virtual unit of measure *won* (元), a cognate of the Chinese *yuan*. For an overview, see Yi, *Kankoku kahei kin'yūshi*, 215–17.

68. "Kahei hō seitei oyobi jisshi hōkoku" 貨幣法制定及実施報告 (Report on the legal framework of the currency law and its implementation), in Nihon ginkō chōsakyoku, ed., *Nihon kin'yūshi shiryō: Meiji Taishō hen*, vol. 17, 159–61.

Table 2.2: Number and type of Korean coins and relative percentage of issuance total, 1894–1900 (in *won*)

Year	5 *yang* silver	1 *yang* silver	2.5 *chŏn* nickel	5 *fun* cuprite	1 *fun* brass	Total
1894	–	–	–	35,610	–	35,610
				(100%)		*(100%)*
1895	–	–	160,869	176,480	4,213	341,562
			(47.1%)	*(51.7%)*	*(1.2%)*	*(100%)*
1896	–	–	34,642	284,354	–	318,996
			(10.9%)	*(89.1%)*		*(100%)*
1897	–	–	17,333	28,409	–	45,742
			(37.9%)	*(62.1%)*		*(100%)*
1898	–	35,789	348,995	248,306	–	633,090
		(5.1%)	*(55.1%)*	*(39.2%)*		*(100%)*
1899	–	62,992	1,281,638	34,202	–	1,378,832
		(4.6%)	*(92.9%)*	*(2.5%)*		*(100%)*
1900	–	–	2,030,463	–	–	2,030,463
			(100%)			*(100%)*
TOTAL		98,781	3,873,940	807,361	4,213	4,784,295
		(2.1%)	*(81.0%)*	*(16.9%)*	*(0.0%)*	*(100%)*

SOURCE: Yi Sŏng-nyun, *Kankoku kahei kin'yūshi*, 215.

sequence of Japan's decision, would make it harder to continue acquiring gold bullion to buttress Japan's currency reserve. (Germany had faced a similar dilemma in the early 1870s.) For Japanese policy makers, it would be quite profitable to have silver coins circulate in Korea in one form or another. But problems for the Korean economy remained, and commodity price instability brought Korea's monetary reform back onto the agenda.

In the years before 1897, Ministry of Finance officials and Shibusawa Eiichi seem to have been in contact on a regular basis, discussing the implications of the adoption of the gold standard. Their schemes were in many ways complementary. Whereas the Ministry of Finance, and especially Sakatani Yoshirō (Yoshio),[69] was concerned with accumulating Korean gold and silver bullion, Shibusawa was focused on the future of his bank. One of the ambitions he expressed was to gradually promote the First Bank "to the central bank of Korea, plan the unifica-

---

69. On Sakatani, see Ko Sakatani shishaku kinen jigyōkai, *Sakatani Yoshirō den*.

tion of its currency, and put its monetary system in order."[70] But how could this be done? The Japanese proposal was a prime example of concession imperialism. Whereas policy makers had once preached a hands-off approach, they now favored a firm hand on the tiller. The idea of Japanese control was revolutionary. Sakatani Yoshio (then head of the tax bureau at the Ministry of Finance) and Shibusawa envisioned a Japan-independent yet Japan-sponsored system.[71] Silver coins would remain in circulation but would be hallmarked with the characters for "Japan" (*gokuin tsuki ginka*). Foreshadowing the First Bank's later role, Shibusawa suggested the issuance of "bearer securities" strictly for circulation in Korea—an idea not unlike Shibusawa's musings of almost twenty years before. In all of its aspects, this proposal had the characteristics of a full-fledged colonial reform effort.

It was one thing to have a plan, but another to realize it. McLeavy Brown left no doubt that the chopped silver coins would continue to be accepted; the exchange rate between chopped and unchopped silver coins would be maintained at 1:1 during the period of transition, in order not to destabilize the exchange markets. He furthermore agreed to invest ¥300,000 worth of chopped silver coins, and simultaneously attempt to stop the outflow of old silver yen to Japan. This not only would drastically reduce costs for reminting, it also again endorsed the importance of the old Japanese yen as trade currency on the peninsula. In February 1898, chopped coins were prohibited from circulation (doubtless under Russian pressure), only to be re-allowed in July of the same year, after the successful conclusion of the Nishi-Rosen agreement.[72]

---

70. See Shibusawa Eiichi kinen zaidan, *Shibusawa Eiichi denki shiryō*, vol. 16, 61–70.

71. For Shibusawa's original proposal, see "Chōsen kokuhei shigi," Shibusawa Eiichi kinen zaidan, *Shibusawa Eiichi denki shiryō*, vol. 16, 61–70. Shibusawa presented this memorandum to then-BOJ governor Iwasaki Yanosuke. It is reprinted in Daiichi ginkō 80-nenshi hensanshitsu, ed., *Daiichi ginkōshi*, vol. 1, 644ff.

72. See Shibusawa Eiichi kinen zaidan, *Shibusawa Eiichi denki shiryō*, vol. 16, 70–84; the Nishi-Rosen agreement, which Rosen himself once called "a rather lame and pointless convention," marks the "exchange Korea for Manchuria" policy (*mankan kōkan*), whereby Russia and Japan came to agreement about their strategic interests in their respective spheres. The consequent occupation of Port Arthur by Russia was perceived not as a threat, but rather as a sign of Russian willingness to abandon furthering her interests on the peninsula. Seung, *The Russo-Japanese Rivalry over Korea*, 264–69.

But what happened to Shibusawa's plan to issue bearer securities? In 1897, Japanese authorities had refused to discuss Shibusawa's scheme on the grounds that it was impractical and that it would offend Korean (and Russian) authorities. It soon turned out to be a much discussed topic. Japanese authorities had not invested much effort in extending any new loan to the Korean government after Inoue's failed loan plan of 1895. But around 1898 the Koreans solicited them to do so, with the express aim of bringing some order to Korea's perennially chaotic currency system. Korea's lack of bullion made any autonomous attempt at reform impossible. Again, Japanese interests had turned against themselves: massive acquisitions of gold dust and silver bullion by the First Bank had effectively undermined a crucial pillar of any monetary sanitation.[73]

Change was looming, however, even (or especially) for the Japanese. The instability of transaction costs had always been a major concern for Japanese merchants. The prospect of the yen disappearing altogether from the peninsula as a result of the decision to adopt the gold standard was even bleaker. Yet Tokyo chose not to address the issue, because of its tight budgetary situation in the aftermath of the war. This stance changed when it became aware of a joint American and British proposal to lend the Korean government ¥5 million, mortgaged against mining rights on royal land. The loan's alleged purpose was to permit the Korean government to issue a new silver currency. Hayashi Gonsuke, then minister to Korea, reacted furiously. Not only had the Koreans approached him in 1898 with a similar loan proposal, he now also perceived the political importance and threat of such a massive amount. From then on, he would relentlessly pursue negotiations with the aim of establishing firmer control over the government and the court. It repeatedly turned out that Japan's own precarious budgetary situation did not permit a firm commitment to Korea's currency stabilization. Nor was there sufficient political will: Itō Hirobumi, in particular, was increasingly sensitive to provoking the Russians.[74]

---

73. This point is also made in Takashima, *Chōsen ni okeru shokuminchi kin'yūshi no kenkyū*, 72ff. For an overview of Japanese bullion acquisitions in the colonies, see Murakami, "Shokuminchi kin kyūshū to Nihon sangyō kakumei"; Kojima, *Nihon no kinhon'isei jidai*, 145–54.

74. Duus, *The Abacus and the Sword*, 157–68; his discussion mainly relies on Moriyama, *Kindai Nikkan kankeishi kenkyū*.

This situation was slightly different for Shibusawa's First Bank. Not a governmental institution, it would gladly undertake efforts at Korean monetary reform if they seemed profitable. This turned out to be the case. In 1900, Shibusawa therefore relentlessly pushed for negotiations with Brown; his proposals ranged from a loan in the form of a ¥1 million overdraft to a loan of ¥2 million (in return for which the First Bank was granted the right to issue custom notes).[75] For Brown, this was unsatisfactory. With a host of questions still unresolved, negotiations broke off. But a new opportunity presented itself as early as 1901. The indefatigable Hayashi suggested that the First Bank issue banknotes, and that it lend them to the Korean government when it was in need of capital. This proved the right idea. Although the Ministry of Finance objected on the grounds that note issuing was reserved to officially established banks, it later approved, with the stipulations that First Bank notes would circulate only under approval of the Korean government and only in Korea, hence not contradicting the legal provision that prohibited privately issued money on Japanese soil.[76] This initiative would, moreover, not require approval of the Korean government.[77] First Bank notes went into circulation in 1902. In order not to compete with other currencies, notably BOJ convertible notes, their denominations were deliberately low. Less fit for international transactions, they were apparently designed for trade with and among the Korean populace; this made them also an ideal vehicle for expanding the use of Japanese currency beyond the port cities. Their issue was an exercise in colonial financial policy. As BOJ convertible notes were counted as an integral part of the First Bank's reserve, the plan effectively made Korea's currency system dependent on Japan's, in clear contrast with the Taiwanese case.[78] But, as Duus has rightly observed, it did not do anything to relieve pres-

---

75. See also Takashima, *Chōsen ni okeru shokuminchi kin'yūshi no kenkyū*, 62ff.; these negotiations occur amid a series of negotiations with several other countries about the very topic of currency reform, listed in ibid., 65–68.

76. "If they are not more than a kind of securities that have credibility and that circulate at one's option, then there is no reason to regard them as breaching Korean sovereignty." Cited in Takashima, *Chōsen ni okeru shokuminchi kin'yūshi no kenkyū*, 69. See also Shibusawa Eiichi kinen zaidan, *Shibusawa Eiichi denki shiryō*, vol. 16, 132ff.

77. Hayashi, *Waga 70-nen o kataru*, 149–52.

78. See Metzler, *Lever of Empire*, 52–55.

sure on the Korean currency system; instead, it "added one more layer of complexity."[79]

Meanwhile, the Korean government had initiated a new campaign in the ongoing reform of the currency. After futile early efforts to adopt the gold standard after the Japanese example,[80] the government had undertaken another attempt at currency autonomy in 1901, this time coupled with the idea of establishing a central bank. The proposal, dubbed the 1901 Currency Ordinance (or *kōmu gonen kahei jōrei*, after the fifth year of Gwangmu rule) was clearly inspired by profound anti-Japanese sentiment. Drawing on the example of Japan's adoption of the gold standard in 1897, it stipulated that Korea (nominally) adopted the gold standard. The new unit of measure was to be the *hwan* 圜 (also pronounced *won*; 1 *hwan* = 100 *chŏn*), a measure of gold; it replaced the *yang* 両, a measure of silver (a cognate of the Chinese *tael*; on the official level, one used the—virtual—unit of *won* 元); 5 *yang* of silver (= 1 *won* 元) was to be exchanged for 1 *hwan* of gold in new money. The ordinance also reserved the right to issue coins solely to the Korean government, prohibited the circulation of Japanese currency, and restricted ownership of stocks in the central banks to Korean citizens.[81]

Aided by an imported German coin press, the authorities ordered the Chŏnhwan'guk to mint a half-*hwan* silver coin with the effigy of an eagle, and subsidiary coinage with a similar figure. It turned out to be another failed reform effort; coinage appears to have been halted at a fairly early stage. In hindsight, it appears that Korean officials did not grasp the cynical parameters within which reform was planned and implemented. In a Korea depleted of bullion and capital, reforms aimed at establishing an autonomous currency system had the perverse effect of

---

79. Duus, *The Abacus and the Sword*, 167.

80. It had, among others, approached Masuda Nobuyuki of the Osaka Copper Company to participate in minting an entirely new silver currency (1998). One year later, it proposed to adopt existing silver coins as the new monetary standard, abolish the minting of subsidiary coinage, and to print paper money instead. Immediately thereafter, it again turned to minting subsidiary nickel coinage and forbid the circulation of silver yen coins. The hastily drawn proposals illustrate the impossible position of Korean policy makers; they came to naught because of the country's poor bullion holdings. Takashima, *Chōsen ni okeru shokuminchi kin'yūshi no kenkyū*, 74.

81. For a good explanation of this ordinance, especially the complexities of units of measure, see Yi, *Kankoku kahei kin'yūshi*, 263ff.

aggravating dependence on foreign countries. After all, foreign powers would have to agree to extend a loan making reform possible—so such nationalist policies by their very nature worked against the objective of autonomy.[82]

As it turned out, by 1904, at the dawn of the Russo-Japanese War, the monetary geography of the peninsula was more fractured and complicated than ever before.[83] As the *Kankoku kahei seiri hōkokusho* makes clear, the country was divided into several currency regions, with competing monies of different kinds and even different functions (see map).[84] Japanese currency, despite the amounts being sent back to Japan for redemption, remained particularly strong in the port cities, where it mainly filled the role of a strong and stable "trade dollar." Korean copper *chŏn*, once the main medium of exchange, had stopped being minted after 1893, but remained in use in more remote regions of the peninsula, especially in the southern provinces (the area around Pusan). Their importance would decline later, ironically due to the rising copper price. After 1902, a large number of copper coins were melted down; the nominal value of copper *chŏn* in circulation fell to 5 or 6 million *won* (from the previous level of 10 million *won*).[85] Segregation between currency regions was more or less complete. People in the copper *chŏn* sphere would not accept the newly minted nickel currency or *paekt'ong*, which was widespread in Seoul and the central regions of the country, and which kept proliferating. Around 1905, it accounted for more than 50 percent of all coinage circulating in Korea. As the profit of coinage was large, the government appeared to have no great interest in controlling its quantity; furthermore, private coinage (*shizō*) and counterfeiting (*gizō*) thrived, and included coins minted in Japan. It was said that around 600 different kind of *paekt'ong* circulated at the same time.

---

82. Also noted in Takashima, *Chōsen ni okeru shokuminchi kin'yūshi no kenkyū*, 77. It appears that the Korean government entered negotiations with Masuda and Yasuda Zenjirō for a loan to save the currency reform; these were broken off because Yasuda could not see sufficient profit in the operation.

83. For an overview of Korean currency before 1910, see Yi, *Kankoku kahei kin'yūshi*.

84. Daiichi ginkō, *Kankoku kahei seiri hōkokusho*, 14–15; see Helleiner, *The Making of National Money*, esp. 19–41.

85. Takashima, *Chōsen ni okeru shokuminchi kin'yūshi no kenkyū*, 91.

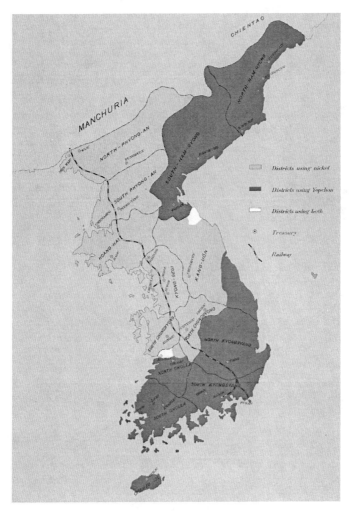

Map 2.1   Circulation of copper and nickel coins in Korea. Reproduced from Daiichi ginkō, *Kankoku kahei seiri hōkokusho*, n.p.

For a host of reasons, but especially because of their overcoinage, *paekt'ong* led the country into soaring inflation.[86] The *Report on the Re-*

---

86. Takashima also mentions the appreciation of Japanese currency due to increased foreign trade as a reason for *paekt'ong* inflation. Ibid., 95ff. According to Helleiner, this complicated relationship between monies of large and low denomination is a typical characteristic of pre-national currency systems. Helleiner, *The Making of National Money*, 66ff.

arrangement of Korean Currency estimates that, in 1905, the number of *paekt'ong* in circulation had reached 11.5 million *won*.[87] It was a truly "schizophrenic" currency, in that nominal value and market value were sometimes far apart. Attempts to stabilize its exchange rate with copper *chŏn* by buying this currency of low denomination met with only limited success, and most probably explain the frantic ups and downs in the exchange rate of both currencies vis-à-vis relative to the Japanese yen.[88] Japanese policy makers were profoundly aware that one day fundamental reform would be inevitable. They did not know that such opportunity would present itself so suddenly and soon, again in the aftermath of a military conflict.

The Russo-Japanese War

The Russo-Japanese War of 1904–05 was an extremely costly undertaking. As Mark Metzler has argued, it confirmed Japan's peculiar financial status in the Darwinian world order of the early twentieth century.[89] Although on the gold standard and thus able to negotiate its war loans on more or less favorable terms, the country could barely carry the tremendous expense of ¥1.9 billion—almost six times the government's national spending in 1903.[90] Forty percent of the cost had to be paid through foreign borrowing. From the humanitarian viewpoint, too, the war's legacy was disastrous. Extensive media coverage, including the new technologies of the telegraph and photography, transmitted the image of the war as a cruel "World War Zero."[91] And last but not least, there was the humiliating aftermath: Russia's plenipotentiary representative to the Portsmouth talks, Count Sergei Witte, very shrewdly managed to suppress the Japanese demand for an indemnity of ¥1.2 billion

---

87. Daiichi ginkō, *Kankoku kahei seiri hōkokusho*, 13–19.

88. A table of fluctuations in the exchange rate of both copper *chŏn* and *paekt'ong* against the Japanese yen is provided in Takashima, *Chōsen ni okeru shokuminchi kin'yūshi no kenkyū*, 94. For this information, Takashima draws on Daiichi ginkō, "Kabushiki gaisha Daiichi ginkō Kankoku kakuten shutchōsho kaigyō irai eigyō jōkyō," 20–28.

89. Metzler, *Lever of Empire*, 45ff.

90. G. Ono, *War and Armament Expenditures of Japan*, 88 (also mentioned in Metzler, *Lever of Empire*, 45). For an analysis of war costs, see Nihon ginkō tōkeikyoku, ed., *Meiji ikō honpō shuyō keizai tōkei*, 143.

91. Steinberg et al., eds., *The Russo-Japanese War in Global Perspective*. See also *The Russo-Japanese War*; Slattery, *Reporting The Russo-Japanese War*.

(= $600 million). Although American sentiment had been with Japan throughout the negotiations, Japanese representatives ultimately had to concede that the Japanese victory had not been decisive enough for their demands to prevail. Still, the Russians' refusal to pay any indemnity at all was considered an affront. On September 5, 1905, crowds of enraged commoners rioted in the streets of Tokyo. It proved to no avail. In the end, Japan had to pay for the whole war effort itself, plus interest. If the war had not yet been cruel enough, the international political arena was.

The postwar financial predicament would continue to dominate Japanese politics for decades to come. In 1904, Takahashi Korekiyo had hailed the war loans as "divine providence."[92] They not only saved Japan's gold standard, he reckoned, they would also be the key to unlock the door to the Asian mainland. Now, however, the loans jeopardized former policies. Two of the 1905 loans, with a combined value of £60 million, were to mature in 1925; only six years later, in 1931, a £25 million loan was to mature. Inability to pay these loans off would lead Japan straight into a new era of borrowing, this time from New York, which had emerged as the world's financial hub. Then, a wholly new generation of policy makers would have to deal with a radically different geopolitical climate—a climate in which American financiers, European economists, and Japanese liberalists alike chose to remember the first gold-standard era nostalgically as an era of international collaboration, a symbol of a seamless world ruled by the values of civilization and free-market capitalism.

This nostalgia would have appeared rather cynical to Japan's leaders in the beginning of the century. Painfully aware of their nation's lesser status in the international arena, they had to settle for a minor monetary award. But there were other spoils of war. Japan inherited rights and concessions that Russia had secretly acquired after Japan had been forced to return the Liadong peninsula to China in 1895. And Korea, now a protectorate, was soon to be under the guidance of a host of Japanese government-appointed advisers. It was also to provide the op-

---

92. The term used for "divine providence" is *ten'yū* 天佑. See Takahashi, *Takahashi Korekiyo jiden*, 205–6; also quoted in Metzler, *Lever of Empire*, 47.

portunity for Japan's first experiment with a full-fledged gold-exchange standard.

The Arrival of Megata Tanetarō

Megata Tanetarō's disembarking onto the peninsula called forth the reiteration of a mantra that had dominated Japanese attitudes toward Korea since the early days of the Meiji reformation. His official biography repeats the claim that Korea and Japan were "as close as lips and teeth," and goes on to argue that Japanese intervention in Korea's domestic affairs was inevitable in view of Korea's recalcitrant political class (a viewpoint that also strongly colored Inoue's perception of Korea's problems).[93] Megata seemed the right man at the right place. His credentials were unblemished.[94] The first Japanese national to graduate from Harvard University, he became a successful bureaucrat in the Ministry of Finance, where, among other responsibilities, he managed the Yokohama Tax Office. But his record of reforming the Japanese tax system as head of the Ministry's Tax Bureau made him ideally qualified for the job.

The following discussion will concentrate on his work as a monetary adviser, or money doctor, in Korea, paying particular attention to the relations among several steps of the monetary and financial reform program. Traditionally, and for understandable reasons, Japanese colonial finance has been a very contentious topic—especially so because of its detrimental consequences. Several Korean commentators have tended to see these consequences as proof of a well-prepared scheme to subdue Korea and "enslave the Korean bourgeoisie upper classes to Imperial Japan."[95] I do not share this analysis, although I certainly do not deny the hardships that were the immediate consequence of the Megata reform.

Instead, here the reform is treated as a case study of the extremely unfortunate interaction of Japanese governmental and private agendas.

---

93. Yoshimura, *Danshaku Megata Tanetarō*, vol. 1, 343. For references to the lips and teeth metaphor, see Duus, *The Abacus and the Sword*, 35, 50.

94. Yoshimura, *Danshaku Megata Tanetarō*, vol. 1, 346–47.

95. Oh, "Currency Readjustment and Colonial System of 1905 in Korea," 54.

Fig. 2.1 Baron Megata Tanetarō, 9 November 1920. Photograph by Bassano.
© National Portrait Gallery, London. Used by permission.

Although sharing the perspective of colonial gain, these agendas were substantially incompatible. On the one hand, those following political logic were certainly limited in their assessment of what was possible, and were probably also unaware of the potential severity of the crisis they were about to set in motion. On the other hand, the agendas of the Japanese (and Chinese) merchants, geared toward economic profit, at different times and to different degrees not only complicated Korea's already troubled economic situation but also disrupted the implementation of a reform operation that was deeply unpopular with Korea's social classes. In the wider context of the other cases discussed in this book, the Megata reform thus becomes the example of colonial monetary leverage par excellence. At the same time, it sharply illustrates the incompatibilities and contradictions in the very design of such a policy.

There were many ways of representing the benefits and disadvantages of the Megata reform. Put in the dispassionate terminology of money doctoring, its core objectives were the thorough uniformization of Korea's money, financial practices, and, by extension, institutions. If we look more critically at its effects and its implementation, though, we are struck by the severity of its societal impact: the disenfranchising of certain Korean classes, especially the bourgeoisie or *yangban*; the confusion arising from neglect of existing financial practices and relief measures; and especially the profoundly deflationary pressure on the Korean economy, with foreseeable consequences.

In order to implement a policy that was expected to be strongly resisted, Megata's prerogatives were defined very broadly. Exactly how sweeping his powers were can be seen in the first three articles of his six-article contract, reproduced in its entirety in his biography:

Art. 1   Megata Tanetarō will adjust and audit the finances of the Korean Government, and will be responsible for the deliberations and plans with regard to all financial facilities in a most trustworthy manner.

Art. 2   The Korean Government will execute all financial measures after obtaining the approval of Megata Tanetarō. Megata Tanetarō will be able to participate in cabinet meetings on financial matters, and may propose his opinions on financial matters to the Government through the Minister of Finance. All cabinet and ministerial decisions with regard to finance will have to receive Megata Tanetarō's consent and will be countersigned by him before being presented to the throne for approval.

Art. 3   Megata Tanetarō may request an audience with the emperor and report on financial matters.[96]

Megata's exceptional position makes the practices of Japanese advisers in Korea worth a study in their own right. But more important for our discussion, the scientific style of his policies, particularly his interest in the statistical documentation of their implementation, produced a wealth of information on Japan's dealings with the protectorate. The

---

96. Yoshimura, *Danshaku Megata Tanetarō*, vol. 1, 346–47. Other articles concern his salary (¥800 plus housing and travel allowances) and conditions voiding the contract.

five-volume *Report on the Reform of Korea's National Finance* and the corollary *Report on the Arrangement of Korean Currency* have unfortunately received scant attention, even from Japanese and Korean scholars.[97] They are, nevertheless, excellent examples of Japanese "scientific" colonialism, as pioneered by Gotō Shinpei in Taiwan and probably surpassed only by the German arch-example.[98] These and other reports include land surveys and reports on the state of commercial banking, foreign trade, infrastructure, the cultivation of tobacco, standards of measurement, so-called Japanese undesirables, and so on.[99] For obvious reasons, I will limit discussion of these reports to their attention to monetary and financial matters.[100]

From the very outset, Megata's ambitions were a total takeover of control over all monetary and financial matters; in that sense, his ini-

---

97. Kankoku seifu zaisei komonbu, *Kankoku zaisei seiri hōkoku; Daiichi ginkō, Kankoku kahei seiri hōkokusho*. Secondary sources on the Megata reform include Hagiwara, *Kankoku zaisei no seiri kaikaku*; Hatori, *Chōsen ni okeru shokuminchi heisei no keisei*; Kang, "Chōsen kahei seiri jigyō ni kansuru kenkyū nōto"; Ueda, *Kankoku ni okeru kahei to kin'yū*. To my knowledge, there is only one study in English: Oh, "Currency Readjustment and Colonial System of 1905 in Korea."

98. See Penslar, "Zionism, Colonialism and Technocracy"; Spidle, "Colonial Studies in Imperial Germany"; Tooze, *Statistics and the German State*.

99. Compare, for instance, H.I.J.M. (His Imperial Japanese Majesty's) Residency General, *Annual Report for 1907 on Reforms and Progress in Korea* (Seoul, 1908) and *The Second Annual Report on Reforms and Progress in Korea (1908–1909)* (Seoul, 1909). Similar reports were published until the outbreak of the second war with China, in 1939.

100. Japanese bureaucratic control was total and grew more intense over the years: Atul Kohli indicates that, in 1937, there were nearly fifteen Japanese officials in Korea for every French administrator in Vietnam (at the same time noting that French control of Vietnam was considerably more intense than, say, the British presence in Nigeria). Kohli, *State-Directed Development*, 35. Japan adopted a type of developmental colonialism, with a large centralist administration and an army of bureaucrats, economic mechanisms as administrative guidance for strategic and infant industries, carefully administered investment programs, and, above all, policies informed by extensive research of Korea's society and its institutions. This streamlined, professional-managerial approach may have been as much a necessity as an example of a consciously selected paradigm. Thomas C. Smith remarked about Japan's own industrialization that the Japanese state had to "act as entrepreneur, financier, and manager" because of Japan's status of a late developer, and the consequent lack of capital-generating capacity: "capital was too weak, too timid, and too inexperienced to undertake development" (*Political Change and Industrial Development in Japan*, 102).

tiative is a conscious prelude to the annexation of Korea in 1910.[101]
Backed by decisions of the *genrō* or "senior statesmen" on the course of
actions Japan should take in Korea, Megata's task was to consider only
the options of monetary dependence and monetary unification—both
of which clearly departed from earlier hands-off policies.[102] Whereas
previously direct political influence had been the objective of only a
limited number of expansionist hawks, successes in the Sino-Japanese
and Russo-Japanese wars had clearly brought about a different climate.

A Gold-Exchange Standard

Megata's most immediate concern was the elimination of several institutions associated with the mismanagement of national finance in Yi
Korea. Megata noted the fundamental distortions of checks and balances
in the Korean political constituency. Although it is probably an exaggeration to view Korean power structures as no different from those
in Heian Japan, as one observer suggests,[103] such imbalances tended to
enrich a very small segment of Korean society, while progressively im-
poverishing the rest. This tendency is especially obvious when considering the extraordinary position of the Korean court. Characterized
by an ever-growing appetite for spending in disregard of the nation's
needs and capabilities, it had drained the country of valuable resources
to a disastrous degree. Megata reckoned that at the time of his arrival
in Korea, the total revenue of the government was around 15 million
won, of which 1.4 million was allocated to the imperial court. But the
court also received the revenues of its monopoly on the ginseng trade
(2 million *won*), the profits of seigniorage (so-called *zōhei ekikin*; amount
unknown), the income from the granting of rights to open certain businesses and rights extended to foreign merchants (amount unknown), the
income of toll rights (620,000 *won*), mining (40,000 *won*) and forestation
(amount unknown), the gold-dust trade (600,000 *won*), and a variety of

---

101. This is also stressed by Takashima, *Chōsen ni okeru shokuminchi kin'yūshi no kenkyū*, 115ff.

102. One finds references to both possibilities in Ōkurashō, *Meiji Taishō zaiseishi*, vol. 13, 398ff.: e.g., "Designing a common currency system for Japan and Korea" ("*Nikkan ryōkoku kyōtsū no kahei seido o shiku*"; 日韓両国共通の貨幣制度を布く).

103. Hagiwara, *Kankoku zaisei no seiri kaikaku*, 6.

special taxes (amount unknown).[104] These aggregated benefits for the court amounted to at least 5.6 million *won* per year, or equivalent to more than one-third of the government revenue. To make matters worse, the court sometimes issued "emergency orders" to the Ministry of Finance for various expenses. The first step in the process of reform was thus to separate the finances of the government and the court.[105] Simultaneously, Megata abolished the Korean Mint, which he identified as a major factor in the currency turmoil, and set up an independent Printing Office; later, he established a budget office and an elaborate tax agency.[106]

Megata's reforms were the prelude to the promotion of Japanese colonial interests. This was to a certain degree unavoidable. As Megata's biographer indicates, close Japanese-Korean trade relations made it obvious to Japanese, if not Korean, policy makers that any readjustment would have to be supervised by Tokyo, and would preferably be implemented by following Japan's monetary and financial model.[107] In an audience with Emperor Kojong on December 31, 1904, Megata therefore proposed to enforce the 1901 Currency Ordinance, the abortive currency scheme by which the Korean government had formerly attempted to adopt the gold standard. After receiving the emperor's informal consent, the way to a full-scale overhaul of Korea's monetary system lay open. In mid-January 1905 the Supreme Administrative Council or Ŭijŏngbu passed resolutions regarding the enforcement of the 1901 Currency Ordinance, a resolution on the circulation of foreign monies, and a draft of an Imperial Ordinance specifying readjustment procedures. In the days that followed, a series of Imperial Ordinances (*choku-rei*) laid the groundwork. Imperial Ordinance No. 2 announced the

---

104. Kankoku seifu zaisei komonbu, *Kankoku zaisei seiri hōkoku*, vol. 1, chapter 4: 1–14 (the report does not have conventional pagination); the yen-*won* exchange rate was then set at roughly 1:2.

105. For an explanation of how Megata proceeded, see Yoshimura, *Danshaku Megata Tanetarō*, vol. 1, 359.

106. Ibid., 408–12; 438ff.

107. Ibid., 476. The density of Japan-Korean trade relations is recognized by Korean commentators: "Imports from Japan during this period [1876–1904] were valued at approximately 130 million yen, which represented about eight-tenths of Korea's total imports, while its exports to Japan during the same period were about 120 million yen, representing around nine-tenths of the total" (Chung, *Korea under Siege*, 47).

adoption of the gold standard and the implementation of Imperial Ordinance No. 4; Imperial Ordinance No. 3 stipulated that monies of the same forms and denominations as Korean currency were to circulate freely (*mugai tsūyō*) and might be used for private and public transactions; and last, Imperial Ordinance No. 4 contained detailed prescriptions for the redemption of the old coins.[108] Importantly, it altered the 1901 provision on the exchange rate of *yang* and *hwan*: 10 *yang* 両 (= 2 *won* 元) of silver was now to be exchanged for 1 *hwan*, instead of the former rate of 5:1.[109]

But was Korea indeed to adopt the gold standard? Although the currency reports of the day indicate that Korea did so, Korea's standard was, by its very design, a gold-exchange standard levered upon the Japanese yen.[110] This can be determined by analyzing institutional preparations for the process of currency readjustment. As Korea did not have a central bank, Megata had, as early as December 1904, charged the Seoul branch of the First Bank with the management of the national treasury, thereby depriving the so-called *ch'ainbae* ("brokers") of the privilege of handling public funds.[111]

Now the First Bank was also to manage the currency readjustment. It is not difficult to perceive Tokyo's interventionist intentions—Jung-en Woo refers to Megata and the First Bank as agents provocateurs.[112] By the provisions of the contract, the Finance Ministry deposited ¥3 million with the bank as a currency readjustment fund; at the same time, the First Bank lent the same amount directly to the government (secured against custom receipts) at an interest rate of six percent; the government then deposited this money in the national treasury (i.e., the First Bank!) as a reserve fund for currency redemption.[113] At the same time, the Japanese government promulgated Ordinance 73, which gave the First Bank the function of Korea's central bank, making it short in name

---

108. On the promulgation and stipulations of these ordinances, see Daiichi ginkō, *Kankoku kahei seiri hōkokusho*, 27ff.

109. Yi, *Kankoku kahei kin'yūshi*, 319ff.

110. For an early analysis, see the work of Matsuoka.

111. In this respect see Yoshimura, *Danshaku Megata Tanetarō*, vol. 1, 353ff.; 370ff.; Kankoku seifu zaisei komonbu, *Kankoku zaisei seiri hōkoku*, vol. 1, chapter 2.

112. Woo, *Race to the Swift*, 25.

113. Contracts pertaining to the reform are reproduced in *Daiichi Ginkō, Kankoku kahei seiri hōkokusho*, 37–42.

only of being the National Bank of Korea.[114] Its notes were to circulate as the country's legal tender, and without hindrance (*museigen hōka*).

Japan's own problems with specie shortage made it a textbook example of a highly leveraged colonial monetary system. Although some gold coins were minted in Korea after 1906, they were never in circulation. Neither did the First Bank hold much gold as a convertible reserve. First Bank notes were convertible into BOJ notes, which were convertible into gold only in Tokyo: "thus there was almost no connection between the issue of Daiichi Ginko notes and the gold reserve."[115] This disconnect was further reinforced by certain amendments that Ordinance 73 introduced to existing First Bank provisions with regard to the issue of notes. Although the bank was in principle backed by a gold money reserve or BOJ convertible notes held at the First Bank's Seoul branch, it was also allowed to issue notes backed by government bonds and other credit securities, and it could issue notes beyond the limits of convertibility on the condition of approval by the Finance Minister.

Redemption of Paekt'ong Coins

The truly detrimental consequences of reform arose from the readjustment of Korea's monetary system. The stipulation that 10 *yang* (= 2 *wŏn*) of silver was to be exchanged for 1 *hwan* of the new gold denominated currency was in itself a seriously deflationary measure. For reasons that are not fully clear, Doo-Hwan Oh has labeled this stipulation "arbitrary." Formerly, 5 *yang* of silver or 1 *wŏn* had been valued at about 1 Japanese yen. Thus, he argues, the radical adjustment of the exchange rate was at odds with the earlier Japanese decision to exchange 1 silver yen for

---

114. Compare Shibusawa Eiichi kinen zaidan, *Shibusawa Eiichi Denki shiryō*, vol. 16, 183–214; this ordinance stipulated that the First Bank was provided with an extra ¥5 million (at 3 percent interest), and that its number of branches was further expanded. The first governor of this central bank was Ichihara Morihiro, who had formerly been employed at the bank's Yokohama branch. See Chōsen ginkōshi kenkyūkai, *Chōsen ginkōshi*, 25–30. Japanese policy makers were not unanimous in their choice of the First Bank—several alternate proposals circulated, the most prominent being that to establish a Sino-Japanese Bank—differences concerned the degree and nature of currency unification. Compare Takashima, *Chōsen ni okeru shokuminchi kin'yūshi no kenkyū*, 119–25.

115. Oh, "Currency Readjustment and Colonial Monetary System of 1905 in Korea," 60.

Table 2.3: Amounts and relative shares of currency in circulation before and after exchange rate stipulations of 1905 reform (in *won* [pre-reform], *hwan* [if converted, post-reform], and yen)

	paekt'ong (*won* / *hwan*)	*yŏpchŏn* (*won* / *hwan*)	First Bank (yen)	Bank of Japan (yen)	TOTAL
Pre-reform	23,000,000 *(53.0%)*	13,000,000 *(30.0%)*	6,068,832 *(14.0%)*	1,300,000 *(3.0%)*	43,368,832 *(100.0%)*
Post-reform	11,500,000 *(45.4%)*	6,500,000 *(25.6%)*	6,068,832 *(23.9%)*	1,300,000 *(5.1%)*	25,368,832 *(100.0%)*

SOURCE: Yi Sŏng-nyun, *Kankoku kahei kin'yūshi*, 320.

1 gold when it had itself adopted the gold standard in 1897.[116] This claim misses the point. In the context of Korea's currency adjustment, the main effect of the new exchange rate was to boost the relative weight of Japanese currency in the basket of all currencies in circulation on the peninsula at the time. A simple analysis of statistics relating to currency in circulation in 1905 shows that it fixed the relative weight of aggregate Japanese currency (i.e., First Bank notes and BOJ notes) at 29 percent of all currency in circulation, whereas its share would have been 17 percent if the original exchange rate had been kept (see Table 2.3).

What was the impact of this abstract stipulation on the redemption of types of coins made of different metals? After all, their bullion prices were not necessarily moving in parallel or fluctuating between the same parameters, especially not at the beginning of the twentieth century. To answer this question we will have to look more closely at these steps in the reform process and attempt to make sense of shifts in the terms of redemption and the methods employed.

The redemption of nickel coins was drastic and spectacular: between July 1905 and November 1909, some 381,051,954 pieces were returned, amounting to no less than 19,052,595 *wŏn*. A number of problems accompanied the exchange process. First, the Ordinance with Regard to the Exchange stipulated that only good-quality coins would be qualified for exchange; it had therefore distinguished between Grade A, Grade B, and Grade C coins (see Table 2.4). The exchange rate of Grade A coins

116. Ibid., 62.

Table 2.4: Numbers and values of recovered *paekt'ong* coins (by period, quality grade, and recovery method)

Period		Exchanged	Redeemed through taxes	Purchased	Transferred by Finance Ministry	TOTAL
07/1905–12/1905	Grade A	157,337,523	6,663,345	14,320,259	23,065,963	201,387,090
	Grade B	1,735,068	273,206	N/A	N/A	2,008,274
	Value	*7,926,814* ¥3,907,412	¥162,486	*716,013* ¥324,567	¥576,649	¥4,971,114
01/1906–12/1906	Grade A	11,208,491	49,459,246	4,417,659	N/A	65,085,396
	Grade B	59,840	5,036,227	N/A	N/A	5,096,067
	Value	*558,768* ¥279,315	¥1,160,937	*220,883* ¥110,167		¥1,550,419
01/1907–11/1909	Grade A	740,766	488,662	113,350,040	N/A	115,079,468
	Grade B	12,903	4,371	N/A	N/A	7,674
	Value	*37,048* ¥18,476	¥12,151	*5,667,502* ¥2,803,071		¥2,833,698
TOTAL	Grade A	169,286,780	56,611,253	132,087,958	23,065,963	381,051,954
	Grade B	1,797,811	5,313,804	N/A	N/A	7,111,615
	Value	*8,522,631* ¥4,205,202	¥1,335,574	*6,604,399* ¥3,237,805	¥576,649	¥9,355,231

NOTES: Values are italicized and given in *won* and yen (denoted with ¥ symbol), when possible. Although estimates for *won* values could easily be made, *won* values are only mentioned when also indicated in the Daiichi ginkō report.

SOURCES: Following Daiichi ginkō, *Kankoku kahei seiri hōkokusho*, 51–110. Comparable tables can be found in Oh, "Currency Readjustment and Colonial Monetary System of 1905 in Korea," 70; Takashima, *Chōsen ni okeru shokuminchi kin'yūshi no kenkyū*, 127.

(*kōshu* 甲種), i.e. old coins of perfect quality, weight, impression, and form, was set at 2.5 *chŏn* (2 錢 5 厘) of the new money; bad old "Grade B coins" (*otsushu* 乙種) could be exchanged for 1 *chŏn* of the new money. If the owner disagreed about the exchange rate for his coins, the money appraiser would cut the coins in half and return them. Last, very bad coins would not be exchanged but would be left for natural extinction.

Further data mining demonstrates an extraordinary bias in favor of members of the Japanese and, interestingly, Chinese merchant classes. They not only were the main holders of Grade A coins, but they also benefited from the system set up to manage the process of redemption. During the first three months, the only applications accepted for currency transactions were for individual exchanges of between 1,000 and 10,000 *wŏn*—amounts that were, for obvious reasons, out of the league of Korean commoners. This resulted in remarkable imbalances in exchange by nationality, with a large number of abstentions by Japanese nationals (131 individuals out of 178 total abstentions). Presumably, they filed their applications with the aim of making a quick profit, but then did not manage to buy the required number of coins by the exchange date.[117] The minor role of Korean nationals (estimated at one-tenth of exchange transactions)[118] in the early months of the exchange process can probably be explained by their longstanding distrust of First Bank notes, into which the old coins were to be exchanged.

Exchange of coins was only one way of redeeming the nickel currency.[119] It accounted for only 47 percent of the total process and appears to have been substantial only in the process's earliest phase. From 1906, its share dropped sharply, making space for other categories such as "paid into the treasury" (*kokko shūnō*) and, especially, purchase (see Table 2.4). The currency paid into the treasury was basically nickel currency received through taxes of all sorts. But what explains the extraordinary share (37 percent) of redemption by purchase?

This shift in means of redemption must be discussed as the outcome of a depression triggered by the prospect of reform itself and exacerbated by uncertainty about which of the so many circulating kinds of

---

117. Gaimushō tsūshōkyoku, "Keijō ryōjikan hōkoku," 15.

118. Oh, "Currency Readjustment and Colonial Monetary System of 1905 in Korea," 67; for the Itō report, see Gaimushō, *Nihon gaikō bunsho*, vol. 38:1, no. 6.

119. Takashima, *Chōsen ni okeru shokuminchi kin'yūshi no kenkyū*, 126ff.

currency would be considered sound.[120] This uncertainty was caused by the conspicuous omission from government instructions of information about whether counterfeit money would be exchanged. At this time, counterfeit money and privately minted coins, often of Japanese origin, circulated widely, especially in the province of P'yŏngan. But even after the government finally committed itself to exchange the counterfeit money as well (renewed instructions were sent on May 16, 1905), former stipulations about the quality of coins remained in place; hence, if a counterfeit coin was considered of a quality too poor to be fit for exchange, it would not be exchanged after all. Rumors that Japanese and Chinese merchants would be given priority and that Korean merchants would be discriminated against—understandable in view of the early rules for exchange applications—fueled a financial panic. Korean merchants frantically sold their *paekt'ong* coins to Japanese and Chinese merchants, who gained by speculation, i.e., by buying only good-quality coins. This panic only exacerbated the depression of Korea's economic constituency, eventually leading to a protest movement directed against Megata.[121]

The resulting difficulty with getting the old nickel coins exchanged at all and the gloomy vision of parallel currencies was the main motivation for Megata and the First Bank to resort to the rather radical policy of buying up currency (the First Bank report refers to it as *tokushu no hōhō*). They turned to middlemen, "trustworthy merchants" (*shin'yō aru shōnin*) and "banks and financial institutions," for whom the exchange rate of 2.5 *chŏn* would be upheld.[122] For both individuals and banks, who received nickel currency through transactions with ordinary Koreans, this was a golden opportunity. This scheme also fit other interests of the government in Tokyo: it assisted directly in boosting the use of First Bank banknotes, as they were given in exchange for nickel coins.

By November 30, 1909, when the circulation of *paekt'ong* was officially prohibited, the process of redemption was more or less com-

---

120. The First Bank report refers to extensive surveys into the regional varieties of nickel currency and their relative purity and quality. See Daiichi ginkō, *Kankoku kahei seiri hōkokusho*, 66–68.

121. Ibid., 70.

122. Ibid., 89.

plete.[123] The Korean and Japanese currency systems, at least in the peninsula's economic centers, were now de facto "harmonized." For many, it had come at the tremendous cost of bankruptcy; the number of discarded *paekt'ong* coins can only be guessed.[124]

Redemption of Yŏpchŏn Coins

The exchange of copper coins or *yŏpchŏn* is a very different story. With them, the problem was not so much inflation, but the continuously rising price of copper after 1900. Their redemption was, according to the Daiichi Ginkō report, "extremely difficult" (*konnanchū no konnan*),[125] for the following reasons:

1. Especially in the *yŏpchŏn* areas people were very stubborn, and they did not easily give up their age-old habits [. . .]
2. In those areas where the new currency was not circulating, one was obliged to pay one's taxes with various kinds of *yŏpchŏn*; but the tax-collecting county magistrates [*Kunsu*], when paying the tax receipts into the treasury, made use of the margin between the market price [*jika*] and the legal ratio [*hōtei kakaku*] of the *yŏpchŏn*. [They did so] by exchanging the tax receipts into new coins, which they then used in payment. As such, the once recovered *yŏpchŏn* flowed out into the market one more time. Consequently, the number of redeemed *yŏpchŏn* was extremely low, and turned the prospect of redeeming the *yŏpchŏn* by means of taxation into an elusive dream [*gabyō*; literally "painted rice cake"].
3. From the spring of 1907, world copper prices gradually rose; at the same time [. . .] the price of *yŏpchŏn* rose; as the margin between their market price and their legal ratio widened, fewer and fewer *yŏpchŏn* pieces were paid into the treasury.[126]

---

123. Ibid., 110.
124. "At the time of the exchange of *paekt'ong* coins, their amount in circulation was 23 million *wŏn*, and their recovered amounts (including exchanges, purchases and taxes) were 19.05 million *wŏn* at the minimum. Out of these amounts 4 million *wŏn* was discarded. Some people say that the amounts of *paekt'ong* coins in circulation was 30 million *wŏn*, so huge amounts of *paekt'ong* coins were left to national abandonment and extinction." Oh, "Currency Readjustment and Colonial Monetary System of 1905 in Korea," 69.
125. Daiichi ginkō, *Kankoku kahei seiri hōkokusho*, 112.
126. Ibid., 120–21.

The drop in use of *yŏpchŏn* coins for these payments was caused not only by the actions of the county magistrates but also by the coins' massive exportation. This outflow had already resulted in a dramatic fall in the amount of the currency in circulation. Over the years, export of the *yŏpchŏn* remained an important mechanism in their redemption. Takashima, basing his estimates on the bullion price of copper in Pusan, asserts that, at the end of the process of their redemption, almost 419 million pieces must have been exported, equivalent to 25 percent of the total of coins taken out of circulation and amounting to 1,617,981 *wŏn*.[127] For this reason, Megata and his personnel at the National Finance Advisory Division (Zaisei komonbu) did not envisage the *yŏpchŏn* coins' complete redemption, but rather hoped to limit their circulation. They would thus be employed as one kind of subsidiary coinage in the newly established gold-exchange standard system.[128]

The rising copper price, however, demanded regular adjustments of the legal ratio. Whereas the *yŏpchŏn* exchange rate had been set at 1 *ri* (厘) per piece in early 1905, the government had to raise it to 1.5 *ri* in October of the same year; in February 1907, it was raised once again, to 1.85 *ri*; in April, to 2 *ri*, still without the desired effect of stimulating redemption. Upward adjustments of the legal exchange rate furthermore translated into distortions of the relative tax burden of *yŏpchŏn* areas relative to *paekt'ong* areas. As long as the 1 *ri* legal ratio was in place, there was no problem. But as soon as the ratio was set at 1.5 *ri*, the relative tax burden shifted: the original 80 *yang* [face value of the old Korean dollar] tax on farm land (*kyŏlse*) then corresponded to 12 *hwan* of the new money (instead of the former 8 *hwan*). In comparison, the *Kyŏlse* of 16 *wŏn* in *paekt'ong* areas remained at 8 *hwan*. Only after the government decided to fix the standard of *Kyŏlse* at 8 *hwan* of the new money do those imbalances seem to have been flattened out.[129]

---

127. In comparison with the *paekt'ong*, buying up currency played a much smaller role, partly because of the credibility this currency held in the regions in which it circulated.

128. Daiichi ginkō, *Kankoku kahei seiri hōkokusho*, 114.

129. Oh, "Currency Readjustment and Colonial Monetary System of 1905 in Korea," 72.

Resistance to Currency Adjustment

The severity of the consequent deflationary pressure must have been enormous. We know this not only from Korean reports, but also from the reactions of some Japanese nationals present in Korea at the time. Nishihara Kamezō, the main actor in the next chapter and not exactly a dove in Japanese Asia policy, was in Korea at the time and appears to have been appalled by the Megata reform. In his autobiography, in which he refers to his attitude as "fighting Megata's finance" (*megata zai-sei o tataku*), he recalls: "The financial crisis following the Megata reform was extreme (*hidoi mono*), and the pitiful voices of Korean commoners could be heard throughout the whole country. When I witnessed this, I could not remain indifferent to what I saw."[130] From his position as adviser (*sōdanyaku*) to the Seoul Chamber of Commerce, he lobbied against Megata as harmful to Korean independence and turned into an ardent antagonist of Japanese efforts to expropriate land to extend railways or build military bases.

So, what exactly was the nature of the economic crisis? As recounted already, the lack of precise regulations for the redemption of *paekt'ong* coins had fueled a panic, during which Korean merchants and commoners frantically disposed of their coins and thus created a brief but serious economic downturn. Many of them, furthermore, had bought real estate. It proved a poor decision; at a time when liquidity was needed, they had fixed their assets and become more vulnerable to further shocks. Soon, however, the tightness of money became an even bigger problem.

This was the result of Megata's plan to reorganize Korea's largely decentralized system of taxation, and of the role of several traditional credit instruments within it. Japanese reformers considered both the taxation system and these credit instruments "primitive" and thus unworthy of a role in the smooth and streamlined (i.e., centralized) modern economy they envisaged. This vision was not necessarily incorrect; the

---

130. Nishihara, *Yume no shichijū yonen*, 33. Nishihara's observations are illustrative of the difficult middle ground occupied by Japanese Pan-Asianists. On the one hand, they were strong supporters of Tokyo's efforts to "uplift" Asia and defend it against Western encroachment; on the other, they naturally opposed measures that estranged public opinion in countries under Japanese dominion.

use of, for instance, *eum*, a sort of promissory note, within commercial circles was directly related to the tightness of money that characterized Korea's pre-reform economy. Such a note made it possible to compensate for a temporary lack of cash money, and guaranteed smooth repayment as soon as monetary conditions had returned to normal; but as it was a rather unsophisticated instrument, it was liable to abuses and was not controlled by even rudimentary regulations.

There was also the old (official) custom of *Oeiheg*, the "order by the Minister of Finance to a county magistrate by which he could lend tax money he had collected directly to a third party"[131] (in practice, a merchant in his particular locality). This practice too was directly related to Korea's illiquid economic periphery: in the hinterland, where shortages of cash were a chronic problem, such loans to privileged merchants (the *ch'ainbae*) could be outstanding for months and even for years.[132] Yet, although it was indeed an old and in many ways outdated financial practice, even some Japanese sources had to concede that *Oeiheg* "had at least one merit: it helped the local economy. Nay, even the irregularity of the taxation period was not without merit, since it did not produce that periodical drain on money to which advanced societies are more or less subjected."[133] But because these practices were prone to abuses and especially because of their nontransparent nature—Korea did not have a budgetary system until the Japanese introduced it in 1905—Megata imprudently prohibited them.[134] He furthermore established a centralized tax agency and tightened Japan's grip on the peninsula's fiscal system by means of supervisory offices (*zeimukanbu*) directly responsible to the Ministry of Finance.[135] Even if these measures were indeed necessary in order to install a sound financial organization, they also compounded the monetary crisis. Continuing shortages of cash de-

---

131. Kankoku seifu zaisei komonbu, *Kankoku zaisei seiri hōkoku*, no. 1, 620.

132. For a concise treatment of *Oeiheg*, see Hatori, *Chōsen ni okeru shokuminchi heisei no keisei*, 44–47.

133. Bank of Chosen, *Economic History of Chosen*, 62.

134. Compare Yoshimura, *Danshaku Megata Tanetarō*, vol. 1, 402ff. For a treatment of this episode, see Hori, "Nihon teikoku shugi no Chōsen shokuminchika katei ni okeru zaisei henkaku."

135. See Kankoku seifu zaisei komonbu, *Kankoku zaisei seiri hōkoku*, no. 4, 39ff.

pressed the prices of farm products, increasing farmers' tax burdens and once more forcing many into bankruptcy.

It appears that Nishihara's role in Korea is directly related to demands for relief from this crisis. After merchants of Seoul's famous Chongno, "Bell Street," had established a Chamber of Commerce, in July 1905, Nishihara assisted them in drafting a petition.[136] The document criticized, among other things, regulations with regard to the classification of grade A and grade B *paekt'ong* coins and the abolition of *Oeiheg*, and it requested, among other things, the establishment of relief centers throughout the country.[137] It was to no avail. Although Megata recognized the hardships related to the reform, he rejected the merchants' proposals.

Megata would eventually unfold his own plan for relief, but one that was once again a means of furthering his designs for a colonial monetary system. He considered it a prerequisite not to rely on or to endorse traditional financial customs, instead creating new organizations that were to function as propellers and mobilizers of credit. Loans from the Korean government were thereby ruled out. In 1905, after obtaining a loan of ¥1.5 million from the Japanese government, he created the so-called "bill associations" (*tegata kumiai*), which included a role, albeit limited, for Korean nationals. Bill associations were allowed to draw bills in the new money for use in transactions between association members.[138]

Megata also addressed the problem of Seoul merchants who had disposed of their *paekt'ong* coin holdings and locked up their capital in real estate. Again in 1905, the reformers set up the Hansŏng Joint Warehouse Company (Hansŏng kyōdō sōko) with ¥250,000 of capital. It was organized "to enable these merchants to get loans on their merchandise by means of the warrants [*azukari shōken*] issued by the company, and so get over the financial embarrassment their shortsightedness had brought

---

136. This petition, called "Kankoku heisei kaikaku ni kan suru jōgansho," was discussed in *Tōyō keizai shinpō*, vol. 360 (December 5, 1905); for a detailed account of this episode, see Namikata, *Nihon shokuminchi kin'yū seisakushi no kenkyū*, 198ff.

137. Nishihara, *Yume no 70-yonen*, 33–34; compare Ōkurashō, *Nihon gaikō bunsho*, vol. 38:1, 744–45.

138. Yoshimura, *Danshaku Megata Tanetarō*, vol. 1, 419–21.

Table 2.5: Estimated trends of currencies in circulation, 1904–1909 (in yen)

Year	First Bank notes	New coin	*Paekt'ong* coins	*Yŏpchŏn* coins	Japanese currency	Total
1904	3,371,817	N/A	11,500,000	6,500,000	1,300,000	22,671,817
1905	8,125,267	367,680	6,530,000	6,393,000	1,300,000	22,715,947
1906	8,245,377	2,137,543	5,000,000	5,823,000	1,300,000	22,505,920
1907	11,807,174	4,100,175	3,285,000	4,704,000	959,000	24,855,349
1908	9,648,764	3,214,515	1,800,000	4,406,000	537,000	19,606,679
1909	12,340,378	5,696,265	1,970,132	2,463,933	848,000	23,318,708

SOURCE: Estimates taken from Oh, "Currency Readjustment and Colonial Monetary System of 1905 in Korea," 74.

upon them."[139] These warrants were issued against merchandise and other holdings and could be used to buy and sell goods, or be employed as securities in order to facilitate a financial credit.[140] In addition, Megata decided to support Korea's two surviving native banks (the Hansŏng Bank and Ch'ŏnil Bank)—although they were put under the supervision of the First Bank and the Ministry of Finance, respectively. In each case, loans were extended in First Bank notes. This policy had an immediate effect on trends in the different amounts of currencies in circulation (see Table 2.5).

Financial Reforms

Monetary reorganization and tax reform were only the start of the complete overhaul of Korea's economic organization. Simultaneous with this "most urgent of urgencies" (*kyūmuchū no kyūmu*),[141] Korea was invaded by a panoply of foreign (Japan-designed) financial institutions, each devoted to a different sector of the banking business, and some surprisingly advanced for the state of the Korean economy at the time. Up to 1900 the country's economy and financial system had been rudimentary, consisting primarily of pawnbrokers, moneylenders for whom

139. Bank of Chosen, *Economic History of Chosen*, 61–62.
140. Compare Yoshimura, *Danshaku Megata Tanetarō*, vol. 1, 417–18.
141. Yoshimura, *Danshaku Megata Tanetarō*, vol. 1, 431.

financial work was only a sideline to other commercial activities,[142] and the *kye* (mutual finance institutions).[143] Typically for such an under-developed system, these were informal operations whose size and trans-actions were insignificant, and whose area of operation was local.[144] There was also a very limited number of indigenous banks, but their capital was insufficient and they appear to have suffered from multiple managerial deficiencies.

Almost overnight, the Megata reform departed from the decentral-ized, even fragmented structure of Korea's economy and attempted to install a modern—and colonial—financial system characterized by sound dealings and *correspondance*, and in which several types of institu-tions were to address different sectors of the credit business.[145] From the surviving reports and articles that Megata and others published at the time,[146] we understand that he envisaged a financial system that was essentially double-layered:

In Korea, we urgently need two types of large financial institutions. One of them, responsible for handling matters related to the national treasury, will be made the bank of the treasury [*kokko ginkō*] [. . .]; it will be given extensive powers, and will shoulder a commensurately heavy responsibility; the other [institution] will [be responsible for] supplying long-term, low-interest loans; it will provide capital for infrastructure, secured against land. In my personal

---

142. This is reminiscent of Japan's system of *sake* brewer-moneylenders who domi-nated the market in the Muromachi period. See Gay, *The Moneylenders of Late Medieval Kyoto*.

143. Itani, "Chōsen ni okeru kei no kenkyū." For their postwar history, see Camp-bell and Ahn, "Kyes and Mujins."

144. This translated, as is so often the case in premodern economies, into rather high interest rates, to be explained by the monopolistic character of financial institutions, the limited availability of funds due to low rates of savings, and the fact that lending was done for consumption rather than for investing in the expansion of productivity.

145. For an overview, see Takashima, *Chōsen ni okeru shokuminchi kin'yūshi no kenkyū*, 139ff., 157ff. A little more than a decade after the Megata reform, the Bank of Chosen would publish *Economic History of Chosen*, reporting on the result of Japanese policies. It provides a detailed overview of the agricultural, industrial, commercial, and financial stimulus programs.

146. See especially the records of Mizumachi Kesaroku, catalogued as *Mizumachi Kesa-roku kankei monjo* (microfilmed), in the Modern Japanese Political History Materials read-ing room of the National Diet Library. It appears there were certain disagreements be-tween Mizumachi and Shōda Kazue when it came to the question of establishing an independent Korean central bank, or employing a branch office of the BOJ.

opinion, [this could be achieved] by establishing Korean Agricultural and Industrial Banks [Kankoku nōkō ginkō] in those regions where this is necessary, which could in turn be supplied with approx. ¥80,000; the latter could then develop branch offices in the principal centers of Korea, which are to be directed from the center to function as industrial banks [*kōgyō ginkō*].[147]

Megata thus proposed a central bank mainly in charge of (re-)discounting bills of exchange. This business separated it from a host of development banks (banks specialized in long-term credit) to which their Japanese peer, the Japan Industrial Bank, would channel funds for the colonization (and exploitation) of Korea. Although this plan was not adopted entirely as presented above, Japanese reformers would never abandon its essentially developmentalist orientation.

Let us for instance look at the Seoul branch office of the First Bank, after 1905 at the apex of the financial system. As soon as currency reform had been implemented, it was transformed into the Bank of Korea (Kankoku ginkō, 1909) and was renamed Bank of Chosen (Chōsen ginkō) in 1911.[148] It fulfilled a series of functions (see Table 2.6). First, its mandate as a central bank gave it an expected range of functions, such as lender of last resort to a host of both Japanese- and Korean-led savings banks, which in turn catered to regional and small-scale credit institutions.[149] Moneylenders continued to operate largely locally, but depended on bank credit as an important source for their operations.

---

147. Megata, "Kankoku kigyō no mokuteki."

148. There were several plans with regard to the establishment of a Korean central bank: some policy makers preferred a branch office of the Bank of Japan, others (e.g., Itō Hirobumi, then Resident-General of Korea), favoring the peninsula's "self-cultivation" (*jichi ikusei*), sought a new institution, which was to be named Bank of Great Korea"(*Daikan ginkō*). Antagonisms between the Resident-General and the Japanese Ministry of Finance were substantial. For an overview of these proposals, see Takashima, *Chōsen ni okeru shokuminchi kin'yūshi no kenkyū*, 144ff. For a description of the evolution of the First Bank into Korea's central bank, see Chōsen ginkōshi kenkyūkai, *Chōsen ginkōshi*, 38–88; see also "Chōsen ginkō no hatten" 朝鮮銀行の発展 (The development of the Bank of Chosen), nos. 1–4, FNN 1915.9.30–1915.10.3, KUDA-ID 00781867; "Saikin 10-nenkan ni okeru Chōsen kin'yūkai no hattatsu: Chōgin no kako oyobi genzai" 最近十年間に於ける朝鮮金融界の発達：鮮銀の過去及現在 (The development of Korea's financial world in the last ten years: the past and the present of the Bank of Chosen), OMS 1919.11.19, KUDA-ID 00472379. For a narrative history of the bank, see Tatai, *Chōsen ginkō*.

149. See Koh, *Shokuminchi kin'yū seisaku no shiteki bunseki.*

Table 2.6: The Bank of Chosen's capital, reserve funds, and limits of fiduciary issue (in yen)

Year	Subscribed capital	Paid-up capital	Reserve funds	Legal limits of fiduciary issue
1909	10,000,000	2,500,000	2,650	20,000,000
1910	10,000,000	2,500,000	2,650	20,000,000
1911	10,000,000	5,000,000	16,150	30,000,000
1912	10,000,000	7,500,000	57,350	30,000,000
1913	10,000,000	7,500,000	134,000	30,000,000
1914	10,000,000	10,000,000	240,000	30,000,000
1915	10,000,000	10,000,000	378,500	30,000,000
1916	10,000,000	10,000,000	518,000	30,000,000
1917	20,000,000	15,000,000	1,683,000	30,000,000
1918	40,000,000	25,000,000	2,333,000	50,000,000
1919	40,000,000	40,000,000	4,820,000	50,000,000

SOURCE: Bank of Chosen, *Economic History of Chosen*, 201.

Remarkably, however, the Bank of Chosen was much more than a "banker of banks." The *Economic History of Chosen*, published in commemoration of the bank's tenth anniversary, could rightfully claim that "so diverse and manifold are the services rendered by the bank that, since its establishment, there has been scarcely any reform undertaken in this country [. . .] which can absolutely disclaim the Bank's assistance given it in one form or another. It has done a great deal more than a central bank, as such is understood in most countries, ought to do."[150] Although a detailed analysis of its balance sheets falls beyond the scope of this study, it is clear that the larger part of its portfolio was invested in extending long-term credit secured against real estate. This included in particular loans to a host of public bodies under Japanese control.[151] Before Korea's annexation in 1910, loans were extended to Japanese municipalities in need of funds to build roads, schools, and so on; after the annexation (coinciding with the abolition of Japanese municipalities), they were transferred to the prefectural governments.

The bank's later problems with capital immobilization and "bad loans" throughout the 1920s can be traced to its conception and the

---

150. Bank of Chosen, *Economic History of Chosen*, 198.
151. Takashima, *Chōsen ni okeru shokuminchi kin'yūshi no kenkyū*, 149–51.

policy of "easy money" that characterized its early career. Curiously enough, its thoroughly developmentalist character also explains its swift venture into the business of a so-called "overseas bank" (*kaigai ginkō*, from the German *Überseebank*).[152] Although such action appears odd in view of Japan's, and certainly Korea's, problems with capital shortage, it was actually directed to the balance-of-payments problem of Korea under its colonial administration. Continuous trade deficits with the Japanese mainland drove Korea into the business of foreign exchange with countries with which it had a trade surplus. This paradoxical policy of importing capital (to Korea) by means of exporting capital (mainly from Japan to Manchuria) is both a symbol of Japan's difficult experiment with expansionism, and the practical consequence of its choice to maintain its easy-money policy in a country it identified as being in dire need of agricultural and (to a lesser degree) industrial development.

South Manchuria in particular proved an attractive partner, especially since the Japanese victory over Russia in 1905 had effectively knocked the bottom out of Russia's territorial claims.[153] The importance of this business can be deduced from the number of Bank of Chosen branches abroad. In the first decade of its operation, this increased from 1 to 28 (18 of these in Manchuria), whereas, over the same period, the number of branches in Korea was reduced to 10.[154] The bank's business activities unrelated to the Korean peninsula's monetary and financial development also expanded rapidly; around 1918, they overtook its business within Korea proper. The consequences were as much political as they were economic. Colonial dominion over Korea provided, indeed almost necessitated, further advances into the Asian mainland.

Agricultural and industrial banks (*nōkō ginkō*) were to be established in accordance with Imperial Ordinance 13 (March 1906); the system of Japan's own agricultural and industrial banks served as their exemplar. These banks are one of the most obscure aspects of the Megata reform. Because source material relating to their establishment and evolution is extremely scarce, one can only guess at the intentions of Megata

---

152. Ibid., 151–55.

153. For the Bank of Chosen's role in Manchuria, see Chapter 4; for a narrative history, see Tatai, *Chōsen ginkō*, 69–85.

154. See Bank of Chosen, *Economic History of Chosen*, 202–7, esp. 207.

and the National Finance Advisory Division. Presumably, these banks' establishment reflects the original conviction that Korea's central bank should not fulfill a role as long-term creditor (and long-term credit did in the end pose serious risks to the Bank of Chosen's business as a central bank, due to the immobilization of resources).

But there may be more to it. Namikata Shōichi's excellent analysis leads one to see that political motives also played an important role in the organization of these banks.[155] Positions within their higher echelons were consistently filled with Koreans from the upper classes of society, and 81 percent of the banks' aggregate stocks were in the hands of only eight wealthy Korean stockholders.[156] With anti-imperialist sentiment mounting, Tokyo would appear to have chosen who was to profit from colonial dominion (mainly landowners) and, in an effort to stay ahead of anti-Japanese protest, attempted to co-opt the elite segments of society. This strategy explains, among other things, why Megata defended the position that such banks should be established in all thirteen provinces (although this eventually turned out to be impossible).[157] Shortly after the promulgation of Imperial Ordinance 13, Megata and his aides took the same approach to establishing regional financial associations (*chihō kin'yū kumiai*) as successors of the *kye*.[158] Created respectively to "aid the intentions of bureaucrats with regard to finance, further understanding about related regulations, and report to the government questions and uncertainties" and to "expand lending by the Agricultural and Industrial Banks and aid in the establishment of agricultural storage," they and the *nōkō ginkō* thus became "lines of defense"[159] in protecting the legitimacy of colonial rule.

---

155. Namikata, *Nihon shokuminchi kin'yū seisakushi no kenkyū*, 204–5.

156. Ibid., 202, 207–15.

157. After the annexation, their number was reduced to six, from the original nine; in 1918, these banks were further amalgamated into the Chosen Industrial Bank. See "Kin'yū kikan seibi keikaku: nōkō ginkō no tōitsu oyobi zōshi to rengō kin'yū kumiai secchi no keikaku" 金融機関整備計画：農工銀行の統一及び増資と連合金融組合設置の計画 (The plan to fix financial institutions: the unification of the Agricultural and Industrial Banks and their capital increase; and the plan for the establishment of financial cooperatives), nos. 1–2, KJN 1917.12.19–1917.12.24, KUDA-ID 00767998.

158. See Shizuta, *Chōsen ni okeru kin'yū kumiai no hattatsu*.

159. Kankoku seifu zaisei komonbu, *Kankoku zaisei seiri hōkoku*, no. 4, 59, 328; for a brief discussion of the function of the financial cooperatives: "Chōsen no kin'yū kumiai

The establishment of these banks is one of the most striking examples of Japan's strategy in matters of colonial management, and one with far-reaching implications for our understanding of not only the relationship between colonizer and colonized, but also of the evolution of Korean capitalism. Whether the *nōkō ginkō* lived up to their mandate is another question. Again, substantial proof is hard to find, but from newspaper articles and other commentaries of the time one gets the impression that *nōkō ginkō* primarily vied with the indigenous ordinary banks in attracting Korean savings.[160] This activity did not translate into a successful business in agricultural credit; again according to Namikata, their share in the total of loans was a mere 17 percent, against commercial credit institutions' 83 percent.

Lasting Effects of the Megata Reforms

How do we relate this early phase of monetary and financial interventionism to the period after the formal annexation of Korea in 1910? How do we interpret the financial aspects of Japan's colonial experience on the Korean peninsula? And what do these financial actions imply for a discussion of Japanese imperialism?

As pointed out earlier, a number of scholars has already corrected the widely held view that Japan's colonial drive had it roots in economic expansion.[161] Kimura Mitsuhiko's excellent quantitative analyses, in particular, show that Japanese imperialism in Korea cannot be explained by economic factors.[162] Japanese exports to Korea accounted for only

---

to wa donna mono ka" 朝鮮の金融組合とはどんなものか (What are the Korean financial cooperatives?), OMS 1930.9.25, KUDA-ID 00474424. Namikata, *Nihon shokuminchi kin'yū seisakushi no kenkyū.*

160. In a newspaper article from 1914, Arai Kentarō, then at the Korean Ministry of Finance explains why this competition made a revision of *nōkō ginkō* regulations necessary: "Ryōrei kaisei no yōshi: Chōsen nōkō ginkōrei oyobi chihō kin'yū kumiairei kaisei" 両令改正の要旨：朝鮮農工銀行令及地方金融組合令改正 (A summary of the amendment of the two regulations: the amendment of the regulation concerning Korean Agricultural and Industrial Banks and the regulation concerning the financial cooperatives), KJN 1914.5.22 KUDA-ID 00750618.

161. Duus, "Economic Dimensions of Meiji Imperialism"; Beasley, *Japanese Imperialism,* esp. 1–13. The topic is also explored by Metzler, *Lever of Empire,* 35ff.

162. Kimura, "Financial Aspects of Korea's Economic Growth Under Japanese Rule," "Standards of Living in Colonial Korea," and "The Economics of Japanese Im-

1–3 percent of Japanese industrial output during the whole colonial period. Cotton textiles, Japan's main export commodity, went mainly to markets in British India, China, and Southeast Asia. Japanese military spending for the defense of Korea amounted to a mere 0.5 percent per annum of the total of products manufactured in Japan for the larger part of the colonial period. By contrast, Japan's share in Korea's exports was substantial (eventually leading to so-called starvation exports [*kiga yushutsu*]),[163] but did not translate into profits for industrialists. Neither was investment a defining factor. Corporate profits in Korea accounted for only 3 percent of all non-agricultural property income generated in Japan. The *zaibatsu* did not show great interest in investment in Korea before the late 1930s, when the government sponsored large-scale arms building programs.

Yet, Kimura's analyses are not sufficiently conclusive. For if the motivation behind imperialism was not primarily economic or financial, what was it? The answer is probably to be found in what I earlier identified as a national security interest in the peninsula. Korea was not to Japan what India was to Great Britain: the relative share in investment, the dedication to infrastructure, and the insistence on multiple reforms is simply too great. Korea was, therefore, not a colony in the conventional sense. Rather, it was a vital thread in the complex fabric that constituted the imperialist project of Japan's modernity. This special function also explains the totality of Korea's transformation: reforms were as much educational as economic, and as much cultural-ideological as political.[164] This was a country to be molded and "assimilated," not just left to the profit of private Japanese interests. Such ambitions are obvious as in the vocabulary of many reports, including those in English, that the Japanese authorities circulated in order to legitimize their activities in Korea.[165] Typically, they report on the "progress" of reforms;

---

perialism in Korea, 1910–1939." He bases his analyses on reports prepared at the time, such as Government-General of Korea, *Chōsen sōtokufu tōkei nenpō* 朝鮮総督府統計年報 (statistical yearbook of the Government-General).

163. See Kimura, "Standards of Living in Colonial Korea."

164. See E. P. Tsurumi, "Colonial Education in Korea and Taiwan"; Oguma, *A Genealogy of "Japanese" Self-Images*.

165. See, for instance, H.I.J.M. (His Imperial Japanese Majesty's) Residency-General, *Annual Report for 1907 on Reforms and Progress in Korea* and *The Second Annual Report on Re-*

the terminology of the "model" (as in "model farm," "model forest," and so on) is at the same time the reflection and rejection of Korea's undeveloped state, and the confirmation of rationalization and mobilization under Japan's leadership.

This politically inspired macroeconomic transformation of Korea into a subsidiary of the Japanese mainland never ruled out the involvement of private interests. As the Megata reforms demonstrate, private interests and profit-seeking could be considered even prerequisite to Japan's broader national security, as Matsukata's phrase of "real rights and interests" reminds us. Private interests were often so prominent as to disturb and even compromise the original political designs and objectives. In describing Japan's thoroughly developmentalist economic agenda for the Korean peninsula, one should never lose sight of this peculiar dynamic between, the interests of the state and those of the business community, even if this tension does not necessarily indicate a conflict between political and economic aims. Indeed, from the viewpoint of a Japanese political planner, these aims could hardly be separated—although a businessman would not always agree. Yet, at least in principle, economics followed political objectives, and in most cases had to accommodate military rule.[166] Japanese encroachment in Korea was therefore total, a matter of self-sufficiency and *Lebensraum*.

Japan's extremely hands-on developmentalist policies make their relations with Korea a sensitive topic for scientific analysis, resulting in a difficult debate about their implications for the development of Korean capitalism.[167] Older Korean studies in particular have dubbed Japan's

---

forms and Progress in Korea (1908–1909). See also Kang, "An Analysis of Japanese Policy and Economic Change in Korea."

166. From reports produced under the supervision of the Government-General, we know that, initially, the main concern had been the development of the agricultural sector. The Oriental Development Company was established with the explicit aim of increasing the production and export of foodstuffs. From 1920 onward, the Government-General initiated a 30-year financial plan to increase rice production (*sanbei zōshoku keikaku*). In the 1930s, Korea, formerly Japan's storehouse, became an entrepôt. With Manchuria now Japan's next line of defense, enormous funds from the Japanese money markets were diverted to Korea for the establishment of machine factories, munitions plants, and heavy industries. In both phases, however, policy makers were driven by concern for economic self-sufficiency.

167. See Eckert, *Offspring of Empire*; Hori, "East Asia Between the Two World Wars"; Kohli, "Where Do High Growth Political Economies Come From?"; McNamara, *The*

policies as a particularly vicious example of "comprador capitalism." They argue that the presence of Japanese businesses in Korea actually prevented national progress, because Japan intervened in Korean sovereignty and destroyed the "roots" of autonomous capitalist development. Military aggression retarded economic progress and made capital accumulation impossible. The effects of Japanese imperialism must be described, they assert, as oppressive, not catalytic.

This view of history has more recently been criticized by Western scholars as nationalistic, and as too simplistic when it comes to the relationship between colonizer and colonized. Scholars such as Carter Eckert and Dennis McNamara have therefore proposed "dependency theory." It may indeed be plausible that Korean society, under the growing influence of internationalization, would eventually have developed a capitalist system and modern economic infrastructure of its own. But what matters is that, largely because of Japanese colonialist intervention, it did not. Korean capitalism was not invented; it was imported. Catalytic and linkage effects were enormous, and stretched into areas of social organization. Such effects are made clear through the Megata reform, as we have seen in the context of relief. Japanese bureaucrats and officials, whatever their strategic objectives of exploitation and control, simply had to create alliances with certain classes of Korean society, as such alliances were in their own interest. It is therefore quite reasonable to speak of

economic modernization within the context of imperialism. Imperialism and colonialism were, in fact, only selectively oppressive and affected different classes of Koreans in different ways. Among the least affected was the nascent Korean bourgeoisie. Indeed, it is questionable whether the Korean bourgeoisie may be justly considered a victim of Japanese aggression at all—at least in the economic sense. [. . .] For their own reasons, the Japanese quite deliberately and purposefully fostered the growth of a Korean bourgeoisie.[168]

The Megata reform itself does however also make clear that dependency theory too needs further modification. Although the latter is certainly right in stressing the complex relation between colonizer and col-

---

Colonial Origins of Korean Enterprise, 1910–1945. On price evolution, see Cha, "Imperial Policy or World Price Shocks?"

168. Eckert, *Offspring of Empire*, 6.

onized with regard to economic development, it does not account for the military rigor with which Japanese reformers sought to control Korea's currency and national finance. The money doctors aspired to direct and total control over their Korean patient, and this aspiration was not only against the latter's will. At times it was simply greater than their concern with the patient's health: "Japanese policy was above all devoted to uplifting Korea, but unfortunately not its people," as Kublin has concluded.[169] Asserting this does not imply a reiteration of the earlier and obsolete "comprador-capitalist" assumptions. It does, however, urge the reconsideration of the imperialist tactics Tokyo pursued, and especially of what it regarded as vital to its own security.[170]

Put somewhat enigmatically, the rationale for the currency bloc here appeared to be the currency bloc itself. This was not a currency bloc in the conventional sense. Unlike, for instance, the Latin Monetary Union, which referred to an agreement among more or less independent nations to keep exchange rates coupled, members of the Japan-led bloc economy did not have the power to choose to remain outside it. In this case, "Japan and the yen ha[d] an overpowering dominance, and arrangements [were] made with an eye to the needs of Japan and the yen, rather than in consideration of the other areas and their currencies."[171]

In the following chapters, we will see how the currency bloc of the embryonic Japanese colonial empire became an insatiable and self-propelling force, eventually growing beyond regions, provinces, and countries that could reasonably be annexed or occupied with military means. In the case of the Nishihara loans, this expansion did not involve a change of the Japanese cast: Megata and Nishihara both had prominent parts, albeit in different roles and in a totally different political context.

---

169. Kublin, "The Evolution of Japanese Colonialism," 81.

170. This is as much as admitted by McNamara: "The model of Japanese capitalism evident in the Korean experience of colonial rule was an odd blend of military priorities, authoritarian rule, and the remarkable mobilization of Korean rule and Japanese capital for the construction of economic infrastructures, Japanese mining, and heavy industrial plants" (*The Colonial Origins of Korean Enterprise*, 50).

171. Hunsberger, "The Yen Bloc in Japan's Expansion Program," 251.

Table 2.7: Chronology of events in Korean financial history

Year	Month/Date	Event
1876	February 27	Conclusion of the Kanghwa Treaty
1878	March	First Bank branch office opens in Pusan
1882		Conclusion of the Regulations of Sino-Korean Maritime and Continental Trade 清韓水陸貿易章程
	December	Appointment of Paul von Möllendorf as adviser to the Korean government
1891	November	Promulgation of the Regulations with Regard to the Currency of Great Korea 大朝鮮国貨幣条例 (alternatively called 新式貨幣条例草案)
1894	May	Outbreak of the Tonghak peasant rebellion 東學農民運動
	July 11	Promulgation of the Regulations with Regard to the Issuing of New Money 新式貨幣発行章程 by the Korean government
	August 1	Outbreak of the Sino-Japanese War
1895	April 17	End of the Sino-Japanese War and conclusion of the Treaty of Shimonoseki 下関条約
	April 23	Triple Intervention by Russia, Germany and France
1897	March	Japan adopts the gold standard
1901		Adoption of the 1901 Currency Ordinance 光武五年貨幣条例 by the Korean government
1902	January 30	Signing of the Anglo-Japanese Alliance 日英同盟
		First Bank notes start circulating in Korea
1904	February 10	Outbreak of the Russo-Japanese War
	February 23	Signing of the Japan-Korea Protocol 日韓議定書
	October 14	Megata signs his employment contract with Finance Minister Min Yŏng-ki 閔泳綺
	November 28	Closing of the Chŏnhwankuk 典圜局
	December	Issuance of Finance Ministry Order No. 2 "Establishing a Treasurer for the National Treasury"
1905	January 31	Conclusion of two contracts between the First Bank and the Korean government with regard to a loan funding currency readjustment
		Conclusion of contract that has the First Bank act as the Treasury for the Korean Government
	March	Promulgation of Japanese Imperial Ordinance 73, which makes the First Bank into Korea's central bank
		Enforcement of 1901 Currency Ordinance with modified instructions for exchange of old coins
	June 24	Finance Ministry Order 1 and 2 with regard to the exchange of *paekt'ong* coins
	July 1	Initiation of the exchange process for *paekt'ong* coins

	September 5	End of the Russo-Japanese War; conclusion of the Treaty of Portsmouth
	September	Promulgation of the regulations with regard to the bill associations 手形組合条例 and regulations with regard to the joint warehouse companies 共同倉庫条例
	November 7	Submission of the first petition 請願書 by the Seoul Chamber of Commerce with regard to problems in relation to the process of currency readjustment
	November 13	Submission of the second petition 情願書 by the Seoul Chamber of Commerce with regard to problems in relation to the process of currency readjustment
	November 17	Conclusion of the Eulsa Treaty 乙巳條約 (Japan-Korea Protectorate Treaty)
1906	March	Promulgation of regulations with regard to the Agricultural and Industrial Banks 農工銀行条例
1907	February	Conclusion of the Gentlemen's Agreement 日米紳士同盟 between Japan and the United States
	May	Promulgation of rules with regard to the regional financial associations 地方金融組合規則
	July 24	Conclusion of the Japan-Korea Annexation Treaty of 1907 第三次日韓協約
	August	Expiration of Megata's contract as monetary adviser
1909		Seoul Office of the First Bank is made Kankoku ginkō 韓国銀行
	November	Termination of the exchange process for *paekt'ong* and *yŏpchŏn* coins
1910	August 22	Conclusion of the Japan-Korea Annexation Treaty 日韓併合条約 (effective August 29)
1911		Kankoku ginkō renamed Bank of Chosen 朝鮮銀行

Table 2.8: Evolution of Korea-Japan trade relations

Year	Exports to Japan (in yen)	Imports from Japan (in yen)	Rice as % of exports	Beans as % of exports	Textiles as % of imports	Gold dust exports (in yen)
1877	151,277	314,170	1.5	3.3	-	35,378
1878	181,469	244,545	27.8	13.8	-	21,806
1879	612,174	566,955	57.4	16.0	-	53,263
1880	1,256,255	978,014	58.1	9.4	-	113,517
1881	2,230,296	1,873,976	27.6	14.3	-	468,378
1882	1,768,619	1,562,169	1.7	25.9	-	529,630
1883	1,656,078	2,178,400	4.4	29.0	-	522,046
1884	884,060	793,734	0.0	0.8	-	-
1885	377,775	1,377,392	-	-	-	-
1886	488,041	2,064,353	-	-	-	911,745
1887	783,752	2,080,787	-	-	-	1,177,975
1888	785,238	2,196,115	-	-	-	1,025,401
1889	1,122,276	2,299,118	6.9	57.5	-	608,414
1890	3,475,098	3,086,897	58.7	28.9	-	275,099
1891	3,219,887	3,226,468	56.5	28.4	-	273,288
1892	2,271,928	2,542,486	46.0	36.7	-	366,960
1893	1,543,114	1,949,043	-	-	-	425,008
1894	2,050,910	3,646,723	-	-	3.5	638,690
1895	2,366,427	5,838,738	-	-	7.3	952,706
1896	4,396,346	4,294,005	-	-	10.6	802,968
1897	8,090,039	6,432,060	-	-	15.5	947,536
1898	4,522,963	6,777,171	-	-	22.1	1,192,588
1899	4,205,382	6,658,200	-	-	20.7	2,049,477
1900	7,232,416	8,241,296	-	-	30.7	3,065,380
1901	7,402,116	9,051,881	-	-	22.3	4,857,201
1902	6,549,646	8,689,220	52.3	-	28.1	5,004,301
1903	7,599,624	11,554,969	54.8	-	18.5	5,456,187
1904	5,697,371	19,007,287	22.7	-	14.7	4,998,646
1905	5,389,914	23,561,899	14.0	-	16.1	5,205,005
1906	6,916,848	22,914,154	18.9	-	14.3	4,601,888
1907	12,767,732	27,381,846	-	-	-	-
1908	10,963,353	24,040,465	43.0	29.4	23.9	4,920,423
1909	12,081,738	21,852,245	32.6	28.8	20.0	6,359,267
1910	15,378,643	25,348,085	27.1	36.0	25.1	10,796,510

NOTES: Percentages are estimates as found in Takashima (see below); hyphens are used for years in which no credible estimates could be made. Textile imports include cotton yarn and other spinning products.
SOURCE: Takashima, *Chōsen ni okeru shokuminchi kin'yūshi no kenkyū*, 218–19.

Fig. G.1   Bank of Chosen in Dairen. Author's collection.

Fig. G.2   Bank of Chosen in Seoul. Author's collection.

Fig. G.3 Bank of Manchukuo in Chifeng (Ulanhad). Author's collection.

Fig. G.4 Bank of Manchukuo in Harbin. Author's collection.

Fig. G.5 Bank of Taiwan in Singapore. Author's collection.

Fig. G.6 Bank of Taiwan in Surabaya. Author's collection.

Fig. G.7   Yokohama Specie Bank in Dairen. Author's collection.

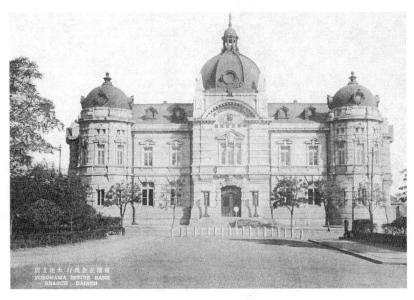

Fig. G.8   Yokohama Specie Bank in Dairen (alternate view). Author's collection.

Fig. G.9   Yokohama Specie Bank in Changchun. Author's collection.

Fig. G.10   Yokohama Specie Bank in Mukden. Author's collection.

SPECIE BANK YOKOHAMA　　横濱正金銀行

Fig. G.11　Yokohama Specie Bank in Yokohama. Author's collection.

THREE

"Separating the Roots of the Chrysanthemum": Nishihara Kamezō and the Abortive China Loans, 1917–1918

At the end of the fortieth session of the Diet, the eminent Noda [. . .] appeared in the ministers' room, handed the ministers a notebook and asked [us] to write our impressions. As I was slightly tipsy and in a good mood, I jotted down the following verse:

> The day to separate the roots of the chrysanthemum has at long last drawn near
> [*sorosoro kiku no newake hi to narinu*]

In the second half of September, when it was to become clear whether the propagated roots of the chrysanthemum would bud or not, Prime Minister Count Terauchi decided to resign. [. . .] Rid of a heavy burden, I spent several days at leisure, but after a while, in mid-November, I decided to recount the things that I had done and thought in as plain a way as possible [*kiwamete tsūzoku ni*], and share them with like-minded people. [The result] is the following pamphlet. It is left to the discerning observer to decide whether the flowers in the story are in full bloom [*dairin*] or rather modest [*shōrin*], and whether they are yellow or white.

—Shōda Kazue, *Kiku no newake*

The First World War turned out to be an unexpected windfall for Japan's financial situation as well as its imperial ambitions. Formerly a debtor

---

EPIGRAPH. Introductory paragraph to Shōda Kazue, *Kiku no newake: Nisshi keizaijō no shisetsu ni tsuite* 菊の根分：日支経済上の施設に就て (Separating the roots of the chrysanthemum: on Japanese-Chinese economic measures) (Tokyo: Nakatomi Shōjirō, 1918); reproduced in Suzuki Takeo, ed., *Nishihara shakkan shiryō kenkyū*, 285.

nation plagued by chronic shortages of capital and specie, its situation radically reversed because of diminished competition from Europe's belligerent powers and the consequent (and unprecedented) demand for Japanese products.[1] European-produced beet sugar, to take one example, more or less disappeared from world markets during the war, thereby greatly increasing the price of cane sugar and the profits of Taiwan's sugar producers—especially the Suzuki concern's sugar interests and its bank, the semi-governmental Bank of Taiwan (BOT). The wartime boost of the Japanese economy began in 1916, just as the Terauchi cabinet came into office. And when the United States experienced its parallel wartime boom, it was ready to absorb more Japanese exports than ever before. Within Japan itself, domestic producers were able to supply the market for many high-technology goods formerly imported from European countries. From whatever perspective, this development was spectacular: "between 1914 and 1918, domestic manufacturing increased by 54 percent in inflation adjusted terms [. . .]; exports increased by three times in money terms and by 47 percent in value."[2]

Through the ingenious financial technologies of its so-called special banks (*tokushu ginkō*), notably the Yokohama Specie Bank (YSB) and the Japan Industrial Bank (JIB), Japan had built up a very large gold reserve, in the form of foreign-held currencies. In 1916, ¥94.4 million of gold poured into the country; in 1917, the number rose to ¥247.2 million (see Table 3.1). According to Inoue Junnosuke, the war economy had supplied Japan with enough financial resources potentially to liquidate all its outstanding debts, both foreign and domestic—an outlook that was in sharp contrast to the prewar debt (1913), which Inoue Junnosuke estimated at ¥2,591 million, of which almost 60 percent was foreign debt.[3]

---

1. For the evolution of Japanese foreign trade during the war, see Metzler, *Lever of Empire*, 91ff.

2. Ibid., 95; compare Allen, *Japan's Economic Policy*, 101; Nihon ginkō tōkeikyoku, ed., *Meiji ikō honpō shuyō keizai tōkei*, 106, 120.

3. Inoue, *Problems of the Japanese Exchange*, 229; Nihon ginkō tōkeikyoku, ed., *Meiji ikō honpō shuyō keizai tōkei*, 158–59, gives a slightly different number (¥2.686 million). Compare Allen, *Japan's Economic Policy*, 22. This debt burden was incurred by favoring industrialization and military buildup and the costly strategy of overseas empire. Empire building brought no return in terms of foreign-exchange earnings, because of the abysmal state of the colonial economies, which demanded further investment and thus,

Table 3.1: Exports and imports of coins and bullion, 1910–1920 (in thousands of yen)

Year	Exports from Japan				Imports to Japan			
	Total	Foreign	Korea	Taiwan	Total	Foreign	Korea	Taiwan
1910	23,577	22,577	–	1,000	21,773	17,494	3,126	1,153
1911	23,713	21,801	1,900	12	17,058	4,938	11,044	1,075
1912	21,399	21,201	5	192	20,416	10,380	9,141	894
1913	21,110	20,704	7	398	11,792	954	9,972	865
1914	26,122	26,039	4	78	18,758	7,103	10,164	1,490
1915	40,729	40,675	20	34	37,930	24,159	11,366	2,404
1916	22,733	22,362	35	336	117,129	99,902	15,623	1,603
1917	151,087	150,639	87	360	398,302	386,990	9,620	1,691
1918	1,393	922	275	195	7,618	829	6,021	768
1919	2,738	1,485	910	342	330,471	325,771	4,415	285
1920	1,140	10	1,088	42	416,628	392,303	23,817	507

SOURCE: Nihon ginkō tōkeikyoku, *Hundred Year Statistics of the Japanese Economy*, 298–99.

At the same time, the war marked a remarkable change in the European presence on the Asian mainland. Most prominently, wartime expediency forced Great Britain to concentrate on the European theater of combat and to abandon its aggressive economic and political activities in China. London soon saw its position endangered by the assertive policies of both the United States and Japan. At stake was the politics of "exclusive rights" that the European powers had wrought upon China, which they regarded as immutable and inalienable. The conclusion of the war heralded a permanent transfer of both economic and political predominance throughout the world from Britain to the United States, accompanied by the powerful and apparently universalist vocabulary of the "Open Door."

This shift in the balance of power in the Far East was the main reason that Japanese policy makers did not follow the American example and liquidate the nation's debts, but instead engaged proactively in foreign lending. Between 1915 and 1918 Japan lent a total of ¥640,627,000 to Great Britain, France, and Russia, with a syndicate of Japanese banks

---

ultimately, foreign borrowing. Profits within this embryonic Japanese empire mainly came in Japanese yen, and this because of colonial administration. Colonial economies were designed as subsidiaries to the economy of the Japanese mainland.

standing as underwriter.[4] It has been made sufficiently clear by Itō Masanao that these loans were primarily economic in nature, and stemmed from problems associated with suspended, or limited, specie exchange. This was especially the case after 1917, when the United States too placed an embargo on the export of gold.[5] It appears that Tokyo faced the prospect of not being able to remit its growing trade surpluses, and thus decided to engage in lending in an effort to "fund its own trade."[6] Imports of raw cotton from India were a key commodity, for they defined the boundaries of repatriating trade surpluses with the United States in gold. Gold shipments were immediately transferred to Indian wholesalers, in order to enable further imports and thus sustain Japan's furious economic growth. In this scheme, extending credit to the European powers was one piece in the larger puzzle of facilitating trade under the difficult conditions of wartime.[7]

There were also other loan schemes, and these carried all the hallmarks of a pronounced political interest. In the period of 1917–18, the Japanese middleman Nishihara Kamezō negotiated a series of loans amounting to the sum of ¥145 million with the government of warlord Duan Qirui. Although contemporary reporting of these loans is spurious, we now know that there were close relationships between Nishihara Kamezō and the Terauchi cabinet in Tokyo, in particular in the person of the Minister of Finance, Shōda Kazue.[8]

---

4. Nihon ginkō 100-nenshi iinkai, *Nihon ginkō 100-nenshi*, vol. 2, 357–63; Ōkurashō, *Meiji Taishō zaiseishi*, vol. 17; Itō, *Nihon no taigai kin'yū to kin'yū seisaku*, 59ff. For the ideological context of these loans, see Kamakura, *Nihon teikoku shugi to shihon yushutsu*, 29ff.

5. This gave rise to quite intricate financial technology. The U.S. gold embargo caused the Japanese government to accumulate payments in the accounts of the Yokohama Specie Bank branch office in New York. When the YSB experienced difficulties maintaining advances to Japanese exporters, the Bank of Japan and the Japanese government purchased the balances to YSB's credit, and thus acquired funds for furthering the economic expansion. These purchases resulted in sharp increases in the Bank of Japan's note issuing, and as such precipitated the postwar inflation and consequent conflict of the so-called positive and negative policies. See Metzler, *Lever of Empire*, 115–58.

6. Itō, *Nihon no taigai kin'yū to kin'yū seisaku*, 25ff.; Nihon ginkō 100-nenshi iinkai, *Nihon ginkō 100-nenshi*, vol. 2, 374ff.

7. On the institutional characteristics of the foreign lending scheme, see Ōkurashō, *Meiji Taishō zaiseishi*, vol. 17, 618ff.

8. This relationship has been highlighted by Shōda's son, Tatsuo, in *Chūgoku shakkan to Shōda Kazue*.

Analyzing the Nishihara loans in geopolitical and historical isolation is, however, to miss the point. In what context(s) were these infamous loans raised? What was their geopolitical climate and their international institutional character? How did the Nishihara loans differ from earlier, more "official" instances of yen diplomacy? In what respect did they represent a break with former administrations, and was there a broad consensus about their objectives and appropriateness? And how did China's turbulent politics contribute to their ill fate?

The Agenda of the Open Door

The broader international context for these loans includes some remarkable developments in American politics at the end of the nineteenth and the beginning of the twentieth centuries. The United States' adoption of the gold standard cannot be seen in isolation from an internationalist strand in American politics, which stressed greater American involvement in international affairs—not by means of heavy-handed European-style military might, but through the beneficial means of free trade and commerce. The U.S. government therefore sponsored the establishment of a Commission on International Exchange whose aim was to investigate the possibility of establishing gold-exchange standards in, among other countries, Panama, Cuba, the Dominican Republic, and Mexico. Their respective currencies would not be based on the pound sterling (the system pioneered by the British in India),[9] but on the U.S. gold dollar. How these changes were brought about has been well documented.[10]

---

9. American policies were so obviously modeled on the British example in India that the economist John Maynard Keynes regarded them with profound contempt: in dealing with her dependencies, the United States had "imitated, almost slavishly, India" (Keynes, *Indian Currency and Finance*, 27). This criticism did not go unnoticed: "[Mr. Keynes's view] cannot be substantiated. The Philippines have a simpler and purer form of the gold-exchange standard than has India. The Indian system has various complicating elements: the sale of council bills for fiscal purposes; the paper money reserve, whose functions decidedly overlap those of the gold standard reserve; and the absence of anything like as rigid and automatic requirements as the Philippines possess for adjusting the monetary circulation to the norms demanded by a strict gold standard" (Kemmerer, "Review: Keynes' *Indian Currency and Finance*," 375).

10. Hollander, "The Finances of Porto Rico"; Kemmerer, "The Establishment of the Gold Exchange Standard in the Philippines," "A Gold Standard for the Straits Settlements I," and "A Gold Standard for the Straits Settlements II."

China remained, however, the nec plus ultra in the Great Power scramble for concessions and favorable trade agreements. It was, unfortunately for U.S. policy makers, also a country whose bargaining position had been substantially weakened. The Japanese victory over China in 1894–95 had effectively eroded the diplomatic leverage of the Chinese government. Toward the end of the nineteenth century, several European countries started to exploit China's limited capability to resist aggressive demands in order to circumvent the earlier relative equality of trade conditions based on so-called most-favored-nation clauses (originally embedded in the treaties of 1842–44).[11] Arguably pioneered by France,[12] this strategy consisted of demanding exclusive concessions, especially in mining and railway building. Such exclusive concessions thus destroyed opportunities for equal investment by other powers, and were consequently capable of destroying equal trading opportunities as well.

The American reaction consisted of the well-known Open Door Policy.[13] The "First Open Door Note" (September 6, 1899), allegedly prepared by Secretary of State John Hay and addressed to Andrew White, was a specific reaction to German exclusivist claims to the Bay of Jiaozhou and the adjacent Shandong Province, but effectively conveys the Open Door's essence:

1. [Each power will] in no way interfere with any treaty port or any vested interest within any so-called "sphere of interest" or leased territory it may have in China.

2. [T]he Chinese treaty tariff of the time shall apply to all merchandise landed or shipped to all such ports as are within said "sphere of interest" (unless they be "free ports"), no matter to what nationality it may belong, and that duties so leviable shall be collected by the Chinese Government.

3. [Each power will] levy no higher harbor dues on vessels of another nationality frequenting any port in such "sphere" than shall be levied on vessels of its own nationality, and no higher railroad charges over lines built, con-

---

11. Prichard, "The Origins of the Most-Favored-Nation and the Open Door Policies in China," esp. 167ff.

12. Ibid., 171; Treat, *The Far East*, 323.

13. For early overviews, see Tomimas, *The Open-Door Policy and the Territorial Integrity of China*; Bau, *The Open Door Doctrine in Relation to China*. On the Open Door's origins and early history, see Varg, "William Woodville Rockhill and the Open Door Notes"; Dennett, "The Open Door Policy as Intervention"; Esthus, "The Changing Concept of the Open Door, 1899–1910."

trolled or operated within its "sphere" on merchandise belonging to citizens or subjects of other nationalities transported through such "sphere" than shall be levied on similar merchandise belonging to its own nationals transported over equal distances.[14]

Formulated in the terminology of freedom, equality of privilege, and progress, the Open Door managed to mobilize not only public opinion but also key players in high finance.[15] Its novelty was not so much the values it claimed to incorporate, but its rhetorical force as an expression of enlightened self-interest. There was, some would say obviously, a strong political aspect to American aid to China.[16] The Open Door endorsed and justified a partnership of government and finance bent upon conquering the "mythical" China market.[17] Frequently, an influential financier such as Thomas Lamont would use it to strike a patriotic chord, stressing his indifference to profits and his dedication to America's superior cause. This American cause proved hard to resist. Appealing to a sort of multinational cooperation, the Jenks mission to China in 1904 was an attempt to bring China onto a gold-exchange standard by establishing an overseas specie reserve held by all international partners. The mission's eventual failure was largely due to external circumstances. The renewed rise in silver prices, which peaked between 1905 and 1907,[18]

---

14. *Papers Relating to the Foreign Relations of the United States, 1899*, 129–30.

15. "Economic institutions and reform organizations interacted with each other and together penetrated China. The people involved in them shared cultural conceptions, political philosophies and bureaucratic backgrounds; they had common outlooks, goals and destinies. In the combination of its parts, not in any single statement, tactic, or motive, lies an understanding of the Open Door in action" (Israel, "'For God, for China and for Yale,'" 796). For examples of praise for the Open Door, see McCormick, "The Open Door"; Prichard, "The Origins of the Most-Favored Nation and the Open Door Policies in China."

16. See T'ang and Miller, "The Political Aspect of International Finance in Russia and China." Paul Reinsch, one of the Open Door's supporters but quintessentially a modern imperialist, once explained the Monroe Doctrine as "an unconscious stroke of genius in statesmanship in that it has preserved South America for us now that we are ready to enter into our possession." Cited in Pugach, "Making the Open Door Work," 161.

17. Compare McCormick, *China Market*; Campbell, *Special Business Interests and the Open Door Policy*.

18. See Kemmerer, "The Recent Rise in the Price of Silver and Some of Its Monetary Consequences," and his subsequent "A Proposal for Pan-American Monetary Unity."

had lifted the pressure on gold payments, thus further reducing the Qing government's already limited attention paid to monetary reform.

In any case, the failure of the Jenks mission did not diminish America's appetite for the Chinese market. In order to befriend the Chinese government and as an apparent symbol of its peaceful ambitions, the United States remitted a portion of the Boxer indemnity to China in 1908.[19] In the same period, U.S. policy makers cleverly exploited disputes about railway concessions among the European financial powers in China (Great Britain, France, Germany, and Belgium) and again pushed for international cooperation, this time with regard to railroad matters. In 1910, after several series of protracted negotiations, the United States signed an agreement establishing a banking consortium with Great Britain, France, and Germany (Russia and Japan were left out of the agreement until June 18, 1912, because of their lack of financial resources).[20] Years later, it was agreed that the consortium would lend the Chinese government gold bonds to the aggregate amount of £25 million. The loan was to be secured upon the entire revenues of China's salt administration and it was to be used mainly for two purposes: the payment of liabilities due from the Chinese government to European powers (including several pre-consortium loans by Belgium and Japan), and various administrative reforms as well as infrastructure improvement.

Around 1913, soon after the signing of the final consortium agreement, however, the reinvented Open Door policy seemed on the verge

---

19. See Hunt, "The American Remission of the Boxer Indemnity." The American share in the indemnity amounted to 7.3 percent, or the yearly sum of £260,000. *The Chinese Student*, a periodical at the time, stated: "America long ago recognized the unfairness of the penalty imposed on China and made amends by returning the unexpected portion of the indemnity without imposing any reservations. China returned the compliment and employed the gift in sending her young sons to study in American Universities and Colleges. The American action at once received the grateful acknowledgement of the Chinese people and had a wonderful effect in promoting good relations between the two countries" (quoted in Scott, "The Boxer Indemnity in Its Relation to Chinese Education," 154).

20. For events leading up to the agreement, see Edwards, *British Diplomacy and Finance in China*, esp. 114–58; Winston, "Chinese Finance Under the Republic"; Field, *American Participation in the China Consortiums*, 1–24. The latter also includes a list of participating banking institutions (Field, *American Participation in the China Consortiums*, 39–40). The sole Japanese bank in the consortium was the Yokohama Specie Bank.

of collapse. Two years after the Revolution of 1911, China's political situation was more troubled than ever. The Manchu empire disintegrated, having fallen prey to warlords, who ruled their territories with the sole aim of exacting tribute to fulfill their obligations toward the imperial court and to enrich themselves and their allies. The central government, led by Yuan Shikai, could hardly claim to possess much central administrative authority. Insofar as it did not interfere with the custom administration—an institution originally associated with foreign financial interests and under foreign management—it merely "functioned as a guarantor to the foreign investor for the maintenance of regular interest and amortization payment on his bonds."[21] Adding to the problem of Chinese instability, President Wilson's fateful decision in 1913 to withdraw from the China Consortium merely convinced the European powers and Japan that America was trying to create the impression that she was China's only true confederate.[22] Consequently, each nation hastened to tighten its grip on its respective spheres of influence. Last but not least, there was the changed geopolitical situation. Although, with the outbreak of the First World War, the United States had effectively outmaneuvered Great Britain in East Asia,[23] it now faced a competitor, Japan, who regarded penetration of China's socioeconomic fabric as vital to its own destiny.

---

21. Bloch, "Warlordism," 692.

22. "The conditions of the loan seem to us to touch very nearly the administrative independence of China itself, and this administration does not feel that it ought, even by implication, to be a party of those conditions. The responsibility on its part which would be implied in requesting the bankers to undertake the loan might conceivably go to the length in some unhappy contingency of forceful interference in the financial, and even the political affairs of that great Oriental State [. . .]" (Woodrow Wilson's reply to the American group of the consortium's demand whether the administration's policy with respect to the consortium was to be the same as that of its predecessor; cited in Field, *American Participation in the China Consortiums*, 111). See also Kimitada, "Japanese Opinions on Woodrow Wilson in War and Peace."

23. Compare Chan, "British Policy in the Reorganization Loan to China 1912–1913"; Davis, "Limits of Effacement"; Scheiber, "World War I as Entrepreneurial Opportunity"; Braisted, "China, the United States Navy, and the Bethlehem Steel Company, 1909–1929"; Hunt, "Americans in the China Market"; Mazuzan, " 'Our New Gold Goes Adventuring.' "

The Plan for a Sino-Japanese Bank

Japanese expressions of interest in a financial presence in China date from the immediate aftermath of the Sino-Japanese War of 1894–95. Several high officials (among them Tomita Tetsunosuke, then governor of the Bank of Japan) pondered the idea of establishing a Sino-Japanese Bank (Nisshin ginkō), with the aim of "facilitating the commerce between the two nations, furthering their industrial development, among other means by documentary bills (*nigawase tegata*), and joining forces in order to develop the commercial situation of all East Asian countries."[24] At the time of its formulation, however, the plan was unrealistic. Japanese industry was still in its infancy, and exports to China were still insignificant—quite apart from the fact that capital exports were a policy issue. Visionary though it may seem in hindsight, this proposal was probably no more than a flight of fancy for its authors.

The plan was taken up again a few years later, in a very different political and economic setting. As we have seen, the adoption of the gold standard was a symbolic benchmark of Japan's entry into the world arena as both a colonial empire and a trading nation. The gold standard was an important step in the history of Japanese capitalism, even more so because it also highlights Japan's peculiar position in Asia. At least for Japanese exporters—Namikata refers to them as the Japanese "bourgeoisie"[25]—the gold standard was a Janus-faced achievement. The Kansai-based spinning companies, from the outset oriented toward the markets of Southeast Asia, now faced formidable export disadvantages. At a time when silver prices were steadily declining, their products were at risk of being priced out of the market by exorbitant transaction costs for Chinese importers. Numerous opinion pieces and solicitations written around 1900 call for "financial institutions concerned with trade toward silver countries, not only to [further the interests of] the spinning industry, but to the advantage of all commercial and industrial interests regarding China."[26] By 1898, Japanese commerce with China represented more than ¥100 million (three-fifths

---

24. Namikata, *Nihon shokuminchi kin'yū seisakushi no kenkyū*, 56.

25. Ibid., 120ff.

26. Ibid., 123; the previous page (122) contains a useful overview of proposals related to a Sino-Japanese bank.

being exports), or approximately a quarter of Japan's total trade volume (estimated at ¥420 million). Japanese exporters thus understandably stressed that China "represents an enormous market for our export products, among which textiles are the most important."[27] Although the YSB was formally in charge of foreign trade, in practice it concentrated on trade with Western countries (that is, countries on the gold standard). In 1894, close to 95 percent of its business was with Europe and the United States, and only 5 percent with China.[28]

Interestingly, it was initiative by the *zaibatsu* that prompted the government to act. These capitalists, whose fates were partially bound up with Japanese exporters through their activities in shipping and international trade, had submitted to the Japanese government their "Tōyō kōro kakuchō oyobi Nisshinkan kin'yū kikan ni kansuru ikensho" (Proposal for the expansion of far eastern shipping routes and the establishment of a Sino-Japanese financial institution) as early as 1899. It has several marked differences with the proposals emanating from the spinning industry, which can be explained by their different activities and interests. Put simply, *zaibatsu* demands were much more strategic. Their proposal notes how the expanded Japanese presence in China after 1895 had not resulted in a commensurate economic flowback or an extraction of special interests. It argues that a Japanese financial presence in China would accelerate the penetration of the Chinese hinterland by Japanese producers, giving them an advantage over the producers of the Western powers. It would also translate into lucrative projects in the fields of railway construction and mining. Such goals considerably affect the nature of the institution proposed. The *zaibatsu* industrialists envisaged an institution that was as much an investment bank as a commercial institution, and a device for extracting concessions from the weaker Chinese. Their proposal was a veritable blueprint for a colonial bank.

This idea resonated with policy circles in Tokyo. Made confident by the Sino-Japanese war indemnity, several politicians took the Sino-Japanese Bank proposal in the direction of a full-fledged real estate bank, with the aim of investing in railroad building and mining. Later, in a grand scheme for the establishment of a so-called East Asian Trad-

---

27. Ibid., 123, citing the original of a request by the presidents of several of Japan's foremost spinning companies.

28. Hijikata Susumu, *Yokohama shōkin ginkō.*

ing Bank (Atō tsūshō ginkō), the Japanese government was urged to expand its political leverage by deepening its commercial interests.[29] The realization of the political value of commercial activity was crucial, if possibly troubling. It highlights a profound awareness of the modern imperialism that dominated Western dealings with China (and as such hints at Japan's own experiment with "yen diplomacy"). It also brings to the fore an important trait of the Japanese policy-making constituency at the time: close attention to the long-term strategic interests of big business, even to the disadvantage of the smaller but nevertheless important exporting industries. Early advocates of Pan-Asianism found the objectives of big business remarkably compatible with their dream of a Japan-led Asian order (*tōa meishu ron*) and effectively neglected the demands of the smaller industries. As Namikata notes, the spinning-industry organizations reacted "coolly" to the political hijacking of their original request for easier access to the China market.[30]

Japanese Investments in China, 1900–1914

Even amid intensifying power competition in China, however, the Katsura cabinet (1901–1905) was unable to act upon the aforementioned requests to make a Sino-Japanese Bank materialize.[31] China nonetheless did not disappear from Japan's financial radar: indeed, the years after the Russo-Japanese War witnessed a dramatic increase in Japanese investments into China. Whereas these occupied an insignificant 0.1 percent (approx. $1 million) of total foreign investment in China in 1902, their share rose to 13.6 percent or $220 million in 1914.[32] These numbers require a great deal of nuance and clarification. First and foremost, Japanese investments in China represented the bulk of Japanese investment abroad—in sharp contrast to the greatly diversified foreign

---

29. Namikata, *Nihon shokuminchi kin'yū seisakushi no kenkyū*, 131.

30. Ibid., 132–33.

31. For an overview of proposals, see ibid., 139.

32. These percentages and numbers are taken from Remer, *Foreign Investments in China*, 76. Remer appears still to be an important reference for Japanese researchers; see Kokka shihon yushutsu kenkyūkai, *Nihon no shihon yushutsu tai-Chūgoku shakkan no kenkyū*, esp. 4. Remer also provides a detailed analysis of Japanese investments from 1897 to 1930: Remer, *Foreign Investments in China*, 408–553. For an early history, see Overlach, *Foreign Financial Control in China*.

investment portfolios of the Western powers. A straightforward comparison of Japanese investment with that of the other colonial powers is therefore impossible.

Nevertheless the growth is remarkable, even more so considering the vast share of state capital (*kokka shihon*) involved, especially through YSB branches.[33] Since the Sino-Japanese Bank plan had been aborted, YSB was given extra facilities for trade with China, among these a China exchange fund (*chūgoku kawase shikin*) to finance cotton exports.[34] (This policy was modified later.) As Taira Tomoyuki has correctly indicated, the crux of YSB's post-1900 activities in China resided in the difficulties the Bank of Japan had maintaining Japan's newly adopted gold standard.[35] In its attempts to do so, the BOJ had decided in 1903 to strictly limit its supply of cheap capital to the YSB. This sudden cut in its liquidity obviously posed problems for YSB's smooth functioning and forced it to find ways to recoup its operating funds. It came up with an astonishing and risky series of solutions. First of all, it reserved a part of its "China exchange fund" (which constituted a portion of BOJ's cheaply supplied money)[36] to fulfill its obligations to Western banks. Second, it resorted to a strategy of collecting deposits through its international branches. In China, its recently opened Tianjin and Beijing branches were exceptionally active in collecting deposits. Apart from the money they used for their day-to-day lending, these banks channeled deposits to the Shanghai branch. There, these funds were used partly for so-called chop-loans extended to the local micro-banks (*qianzhuang*), in an effort to control the Shanghai capital market.[37] The remaining share was used to buy exchange bills that were payable to YSB's London branch—the heart of its operations as an international exchange bank.

This was only the start of the monetary alchemy. YSB also engaged in large-scale lending in China, which might seem paradoxical given its

---

33. For a brief discussion of loans by other banks, see Metzler, *Lever of Empire*, 50–52.

34. These extra facilities were grants of ¥3 million (in 1897) and ¥10 million (in 1899). See Wray, "Japan's Big-Three Service Enterprises in China, 1896–1936," esp. 34–38. This otherwise excellent collection does not include papers on the Nishihara loans or on the Pan-Asianist aspirations of the Terauchi cabinet.

35. Taira, "Dai ichiji taisen izen no tai-Chūgoku shakkan to tōshi shutai."

36. The fund was ultimately liquidated in 1913. Ibid., 20.

37. Compare Nishimura, "Zai-Shanhai gaikoku ginkō to genchi ginkō."

collection of deposits from the same source. This lending strategy was fueled by a newly developed political interest in what was referred to as "weapons independence" (*gunki no dokuritsu*), or, in twenty-first-century parlance, "indigenization" (*kokusanka*) of military technology and technologies associated with heavy industrialization.[38] Such a policy translated into attempts to gain a stronger economic grip on countries that were geographically close to the Japanese mainland. Its effect on YSB's China portfolio was direct and enormous. Between 1906 and 1914, YSB invested aggressively and almost exclusively in China's mining sector. In efforts to sustain lending in the face of German competition, in particular for the strategic objective of developing the Hanyeping Coal and Iron Company, YSB would go to great lengths: in several cases, the Japanese government guaranteed the loans; in other instances, it even provided direct funding. In total, 26 loans materialized (10 of them for the Hanyeping Coal and Iron Company; Remer estimates their total value at around $15 million), some of unprecedented size.[39]

Together with the bank's eventual entry into the international China Consortium, in 1913, these loans heralded a new era: by 1914, China had become "the propelling power of YSB's exchange cycle" (*kawase shikin junkan no kidōryoku*).[40] The YSB had also become the stronghold of Japan's "political" loans to China,[41] even though the Japanese share of, for instance, the Reorganization loan was not issued in Japan. [42]

---

38. For an account in English, see Samuels, *"Rich Nation, Strong Army."*

39. See Jansen, "Yawata, Hanyehping, and the Twenty-One Demands"; Remer, *Foreign Investments in China*, 439ff. See also Bratter, "The Role of Subsidies in Japan's Economic Development;" Wilkins, "Japanese Multinational Enterprise Before 1914."

40. Taira, "Dai ichiji taisen izen no tai-Chūgoku shakkan to tōshi shutai," 20.

41. YSB gained this position through its entanglement in the China Consortium and its handling of Japan's share of the Boxer indemnity. The principal of the Boxer indemnity obligation to Japan was $24.5 million on January 1, 1902, before payments began. Another instance of YSB's political lending was its obligation in the context of the 1913 Reorganization loan to China. The loans' total amount was £25 million, the Japanese share of which was £5 million (roughly equivalent to ¥50 million). Other overtly political loans, for ¥2.5 million and for ¥10 million, were made to the Chinese Ministry of Communications (Shinkoku seifu yūdenbu).

42. Remer, *Foreign Investments in China*, 433: "While it is true that the legal obligation to make payment to the Yokohama Specie bank exists, it is also true that the whole of the Japanese share of the Reorganization loan was issued outside of Japan. It is unusual [. . .] for a legal obligation to exist to pay a bank in one country when the whole of the

Nishihara Kamezō

The distinction between "political" loans and "economic" ones is problematic at best. Such a distinction was, however, the rhetorical strategy explored by a host of Japanese policy makers, bureaucrats, and businessmen, especially after 1914—which marked the beginning of a boom for Japan's industries. It is also in this period that we encounter the protagonist of later financial negotiations with China.

Although Nishihara Kamezō is primarily known as the middleman who negotiated the series of Japanese loans to China that are the subject of this chapter, his prior history was not unrelated to the infamous "Nishihara loans." His early life, documented in his (largely self-serving) autobiography, is not of immediate concern here.[43] More significant are his activities in Korea. Nishihara, in his own words a "restless wanderer," arrived in Korea for the third time in 1904, with the intention of settling there for good. Like so many Japanese migrants, he was motivated by both a dream of easy profits and a paternalistic desire to work with the Koreans. What distinguished him from so many others, however, was his extraordinary penchant for social networking. A natural political "fixer,"[44] he soon found himself acquainted with many members of Korea's pro-Japanese political establishment. His activities after being appointed adviser to the Korean Chamber of Commerce in 1905 are illustrative of his career. At the chamber, he lobbied for an active Korean voice in Japanese policy toward the peninsula. Typically, he was in the forefront of resistance against the Megata reforms, which he believed to be at the root of Korea's economic malaise. As so often in similar incidents throughout his life, his stance earned

---

funds have come from investors in other countries [. . .]. The explanation for such transactions lies in the political field. Concerning the Japanese share of the Reorganization loan, the fact is that the funds came from England, France and Germany, and that the payments of the service of the loan were made through the Yokohama Specie Bank and through the banks in these European centers to investors in England and on the continent of Europe. Upon the principle of place of issue *the Japanese had no share in the loan.* [. . .] As a matter of fact, the financial transactions connected with the Reorganization loan *probably meant a transfer of funds from Europe to Japan rather than from Japan to China*" (italics added).

43. Nishihara, *Yume no 70 yonen*, esp. 3–30. For a summary of Nishihara's youth, see Duus, *The Abacus and the Sword*, 347–50.

44. Ibid., 347.

him both friends and enemies—most prominently Megata himself, who allegedly tried to have Nishihara expelled from Korea.[45]

This is not to say that Nishihara was anti-imperialist. After all, he later befriended members of the higher echelons of the Japanese colonial administration and appears to have been particularly close to Governor-General Terauchi Masatake, for whom he acted as a policy adviser.[46] While still in Korea, he also met Shōda Kazue, then governor of the Bank of Korea. Yet he was not the mere opportunist several commentators have made of him. Nishihara was, rather, an ideologue, and the quintessential Pan-Asianist: a staunch believer in the potential success of Asian unity and in the need for Asian peoples to work together as much as possible.[47] A Pan-Asian government would have to follow the principle of *wang dao*, the rule of right, rather than the (Western) rule of might. This belief also explains his (and Terauchi's) bitter resentment of the policy of the "Twenty-One Demands" forced upon China by the Ōkuma cabinet.[48] In a dramatic depiction of an encounter with Count Terauchi, Nishihara quotes the latter as saying: "What the Ōkuma cabinet is doing is the annihilation of eternal peace in East Asia. [This is] unforgivable. It may be easy to invade territory, but it is not going to win you the hearts of the people."[49]

Nishihara was particularly concerned with schemes for economic cooperation and the need to develop a unified currency zone—the "yen bloc" (*en burokku*). This idea may have originated in a very practical concern: as a frequent traveler along the borders of China, Manchuria, and Korea, he must have been painfully aware of how the congeries of different currency systems and local monies hampered his dream of

---

45. Nishihara, *Yume no 70 yonen*, 35.

46. Nishihara earned the name "Terauchi's pearls of wisdom" (*Terauchi-san no chie-bukuro*). Ibid., 46.

47. For an overview of the literature, see Nishikawa J., "Nishihara Kamezo and His Age."

48. This defining incident in the history of Sino-Japanese relations is well known and has been much commented upon. In this respect, see Dull, "Count Kato Komei and the Twenty-One Demands"; North, "The Negotiations Between Japan and China in 1915"; Elliott, "The Shantung Question"; Jansen, "Yawata, Hanyehping, and the Twenty-One Demands"; Luo, "National Humiliation and National Assertion: The Chinese Response to the Twenty-One Demands."

49. Nishihara, *Yume no 70 yonen*, 72.

a self-sufficient Asian socioeconomic fortress.[50] As early as 1912, Nishi-hara wrote a pamphlet entitled "Currency Unification in Manchuria and Measures for the Development of Trade Among Japan, Korea, and Manchuria" (*Manshū ni okeru tsūka tōitsu to Nissenman bōeki hattensaku*), most probably commissioned by Korea's Government-General or by the Bank of Korea.[51] The proposal is not radically new. It echoes and appropriates earlier ideas concerning currency unification that were cir-culating in certain policy circles in the Bank of Taiwan and the Bank of Chosen (BOC). Yet his pamphlet also conveys a clear sense of the so-called yellow man's burden, the Japanese responsibility for uplifting Asia and defying the West. "As we cannot expect the newly established Chinese government to unify the currency in Manchuria overnight," he explains, "it is up to us [Japanese] to unify Manchuria's currency, fur-ther trade among Japan, Korea, and Manchuria, and gradually expand our economic zone to the south." The means to do so is Japanese pa-per money: "It cannot be difficult to circulate gold coins and paper money in the whole of Manchuria. There is no doubt that this will trig-ger a process that is antithetical to Gresham's law: good coinage will drive out bad coinage. [As a result] our economic zone will not only encompass Manchuria, but will also stretch much further, beyond Zhili and Shandong, and beyond the Yellow and Blue River."

Many a bureaucrat or politician at the time would have immediately recognized the explosiveness of any such plan. Was YSB not legally prohibited from issuing gold bills? And was the BOJ not bound by the provision to keep its supply of convertible money in line with its specie reserve? These need not be obstacles, Nishihara insists: as in Korea, BOC bills will naturally proliferate.[52] The document thus marks the birth of the "Korea connection" (*Chōsengumi*) of Terauchi, Shōda, and Nishi-hara.[53] More important, it also signals Nishihara's interest in the grand

---

50. Namikata draws particular attention to his travel experience; ibid., 326. He shared this experience with Shōda Kazue, who carried out a prospectus of China and Korea in 1909 and published his findings in 1910 as Shōda Kazue, *Shinkan man'yū yoreki.*

51. See Namikata, *Nihon shokuminchi kin'yū seisakushi no kenkyū,* 326–33.

52. Ibid., 326.

53. Hayashi Gonsuke appears to have referred to them as such in a telegram of 1918 to Minister of Foreign Affairs Gotō Shinpei. See Gaimushō, *Nihon gaikō bunsho,* Taishō 7 (1918), vol. 2, 811–12. Hatano, *Chūgoku kindai gunbatsu no kenkyū,* 313; also mentioned in Namikata, *Nihon shokuminchi kin'yū seisakushi no kenkyū,* 332–33.

scheme of "Sino-Japanese economic cooperation" (*nisshi keizai teikei*)—
an objective that he envisaged being attained through the establishment
of a Sino-Japanese mining trust and the creation of a Chinese central
bank with Chinese and, more remarkably, Japanese capital.[54] In his
own words, and probably blind to the irony, he proposed a "Monroe
Doctrine for East Asia, or Pan-Asianism" (*Tōyō no Monrō sunawachi zen-
Tōyō shugi*).

"Divine Providence"

Although the Twenty-One Demands dealt a severe blow to the vision
of Sino-Japanese cooperation, Nishihara's ideas again came to the fore
in 1916. Once more, international events supported a proactive China
policy. Although the United States had effectively stepped out of the
China Consortium in 1913, it did not reduce its efforts to gain more influence in China. On the contrary, 1916 was "the year of American
loans" (*Beikoku shakkan no toshi*), as Higuchi Hiroshi asserted in 1939.[55]
In something of a lending frenzy, the United States provided money for
canal projects in the provinces of Shandong and Jiangsu ($6 million)
and for several railroads ($10 million), and concluded a loan contract
($5 million) through the Bank of Chicago. Japan would have to act
swiftly if it did not want to lose momentum in China. China's domestic
politics made action even more imperative. The sudden death of Yuan
Shikai had plunged China into the dark era of the warlords, whose ri-
valries colored their dealings with foreign countries.

The time proved right for Nishihara Kamezō. Typically, he perceived Yuan Shikai's death not as a crisis, but as "divine providence"
(*ten'yū*),[56] a situation that could be turned to Japan's advantage. Japan
would have to play rival parties off against one another. In his famous
"Jikyoku ni ōzuru tai-Shi keizaiteki shisetsu no yōkō" (Outline for op-

---

54. Ōmori Tokuko has argued that access to iron ore and steel, and monetary influence, were the ultimate rationale of the Nishihara loans. See Ōmori, "Nishihara shakkan ni tsuite." She thus corrects the rather naive view that the Nishihara loans were inspired by Japan's desire to establish friendly relations with its much larger neighbor
after the predicament of the Twenty-One Demands. See Langdon, "Japan's Failure to
Establish Friendly Relations with China in 1917–1918."

55. Higuchi, *Nihon no taishi tōshi kenkyū*.

56. Nishihara uses the characters 天祐. Nishihara, *Nishihara Kamezō nikki*, 129.

portune economic facilities regarding China), he calls for the following steps to be taken:

1. Establish a concern for business investment in China, in order to acquire an imperial economic base in China.
2. Establish provincial banks in the Three Eastern Provinces[57] and Zhili to issue gold paper currency.
3. Have the Japanese business investment concern provide the capital of the provincial banks, in the form of not BOJ paper currency, but paper currency issued by a "special bank" [*tokushu ginkō*; Nishihara obviously looking to the example of the Bank of Chosen].
4. Make sure that the provincial banks invite "financial advisers" (*zaisei komon*) recommended by the Japanese business investment concern, or that such advisers are placed in the finance departments of the Chinese government, or in the financial administration of the provinces.
5. Prepare regulations that would add gold coinage, *similar in form/weight/ denomination to Japanese coinage*, to the existing system of silver standard money; to promulgate regulations determining the legal ratio of gold specie to the amount of paper money to be issued. And . . .
6. [. . .] Make sure that paper money can be exchanged for gold coins in the bank's reserve, or for gold bills of identical value, to put paper money at par with Japanese currency.[58]

Nishihara's strategy, although never carried out in the form outlined above, must have been immediately clear to any official involved at the time. By mentioning "business investments" and the role of "special banks" he exposed a schism in Japan's policy-making constituency. Indeed, the Yokohama Specie Bank (and the Ministry of Finance) had from the very outset been highly critical of the Korea connection; they judged an independent Japanese financial position in China to be reckless. Now Nishihara even sought to bypass the established framework of the multinational China Consortium and YSB's "political" loans by setting the latter apart from the (imaginary) category of business loans.[59]

---

57. The Japanese term for the provinces of Liaoning, Jilin, and Heilongjiang.

58. Nishihara, *Yume no 70 yonen*, 83–86.

59. Hayashi Gonsuke's description, in a 1917 telegram to Minister of Foreign Affairs Motono Ichirō, is apt: "political loans masked as business loans." Gaimushō, *Nihon gaikō bunsho*, Taishō 6 (1917), vol. 2, 270. See also Remer, *Foreign Investments in China*, 540–41: "It is difficult to find a name for these transactions. They were hardly investments in any usual sense of the word. In attempting to state their nature carefully and accurately,

Several surviving communications from the time show the irritation this caused to YSB bankers and officials from several ministries.[60] However, when the Terauchi cabinet entered office (after a showdown about a Russo-Japanese Convention which the military-bureaucratic faction in Tokyo perceived as an opportunity for consolidating its advances into Asia),[61] those who stuck to the multinational China Consortium saw their position compromised. The situation in China only exacerbated matters for them. When the mounting costs of internal war forced China's largest banks—the Bank of China and the Bank of Communications (Kōtsū ginkō)—to suspend convertibility and to block the withdrawal of deposits in May 1916, the road to new China loans was opened wide. During a series of six (partially secret) missions to China, Nishihara would negotiate several loans on behalf of the Japanese government, every one of which would resonate in Sino-Japanese relations for two decades to come.

For the Korea connection, however, this was the realization of a dream that had seemed shattered only shortly before. After legal arrangements for the government securitization of the JIB bonds were in order, Shōda was therefore nothing short of ecstatic. Later, in 1928, he magnanimously claimed and explained in an *Ōsaka shinbun* column:

"The day to separate the roots of the chrysanthemum has drawn near"—.

As it was immediately after the proposal for the China loans had passed the Diet—which had been quite some work—I chose the phrase "propagating the roots of the chrysanthemum" to convey my joy that the days in which Japan's economic power would take root on the Asian mainland were approaching.[62]

---

one might say this: they were a series of payments of Japanese funds to a group of Chinese officials then in power in exchange for agreements which gave Japanese interests certain claims, particularly in Manchuria, and so advanced the policy of the Japanese government." A similar appraisal of the Nishihara loans can be found in C. W. Young, *Japan's Special Position in Manchuria*, 239ff.

60. Namikata, *Nihon shokuminchi kin'yū seisakushi no kenkyū*, 374ff. For an analysis of the role of domestic politics in Japanese foreign policy under the Terauchi Cabinet, see Dickinson, *War and National Reinvention*, 164ff.

61. See Dickinson, *War and National Reinvention*, 138–52.

62. Shōda Kazue, "Sono koro o kataru / Nishihara shakkan no ben / hinan no riyū wa nai" その頃を語る / 西原借款の弁 / 非難の理由はない (Talking about what happened back then / the case of the Nishihara loans / no need for condemnation), OAS 1928.9.21, KUDA-ID 00800368); the citation can also be found in: Suzuki (ed.),

Early Loans

After 1916, Nishihara's activities both accelerated and intensified. When both Ōkura and Co. and YSB proved unwilling to lend to the Bank of Communications (which had approached them in 1915),[63] Nishihara—now on a second trip to China—chose to side with Transportation Minister Cao Rulin in the new regime led by Duan Qirui. He signed a preliminary loan for ¥5 million; the final contract with the three-bank group that would become the Korea connection's favored vehicle was executed on January 20, 1917.[64] The JIB put up ¥3 million, whereas the BOC and the BOT put up ¥1 million respectively.[65] This first Bank of Communications loan (*daiichiji Kōtsū ginkō shakkan*) was the only one of the ensuing series of loans for which the banks bore the full risk; it was also the only one to be repaid when it matured. In design, it was one of the most obviously colonial loans. Gold currency notes of the same type as Japanese currency (and convertible into it) were to be issued, backed by Japanese gold notes. This not only would favor Japanese commerce at the expense of the Western powers, it also would be a first step toward incorporating China into a yen exchange-standard zone. Nishihara had long believed that this was the only method of overcoming Japan's financial inferiority to the Western powers.[66] The loan contract also stipulated the appointment of a Japanese financial adviser: after the conclusion of the second Bank of Communications loan, in October 1917, Fujiwara Masafumi was dispatched to China to oversee the bank's operations.

The year 1917, however, saw more than the first Nishihara loan. To the alarm of Japanese expansionists, and the Terauchi cabinet in particular, it was also the year in which the United States entered the war.

Nishihara shakkan shiryō kenkyū, 16. The reader may be aware that Shōda had used the metaphor of propagating a chrysanthemum by separating and transplanting the roots in a booklet he had published 10 years earlier (*Kiku no newake*).

63. YSB's management appears to have feared the upheaval that would ensue if the bank were known to be engaging in lending schemes outside the framework of the multinational China Consortium. See Namikata, *Nihon shokuminchi kin'yū seisakushi no kenkyū,* 376.

64. See MacMurray, ed., *Treaties and Agreements with and Concerning China,* vol. 2, 1345–46.

65. For the Bank of Chosen's role, see Tatai, *Chōsen ginkō,* 88–109.

66. Nishihara Kamezō, in the appendix to the "Outline for Opportune Economic Facilities vis-à-vis China." See Nishihara, *Yume no 70 yonen,* 85–86.

America's new voice in international affairs did far more than contribute to another shift in the balance of power in Asia. It also marked the introduction of a policy vocabulary that broke with the conventional power-political rhetoric of the old European powers and instead took up the concepts of peace, cooperation, and unilateralism—if not in substance, then at least in form.[67] Thus, President Woodrow Wilson's invitation to all neutral countries to sever relations with Germany also affected Japanese relations with China, as the Chinese were promised considerable financial assistance if they chose to ally themselves with the United States. For the Terauchi cabinet's foreign policy, the timing of this invitation could not possibly have been worse.

Realizing that Japan was steadily losing its foothold in China, Nishihara traveled there for a third time, in an effort to ensure that China's entry into the war would be counted to Japan's credit.[68] China severed relations with Germany on March 14.[69] Negotiations for the second Bank of Communications loan (*dainiji Kōtsū ginkō shakkan*) were infinitely more difficult than those for the first. These negotiations highlight Nishihara's character as a true visionary, albeit an expansionist one. This time, he had to come up with a scheme that would be more lucrative to the Chinese than the previous one-off loan of ¥5 million. With unbounded ambition, he proposed a loan that was four times the size: ¥20 million for securing Chinese participation in the Great War. This was not all. In his talks with members of the Duan clique, he also created the contours of a debate (and subsequent policy) that would come to maturity only in the 1930s.

The notion of an "East Asian self-sufficient zone" (*Tōyō jikyūken*) was a radical departure from former foreign policy ideology.[70] Nishihara insisted on promising Japanese assistance in increasing Chinese custom duties with the aim of stimulating the country's domestic de-

---

67. For an explanation of the impact on Japanese foreign policy of the U.S. entry into the war, see Dickinson, *War and National Reinvention*, 176–79.

68. Nishihara vividly describes his meeting(s) with Duan Qirui in his autobiography, *Yume no shichijū yonen*, 140–45. Namikata provides a good analysis of the evolution in Nishihara's thought. Namikata, *Nihon shokuminchi kin'yū seisakushi no kenkyū*, 383.

69. Dickinson, *War and National Reinvention*, 169.

70. Compare Morikawa, "Terauchi naikaku-ki ni okeru Nishihara Kamezō no tai-Chūgoku 'enjo' seisaku kōsō."

velopment and trade, in exchange for "the abolition of export tariffs on cotton, wool, iron, and copper, and possibly two or three other commodities."[71] It was difficult not to see the political implications of such an arrangement. Yet Nishihara avoided any reference to the political nature of this loan, insisting on the borrower's "sound judgment" about the opportune application of the money (although ultimately any "reform effort" was postponed, and at least ¥10 million was used for battling the southern revolutionaries).[72]

Domestically, Nishihara was also making enemies. Spinning companies reacted fiercely to the prospect of higher Chinese custom duties, as they had since earlier Chinese requests for tariff reform.[73] In attempting to explain the necessity for the duties, Nishihara's arguments foreshadow the grim realities of the 1930s and prefigure the German and Japanese militarist belief that war was inevitable.[74] After this war, he predicted, the world would fall apart into several blocs, "be it in the form of economic wars between the powers, or [in the form of] the unification of one British empire, or realized through extreme protectionist measures [*kyokutan naru hogo seisaku*]."[75] It would thus be in Japan's interest to form one such bloc with China, in which both Japan

---

71. Telegram to Foreign Minister Motono, in Gaimushō, *Nihon gaikō bunsho*, Taishō 6 (1917), vol. 2, 635–40.

72. Estimate by Okabe Saburō, *Nishihara shakkan o ronsu*. See Suzuki Takeo, ed., *Nishihara shakkan shiryō kenkyū*, esp. 493. The original version of this "top secret" (*gokuhi*) booklet was circulated in 1931 within the Japan Industrial Bank.

73. Compare "Waga hōsekigyō to Shina kanzei: tōgyōsha no shoken" 我紡績業と支那関税 : 当業者の所見 (Our spinning industry and China's customs: opinions from people in the industry), nos. 1–5, CSS 1917.2.27–1917.3.4, KUDA-ID 00858789; "Waga sangyō hatten to kanzei mondai: hōsekigyō no dageki" 我産業発展と支那関税問題 : 紡績業の打撃 (The development of our industries and the customs problem: a blow to the spinning industry), nos. 1–2, CSS 1917.3.8–1917.3.9, KUDA-ID 00858791; "Shina kanzei mondai: hōseki rengōkai ketsugi" 支那関税問題 : 紡績連合会決議 (China's customs problem: the decision of the Spinners' Association), in CSS 1917.4.13, KUDA-ID 00858815.

74. The notions of *Lebensraum* and the "East Asian self-sufficient zone" both anticipated and accelerated this militarism.

75. Nishihara, "The China Customs Problem and Japan" ("Shina kanzei mondai to Nihon"; May 1915). This pamphlet is among the Shōda Family Papers 勝田家文書, vol. 97; 18 (preserved in the National Diet Library of Japan).

and China would profit equally.[76] It would not be until September 20, 1917, that the Japanese government endorsed its support for Duan Qirui.[77] The familiar three-bank group signed a ¥20 million loan contract on September 29; the total amount would be taken out of the Deposit Fund (Yokinbu) of the Ministry of Finance.[78]

Japan Supports Chinese Monetary Reform

Although Nishihara had been relatively successful in buying friendship from Duan, Cao, and other members of the Duan clique, he had not yet been able to build upon this success to achieve his ultimate objectives of securing (exclusive) access to Chinese iron ore and steel and, as a corollary, propagating the yen within China's borders—two pillars for the establishment of an autarkic empire. Both securing exclusive access to Chinese iron and propagating the yen would be on the table after the Chinese government officially applied to the multinational China Consortium for a second reform loan of £1 million in 1916 (the consortium had earlier lent £2.5 million; because of the war, this Chinese idea of a second loan went nowhere).[79] European countries, caught up in the ongoing war effort, realized that their once preeminent position in China had been seriously weakened. Japan was the only country to furnish the required funds; consequently, it would acquire a dominant position in Chinese financial affairs.

With the United States as yet unwilling to return to the multinational consortium,[80] the Chinese government also understood that Japan was the source to turn to. However, Japanese negotiators of the Ōkuma cabinet insisted on securing any loan against the revenue of Chinese land taxes; they also pushed for Chinese acceptance of a Japanese ad-

---

76. In the China Customs pamphlet, Nishihara uses the words *higa kyōeki no mi o akuru.*

77. For Japanese domestic political affairs and the confused events in China at the time, see Dickinson, *War and National Reinvention*, 173ff.

78. For a history of the Deposit Fund, see Ferber, "'Run the State Like a Business.'"

79. In Japanese, the loan is referred to as *dai niji zengo shakkan.*

80. Japanese negotiators and ambassadors understood that any American return to the multinational consortium would severely damage Japan's position in China. Compare Namikata, *Nihon shokuminchi kin'yū seisakushi no kenkyū*, 401–8.

visor to supervise the loan's administration.[81] The Chinese regarded the first provision as too harsh a condition, because collateralizing land taxes, which were the pillar of Chinese national finance, would constitute a serious threat to Chinese integrity and sovereignty. Yet China, convinced that Japan was eager to provide a loan and realizing that its government was in need of money, came up with a revised loan scheme and conditions. Carefully avoiding reference to collateralizing the revenues of land taxes, Liang Qichao, the acting minister of finance, suggested in August 1917 that the multinational consortium issue a loan of £20 million for purposes of administrative and monetary reform, and the government chose to "invite" Sakatani Yoshirō, Japan's former finance minister, as an adviser. The monetary reform was envisaged as follows:

1. Regulate monetary reform centrally and independently, put it under the supervision of the prime minister or minister of finance, and invite one adviser from a member country of the multinational consortium. [. . .]
2. Give the country's mint bureaus the sole authority (*kankatsu*) for regard to matters of monetary reform [. . .].
3. Pursue a gold-exchange standard; use three-fourths of the loan [. . .] to establish an exchange fund (*taigai kawase shikin*).
4. Send one-fourth of the loan to China [. . .].
5. Issue gold notes [*kinpyō*] first in the main trading ports and have them circulate on the market, through tariffs, and in railway offices. [. . .]
7. As collateral for the loan, use (1) the assets of the mint bureaus, (2) seigniorage and [other] profits, (3) the profits of recoining *sen*. [. . .][82]

Namikata persuasively characterizes this proposal as an almost desperate attempt to apply for a large foreign loan without being driven to collateralizing the revenues of land taxes.[83] The idea of a loan also appealed

---

81. The revenue of the salt administration had been used as collateral for the first reform loan.

82. See "Heisei no kaikaku oyobi shakkan ni kansuru Ryō zaisei sōchō no kōsō" 幣制の改革及借款に関する梁財政総長の構想 (Monetary reform and governor Liang's ideas about loans), in Gaimushō, *Nihon gaikō bunsho*, Taishō 6 (1917), vol. 2, 201–2.

83. Namikata, *Nihon shokuminchi kin'yū seisakushi no kenkyū*, 403–5.

to Japanese negotiators.[84] Shōda almost immediately responded that Japan could provide half of the amount, £10 million or the equivalent of close to ¥100 million. He was, however, far less enthusiastic about the gradual reform plan put forward by the Chinese side, which would mean the establishment of a gold-exchange standard. He and Nishihara envisaged a more radical connection between the Chinese and Japanese monetary systems than a monetary bloc merely based on the yen (*engawase ken*). What they had in mind was a full-fledged yen bloc, encompassing all the countries in Japan's sphere of influence, in which the Japanese yen would be the sole standard against which other currencies would fluctuate (*enkei tsūkaken*).[85] Therefore, Japan would insist on the issuing of gold bills (*kinken*), similar to those issued in Korea by the BOC, which were to circulate in China together with the BOC bills.

The Lending Frenzy in the Wake of the Bolshevik Revolution

The revised loan plan was being discussed after another dramatic shift in world events: the Russian revolution. In Japan, the consequent fear that the Bolshevik revolutionary spirit would contaminate other regions of the world led, among other things, to the promulgation of the Munitions Industry Mobilization Act (Gunju kōgyō dōin hō, April 1918) and the conclusion of the Sino-Japan Joint Defensive Military Agreements (Nikka kyōdō bōteki gunji kyōtei, May 1918). These were tumultuous times. In August 1918, Japan participated in an Allied Expeditionary Force to destroy the Bolsheviks. The top brass even envisaged occupying a large area of Siberia[86]—a dream curtailed by rice riots on the Japanese mainland, which eventually caused the fall of the Terauchi cabinet.[87]

---

84. According to Ōmori, "Nishihara shakkan ni tsuite," 47.

85. Tsurumi Masayoshi, "En burokku no keisei."

86. The Siberian expedition may have been intended as a way to recoup losses incurred by lending to Russia: Japan would have regarded it as legitimate to go into Siberia and take Siberian railways as collateral for the loans to the Tsar's regime on which the Bolsheviks had defaulted.

87. The hike in rice prices came at the peak of a post–World War I inflationary spiral that affected most consumer goods and rents; undertaking the Siberian intervention further exacerbated the situation, as the government bought up existing rice stocks to supply the troops overseas. See Lewis, *Rioters and Citizens*. On the rice riots, see Ichibangase, "Kome sōdō to Nihon shakai jigyō."

For the Japanese initiatives in Korea, the strategic anxiety surrounding the threat of revolution proved to be an opportunity. It is during this period that Nishihara turned into a prolific writer of the pamphlets for which he is still known. After the aforementioned "About China's Customs Problem and Japan" (*Shina kanzei mondai to Nihon*) of May 1917, he wrote, in immediate succession, "A Policy for the Eternal Peace of East Asia" (*Tōyō eien no heiwasaku*) and "An Opinion About a Plan for the Mobilization of a Wartime Economy" (*senji keizai dōin keikaku shigi*), both in November 1917; "Current Issues" (*jigen*) in December 1917; and ultimately the rather chimerical "The Cardinal Point of China Policy" (*tai-Shi seisaku no yōtei*) in January 1918—elaborating on the desirability and concrete meaning of an East Asian self-sufficient zone.[88] It is clear from these pamphlets, and especially from the last, that Nishihara believed that massive financial support for China was the only way to solidify Sino-Japanese relations and ensure long-term peace.[89]

But how to deliver such far-reaching support without being seen to do so? Secrecy was the easy part. The Korea connection urged the establishment of the Exchange Bank of China (Chūka kaigyō ginkō),[90] which was to act as a middleman between the Chinese government and the three-bank group. Instead of the traditional three-bank group, Nishihara proposed a countrywide "capital trust" (*shihondan*) to enable the raising of large railway loans. In February 1918, the Terauchi cabinet paved the way by planning the issue of government-secured "industrialization bonds" for up to ¥100 million, specifically to be used for foreign investment. (This was the moment Shōda referred to as the time that the roots of the chrysanthemum would be separated.)[91] In April of the same year the foreign investment trust was established, comprising eighteen banks that included even the Nishihara-averse YSB.

Yet tensions within the Japanese government remained. As already indicated, the Korea connection had powerful adversaries. With regard

---

88. Namikata, *Nihon shokuminchi kin'yū seisakushi no kenkyū*, 410.

89. Nishihara proposed that, as a gesture of friendship and good intentions, China be excused from the Boxer indemnity payments due to Japan; this policy may have been inspired by the American decision to do the same.

90. Namikata refers to the bank's English name as the Chartered Exchange Bank of China. Namikata, *Nihon shokuminchi kin'yū seisakushi no kenkyū*, 411.

91. Suzuki Takeo, ed., *Nishihara shakkan shiryō kenkyū*, 14–16.

to its China policy, Japan's Ministry of Foreign Affairs was especially antagonistic to working outside the framework of the multinational banking consortium and pushing forward reforms in a manner "insensitive" to international pressure. The Ministry of Foreign Affairs, furthermore, already had a foothold in China. After China's official application to the multinational consortium for a second reform loan, it had pressured Minister of Finance Cao Rulin into inviting Sakatani Yoshio to conduct preparatory surveys regarding monetary reform.[92] Sakatani arrived in March.[93] He investigated China's monetary situation, the state of its mint bureaus, and so on. On returning to Japan three months later, he submitted several reports on monetary reform that departed from Nishihara's line of thought in at least two radical ways: he proposed that any reform should proceed gradually, and that the end of the reform road was to be a gold-exchange standard.[94]

During Sakatani's stay in China, Nishihara again traveled to Beijing, with the intention of amplifying his plan for the monetary and economic takeover of China by means of the Japanese yen. By April 10, he had already reached an informal agreement with the Chinese government and the Exchange Bank of China concerning a telegraph loan (the so-called *yūsen denshin shakkan*), the contract for which was signed on April 30.[95] Soon thereafter, however, events turned against Nishihara. On his arrival in Beijing, he must have been stunned to find that the Chinese government had already drafted the bill with regard to the issuing of gold notes, but with the stipulation that their denomination was to be 0.5 percent lower than the official Japanese rate of ¥1 = 0.75 grams of gold—Chinese gold notes were to be set at 0.746 grams. Ap-

---

92. Shimazaki, *En no shinryakushi*, 119ff, is especially helpful for understanding the complicated relationship between Nishihara and Sakatani.

93. I follow the discussion as presented by Namikata, *Nihon shokuminchi kin'yū seisakushi no kenkyū*, 414ff. For official documents relating to Sakatani's dispatch, see JACAR Ref. A04018134600: "Shina seifu o shite heisei komon ni nin'yō seshimuru shushi o motte Sakatani danshaku o beijin ni shucchō seshimuru no ken" 「支那政府ヲシテ幣制顧問ニ任用セシムル趣旨ヲ以テ阪谷男爵ヲ北京ニ出張セシムルノ件」 (On sending Baron Sakatani to Beijing with the aim of acting as monetary adviser to the Chinese government); and the following documents: JACAR Refs. B04010809800, B04010839300, B04010839400, B04010839600, and B04010839700.

94. See Metzler, *Lever of Empire*, 106–8.

95. Langdon, "Japan's Failure to Establish Friendly Relations with China," 251.

parently, Chinese officials were less enamored of the idea of a mingled currency than Nishihara was.

In Japan too, considerable doubts had arisen about the viability of the loans. The Ministry of Foreign Affairs had opposed Nishihara's plans from the outset. But now there were problems with the commercial participants of the eighteen-bank trust as well. For the likes of Ōkura, Kurihara, Mitsui, and their peers, notions of "mutual benefit" to Japan and China or an "East Asian autarkic zone" were the proverbial "painted rice cake" (*gabyō*), a mask for covering the expansion of their managerial grip on China's iron and steel companies. There were problems with this strategy: Ōkura's problems with the Fenghuang Iron and Steel Company were only one sign of the gravity of Chinese opposition.[96] With the aim of their investments compromised, the Chinese naturally allied with the Ministry of Foreign Affairs.

These problems spilled over into the negotiations about currency reform and led to a painful turning point in relations between Nishihara and Shōda.[97] Nishihara, in China for the sixth and last time, insisted that Japan be forthcoming with shipments of bullion in order to back the Chinese gold bills to be issued. Back in Tokyo, however, Shōda realized how inopportune such an action had become. Now not only the Ministry of Foreign Affairs, but even the Ministry of Finance, along with the BOJ and the YSB,[98] were vehemently opposed to the shipping of bullion to China. For the future of Japan's own financial situation, they reckoned that Japan could not and should not assist China's currency reform by such means.[99] When Shōda replied to Nishihara that bullion shipments were impossible, Nishihara wrote in his diary: "I have serious doubts as to whether Finance Minister Shōda is committed to the friendship and prosperity of China, whether he favors eco-

---

96. Namikata, *Nihon shokuminchi kin'yū seisakushi no kenkyū*, 418. The discussion must be seen in the wider framework of U.S.-Japan relations, in which America had tried to contain Japan through a steel embargo. See Safford, "Experiment in Containment."

97. See Suzuki Takeo, ed., *Nishihara shakkan shiryō kenkyū*, 20–22.

98. Ibid., 21–22.

99. Namikata assumes that Sakatani was a catalyst in this decision. Namikata, *Nihon shokuminchi kin'yū seisakushi no kenkyū*, 420.

nomic rapprochement, and whether he desires the eternal benefits to both countries."[100]

From there, the decision-making process becomes unclear. Shōda eventually reversed his stance and instructed Nishihara to continue the negotiations. The progress of the negotiations was slow at first, but they were concluded rapidly—indeed, frantically. The loans were, in chronological order:

1. The Kirin–Hueining Railway Primary Loan (June 18, 1918): ¥10 million for linking Manchuria and northern Korea
2. The Mine and Forestry Loan (August 2, 1918): ¥30 million for developing gold mines and forests in the Russian zone of northern Manchuria
3. The Manmō Four-Railway Loan (September 28, 1918): ¥20 million for linking Manchuria and Mongolia
4. The Shandong Two-Railway Preliminary Loan (September 28, 1918): ¥20 million for linking Shandong with central and southern China; the railway was to be a jointly-owned Chinese and Japanese line; and
5. The War Participation Loan (September 28, 1918): ¥20 million.[101]

These, together with the earlier loans, amounted to no less than ¥145 million.[102] Interestingly, three of the loans had been hastily concluded on the Terauchi cabinet's final day in office. When confronted with the question of why these loans had been pushed through at the last possible moment, Terauchi declined to answer.[103]

Once the foreign powers had been alerted to the magnitude of the Nishihara loans, they conspired for the loans' immediate termination. The Japanese government was pressured into writing them off completely, with the exception of a token repayment of ¥5 million. This left

---

100. Nishihara, *Nishihara Kamezō nikki,* 262–63.
101. For the English text of the separate agreements, see MacMurray, *Treaties with and Concerning China,* 1430–32, 1434–40, 1446–52. The Japanese text is in Suzuki Takeo, ed., *Nishihara shakkan shiryō kenkyū,* 152–65.
102. For documentation on the use of the loans, see Keizai chōsakai 経済調査会, "[Gokuhi] Nishihara shakkan riyō mondai ni tsuite" [極秘] 西原借款利用問題について ([Top Secret] About the problem of the use of the Nishihara loans; December 1932); Mantetsu sōmubu chōsaka 満鉄総務部調査課, "Nishihara shakkan shijo ichiranhyō" 西原借款使途一覧表 (A schematic overview of the spending of the Nishihara loans); both in the Library of Congress, Washington, DC.
103. This episode is related in Suzuki Takeo, ed., *Nishihara shakkan shiryō kenkyū,* 6–7, as "the mystery of September 28" (*nazo no 9-gatsu 28-nichi*).

¥140 million unaccounted for, which probably went to line the pockets of corrupt Chinese officials. John MacMurray, reporting from China in 1918, states that, with regard to the projects in the industrial field, "the contemplated industrial development has made no progress towards a beginning."[104] The main effect of the Nishihara loans may thus very well have been merely to prolong China's civil war. This example of yen diplomacy generated an immense antipathy for things Japanese. Worse still for Japanese financiers, Japan's international status as a creditor nation had been tarnished. Of the total foreign loan portfolio it had built up, another ¥220 million, lent to Tsarist Russia, was unrecoverable.[105] Both Russia and China had defaulted, for different reasons. Later, Shōda would return to his earlier metaphor: "The sprouts of the chrysanthemum have been trampled upon. I have heard that a very beautiful chrysanthemum is blooming in America. I would just like to meet an old man who grows a chrysanthemum. The following year, there will be this verse: '—the leaves of the winter chrysanthemum wither, its stem is wearing thin; the year must be coming to a close.'"[106]

International Condemnation and Aftermath

In the international press, the Nishihara loans were rebuked as vile examples of "German-inspired" methods. "Japan Ousts Pro-Hun," the *Washington Post* announced in the typical rhetoric of the day; Nishihara's actions had been a "menace to American, allied and Japanese comradeship." This comradeship was, however, not to be considered broken. Japanese and American cooperation had never been stronger, because both sides understood its importance: "the voice was Nishihara's, but the hand was the horrid hand of the Hun. [. . .] The part played by Nishihara was a true copy of the 'script' given by Bismarck, through Bleichröder to Herr Justizrath Primker. Count Terauchi repudiated Nishihara when the loan scandal was aired in the Diet, and the count is a soldier and a gentleman—a Japanese, not a German."[107]

---

104. Quoted in Remer, *Foreign Investments in China*, 542.
105. Inoue, *Problems of the Japanese Exchange*, 38.
106. Quoted in Shōda, *Chūgoku Shakkan to Shōda Kazue*, 181.
107. Gallagher, "Japan Ousts Pro-Hun: Disowns Tricky Financier Who Aids Germans in Plots," *Washington Post*, October 27, 1918.

Months earlier, Japan's Ministry of Foreign Affairs had attempted to mitigate any bad publicity associated with the China policies of the Terauchi cabinet. On September 12, 1917, Imperial Ordinance No. 144 called for the establishment of a Special Finance and Economic Commission (Kaigai tokuha zaisei keizai iinkai), apparently in an effort to give the Ministry of Foreign Affairs its own finance forum without directly clashing with Nishihara.[108] A first mission, led by Megata Tanetarō (then a member of the House of Lords), was sent to the United States,[109] acknowledging that America's financial position in the world would remain dominant after the war and arguing that "to strengthen the basis of cooperation with her is tantamount to advancing the economic position of this Empire."[110]

What is the legacy of the Nishihara loans? Ultimately they became widely regarded as a symbol of the perversions of prewar Japanese imperialism.[111] Okabe Saburō's 1931 description leaves no room for am-

---

108. Namikata, *Nihon shokuminchi kin'yū seisakushi no kenkyū*, 383–84.

109. Yoshimura, *Danshaku Megata Tanetarō*, 603ff. There is also a very rare English report of this mission: *The Imperial Japanese Government's Special Finance and Economic Commission to the United States, Headed by Baron Tanetaro Megata*. Other members of the commission were Matsumoto Osamu, Sakaguchi Takenosuke, Baron Itō Bunkichi, Dr. Hishida Seiji, Yoneyama Umekichi, Yamashita Yoshitarō, Koike Chōzō, and Matsumoto Kenjirō. The American press also covered the mission: "Why Japan Sent Finance Mission; Baron Megata Says His Country and America Need Better Understanding in Trade," *New York Times*, December 2, 1917; "Japan Seeks Trade Union with America; Baron Megata, Replying to City's Welcome, Tells of Commission's Aim," *New York Times*, November 24, 1917.

110. *The Imperial Japanese Government's Special Finance and Economic Commission to the United States*, 4. For Japanese newspaper reports of the time: "Nichibei kin'yū teikei / Nihon ginkō happyō / Nichibei ginkō (1)" 日米金融提携 / 日本銀行発表 / 日米銀行（一）(American-Japanese financial cooperation / presentation by the Bank of Japan: An American-Japanese Bank [1])," OAS 1918.1.24, KUDA-ID 00782197; "Nichibei kin'yū kyōtei / rengō kakkoku no teimei / Nichibei ginkō (4)" 日米金融協定 / 連合各国の締盟 / 日米銀行（四）(Japanese-American financial cooperation: an alliance of these countries: An American-Japanese Bank [4]), KMS 1918.1.25, KUDA-ID 00782200.

111. The Nishihara loans were widely commented upon in Japanese newspapers at the time. For a fairly representative digest, see "Tai-Shi seiri daishakkan / jitsugen no ki chikakaran" 対支整理大借款 / 実現の期近からん (Consolidating the big China loans: time for realization is approaching), nos. 1–3, JJS 1922.10.21–1922.10.23, KUDA-ID 00798433; "Izen ikinayameru Nishihara shakkan / seiri kōsai no seihi ga mondai / Seiyūkai ni mo sekinin ari" 依然行悩める西原借款 / 整理公債の成否が問題 / 政友

biguity: "The bad reputation of the Nishihara loans. A subsidy for civil war; high treason (*baikoku*). The questionable credentials of the people involved. The waste of means. [The fact these loans were] unsecured (*tanpo fukakujitsu*). The shameless search for profit. Rogue loans (*yashin shakkan*). The Nishihara loans have a very bad reputation, of course in China and Japan, but even in the public opinion of the Western countries which have no direct relationship with them."[112] Yet, throughout the 1920s and 1930s, successive Japanese governments sought to undo the financial damage wrought by the loans. At the Tariff Conference in Beijing, held from October 1925 to October 1926, Japanese authorities lobbied strongly to recover the Nishihara loans, but the meeting was broken off before the matter could be formally discussed.[113] Remer furthermore reports that, in an exchange of notes in connection with the Customs Agreement of May 6, 1930, the Japanese government "asked for a 'speedy consolidation' of the unsecured and inadequately secured obligations of China due to Japanese creditors."[114] Although the Chi-

---

会にも責任がある (Nishihara loans remain headache / success of consolidating government bonds in doubt / Seiyūkai is also responsible), JJS 1923.1.11, KUDA-ID 00798454; "Nishihara shakkan no zengo / gankin wa kōsai no karikae hakkō / rishi wa seiri shakkan enjo" 西原借款の善後 / 元金は興債の借替発行 / 利子は整理借款援助 (Reconstruction of the Nishihara loans / original amount based on issuing of industrial bonds / interest used as means of consolidating loans), TAS 1923.2.4, KUDA-ID 00798463; "Nishihara shakkan seirian / kyō honkaigi ni jōtei" 西原借款整理案 / きょう本会議に上程 (Plan for consolidation of the Nishihara loans / today on the agenda of the summit), KYN 1926.2.3, KUDA-ID 00800336; "Shina gaisai seirian Nihon ni tori daieikyō / Nishihara shakkan wa zettai ni mitomezu / Mantetsu shakkan wa chūō ni utsusu / Nankin honsha tokuden" 支那外債整理案日本に取り大影響 / 西原借款は絶対に認めず / 満鉄借款は中央に移す / 南京本社特電 (Plan for consolidation of China's foreign debt: great implications for Japan: no recognition of the Nishihara loans: move South Manchurian Railway loans to the center : special telegraph from our Nanking main office), OMS 1930.11.20, KUDA-ID 00811061; "Nishihara shakkan dake demo 3-oku sū senman'en / sore o fumitaosu tsumori ja naika? / mondai no saimu seiri kaigi e no teian / odoroku beki Shina no museii" 西原借款だけでも三億数千万円 / それを踏み倒す積りじゃないか / 問題の債務整理会議への提案 / 驚くべき支那の無誠意 (More than 3 hundred million yen for the Nishihara loans alone / don't they intend to default on that? / Proposal to put this problem to the summit concerning the consolidation of debts / the incredible insincerity of the Chinese), OMS 1930.11.21, KUDA-ID 00478613.

112. Introductory paragraphs to Okabe, *Nishihara shakkan o ronsu.*
113. Nish, *Japanese Foreign Policy in the Interwar Period*, 54–55.
114. Remer, *Foreign Investments in China*, 544.

nese originally agreed to call a conference by October 1, 1930, there would be no repayments.

Thus, although the government's official position remained that "Japan will never consent to China's demand for . . . cancellation,"[115] it also realized that the whole episode was a folly and a lost cause. The financier and statesman Inoue Junnosuke understood this as early as 1926: "these investments with the central and provincial governments of China—investments running to several hundred million yen—resulted in a dead loss, and today Japan can recover neither the capital which she thus locked up nor one penny of interest on it. To put the matter in a nutshell, I would say that foreign investment was not practiced by this country, and that such trifling investments as were effected might just as well have been thrown into the sea."[116]

---

115. Shidehara Kijūrō, quoted in ibid., 545.

116. Inoue, *Problems of the Japanese Exchange, 1914–1926*, 37; also cited in Moulton, *Japan: An Economic and Financial Appraisal*, 284. See Remer, *Foreign Investments in China*, 544.

FOUR

"To Dream the Impossible Dream":
Ideological Controversy in Manchukuo

We pioneered a new realm [*atarashii tenchi*], and had the genuine intention of partaking in the building of a new country. Owen Lattimore called Manchuria the "cradle of conflict" in East Asia. Until the construction of Manchukuo, it was just that. But turning [that situation] around, and making it into the cradle of East Asia's peace was the honest intention of those who took part in the building of Manchukuo. In the history of Manchukuo there were no scandals of the kind one constantly encounters in overseas territories or colonies, and that its bureaucrats were incorruptible from beginning to end certainly had to do with this. Surviving approximately thirteen years, Manchukuo's establishment ended as an impossible dream [*mihatenu yume*]. Yet I am convinced that all the efforts and all the hard work of Japan's youngsters at the time will forever be the pride of the Japanese race. I am sure that I am not the only one who prizes his luck for having had the chance to participate in the founding of Manchukuo.

—Hoshino Naoki, *Mihatenu yume*

Manchuria figured prominently in Japanese foreign policy from the beginning of the twentieth century onward, in a context never devoid of monetary preoccupations. The Bank of Chosen developed its function as an overseas bank or *kaigai ginkō* because Korea's trade deficit with the Japanese mainland and its consequent balance-of-payments problem made it necessary for the bank to venture into those countries with which it had a trade surplus. Bank of Chosen bills thus almost necessarily came to circulate in the adjacent territory of South Manchuria. Yet, rising

---

EPIGRAPH. From the epilogue of Hoshino, *Mihatenu yume*, 320.

Japanese militarism and diminishing civilian control over it (culminating in the politics of "government by assassination" and the infamous Mukden or Manchurian Incident in 1931)[1] did radically alter Japanese-Manchurian relations. The establishment of Manchuria as the semi-autonomous puppet state (*kairai kokka*) of Manchukuo,[2] or Manshū-koku, is both the hallmark of Japan's departure from the norms of the international arena and the consolidation of the self-enclosed political and economic zone of the yen bloc.

There are yet other reasons to treat Manchuria and the later Manchu-kuo separately. As Peter Duus stresses in the introduction to *The Japanese Informal Empire in China*, Tokyo's prewar interest in China proper was sharply different from its interests in Taiwan and Korea.[3] Earlier chapters have emphasized that, although distinct in their degree of strategic importance, both the establishment of Taiwan as a colony and Korea's annexation were quintessentially political or military decisions. China (including Northeast China) was different. A panoply of interests and concerns appear in different constellations at different points in the pre-war Sino-Japanese relationship. China prided itself on a venerable cultural tradition that did not lend itself easily to the discourse of assimilation that was so prominent in Japan's colonies. Although the Japanese expressed contempt for China's political situation in the 1930s, it was always mixed with a strong respect for its past. As Duus has said, people as different in viewpoint as Okakura Tenshin and Yamagata Aritomo frequently referred to the countries' shared histories, their relationship of "common script—common stock" (*dōbun dōshu*).[4] Quite a few Japanese believed that China, currently "backward," could benefit from coopera-tion with the "superior" Japanese in pursuit of the common objectives

------

1. Byas, *Government by Assassination*, a caricature of "government by representation." Compare Berger, *Parties Out of Power in Japan*. For early reports on the Manchurian Inci-dent, see Green, "Crisis in Manchuria"; Q. Wright, "The Manchurian Crisis"; Kuhn, "The Lytton Report on the Manchurian Crisis." See also Ferrell, "The Mukden Incident: September 18–19, 1931"; Smith, *The Manchurian Crisis, 1931–32*; Weland, "Misguided In-telligence: Japanese Military Intelligence Officers in the Manchurian Incident, September 1931."

2. In Chinese, it is still referred to as "False Manchuria" (*wei Manzhou guo*).

3. Duus et al., *The Japanese Informal Empire in China*, xi–xxvii.

4. See in this respect also Tankha, *Okakura Tenshin and Pan-Asianism*.

of wealth, national strength, and civilization. (Nishihara Kamezō, as we have seen, was one holder of this curious mix of attitudes.)

This peculiar definition of solidarity was not shared by many Chinese. Over the years, Chinese nationalism and anti-Japanese sentiment only increased, making the two nations' positions irreconcilable—"what the Japanese regarded as political intransigence or backwardness, the Chinese saw as patriotic resistance."[5] The "China problem" thus precipitated a sea change in Japan's descriptions of its purpose.[6] More and more people in the "inner sphere" (*naichi*) of the empire came to stress the importance of unilateral Japanese action for the benefit of Asia. Ultimately, this belief culminated in several versions of the Ōkuma doctrine or the idea of the "yellow man's burden": a reiteration of the notion of Asia's innate unity, but with a pronounced role for a strong and dominant Japan. This notion could be called the cultural or ideological dimension of Japan's unique relationship with China.

Culture and ideology, however, cannot be isolated from other spheres of social organization. The different nature of Japan's cultural relationship with China compared to its relations with Taiwan and Korea was also reinforced by the geopolitical environment. Tokyo's dealings with successive Chinese governments were crucially affected by the imperialism of the Western powers. Around 1900, this influence contributed to a case study in the emergence of semi-imperialism,[7] or the strategic necessity of establishing "informal empire" as a cooperative, collective effort.[8]

---

5. Ibid., xiii.

6. For a convincing history of ideas about the Japanese empire at the time, see Oguma, *A Genealogy of "Japanese" Self-Descriptions*, 156ff.; Saaler and Koschman, eds., *Pan-Asianism in Modern Japanese History*; Hotta, *Pan-Asianism and Japan's War, 1931–1945*.

7. The notion of "semi-imperialism" has received ample attention thanks to the work of Gallagher and Robinson: "For purposes of economic analysis it would be clearly unreal to define imperial history as the history of those colonies coloured red on the map" ("The Imperialism of Free Trade," 1); for a critique, see MacDonagh, "The Anti-Imperialism of Free Trade." In the context of Chinese history, see the following thoughtful analyses: Osterhammel, "Semi-Colonialism and Informal Empire in Twentieth Century China"; Osterhammel, "Imperialism in Transition: British Business and the Chinese Authorities, 1931–37."

8. Duus et al., *The Japanese Informal Empire in China*, xviii. Descriptions of informal empire in China include: Wilgus, *Sir Claude MacDonald, the Open Door, and British Informal Empire in China*; Edwards, *British Diplomacy and Finance in China, 1895–1914*; McCormick, *China Market: America's Quest for Informal Empire*.

China's magnitude and its clever diplomatic technique of playing the powers off against each other effectively prevented unilateral action by any one power.[9] Everybody, including the Chinese, had a stake in maintaining the treaty structure and the balance of power that it preserved. Japan, both politically and financially a far lesser player in the international arena, simply had to settle for an informal style of imperialism in China. It had to accommodate itself to the fact that Chinese sovereignty, however tenuous, was nevertheless incorporated in the complicated web of the unequal treaty system. The aftermaths of both the Sino-Japanese War and the Russo-Japanese War had clearly demonstrated that Japan neglected the demands of the Great Powers at its peril.

The situation in Asia changed due to a mix of international and domestic political factors. The coinciding of the European powers' retreat from the Asian theater because of World War I with the effects of the Chinese revolution of 1911 fundamentally recast China's international position (just as it heralded the recession of the waters of heavy-handed imperialism in favor of more subtle tactics). Abolishing the unequal treaties became the key demand of Chinese nationalism.[10] The European powers at first reacted ambiguously to national resistance movements, and began to experiment with neo-imperialist devices such as concession hunting. But the apparent legitimacy of internationalist, universalistic, and cooperative discourses—those associated with the Open Door Policy—was to the advantage of the United States.[11]

---

9. For the Korean case, compare M. Wright, "The Adaptability of Ch'ing Diplomacy."

10. Fung, "The Chinese Nationalists and the Unequal Treaties 1924–1931."

11. Indeed, the latter's impact was so strong that, in the years leading to 1930–31, the "race for concessions" had turned into a "race for rights recovery." Typically, the British were quick to grant the Chinese government autonomy of taxation (1928) in an effort to preempt the Americans from doing so; long before that, the United States had resorted to the policy of remitting their share of the Boxer Indemnity (1908); a second remission (1924) was used for the establishment of the *China Foundation for the Promotion of Education and Culture*; the British in turn invested their share in a fund to support cultural and educational work in China (1930), and, in 1931, they turned the Salt Administration over to Chinese control. In this respect, see Finch, "Remission of the Chinese Indemnity"; Malone, "The First Remission of the Boxer Indemnity"; Hunt, "The American Remission of the Boxer Indemnity: A Reappraisal"; Scott, "The Boxer Indemnity in Its Relation to Chinese Education"; Fan, "Eastern Trends in the New Sciences. The China Foundation for the Promotion of Education and Culture."

It is remarkable that Tokyo in the same period opted for an opposite course of more political and military intervention in China. Originally resembling a cacophony of as many ideas as ideologues, China's policy-making constituency gradually evolved toward more assertiveness and less compromise.[12] At the time of the assassination of Manchurian warlord Zhang Zuolin in 1928 and again at the time of the Manchurian Incident, Japanese politics skewed dangerously toward militarism.[13] The country's China policy had taken a sharp turn; whereas accommodating the Western powers had earlier been Japan's central tenet in its dealing with its immediate neighbors—hence its joining the League of Nations[14]—its military class now decided differently. It directed the country in the direction of conflict with the main ideological strands in international political opinion. Politics is the second dimension setting Sino-Japanese relations apart from Tokyo's relations with other countries in its sphere of influence.

Japanese Economic Interests in Manchuria

But there also was an important economic dimension to this relationship. Japanese investments in China were substantial—which was not the case for Taiwan and Korea. In Korea, political action had been prompted by strategic concerns but the Japanese interest in (especially) post-Restoration China, was at least as much economic-commercial as it was concerned with national security. Although one might doubt Duus' claim that the total China-Japan commodity trade was already in 1910 five times that with Korea and Taiwan combined, it was nonetheless at least several times greater.[15] Differences in the economic makeup of these countries go a long way toward providing an explanation for the disparity. Whereas the colonies mainly produced foodstuffs for the metropolis, China provided the raw materials Japan so urgently needed for its industrial production. Furthermore, it held the promise of a giant marketplace with an almost unlimited number of consumers of Japanese

---

12. On different opinions, see Duus et al., *The Japanese Informal Empire in China*, xxvii.

13. Zhang Zuolin was killed by the bombing of his railroad car, in a plot by officers of the Japanese Kwantung Army. See Dull, "The Assassination of Chang Tso-lin."

14. Burkman, *Japan and the League of Nations*.

15. Duus et al., *The Japanese Informal Empire in China*, xiii. See also Mizoguchi, "The Changing Pattern of Sino-Japanese Trade, 1884–1937."

products. Hence the history of Mitsui bussan can hardly been seen separately from that of Japanese empire in China, be it informal or formal.[16]

A particular instance of the economic dimension of this relationship
was the network of railroads in the region of Manchuria. Nowhere else
in Asia were imperialist doctrine and planning so clearly incarnated in
the technology of the railway. If one element has to be singled out as the
defining vector of Japanese encroachments into China, it would be the
South Manchurian Railway Company (SMRC), or Mantetsu.[17] Although
railroad technology's infrastructure and conception were inherited from
the Russians, the Japanese quickly carried it beyond its original scope
through sustained political and financial efforts. By its very nature,
SMRC grew into a semi-official organization with a considerable degree
of autonomy and, indeed, authority. Steven Ericson has therefore proposed that the locomotive was as much the symbol of Japan's own modernization as the expression of the country's political sway in Asia.[18]
In a way, SMRC was a tangible expression of Gotō Shinpei's credo of
"military preparedness in civilian clothes" (*bunsōteki bubi*).

The railway's expansion had a significant political-economic impact, especially in combination with Mitsui bussan and Japan's "colonial
banks." By virtue of its effective monopoly on commercial transportation, SMRC embodied the potential for diverting the region's economic
growth, directing the development of its natural resources, and, as many
a Japanese imperialist dreamed, determining patterns of settlement and
migration.[19] As a quintessentially imperialist corporation with the commercial mission of making a profit, it spearheaded both the politico-
strategic and business interests of Japan's imperialist constituency. This
is not to say that strategic and commercial interests always reinforced
each other, or that soldiers and railway managers necessarily agreed on

---

16. This has been very well treated by Sakamoto, *Zaibatsu to teikoku shugi*. For a more
general discussion of the business of Japanese multinationals, in China as well as elsewhere, see Wilkins, "Japanese Multinational Enterprise Before 1914."

17. This has been extensively documented. For a recent account, see Matsusaka, *The
Making of Japanese Manchuria*.

18. See Ericson, *The Sound of the Whistle*.

19. For an example of a Chinese business with a similar agenda, see Rosenbaum,
"Railway Enterprise and Economic Development." For overviews of Manchurian development in English, see Eckstein, Chao, and Chang, "The Economic Development
of Manchuria"; Bix, "Japanese Imperialism and the Manchurian Economy."

the railway's mission or its investment choices and business opportunities. As in Korea and with the Nishihara loans, conflict between raison d'état and raison d'affaires[20]—this time concerning the feasibility of integrating the Korean and Manchurian economies—once more constituted a core predicament of Japanese monetary imperialism.

Without wanting to minimize the SMRC's formative role in Japanese imperialism in Manchuria, I will touch on the SMRC only insofar as its activities relate to monetary and financial issues. To continue investigating Tokyo's financial policies and reforms, we will look more closely at such institutions as the Yokohama Specie Bank and the Bank of Chosen. Their presence may have been less visible than the railways', but by supplying capital to the SMRC or to its subsidiaries, Japanese businesses that aimed at penetrating the Chinese market, and smaller Japanese and Chinese manufacturers, they played a role of formidable importance in the Japanese imperial project—a role Shibata Yoshimasa has dubbed "currency imperialism."[21] As with the banks' activities in Korea, their interest lay in molding Manchuria to specific needs, whether commercial or political or both. I will describe their activities and their respective allegiances to (often different) political groups in the Japanese metropolis, and highlight their conflicts and their sometimes contradictory policies.

Manchuria's Muddled Currency Situation

The origins of Japanese financial interest in Manchuria must be placed around 1895, at the end of the Sino-Japanese War and only a few years after the first economic relations were established between the Meiji state and Northeast China.[22] The Manchurian economy had been

---

20. Following Matsusaka, *The Making of Japanese Manchuria*, 146. Compare, furthermore, 141: "Harmony between railway management and colonization and, more broadly, between profits and policy, of course, had limits. In the final analysis, sound business strategy and empire-building operated within different frameworks of logic."

21. Compare Shibata, *Senryōchi tsūka kin'yū seisaku no tenkai*, 4–5.

22. For a brief overview of Japanese financial policy toward Manchuria from its beginnings to the mid 1920s, see Shibata, "Nihon no tai-'Manshū' tsūka kin'yū seisaku no keisei to sono kinō no jittai." An exhaustive treatment of policy after the Manchurian incident can be found in Shibata, *Senryōchi tsūka kin'yū seisaku no tenkai*, 15–205. For the following paragraphs, the analysis by Kaneko Fumio proved extremely useful: Kaneko, *Kindai Nihon ni okeru tai-Manshū tōshi no kenkyū*, esp. chaps. 3, 6, and 9. Older but nevertheless still useful treatments include Kin'yū kenkyūkai, *Manshū kokuheisei to kin'yū*; Minami

opened by the Tianjin Treaty, forced upon the Chinese by the British. Typical of many a treaty at the time, the British had used it to urge the opening of trading ports. The port of Niuzhuang, on the left bank of the River Liao, became the economic pathway to South Manchuria.[23] Its trade volume alternately expanded and stagnated until it began to boom around 1890-91. According to Komine Kazuo, Japanese commercial relations with Manchuria received a boost around 1892, when Chinese traders chose to trade their beans, beancake, and bean oil—the three products of Manchuria's "soybean economy"[24]—not only via Korea, but also via a maritime route.[25] The Sino-Japanese War provided momentum for this trade expansion. Not only did exports to Japan, already substantial, more than double; Japan also took the lion's share of all transactions (in 1896, some 3,104,000 *taels* or approximately 87 percent of total exports, a portion that would not decline until just before the Russo-Japanese War).[26]

With such a startling increase in transactions and the enhanced involvement of major corporations, monetary and financial issues were bound to appear on the radar of policy makers in Tokyo. As we have

---

Minami Manshū tetsudō keizai chōsakai, *Manshūkoku tsūka kin'yū seido tōitsu ryakushi*; Kawashima, *Manshūkoku tsūka mondai no kenkyū narabi ni shiryō*. See as well Nangō Tatsune's writings, reprinted in: Kobayashi, Nangō, and Katō, *Mantetsu chōsakai to Nangō Tatsune*, 319–77.

23. Geographically, this is not wholly correct. The place of Niuzhang indicated in the Tianjin treaty refers to the old town of Niuzhang. The British recognized, however, that the port of Yingkou, 50 miles farther down the river, was a more fitting place as a trading port. In Yingkou they set up a consulate which they called the "Newchwang Consulate"—hence the misunderstanding. Compare Bank of Chosen, *Economic History of Manchuria*, 16.

24. In Japanese, *daizu keizai*. The term is taken from Kaneko, *Kindai Nihon ni okeru tai-Manshū tōshi no kenkyū*.

25. Komine, "Reimeiki no Nichiman bōeki," 16–17. For Japanese-Manchurian trade after the Sino-Japanese war, see Komine, "Nisshin sensōgo no Nichiman bōeki no seichō."

26. Interestingly, imports from Japan were considerably smaller (in 1896 approx. 423,000 *taels* or 22.4 percent of total imports through Yingkou). These numbers are taken from Kaneko, *Kindai Nihon ni okeru tai-Manshū tōshi no kenkyū*, 21ff. Kaneko provides a seminal analysis and statistics of the early economic history of Japanese-Manchurian relations. Comparable numbers are given in Bank of Chosen, *Economic History of Manchuria*, 28ff.: "Japan was yet in no position to compete with England, America, and India in that respect" (29).

seen, this was a period that saw several proposals for the establishment of a Sino-Japanese Bank.[27] Although these proposals eventually came to naught, they highlight an ambition that was paramount to Russia's in the years before direct Russo-Japanese conflict. Russia considered itself to have a mission of its own in Manchuria.[28] This went beyond the Siberian Railway and Chinese Eastern Railway (although railways were of the most obvious strategic concern to the Japanese military, and a direct reason for hostilities).[29] Russia also invested heavily in other types of infrastructure: the radial street grid of the city of Harbin, for example, is wholly of Russian design, as are the fortifications of Port Arthur and the Port of Dairen (referred to in Russian as Dalny).

Russia also attempted to create an economic network in China, for instance through afforestation and monetary policy.[30] Again according to the *Economic History of Manchuria*, in Northern Manchuria the Russian ruble became "the coin of the realm in the same sense in which the pound sterling is the coin of England"—no doubt a result of the efforts of the Russo-Chinese Bank to unify Manchurian currency.[31] For a variety of reasons, however, currency in the whole of Manchuria was muddled to a degree not unlike that in Korea around 1900.[32] Manchuria's monetary geography at the time can be deduced from a 1904 report by Arthur Henckendorff, then agent of the Russo-Chinese Bank in Niuzhuang:

I think it would not be possible to find a more intricate or complicated money system than that at present in vogue in Manchuria. This is owing, I should say, to the fact that they have not there a fixed recognized standard of silver which can be taken as a basis for exchange operations. Although China's currency is

---

27. An overview of proposals can be found in Namikata, *Nihon shokuminchi kin'yū seisakushi no kenkyū*, 122.

28. Ironically, this is noted in Bank of Chosen, *Economic History of Manchuria*, 49.

29. Compare, for instance, Patrikeeff and Shukman, *Railways and the Russo-Japanese War*.

30. I surmise this Russian policy also served as an example for the later Japanese policy of afforestation. There is a hint of this in Bank of Chosen, *Economic History of Manchuria*, 48.

31. Bank of Chosen, *Economic History of Manchuria*, 45. Compare as well: Matsusaka, *The Making of Japanese Manchuria*, 81.

32. For a helpful English guide (with Chinese characters) to currency circulating in Manchuria at the time, see Bank of Chosen, *Economic History of Manchuria*, 233ff. For a study of the complementarity of currencies in the whole of China at the time, see Kuroda, "Concurrent but non-integrable currency circuits."

on a silver basis, yet there is no standard of silver common to all their provinces.

1. For instance, the silver of Niuchwang has a touch of 99.2—or, in other words, 8 ounces of alloy to 992 ounces of pure silver. The touch of the silver of Liaoyang, Mukden, Kirin, and Tieling is supposed to be the same as that of Yingkou, but it never is, Yingkou silver usually being finer by 1 or 2 ounces in the thousand. Kwangchingtsu silver has a touch of 99, which puts it below Yingkou silver, while, on the other hand, Harbin silver has a touch of 99.8, which puts it above that of Niuchwang. When we think that the touch is only one of the items which has to be taken into consideration in the everyday exchange operations between the Manchurian towns, we can understand that the negotiating of a rate between Chinese currency is not a simple matter. [. . .]

The hard-coin currency in Manchuria consists of the sychee, small coin, and, of late, the ruble; yet the bulk of the merchandise bought and sold is not bought or sold against these hard effectives. All prices and rates quoted are against transfer money or mo-lu yingtzu.[33] [. . .]. The transfer is a peculiar and muddled system. [. . .] Transfer money is a purely nominal currency and not substantiated in any way by an effective.—in other words, it is a credit.[34]

This system was continued until about two years after the Japanese war. During this period the effective currency was sycee and copper cash, small coin not having then made its appearance in large amounts.

Tiao notes[35] were largely issued by bankers and merchants of good standing.

Of late the ruble has been a very important factor in the Manchurian currency. The ruble was brought into circulation by the Russian railway and the troops. The Chinese took it readily, owing to the ease with which it could be carried backward and forward, thus saving the expense of shipping specie.

2. The currency of Laioyang is slightly different from that of Niuchwang. The effectives here are small coin, sycee, copper cash, and rubles. They

---

33. The reference is to the "transfer *tael*" or *guoluyin*. See Ishida Kōhei, "Eikō ni okeru karogin no kichō to sono suii" and "Eikō ni okeru karogin seido no seiritsu to kikō."

34. This is now referred to as "imaginary money." See Einaudi, "The Theory of Imaginary Money from Charlemagne to the French Revolution."

35. The author probably means government notes or *guantie*; such notes were denominated in *diao* 吊.

have here also a system very much like the transfer money of Niuchwang—that is, the tieh yingtzu, or note money. [. . .]
3. The money system of Moukden and Tieling is practically the same as
that of Liaoyang.
4. The system in Kwangchingtsu and Kirin is quite different again. There
they have a system of transfer money very much like the system in Niuchwang.[36]

The Role of the Yokohama Specie Bank, 1905–1914

Reports of discussions about the establishment and functions of a Sino-
Japanese Bank indicate that currency reform (together with the construction of a customs union) was as much on the Japanese agenda as it
had been on the Russian. In the aftermath of the Russo-Japanese War,
Tokyo got its chance. Plans for a Sino-Japanese bank were shelved, and
early reform efforts were assigned, somewhat surprisingly, to the Yokohama Specie Bank.[37] As an exchange bank, YSB might not be considered fit for undertaking a task such as currency reform.

However, YSB was not solely engaged in the business of foreign exchange. As one of the many foreign banks with a presence in Northern
Manchuria, it had monetary experience from issuing so-called bearer
notes (*ichiranbarai tegata*). YSB bearer notes appear to have been issued
for the first time in 1902 in Tianjin and Shanghai; in 1903 YSB started
to issue them in Manchuria as well, particularly through its Niuzhang
branch office.[38] This experience turned out to be an asset. After the
conclusion of the Russo-Japanese War, the Japanese government entrusted YSB with the task of redeeming the large amounts of military
scrip or *gunpyō* circulating in Northeast China. Issued by the Japanese
government for use by the army divisions in Manchuria, they became
a cumbersome relic of the military conflict: although defined as convertible, these notes had a low credit status.[39]

In any case, this postwar assignment conferred on YSB the privilege
of note-issue in Manchuria and marked the start of its important (if of-

---

36. The report is reproduced in its entirety in Hanna, Conant, and Jenks, *Gold Standard in International Trade*, 276–78.
37. Kaneko, "Nichiro sengo no 'Manshū keiei' to Yokohama shōkin ginkō."
38. Compare Yokohama shōkin ginkō, ed., *Yokohama shōkin ginkōshi*, 227–28.
39. Kaneko, *Kindai Nihon ni okeru tai-Manshū tōshi no kenkyū*, 132–34.

ten contested) role in Manchuria policy. Its authoritative success in redeeming military scrip was effectuated in part by financing Japanese
cotton exports to Manchuria. According to the *Economic History of Manchuria*, of the ¥15 million circulating in July 1906, only ¥900,000 could
not be redeemed; the remaining amount of military notes actually in
circulation was doubtless much lower.[40] As in the case of the First Bank
in Korea, a Japanese bank again de facto became a colonial "central
bank," not incidentally again in the aftermath of a military campaign.[41]
From around 1906, YSB would greatly expand its network of branches
and engage in a wide range of activities with the objective of expanding
Japanese-Manchurian trade.[42]

Seemingly in accordance with a plan by Minister of Finance Sakatani
Yoshirō, this was a hands-on operation, in which financial sanitation
was to be backed by military support. The result was felt immediately.
Already in April 1906, the Mukden (Fengtian) Provincial Bank lost the
right to issue notes in the Kwantung Leased Territory and the SMRC
zones; all Japanese banking institutions present in China were ordered
to assist YSB. In August, Imperial Ordinance no. 247 officially recognized YSB bearer notes as banknotes. But just how successful was YSB,
in particular in its early attempts at monetary reform?

To be sure, Tokyo's wider macroeconomic ambitions and influence
encompassed the objective of currency unification.[43] For instance, YSB's
engagement in the financing of Japanese cotton exports to Manchuria
would result in greatly expanded trade, at the expense of American and
British exporters. But YSB also fit into a larger scheme of taking control

---

40. Bank of Chosen, *Economic History of Manchuria*, 258. Kaneko's statistics show that
the amount was originally much higher, topping ¥88,388,000 in June 1905 (*Kindai Nihon ni okeru tai-Manshū tōshi no kenkyū*, 133).

41. Several Japanese scholars discern an imperialist pattern here: Kaneko, *Kindai Nihon ni okeru tai-Manshū tōshi no kenkyū*, 133; Shibata, *Senryōchi tsūka kin'yū seisaku no tenkai*,
3–7.

42. At the outbreak of the war, new YSB branches had been established in Dairen,
Liaoyang, Mukden (Fengtian), and Tiehling; after the war, new branches were established in Changchun, Harbin, and Kaiyuan.

43. Originally, Sakatani's plan envisaged this role for the Japan Industrial Bank (Nihon kōgyō ginkō). This made sense if one realizes the long-term aspects of this financial strategy. In the end, however, preference was given to YSB in view of its presence
in Manchuria.

of the soybean economy, by taking it out of the hands of the *liangzhan* (crop dealers) and simultaneously getting rid of the chaotic and locally oriented currency systems associated with their practices.[44]

Liangzhan functioned as middlemen between the local farmers and the large exporters. As is typical in premodern economies, their crucial role as capital supplier and go-between gave them significant power, and they were accordingly vigorously resistant to change.[45] Reports prepared by SMRC document that bypassing the *liangzhan*'s monopoly would be extremely difficult if not impossible, not only because it was considered dangerous to take large amounts of cash into the Chinese hinterland, but especially because of the farmers' fundamental reluctance to deal with anybody other than the *liangzhan* and their mistrust of foreign monies.[46] As could be expected, YSB's policy of subjugating Manchuria by monetary means was not very successful. Until long after 1906, the middlemen had to be accepted as a necessary evil, as did a variety of privately issued and strongly locally bound currencies or *sitie* in the lower strata of the soybean economy. Currency unification thus remained elusive. Especially after several Chinese "provincial banks" or *guanyinhao* entered into competition with YSB in an attempt to regain their share of control over the soybean economy,[47] Manchuria's multiple monetary differentiation was only reinforced. Although Manchuria's economic ties with the international markets has deepened, its commercial centers still possessed their own currency types and credit idiosyncrasies: the silver yen in Dairen, the transfer *tael* in Yingkou, the ruble in Harbin, and so on.[48]

---

44. For more information, see Ishida Takehiko, "Chūgoku tōhoku ni okeru ryōsan no dōkō."

45. Kaneko dubs the nature of the Manchurian economy feudal and colonial at the same time: Kaneko, *Kindai Nihon ni okeru tai-Manshū tōshi no kenkyū*, 144.

46. Compare, for instance, Minami Manshū tetsudō keizai chōsakai, ed., *Manshū ni okeru ryōsan*.

47. For an overview of Chinese banking institutions present in Manchuria, see Yasutomi, *"Manshūkoku" no kin'yū*, 12–17. Yasutomi lists as the most important banks: the Provincial Bank of the Eastern Three Provinces, the Frontier Bank, the Kirin Yong Heng Provincial Bank, and the Amur Provincial Bank. These banks were allowed to issue coins and notes in small-coin denominations. Modeled upon foreign examples (unlike traditional Chinese coins, for instance, these coins did not have a hole in the center), these were somewhat confusingly referred to as "foreign monies" or *yangqian*. A list of currencies is given in Bank of Chosen, *Economic History of Manchuria*, 237ff.

48. Following Kaneko, *Kindai Nihon ni okeru tai-Manshū tōshi no kenkyū*, 147.

Nonetheless, YSB and SMRC's attempts to break the economic linkages with China proper did succeed in bringing about a sea change in
Manchuria's economic geography. The original economic backbone was
the River Liao, its harbor of Yingkou, and the Chinese-owned Peking–
Mukden Railway (PMR). This geographic dominance was resented not
only by SMRC officials but also by Japanese policy makers in Tokyo, for
it meant that the soybean trade was firmly anchored within traditional
Chinese merchant channels and local business communities. Yet the
Chinese route had one important disadvantage: the harbor of Yingkou
was icebound during winter.[49] Shippers choosing Yingkou therefore
faced the costs and risks of stockpiling goods during three months of the
year. Using this inconvenience as a political pretext as well as a commercial opportunity, the Japanese were quick to propose the Dairen strategy
or "Dairen-centrism" (*Dairen chūshin shugi*).[50] The harbor of the newly
built city of Dairen was not only ice-free but also deep enough to accommodate oceangoing freighters. Even if Yingkou might suffice for
the time being, Dairen was more suitable for future expansion. YSB,
through its extensive facilities for lending (made possible by the system
of special loan facilities or *tokubetsu kashitsuke*, for which the Bank of
Japan had been commissioned to extend a low interest loan to YSB),[51]
discounting, and so forth, was essential in accelerating the port's expansion: a brief look at YSB's portfolio reveals the obvious concentra-
tion of its capital and activities in Dairen.[52] Aggressive managerial and
financial measures, including a superior infrastructure but also more-
contested measures such as reduced rates and tariffs,[53] and even tax ex-

---

49. For an overview, see Hitch, "The Port of Tientsin and Its Problems."

50. Following Matsusaka, *The Making of Japanese Manchuria*, 130ff.

51. This is one of the many measures indicating the Japanese government's strong
engagement in expanding trade with Manchuria. Compare, in this respect, Kaneko, *Kindai Nihon ni okeru tai-Manshū tōshi no kenkyū*, 139–42, who also speaks of "government
backup" (*kokkateki bakku appu*), and characterizes measures as "dumping." For more
information on the *tokubetsu kashitsuke* system, see ibid., 155–56. On the concrete use
of these loans and the use of postal savings (*yokinbu*), see the present book's chapter on
the Nishihara loans, above, especially with regard to the Hanyeping Coal and Iron
Company.

52. For an overview, see Kaneko, *Kindai Nihon ni okeru tai-Manshū tōshi no kenkyū*, 135,
tables 3–4.

53. This produced rather complicated rate schedules. It was, for instance, not uncommon to find different rates for the same itinerary, if traveled in the opposite direc-

emption,[54] were to do the rest: "The creative exploitation of Dairen's superiority as port alone would go a long way toward enticing even those shippers closely tied to the Yingk'ou business network. The development of attractive, alternative services in the Japanese-controlled port would strengthen its drawing power. Commodity exchanges, banks, insurance agencies, international trading companies, and bonded warehouses would provide bean merchants with access to better prices, wider markets, and new sources of finance, as well as reduce the risks of business."[55] Roughly by the beginning of World War I, the groundwork for Japan's economic takeover had been laid, and the role of a Japanese bank had once more proved to be substantial.

The Silver and Gold Factions

From the very beginning, however, the role of YSB in Manchuria was also considerably contested by the Japanese community. Because of YSB's original function as an exchange bank and the demands on liquidity this posed for the bank's operations and business strategy, many commentators raised concerns about whether YSB was up to the task of engaging in long-term lending, or even willing to immobilize a substantial portion of its assets in order to finance the Japanese corporations in Manchuria. Some analysts also doubted YSB's commitment to this new task.[56] Other, even more fundamental reservations concerned the role of the bank's silver notes in monetary reform and constituted the core of the debate about the desirability of taking Manchuria onto a silver standard or a gold standard.

Namikata has correctly identified the dispute as one between two different strands in Japanese imperialism.[57] On the one hand were the

---

tion (i.e., from city B to city A instead of from city A to city B). This highlights the Japanese preoccupation with macroeconomic control. A similar concern was held by the Russians; similar to Japanese "Dairen-centrism," they developed a Vladivostok strategy. See Matsusaka, *The Making of Japanese Manchuria*, 134.

54. Kaneko, *Kindai Nihon ni okeru tai-Manshū tōshi no kenkyū*, 141.

55. Matsusaka, *The Making of Japanese Manchuria*, 131–32.

56. Kaneko, *Kindai Nihon ni okeru tai-Manshū tōshi no kenkyū*, 139.

57. Namikata, *Nihon shokuminchi kin'yū seisakushi no kenkyū*, 178. The origins and nature of this issue receive a lot of attention in almost all related works: Kaneko, *Kindai Nihon ni okeru tai-Manshū tōshi no kenkyū*, 162–64; Shibata, *Senryōchi tsūka kin'yū seisaku no tenkai*, 15ff.

silver proponents, most forcefully represented by YSB president Takahashi Korekiyo. For them, any form or instance of monetary unification should be directed solely by business interests, and more specifically in the wider framework of Sino-Japanese trade. Their position was
thus a more or less pragmatic one. Not only did silver proponents express concern about the strain monetary reform by means of gold
might place upon the BOJ's specie reserve.[58] They also concluded that
because in terms of capital, labor, business organization, and so on,
Manchuria was indeed very much linked with (silver-standard) China
proper, it therefore was in the interest of commerce to divide exchange
costs evenly between Japanese and Chinese businesses.

On the other hand were the proponents of gold, personified by
SMRC president Gotō Shinpei and by Shōda Kazue, at the time director of the Bank of Chosen. Because SMRC was highly dependent on
foreign capital, Gotō and others stressed that silver would translate into
substantial extra costs for running its operations and a panoply of side
businesses.[59] As soon as 1906, SMRC therefore allowed the use of
(gold-denominated) Bank of Japan convertible notes; in 1907 it decided
to quote its fares in gold.[60] But fundamentally, the pro-gold group articulated a quintessentially different outlook on the nature of the Japanese empire. For them, gold was a prerequisite to eliminate transaction
costs for Japanese merchants and guarantee them an exchange advantage over Chinese merchants. This position could be described as proactive and even political-ideological. One publication typically claimed
that "rather than regarding Kwantung and the SMRC railway zone as
part of Manchuria, it should be seen as part of the Japanese mainland,"
in other words as an "extension" (*enchōchi*) of Osaka and Kobe.[61] In any
case, the debate was never really resolved, and Tokyo's policy toward

---

58. This was by no means a hollow argument. In the former chapter we have already discussed BOJ's difficulties in keeping Japan on the gold standard after its adoption in 1897. Compare also Taira, "Dai ichiji taisen izen no tai-Chūgoku shakkan to tōshi shutai."

59. Kaneko, *Kindai Nihon ni okeru tai-Manshū tōshi no kenkyū*, 162–64. On SMRC's
side businesses, see Matsusaka, *The Making of Japanese Manchuria*, 135ff.

60. Shortly before, the Kwantung government had made gold the basis of its accounts. Namikata, *Nihon shokuminchi kin'yū seisakushi no kenkyū*, 175–76. In Japanese this
"quoting in gold" is called *kindate*, and in silver *gindate*.

61. Quoted in Namikata, *Nihon shokuminchi kin'yū seisakushi no kenkyū*, 178.

Manchuria was ambiguous at the least. In 1913, when it was clear that the Bank of Chosen and its gold notes would also play an important role in Manchuria, YSB was made to issue a gold note convertible into gold coin or Bank of Japan notes. This action only compounded monetary trouble.

This debate about who was to profit from (monetary) reform can also be traced in broader macroeconomic policy issues affecting the region. It is important to be aware that the Dairen strategy affected Chinese and Japanese merchants to the same degree. As Matsusaka has argued, "the fact that the Japanese controlled one port and the Chinese, the other, represented [to SMRC] an incidental circumstance."[62] Yet, at Dairen, everybody, including the Chinese, received preferential treatment, and every commercial enterprise in Yingkou, including Japanese businesses, received discriminatory treatment. The long-term desire to establish a unified trade and currency zone in the whole of Northeast Asia (embodied, for instance, in doctrines such as "Sino-Japanese economic cooperation" [nisshi keizai teikei]) had a blind spot about exactly this issue. Such a bloc would work against the interests of Japanese enterprises in regions adjacent to but outside the bloc, by its very nature. This circumstance is the embodiment of many incompatibilities in the practices demanded by profits on the one hand and by policy on the other.

Predominance of the Bank of Chosen

The dispute over silver versus gold would first be decided to the advantage of the "ideological" gold faction. Perhaps this was less ideological than thought, as gold notes had sharply grown in importance.[63] This growth was directly related to a policy of the Bank of Chosen, which was, in turn, caused by the bank's situation on the Korean peninsula. Around 1910, Korea's industrial and commercial base was still very weak; the previous discussion of Megata Tanetarō therefore highlighted the sharp divide between the peninsula's economic development and its financial system. Currency was more or less unified, but a large amount

---

62. Matsusaka, The Making of Japanese Manchuria, 144.

63. Ishikawa, "1910 nendai Manshū ni okeru chōsen ginkōken no ryūtsū to chiiki keizai." For an analysis of the restructuring of the Japanese financial presence in Manchuria in the period, see Kaneko, "Dai ichiji taisenki ni okeru shokuminchi ginkō taikei no saihensei."

of the old coinage remained in circulation, often with detrimental effects such as money tightness, slumbering credit, recurrent speculative frenzies, and consequent occasional business depressions. Directly impeding the smooth operation of the Bank of Chosen as the peninsula's national bank was the problem of import excesses relative to the Japanese mainland. This imbalance resulted in difficulties in maintaining the required ratio of specie reserve. To avoid problems of liquidity and the excessive raising of interest, the bank had to look for ways to make up for what it was losing on its balance sheets.

Venturing into the business of an overseas bank and, specifically, into Manchurian territory turned out to be the solution.[64] Here, the situation was very different from that in Korea: "the demand was always present, and the Bank in most cases had simply to follow it."[65] Especially after the Yalu bridge had been completed and after the tariff for overland trade had been reduced by one-third (a policy that fitted into the framework of shifting Manchuria's economic mainstay to the advantage of SMRC), Chōsen-Manchuria trade was boosted. The strategy was simple: the Bank of Chosen bought Manchurian export bills and could thus create a balance abroad to meet its ever increasing obligations as national bank on the Korean peninsula. At the same time, it greatly expanded its network of branches in Manchuria. Since the outset of its establishment, it had maintained a branch in Andong (immediately over the Yalu River); to this were added branches in Mukden, Dairen, and Changchun (all founded 1913), and, later, Sipingjieh (1914), Kaiyuan (1915), Harbin (1916), Fujiadian (1916), Yingkou (1916), and Longjing (1917). Business growth after 1913, but especially during World War I caused a sea change in the relative positions of gold and silver. Whereas, in terms of transactions, both silver and gold increased, the latter increased roughly fifteen-fold as against five-fold for silver.[66] It is the clear expression of the fact that, as Kaneko put it, "the Bank of Chosen was in the forefront of Japanese policy towards the conti-

---

64. Kaneko, *Kindai Nihon ni okeru tai-Manshū tōshi no kenkyū*, 252–60.

65. Bank of Chosen, *Economic History of Manchuria*, 285.

66. Ibid., 297. These numbers need further modification. YSB notes had a greater velocity, and were thus a more sound indicator of (and a superior corrective mechanism for) volatilities in trade.

nent."[67] Remarkably, from 1918 onward, the bank's business in Manchuria (and mainland Japan) equaled and even overtook its business in Korea proper, in terms of both deposits and loans.[68]

Kaneko's remark also indicates that it would be unfair to credit mere economic factors for the Bank of Chosen's expanding influence, which was also helped by a shift in the political constituency in Tokyo. Earlier Japanese policy toward China had been one of concession imperialism, which strove for the recognition of Japan's special rights and an (exclusive) sphere of influence, but always in strong consideration of its Western competitors and, more broadly, the existing geopolitical order. This pattern was abruptly broken by the Terauchi cabinet. Terauchi and the "Korea clique" represented the birth of a strand in Japanese politics that (1) expressed its discontent with the existing balance of power in Asia; (2) therefore stressed a more proactive expansionism with totalitarian traits;[69] and (3) perceived it to be in Japan's interest to establish an economically and politically self-sufficient regional bloc that was principally anti-Western.

As we have seen, these ideas formed the core of the Nishihara loans debacle.[70] Less visibly, but equally forcefully, they also heralded important changes in policy toward Manchuria. In 1917, the privilege of issuing notes and the right to manage the treasury were taken away from YSB and transferred to the Bank of Chosen. YSB's branches at Port Arthur (Lushun), Liaoyang, Tiehling, and Andong were made over at the same time; the bank's lending activity (and the special credit facility called *tokubetsu kashitsuke*) was assigned to the Oriental Development Company (Tōyō takushoku gaisha). Among YSB employees, these deci-

---

67. Kaneko, *Kindai Nihon ni okeru tai-Manshū tōshi no kenkyū*, 254.

68. Ibid., esp. 255. Kaneko's statistics are based on monthly reports prepared by the Bank of Chosen (the so-called *Chōsen ginkō geppō*). Whereas, in 1918, deposits in Korea and Manchuria both stood around ¥31 million, lending in Manchuria approached ¥70 million (as against ¥65 million in Korea). In the next year, they would climb to ¥114 million. Obviously, the role played by the Nishihara loans must be considered substantial.

69. Think, for instance, of the rise of a vocabulary closely associated with the mobilization of all aspects of society (e.g., *sōryokusen/kokkasōdōin*) and the subjugation of all interests to the national interest. Typically, this vocabulary was very strongly present in varieties of Pan-Asianism.

70. See also Morikawa, "Terauchi naikaku-ki ni okeru Nishihara Kamezō no tai-chūgoku 'enjo' seisaku kōsō."

sions to strip YSB of its role as Japan's foremost colonial bank in China were deeply resented. YSB-BOC competition was to resonate for years to come.

The Chinese Reaction

Amidst YSB-BOC infighting for monetary dominance in Manchuria, the Chinese side could also be expected at least to attempt to regain control of the region's economy and currency system. The Chinese government would not disappoint administrators and the business community. Its efforts were aided by Manchuria's economic geography. We have already discussed how Japanese efforts to cut short the power relationships between Manchurian farmers and *liangzhan* proved extremely arduous and eventually futile: the farmers' ties with the local business infrastructure and its customs, and their distrust of everything foreign, made the use of local currencies, at least for Japanese merchants, a necessary evil. The Chinese actively stepped up their efforts by establishing a series of provincial banks or *guanyinhao*, whose mandate was expressly political. Kaneko, drawing his conclusions from reports prepared at the time, stresses that one objective in the strategy of granting these banks the right to issue notes was to "counter foreign banks and assign the right to issue notes to [an institution of one's own] country."[71]

Yet installing a stable currency in a territory characterized by monetary differentiation and political instability was not an easy task. One enormous problem was the variety and incalculable amounts of monies already issued by local banks, exchange shops, pawnshops, and other businesses. These local monies continued to exist alongside the newly issued notes of the provincial banks and reinforced monetary mechanisms that strike financial historians and students of macroeconomics as Byzantine. One example is the daily meetings of Chinese chambers of commerce whose sole aim was determining the relative value of currencies in their immediate area of circulation.[72] Yet in the immediate aftermath of the provincial banknotes' creation, they did enjoy a rela-

---

71. Kaneko, *Kindai Nihon ni okeru tai-Manshū tōshi no kenkyū*, 168. It appears that this strategy was originally directed toward the Russo-Chinese Bank, established in 1897 and issuing notes in China proper.

72. Compare the quote from the report by Arthur Henckendorff referred to earlier. The reader will understand that these practices continued long after 1904.

tively favorable credit status and even became an indispensable ingredient in Manchuria's still diffuse economy.[73]

The banknotes' situation deteriorated around the start of World War I, mainly due to two developments. One of these was the imposition of restrictions on the international movement of metals such as silver and gold by the warring European nations. Because provincial banknotes had been issued against reserves of valuable metal (mainly silver and copper), the difficulty of importing those metals from the West gave rise to suspicion that notes were issued without adequate reserves. Possibly more important, and typically hidden in many Japanese reports of the time, is the role of more-or-less concerted efforts to cause these currencies to depreciate.[74] Japanese merchants in particular, were quick to point out that provincial banknotes might be inconvertible.[75] Acting on the advice of Japanese chambers of commerce, they resorted to the practice of presenting their notes at Chinese banks and demanding payment in silver or copper, thereby causing severe instabilities in these notes' exchange rate, a phenomenon that peaked around 1917.[76]

Around this time the Mukden provincial government made efforts to alleviate pressure from Manchuria's strained monetary system and bring the Three Provinces under its monetary control. It would do so by adjusting the system in use (mainly through halting the depreciation of the many provincial currencies in the region) and by creating a stable

---

73. Typically, notes of the Mukden Provincial Bank continued to be used by several Chinese merchants also in Dairen, even though Japanese notes (first YSB, and after 1917 BOC-issued) had been proclaimed standard currency there. Even the *Economic History of Manchuria* stresses the early soundness of some of the provincial notes and their role in Manchuria's economic fabric. Bank of Chosen, *Economic History of Manchuria*, 250.

74. See, for instance, ibid., 247ff. Instead, the authors stress that "the Manchurian provinces were among those that issued [notes] most recklessly" (247).

75. Suleski, "The Rise and Fall of the Fengtien Dollar," esp. 647–49. I have not found direct evidence of such Japanese efforts, but they are certainly not unthinkable. The reader may remember the role of Japanese speculators in carrying out reform efforts in Korea (see above). For more information, see the article by Suleski. Kaneko does not find evidence either, but speaks of "friction between Japanese and Chinese merchants." Kaneko, *Kindai Nihon ni okeru tai-Manshū tōshi no kenkyū*, 261. It is undeniable, however, that BOC used the situation in order to push for a loan aimed at aiding currency reform (obviously with the intention of establishing a gold exchange standard).

76. Suleski, "The Rise and Fall of the Fengtien Dollar," 649. See also Kaneko, *Kindai Nihon ni okeru tai-Manshū tōshi no kenkyū*, 260–66.

note in 1917 to be issued as an alternative to the existing system. One novelty was that the Mukden provincial government chose to abandon the small-coin standard (in use since 1905) and adopt the silver *yuan*-standard (alternatively called *dayang*-standard) instead.[77] This action not only brought Northeast Chinese currency in line with the system of the central government; it also, by choosing silver, opted for an internationally recognized metal whose value (at least in 1916–17) was on the rise.[78] But the greater innovation was the choice to have the Provincial Bank of the Eastern Three Provinces issue exchange notes (*hui-tui-p'iao*).[79] This strategy was aimed at undercutting efforts to discredit the currency by invoking chronic and large-scale demands for conversion. Exchange notes were issued against silver reserves held by the provincial government, but were, contrary to the older provincial banknotes, not convertible into silver coin.[80] In a way, these notes reversed the process of conversion, as they were issued against deposits of silver or coin at the official bank. They were available as cash only when making a remittance, "strange as it may seem, from Tientsin or Peking [and later Mukden] to Shanghai."[81] Not only was the problem of massive conversion effectively solved; by establishing direct contact with the Shanghai *kuei-yuan tael*, a purely nominal measure of value used only in international trade, these exchange notes also made one-sided local efforts at disturbing its value highly improbable. Because they were able to

---

77. This *yuan*-standard had been adopted by the government of Yuan Shikai in 1914. For more information, see T'ang, "The Problem of Chinese Currency." A contemporary overview is "Manshū tsūka no shurui" 満洲通貨の種類 (Types of Manchurian currency), nos. 1–3, KJN 1917.12.11–1917.12.15, KUDA-S ID 00814288.

78. Hence, its conversion rate was set unusually high. The small-coins value was put at 8.33 cents per *chiao* 角 instead of the usual 10 cents per *chiao*. The new *yuan* was put at a ratio of 1 *yuan* = 12 *chiao*. Suleski, "The Rise and Fall of the Fengtien Dollar," 651.

79. In 1919, the privilege to issue exchange notes was also extended to the Bank of China and the Bank of Communications.

80. According to Suleski, this "new exchange note, which was soon to become the most widely circulated banknote in Manchuria, can be termed the Fengtien dollar" ("The Rise and Fall of the Fengtien Dollar," 652). However, this terminology is unfortunate at best. It does not distinguish this note from the so-called *Fengtianpiao*, already circulating long before 1917 and also dubbed "Fengtian dollar."

81. Bank of Chosen, *Economic History of Manchuria*, 254.

maintain a 1:1 ratio with the Japanese gold yen note, they were a powerful competitor to it in Manchuria for several years to come.[82]

Problems of the Gold Faction

The preceding chapter showed that the Nishihara loans were Japan's extraordinarily assertive reaction to China's thrust toward currency autonomy. BOC's activity in Manchuria further increased. Its gold notes even played an important role in the Siberian intervention, as currency domination extending deep into the continent became a clearly articulated strategy.[83] It is also around this time that BOC's leverage came under considerable pressure. In a way, it was the victim of its own expansion. Few BOC directors would have predicted in 1915 that, within a few years, the BOC's balance sheet would further deteriorate, ironically due to its business in Manchuria. Not only were its Korean branches running a balance-of-payments deficit with Japan proper; its Japanese branches were also running a deficit with Manchuria. Again the bank faced problems with its currency reserve: amid the complexities of the exchange circle sketched above, it had overstretched its lending portfolio, and was furthermore plagued by jumps in the price of silver.[84] As Japanese exporters to China thrived, the country's most important bank in Manchuria suffered. In a way, the relative depreciation of its gold notes because of the rising silver price fed back into its status as lender, fueling the issuing of further or different loans and ultimately leading to inflation. It is not difficult to regard this situation as the seed of BOC's predicament with bad loans (*furyō saiken*) in the 1920s.[85] When it faced the bust after the early postwar boom, a number of these loans—even some that had originally been sound—immobilized the bank's capital or had to be written off.

Several years before this, however, Japan's policy in Manchuria remained to push gold as the standard medium of exchange. This position is especially clear in the debate on whether to quote prices on the Dai-

---

82. Suleski, "The Rise and Fall of the Fengtien Dollar," 653ff.
83. In this context, see Nihon ginkō chōsakyoku, *Nihon kin'yūshi shiryō*, vol. 22, 96.
84. Kaneko, *Kindai Nihon ni okeru tai-Manshū tōshi no kenkyū*, 289.
85. For analysis, see Itō, *Nihon no taigai kin'yū to kin'yū seisaku*, 82–88.

ren Commodity Exchange in gold or in silver.[86] The arguments are the quintessential illustration of the ideological bias of the gold faction: First of all, as BOC gold notes had de facto overtaken YSB silver notes, it was simply a matter of consistency to adapt to that reality. Second, and more important, adopting gold would give Japanese merchants in Manchuria an exchange advantage over their Chinese counterparts. And third, this action also fitted into the Terauchi cabinet's wider policy of favoring gold. On the ground, however, the decision to quote the Exchange's prices in gold led to strong protests in Manchuria's main commercial centers;[87] some local authorities went so far as to call for the boycott of several Japanese products and even the use of BOC gold notes. The gold faction had furthermore overlooked an important facet of the still existent silver notes. Although fewer in number, YSB notes had a higher velocity and probably also had a higher corrective potential for creating price stability.[88] This capacity did not deter gold's proponents. In 1921, the Japanese government confirmed its support for gold. Only in 1923, after the troubled postwar situation had made it painfully clear that Japan could not unilaterally pursue a gold standard in Manchuria, was it decided that prices were to be quoted in both of the metals.[89]

Throughout the 1920s, a number of fundamental problems and even contradictions in the thinking of the "gold proponents" surfaced regarding the strategy of the "Korean-Manchurian nexus" (*Sen-Man ittaika*). First, problems with penetrating the hinterland of the Manchurian economy persisted; a relatively recent Japanese claim that BOC gold notes were, already in the 1910s, sound enough to have been capable of controlling the issuing of indigenous currencies and strong enough to reinforce their acceptance throughout the Three Provinces, is a gross overestimation.[90] One decade later, it became obvious how arduous the

---

86. See Namikata, *Nihon shokuminchi kin'yū seisakushi no kenkyū*, 459ff.; Shibata, *Senryōchi tsūka kin'yū seisaku no tenkai*, 26–29.

87. This is well documented in several newspapers at the time. See, in this respect, many entries in KUDA-S (retrievable with search terms 大連 and 金建): e.g., "Gindate ijigawa no un / Dairen torihikijo to kindate mondai" 銀建維持側の運／大連取引所と金建問題 (Luck for those upholding quoting in silver / the Dairen Commodity Exchange and the problem of quoting in gold), OJJS 1921.4.21, KUDA-S ID00074819.

88. Kaneko, *Kindai Nihon ni okeru tai-Manshū tōshi no kenkyū*, 296–97.

89. Namikata, *Nihon shokuminchi kin'yū seisakushi no kenkyū*, 464.

90. For such a claim, see Kojima, *Nihon no kinhon'isei jidai*, esp. 213–15.

struggle for monetary control had been and continued to be. The "solution" to the case of the Dairen Commodity Exchange, to give just one example, cannot have been to the liking of BOC directors. Eventually, the bank would as good as admit that its ambitions had been overweening. Coinciding with the decision to quote prices in silver and gold, this action also allowed the opening of silver accounts (*ginkōza*).[91]

Second, and equally illustrative of cracks in the *Sen-Man ittaika* strategy, was the phenomenon of arbitrage in the Chinese money market, more especially between Shanghai and Dairen. For a host of reasons, gold was traditionally the relatively high-priced metal in Shanghai, and silver the relatively low-priced metal;[92] in Dairen, the reverse was the case. Japanese or Chinese businessmen in Shanghai, when remitting gold to Japan, could thus make a profit by remitting their funds through Dairen. Directors of BOC, the bank in charge of remittances from Dairen to Japan, soon realized the devastating consequences of this mechanism—ironically enough, the indirect effect of their own efforts to create a Manchurian gold zone separate from China proper. Once more, the required specie reserve was under strain. Only after deliberations with the Japanese Ministry of Finance could a strict quota on remitting money to Japan be imposed.[93]

---

91. Compare Shinozaki Yoshirō, "Gin shihon ginkō setsuritsuron to Manshū chūō ginkō mondai" 銀資本銀行設立論と満洲中央銀行問題 (The idea of establishing a bank with silver capital and the problem of the establishment of the Central Bank of Manchuria), nos. 1–2, MNNS 1924.2.7–1924.2.8, KUDA-ID 00784861. Shinozaki was the then secretary-general of the Dairen Chamber of Commerce.

92. The period from 1917 to 1920 was an exception to this rule because of the extraordinarily high silver prices. The main reason for gold normally being priced higher in Shanghai than in Dairen was presumably the persistent import surplus vis-à-vis the Japanese mainland. This is also the reason given in Kaneko, *Kindai Nihon ni okeru tai-Manshū tōshi no kenkyū*, 462. See also Matsuno, "Dai niji sekai taisen mae Chūgoku tōhokubu ni okeru Nihon no kin'yū shokatsudō ni tsuite" and "Teikoku shugi kakuritsuki Nihon no tai-Manshū tsūka kin'yū seisaku." On the intricacies of the Shanghai-Dairen-Japan exchange triangle, see Kojima, *Nihon no kinhon'isei jidai*, 218–31.

93. See, for instance, "Manshū kara Nihon e no sōkin seigen mondai funkyō sen" 満洲から日本への送金制限問題紛糾せん (Do not complicate the problem of limited specie remittances from Manchuria to Japan), OAS 1924.7.17, KUDA-ID 00822714; "Sengin no sōkin seigen / kawase sayatori gyōsha no katsuyaku o soshi sezu" 鮮銀の送金制限／為替鞘取業者の活躍を阻止せず (Limited specie remittances from the Bank of Chosen / it does not hamper the activities of the exchange brokerage firms), MNNS 1928.9.20–1928.9.21, KUDA-ID 00474289. The problem is also treated in Yasu-

But BOC's real predicament lay with the impact of the post-World War I economic downturn in Manchuria. The postwar bust set in on the Japanese mainland around 1920 and almost immediately spilled over into the Manchurian economy. As Japan had profited more than other countries from the war and the steep economic growth that followed it, the subsequent decline was also much sharper. Japan's situation was certainly not helped by its strong dependence on demand from the United States, the other real victor of World War I.[94] Shortly before panic selling overtook Japan's financial market, the Bank of Japan, perceiving a speculative bubble, had forcefully raised its discount rate to 8.03 percent, a rate that would not be imposed again until the inflationary 1970s. Soon, Manchuria was to experience an even stronger backlash.[95] It suffered a long and painful financial contraction and restructuring.[96] After the boom years (peaking in 1922), the number of banks and their branches was drastically reduced; the amount of paid-up capital also fell dramatically. As lender of last resort, BOC could not escape from this downward credit spiral. Indeed, BOC was among those hardest hit by the anti-expansionary, liquidationist climate of Japan's economy.[97]

The most striking economic fact of the period is however the predicament of so-called frozen loans (*koteikashi*) made by Japanese colonial institutions in Manchuria. YSB was the only and remarkable exception. According to several estimates, frozen loans in the December 1924 portfolio of Manchurian branches of BOC amounted to 67.5 percent of outstanding loans, or ¥84.62 million; the amount lost to nonpayment was projected to be around 38.9 percent or ¥46.27 million of

---

tomi, *"Manshūkoku" no kin'yū*, 35ff.; and Shibata, *Senryōchi tsūka kin'yū seisaku no tenkai*, 29–33.

94. See Metzler, *Lever of Empire*, 115ff.

95. Ibid., 135: "At the peripheries of Japan's empire, the effects of Japan's boom-bust cycles were often magnified. 'The speculative fever did not stop at the home islands [. . .],' Inoue later explained, 'Wherever Japanese people go, they set up exchanges and speculate.' They had done so in every Manchurian town, 'and speculation there reached an even higher fever pitch than in Japan.' By 1919, land prices in Dairen were six times the level of 1917."

96. A similar restructuring, i.e. a process of bank consolidation through merging, occurred in Japan proper at a later date (1927) and was accelerated judicially. In this respect, see Okazaki and Sawada, "Effects of a Bank Consolidation Promotion Policy."

97. For a thorough explanation of the liquidationist character of the "negative" policy, see Metzler, *Lever of Empire*, 67ff.

the same portfolio. In a headlong commitment to its developmentalist strategy, BOC had recklessly overextended itself.[98] As it had done before in similar situations, Tokyo bailed the bank out by resorting to BOJ and its "second budget" of the Postal Savings (*yokinbu*). The price of the rescue operation was restructuring.[99] In 1925, three of the bank's branches were closed, but even this was not enough to bring fundamental relief. The March 1927 portfolio records a further increase in the frozen loan amount, to ¥81.83 million, although we must add that this amount also reflects the bank's role as a central bank.[100]

In many ways, the 1920s thus dealt a decisive blow to the once strong aspiration to integrate the Manchurian and Korean economies by means of gold notes. What was left was not a "leveled" economy,

---

98. Shibata, *Senryōchi tsūka kin'yū seisaku no tenkai*, 33–37. Takeda Haruhito also perceives problems in the highly speculative nature of Japanese investments in Manchuria at the time. Compare Takeda, "Furukawa shōji to 'Dairen jiken.'" In this respect, see also "Mamekasu jiken no keika / jiken hottan to kaiketsu / shōrai ni kakawaru shomondai" 豆粕事件の経過／事件発端と解決／将来に係る諸問題 (Evolution of the beancake incident / the outburst of the scandal and its solution / problems for the future), nos. 1–8, MNNS 1920.5.8–1920.5.16, KUDA ID 00496606.

99. See, for instance, "10-nen keikaku no Sengin seiri gutaian / seifu Nichigin no shikin yūzū wa jōken tsuki" 十年計画の鮮銀整理具体案／政府日銀の資金融通は条件付 (Concrete proposal for the adjustment of the Bank of Chosen in a 10-year plan / conditions imposed with regard to capital injection from the government and the Bank of Japan), CSS 1924.2.16, KUDA-ID 00784864; "Gyōzai seiri no futettei to Sengin genshi mondai / dōkō no kinō shittsui wa Mansen sangyō kaihatsujō ni ichidai shōgai / kekkyoku hakkenken wa Nichigin ni tōitsu" 行財整理の不徹底と鮮銀減資問題／同行の機能失墜は満鮮産業開発上に一大障害／結局発券権は日銀に統一 (The incompleteness of the adjustment of financial administration and the problem of the Bank of Chosen's capital losses / decreased functioning of this bank is a big blow to the industrial development of Chosen and Manchuria / ultimately right to issue notes is unified under Bank of Japan), KMS 1925.3.12, KUDA ID00785091; "Sengin ga gutai seirian o teiji / kekkyoku wa Nichigin no enjo ga hitsuyō" 鮮銀が具体的整理案を提示／結局は日銀の援助が必要 (Bank of Chosen submits concrete plan for [its] reorganization / ultimately, support of Bank of Japan is necessary), OMS 1925.5.10, KUDA-ID00785139; "Taisen ryōgin seiri yōkō / yokinbu un'yō iinkai / kakuiin ni haifu saretaru" 台鮮両銀整理要綱／預金部運用委員会／各委員に配布されたる (Outline of the plans for the reorganization of the Bank of Taiwan and the Bank of Chosen / plans are distributed to all members of the management council of postal savings), OJJS 1925.8.6, KUDA-ID00785235.

100. Numbers taken from Kaneko, *Kindai Nihon ni okeru tai-Manshū tōshi no kenkyū*, 458.

dominated by Japanese banks and characterized by a containable degree of monetary differentiation. Instead, a gold and silver dual-economy system (*nijū keizai*) was consolidated. In this system, BOC's role was more-or-less confined to managing the economy's troubled financial sector. In offering short-term credit, it catered to only one segment of the "soybean economy," and BOC furthermore never managed to expand its relations with indigenous Chinese banks.[101] The Japanese business community could not remain indifferent to this shift, and even expressed open disapproval of the Terauchi-BOC policy line.[102] During this period it made recurrent demands to Manchurian political and financial authorities to establish a Manchurian central bank and real estate bank, which were to replace respectively BOC and the Oriental Development Company—to no avail.

The Silver Clique Rebounds

The other role in the dual economy was played by BOC's longstanding antagonist: YSB. Kaneko follows Shinozaki in his assessment that YSB's "management had been relatively healthy, hence its favorable business record."[103] Although the bank's former prerogatives had been forcefully taken away in 1917, it made a remarkable comeback in the 1920s. Unlike BOC, it had not engaged in an aggressive developmentalist strategy. Instead, it explored and cleverly exploited the Chinese silver deposits while at the same time successfully fine-tuning its core business—foreign exchange—within the larger Chinese economy.

The bank's success in increasing its silver holdings had been a direct effect of North China's volatile situation. Chinese efforts to regain control by means of so-called exchange notes had posed a competitive threat to Japanese gold notes around 1920. After 1924, however, the stability of the exchange notes was once more lost.[104] Large-scale fight-

---

101. Ibid., 455.

102. Namikata is very detailed in this respect: Namikata, *Nihon shokuminchi kin'yū sei-sakushi no kenkyū*, 459ff.

103. Kaneko Fumio, *Kindai Nihon ni okeru tai-Manshū tōshi no kenkyū*, 464; for Shino-zaki's original assessment, see Shinozaki, *Manshū kin'yū oyobi zaikai no genjō*, vol. 2, 1.

104. Compare Suleski, "The Rise and Fall of the Fengtien Dollar," 659: "In contrast to the four years it had taken the Official Bank to slowly double the annual issue of notes, in the single year of 1925 the amount of Fengtien dollar notes issued by the Of-

ing broke out in the region, and Zhang Zuolin, who had, in a way, turned into a "satrap" of Japanese imperialist interests in the region, became ever more entangled in political affairs in China proper.[105] When he interfered in the banknote-issuing business of the Provincial Bank of the Eastern Three Provinces (a decision that led to the predicament of inconvertible notes for years to follow), his actions caused a large-scale defection of Chinese account holders to YSB. Foreigners in China also preferred YSB as their bank, probably due to its internationally established reputation as an exchange bank.[106]

YSB also carefully monitored its lending and effectively avoided immobilizing its assets in loans. Its notes had a strikingly high volatility in comparison with BOC gold notes, but it also had a policy of discouraging lending to its customers. We know that it was the only Japanese bank in Manchuria at the time whose balance sheets recorded more deposits than loans.[107] It also expanded its foreign exchange business with Shanghai, for a practical reason. As it could not convert its silver notes to silver yen, it managed its silver bullion holdings by selling drafts drawn on Shanghai (so-called *shenhui* or, inverted, *huishen*),[108] and keeping what it received in silver as reserve for the paper money it issued in Manchuria. This action was relatively easy because of Japan's favorable balance of trade with China proper.[109]

At the same time, YSB carefully monitored the price stability of these drafts. Because the yen-*tael* exchange rate was around 100 yen = 72.2 *tael*, YSB intervened as soon as it perceived that this rate was approaching the "silver export-import point" (*gin gensōten*, i.e., the point where it be-

---

ficial Bank jumped by over 100 per cent to 134 million *yuan* by the end of the year. Almost automatically the value of the notes began falling. On 16 October 1925 one Japanese gold yen note cost 1.59 *yuan* and by 19 October it cost 1.76 *yuan*. The decline in value continued during late November and early December. One Japanese gold yen note went from 1.87 *yuan* on 21 November 1925, to 1.99 *yuan* on 29 November, to 2.1 *yuan* by 12 December 1925."

105. In this respect, see Suleski, "The Rise and Fall of the Fengtien Dollar," 658ff.; for a more comprehensive account, see McCormack, *Chang Tso-lin in Northeast China.*

106. Kaneko, *Kindai Nihon ni okeru tai-Manshū tōshi no kenkyū*, 465.

107. Ibid., 454.

108. Japanese newspapers of the time consistently refer to these drafts as *huishen* (*shen* being an alternative name for Shanghai). A reference to the term *shenhui* can be found in Sheehan, *Trust in Troubled Times*, 154.

109. Kaneko, *Kindai Nihon ni okeru tai-Manshū tōshi no kenkyū*, 466–67.

comes profitable to melt down silver coins and ship silver bullion in order to make an exchange profit). When the rate went down—i.e., when the Shanghai *tael* became more expensive relative to the yen—it would sell drafts, collect silver notes, and withdraw them from circulation, and thus return the price of drafts to its stable value. When the rate went up, it would do the reverse. YSB silver notes thus became an important stabilizing monetary factor for the soybean economy in South Manchuria, especially at a time when the region's economy was increasingly plagued by inconvertible indigenous monies (in particular the *Fengtianpiao*)[110] and

---

110. Indeed, the complex nature of Chinese indigenous currency cannot possibly be overestimated. Not only was there an enormous variety in coins and their issuing banks, North and South Manchuria were also characterized by a different credit structure, i.e., in terms of differentiation between rural and urban areas. Kaneko, drawing on reports by the SMRC research bureau, provides a detailed analysis: Kaneko, *Kindai Nihon ni okeru tai-Manshū tōshi no kenkyū*, 498–519. Compare also "Keizai no Manmō / sono genjō to kōseisaku" 経済の満蒙/其の現状と更生策 (Manchuria and Mongolia in an economic perspective / their present state and policies for their revival), nos. 1–77, CSS 1928.1.31–1938.4.25, KUDA-ID 00474240, esp. 66; "Manshū heisei kaikaku to yoron no kanki / Dairen shōkōgi no teigi / Nihon shōkō kaigisho sōkai ni" 満洲幣制改革と輿論の喚起 / 大連商工議から提議 / 日本商工会議所総会に (Currency reform and Manchuria and the arousal of public opinion/a proposal from the Dairen Chamber of Commerce/to the general council of Japan's chambers of commerce), MNNS 1928.10.14, KUDA-ID 00478396; "Manshū ni okeru kin'yū seido to tsūka (1) / kin'yū to tsūka Manshū no heisei tōitsu mondai (5)" 満洲に於る金融制度と通貨(一) / 金融と通貨：満洲の幣制統一問題(五) (The financial system and currency of Manchuria (1) / finance and currency: the problem of the unification of Manchurian currency), MNNS 1928.8.24–1928.8.30, KUDA-ID 00771014; "Tōsanshō no heisei / mazu engin junbi de tōitsu o" 東三省の幣制 / 先ず円銀準備で統一を (The currency of the three eastern provinces: first unification on the basis of a silver yen reserve), MNNS 1928.8.31, KUDA-ID 00771015; "Manshū zaikai no byōkon / fukan shihei no seiri / keizai mondai kaisetsu / Manshū heisei kaikaku mondai" 満洲財界の病根 / 不換紙幣の整理 / 経済問題解説 / 満洲幣制改革問題 (The root of the problem of Manchuria's financial world / adjustment of inconvertible paper money / an explanation of economic problems / the problem of Manchuria's currency reform), TAS 1928.11.22, KUDA-ID 00478409. On the Mukden Fengtian dollar in particular, see "Hōhyō sanraku no eikyō / Hōten sōryōjikan hōkoku" 奉票惨落の影響 / 奉天総領事館報告 (The impact of the slump of the Fengtian dollar/a report by the Mukden consulate), MNNS 1926.4.8, KUDA-ID 00817443.

corollary inflation; eventually the YSB silver notes would become a medium for collecting taxes in Dairen.[111]

The Early 1930s: A New Course

A few years later, when Japan became aware of its own deteriorating economic situation in Manchuria, it chose to end China's turbulent political (and monetary) situation by heavy-handed unilateral action.[112] Japan had rid itself of Zhang Zuolin by blowing up his train in 1928. When his son, Zhang Xueliang, turned out not to be sufficiently accommodating to the demands of Japanese negotiators, the military's stance hardened.[113] In 1931, using an alleged Chinese provocation as pretext, the military began an occupation of cities and towns along the line of the South Manchurian railway, which soon extended to all of Manchuria. Shortly thereafter, they created the semisovereign state of Manchukuo, with the aim of turning it into an industrial powerhouse for the militarists.

This is probably the event that sealed the fate of the last openly internationalist element in Japanese politics and unleashed the brutal tactics of domestic and foreign oppression that would come to an end only thirteen bloody years later. In 1933, after strong criticism from the Lytton commission, among others,[114] Tokyo confirmed its isolation by withdrawing from the League of Nations. The unilateral character of these events caused many to see them as a dramatic turning point in Japan's political development. A statesman as eminent as Takahashi

---

111. Kaneko, *Kindai Nihon ni okeru tai-Manshū tōshi no kenkyū*, 467ff. For a very good and more extensive treatment, see Li and Shimomura, *Dairen o chūshin to suru Shanhai-Nihon kan kawase sankakkei*.

112. This has been widely documented in Japanese and Western sources. For a contemporary analysis, again see Matsusaka, *The Making of Japanese Manchuria*, 349–87.

113. Between 1929 and 1931, a Sino-Japanese "railway war" scuttled any hope of bilateral cooperation between the two countries, and destroyed the imperialist middle ground in Japanese politics. Akira Iriye explains the complex dynamics of Chinese nationalism, the Tanaka cabinet's "positive policy," and the power struggle within the Three Provinces, in "Chang Hsüeh-Liang and the Japanese."

114. Earl of Lytton, "The Problem of Manchuria"; Dennett, "The Lytton Report"; Memorandum, "Memorandum on the Report of the Lytton Commission"; Kuhn, "The Lytton Report on the Manchurian Crisis"; for a historiographical assessment of the event, see Nish, *Japan's Struggle with Internationalism*.

Korekiyo regarded the whole affair with abhorrence. In the words of
Arai Seiichirō, one of his aides, "Takahashi hated Manchuria. [. . .] The
militarists wanted to take over Manchuria and China for Japan, but Takahashi absolutely opposed this."[115]

Economically too, Japan went through difficult times. After its return to the gold standard on January 11, 1930, and after the contractionary policies of BOJ governor Inoue Junnosuke had raised the yen's
value relative to other currencies, gold and specie flowed out of Japan.
Shortly before that, in October 1929, Wall Street's Black Thursday had
made it clear how close the ties of the international economy really
were—ties that Tokyo, for better or for worse, would increasingly seek
to sever. In December 1931, Takahashi effectively removed Japan from
the gold standard and, by doing so, probably isolated Japan's economic
performance from the effects of the Great Depression.[116]

How did these events affect monetary policy in Manchuria?[117] Asserting that it meant the outright subordination of economic objectives
to military priorities tends to obscure much of the discourse at the time.
The totalitarian nature of Japanese militarism did not permit a clear-cut
distinction between economics and politics, or, for that matter, finance
and strategy. The conflation of economic and military means and objectives was remarkably strong, if inherently problematic; the same conflation makes understanding the period difficult from a twenty-first-
century perspective.[118]

---

115. Quoted in Smethurst, *From Foot Soldier to Finance Minister*, 250.

116. On how the gold standard played a role in deepening the effects of the Great
Depression, see Eichengreen, *Golden Fetters*. The theme is further explored from a macroeconomic viewpoint in: Bernanke, *Essays on the Great Depression*. Takahashi's policies are
explained in Smethurst, *From Foot Soldier to Finance Minister*, 238–67. For a very recent (and
partially corrective) reassessment of Takahashi's policies, see Utsunomiya, "Economic
Fluctuations in Japan During the Interwar Period."

117. "Nisshi shōtotsu jihen de Manshū heisei kongo dō naru? / sekai heiseishi no
epokku" 日支衝突事変で満洲幣制今後どうなる？／世界幣制史のエポック
(What will happen to Manchurian currency after the Sino-Japanese conflict? / an epoch
in the history of the currencies of the world), no. 1, MNP 1931.10.11–1931.10.14
KUDA-ID 00458246.

118. A very good cultural history of Manchuria is L. Young, *Japan's Total Empire*. In
order to grasp the difficult totalitarian nature of Japanese imperialism at the time, she
hints at the "paradox of total empire."

Together with establishing Japanese military and political dominance, the occupying forces set out to control the region by economic and monetary means. They immediately confiscated all banks that functioned as the monetary pillars of the Mukden *gunbatsu*,[119] put them under the supervision of employees of SMRC, YSB, or BOC, and seized both their assets and ledgers. These records were studied to determine how the banks could be put to use for Manchuria's economic unification and, by extension, for the further integration with the economy of the Japanese mainland.[120] But even in the aftermath of an event as irreversible as Japan's military intervention, old habits died hard. As a matter of fact, the controversy between YSB and BOC returned with renewed vigor. Already in the very early days of the construction of Manchukuo, documents circulated arguing for BOC leadership in the new country's monetary organization. In a typical example, "About the Currency System of the New State of Manchuria and Mongolia" (*Man-Mō shinkokka no heisei ni tsuite*; undated) urges the "immediate adoption of the gold standard," especially in view of the envisioned "strengthened economic ties between Manchukuo and Japan."[121] If the establishment of an autonomous monetary system proved to be elusive ("as history had proved so many times," in the report's words), it would always be possible to circulate BOC gold notes.

This time, however, the proponents of gold found it harder to present their case as a plausible strategy. For one, the "golden fetters" of the gold standard seemed to have been severely damaged. Great Britain's suspension of gold shipments in 1931 had shaken the faith of many Japanese policy makers in the working and future of this international monetary system. For many a Japanese observer at the time, this was an event as important as the Manchurian Crisis.[122] But gold proponents

---

119. Namely, these banks in Mukden Province were the Bank of the Three Provinces, the Frontier Bank, the Bank of China, and the Bank of Communications; in Kirin, the Kirin Provincial Bank; and finally in Amur Province, the Heilongjiang Provincial Bank. For a brief overview of events in English, see Yasutomi, "Finance in "Manchukuo.""

120. On the study of these ledgers, see Minami Manshū tetsudō keizai chōsakai, *Manshūkoku tsūka kin'yū seido tōitsu ryakushi*.

121. Shibata, *Senryōchi tsūka kin'yū seisaku no tenkai*, 46.

122. Of great importance to the following discussion is Nangō Tatsune's assessment, reprinted in Kobayashi, Nangō, and Katō, *Mantetsu chōsakai to Nangō Tatsune*, 343: "In the sixth year of Shōwa, two events happened that should be engraved in the memory of our

also faced vigorous institutional hindrances. From the very outset, expertise on monetary and financial matters was firmly concentrated in the hands of a few silver proponents. Shutō Masatoshi was the most senior of them. As administrator of SMRC, he was responsible for supervising the (newly reopened) Bank of the Three Provinces and the Frontier Bank; but as his career background was with YSB, he was very skeptical if not hostile to BOC currency schemes. He could furthermore draw on the skills of a few pro-silver aides who enjoyed considerable prestige in the Governing Division of the Kwantung Army (Kantōgun tōchibu). One of them was Igarashi Yasushi, of the division's section of finance; another was Yasumatsu Morinosuke, of the influential SMRC Bureau for Economic Research (Mantetsu keizai chōsakai), a bureau that had been established in 1932 with the explicit aim of formulating economic policy.[123]

Another employee of the same bureau was Nangō Tatsune. Born in Kagoshima prefecture in 1901, he had joined SMRC at the young age of 21; he then worked for the research bureau of the director's office. In 1932 he moved to the SMRC Bureau for Economic Research, where he would eventually lead subdivision 4, the Finance subdivision. He is of particular importance for this discussion, not simply for his role in formulating the future of Manchurian finance, but especially because of his many publications, his partially preserved diary, and his transcripts of many discussions at the time. These documents have been an indispensable tool for much of the following reconstruction of debates, ideological cleavages, and other developments.[124]

Nangō Tatsune and the Technocratic Reformists

From Nangō Tatsune's writings we understand that, in January 1932, consultation among a small cluster of economic experts led to the formulation of "Honjō gunshireikan kyakka ni teishutsu seru Manshū no

---

people: one is Great Britain's abandonment of the gold standard, the other is the occurrence of the Manchurian Incident."

123. For discussions of the economic policy bureau, see Kobayashi, *Mantetsu "chi no shūdan" no tanjō to shi*; idem, *Mantetsu chōsabu "ganso shinkutanku" no tanjō to hōkai*; idem, *Manshū to jimintō*; and idem, *Mantetsu chōsabu no kiseki*.

124. A more or less definitive account of these is Kobayashi, Nangō, and Katō, *Mantetsu chōsakai to Nangō Tatsune*.

heisei narabi ni kin'yū ni kansuru ikensho" (Opinions with regard to currency and finance, presented to His Excellency Commander Honjō).[125] What sets this report apart from, for instance, the aforementioned *About the Currency System of the New State of Manchuria and Mongolia* is its explicitly pragmatic, one would almost say anti-ideological and technocratic stance. As could be expected, it most fundamentally addresses two questions: gold versus silver as the standard metal for the monetary system; and the central bank system to be adopted (the nature of its capital, shareholders, mandates, and so on).

In turn, this document functioned as a working paper for a series of heated debates by the Commission for Monetary and Financial Affairs (Heisei oyobi kin'yū shimon iinkai), summoned by the Kwantung Army's Governing Division and held January 15–20, 1932, in the Mukden Yamato Hotel. The gold versus silver debate was far from settled, as we understand from the transcripts that Nangō meticulously kept.[126] The BOC faction, represented by Irobe Mitsugi and Matsusaki Hisashi, was ardently in favor of the immediate adoption of the gold standard. Its members' arguments were not fundamentally different from earlier BOC viewpoints and arguments, as is evident from the following medley of quotations:

For more than twenty years now, our imperial army has striven to establish Manchuria and Mongolia as a first line [of defense]. It is simply a matter of common sense that the country should adopt an infrastructure that benefits our nation and our people as much as possible; an economic system, or, to be more specific, a monetary system is clearly a matter of paramount importance in this respect.[127]

[Another] reason [we] believe it is important to lay the groundwork of the gold standard [in Manchuria] is that, apart from showing the determination to differ from China proper in a political way, it is also indispensable that it shows itself to be determined to separate from China economically.[128]

----

125. The official author of this document is Shutō Masatoshi. See also Shibata, *Senryō-chi tsūka kin'yū seisaku no tenkai*, 45.

126. Reprinted in Kobayashi, Nangō, and Katō, *Mantetsu keizai chōsakai to Nangō Tatsune*, 161–287.

127. Ibid., 218.

128. Ibid., 192.

I think it would furthermore be absurd [to adopt the silver standard and] demand that Japanese use silver in their dealings with the Chinese. One cannot ask a people with such an advanced monetary system to take a retrograde step. That is simply absurd. Would it not be better instead to have the Chinese advance? That appears to be the obvious course to adopt. Rather than have the Japanese people take a backwards step and participate in Chinese practices, [adopting the gold standard] will educate the Chinese. [. . .] It cannot be helped that one will have to deal with some imperfections when establishing this new monetary system.[129]

Once more, gold proponents viewed the debate through the prism of Japanese investments in Manchuria and, as Nangō's transcripts make clear, with the final goal of monetarily uniting the newly established state with the Japanese metropolis or *naichi*.

As was to be expected, Shutō and his aides were not convinced. The central question of monetary reform, they argued, was not Japanese investments. Rather, what had to be considered before all else was the country's stabilization. In Shutō's words:

Concerning how to fix the monetary system of Manchuria, [our decisions should be led by] *what we are able to do.* This being said, I think that we should give priority to stabilizing its business and financial world. Just consider the unequal distribution of gold throughout the world, and [it will be clear that] bringing Manchuria on a pure gold coin standard is out of the question. Or, an abrupt change like having Japanese coins circulate into Manchuria is something we should only start to consider *after* political and economic affairs have settled down. I furthermore think that, from a political viewpoint too, it is not advantageous to implement those large changes in a climate of severe financial and economic distress. Indeed, I believe that, precisely because of this [instability], their [very implementation] would meet enormous problems and thus rather be unattainable.[130]

It is instructive to keep in mind the discussion's rhetorical subtleties. Silver advocates did not necessarily disagree about Manchuria's eventual fate. In the end, as they explained on several occasions, they would not disagree with the adoption of the gold standard at a different, future point in time. Rather, their objections were tactical. Was the gold

129. Ibid., 245.
130. Ibid., 174 (italics added).

faction not mistaken in its assessment of the nature of the Manchurian economy? Was it really aware of the difficulties that reform efforts might face? This went well beyond the culturalist bias—an assertion of the Chinese people's "preference for silver"—that several members of the gold faction would from time to time ascribe to their counterparts. Instead, Shutō and his aides urged an open and pragmatic, yet equally imperialist, outlook on what the Japanese leadership faced. Consider, for instance: "Until now, we have made a distinction between Japan's trade with Manchuria on the one hand, and China's trade with Manchuria on the other, but when it comes to Manchuria's monetary system, one may wonder [whether it is justified to] differentiate between unifying it with Japan or with China."[131]

Did exchange relationships with China make it impossible to present monetary matters in those simple terms? This statement was a clever nod toward the situation of the Japanese economy at the time. Indeed, the gold advocates may not have paid sufficient attention to the complexity of Manchuria's and Japan's economies in terms of their international position, especially in their evolving relationship with China (through the Shanghai market):

In the last two years or so, after Japan lifted the ban on gold exports, [it] has run a balance of payments deficit, i.e., a deficit with gold-standard countries. [It appears that, at the time,] the Chinese [i.e., the government of Zhang Xueliang], when buying goods from abroad—in order to pay for its military arsenal acquired abroad [i.e., mainly in England and the United States]—have converted [Bank of Chosen bills] through Shanghai. In other words, it seems that the Chinese have heavily drawn on Japanese specie [in order to obtain] the necessary gold. So, although China's balance of trade has been running a balance of payment deficit, the fact that Japan has been running a balance of payment deficit with China [must] actually [be explained as the outcome of] China drawing on Japanese gold. [In other words, it seems that] Japan has in the past provided China's specie reserve. [. . .] When discussing the new rule and monetary issues of Manchuria and Mongolia while keeping their relationship with Japan's own monetary problems in the back of our minds, it appears that one should distinguish sharply between *what has been* and *what will be*.[132]

---

131. Ibid., 203.
132. Ibid., 203 (italics in original).

To Shutō and his aides, it was clear that Manchuria's monetary future would largely be determined by both the size and the proximity of the Shanghai market. Speculation in gold and silver was a particular concern, not least because it would in turn be affected by the monetary standard Manchuria was eventually to adopt. How would the relatively minor Manchurian economy react to massive speculation in the biggest marketplace of silver-standard China? It is one of the most intricate riddles for the negotiators, and possibly even a turning point in the discussions. Nangō's studies, apparently aware of shortcomings in statistics at the time,[133] point out that this speculation may well be sufficiently large-scale to rule out the gold standard as an option for the near future.[134] It would put severe, if not impossible demands on amounts of specie reserve to be held. Shutō, irritated by continuing resistance to his vision of a silver-bullion standard, explains: "It seems I must stress this over and over again. In the case of gold or in the case of silver, [the amount of specie to be held] is radically different. [If we opt for] a silver-bullion standard, I think it will not be necessary to have a large reserve. It is hard to be more specific about this [at this point], but if I would have to give a concrete estimate, I would say that a ratio of 40 percent would be sufficient. Now, in the case of gold, 50 percent would absolutely be insufficient. If [the reserve] would not be something around 70 percent, I think we cannot be reassured."[135]

These numbers were hard to ignore. Ultimately, Shutō's original proposals were accepted, although even his hints about the adoption of a silver-bullion standard were eventually rejected. Instead, the Central Bank of Manchou (established June 15, 1932, and opening for business exactly one month later)[136] speaks of the adoption of a "silver standard

---

133. Shinozaki speaks of deceitful statistics (*uso no tōkei*): ibid., 221–22.

134. Minami Manshū tetsudō kabushiki gaisha, ed., "Shanhai shijō no engawase to Manshū no tsūka."

135. Kobayashi, Nangō, and Katō, *Mantetsu keizai chōsakai to Nangō Tatsune*, 241.

136. For documents relating to the bank's establishment, see "Manshūkoku kahei hō / Manshū chūō ginkō hō / Manshū chūō ginkō soshiki benpō" 満州国貨幣法 / 満州中央銀行法 / 満州中央銀行組織弁法 (Currency Act of Manchukuo / Central Bank of Manchou Act / Laws with regard to the structure of the Central Bank of Manchou), JACAR Ref. B02032053300.

controlled currency"[137] (a silver-exchange-standard managed currency or *gin kawase kanri tsūka*, to be more precise). This proposal was extraordinary. In the charter of the Central Bank of Manchou, all references to the issue of convertibility were omitted. Instead, the bank was simply requested to hold, as reserve, a sum equivalent to 30 percent or more of the total amount of notes issued, either in silver or gold bullion, or as foreign currencies and deposits with foreign banks in silver or gold accounts. Thus, from a rather optimistic assessment of Manchuria's monetary and financial future, even the gold proponents made a complete U-turn.

It would soon become clear how important the Shanghai market really was. Shutō's proposal already mentioned the necessity of maintaining a reserve of silver specie in Shanghai for the settlement of the country's balance of payments accounts.[138] (In his diary, Nangō typically refers to this as the "problem of balance of payments" or *kokusai shūshi mondai*.) This clause was ultimately deleted; yet, tying Manchurian currency to the Shanghai *tael* in an indirect way would, at least in the early years of the bank's operation, become the foundation of the stability of the country's currency. In the early 1930s, the Central Bank of Manchou sold Japanese silver yen (YSB notes or *shōhyō*, issued by the Dairen branch of YSB against a silver fund held in Shanghai) in order to withdraw Manchurian currency, which could thus be bought at par with the "big money notes" or *dayang*.[139] In turn, YSB would react to changes in the market price of its notes through exchange operations in Shanghai. Yasutomi Ayumu explains that this was fundamentally similar to the situation in the 1920s, when the region—just as in the early 1930s—faced an export excess with Japan and an import excess with China

---

137. From a pamphlet of the time: The Central Bank of Manchou, *The Central Bank of Manchou and Appendix of Laws Pertaining Thereto*, 13. Concretely, this means that the stability of the currency was to be maintained by control of the note issue, and by purchases and sales of silver bullion. The exchange rate is therefore influenced by central bank intervention in the exchange markets, as opposed to the interaction of supply and demand in the free market.

138. Manshū chūō ginkō, *Manshū chūō ginkō 10-nenshi*, 77–78; Kobayashi, Nangō, and Katō, *Mantetsu keizai chōsakai to Nangō Tatsune*, 17; Kobayashi, *Mantetsu chōsabu no kiseki*, 199; Shibata, *Senryōchi tsūka kin'yū seisaku no tenkai*, 49.

139. For the share of YSB silver notes in the reserve of the Central Bank of Manchou, see Yasutomi, *Manshūkoku no kin'yū*, 20–21 (appendix).

proper. At that time, Manchurian bankers exchanged surplus Japanese capital for Shanghai silver capital by means of selling bills of exchange drawn on Shanghai, in order to make up for the difference and stabilize the price of their notes at the same time.[140] YSB's "advanced" version of this policy would work relatively smoothly until early 1935.[141]

Constant monitoring and cooperation with YSB was central for this arrangement, particularly because of consequences for the circulation of the latter's notes. Yasutomi stresses that this policy caused a shrinkage of note issuance from the original 14 million yen in 1931 to a mere 3 million yen in 1933, from which we can also infer that managing Manchurian currency caused a serious drain on the central bank's holdings of YSB silver notes.

The Adjustment of Manchurian Currency

After fixing the silver unit, the reformers faced a task that may have looked harder than the one undertaken by their peers in Korea three decades before: adjustment of the old banknotes. In the parlance of the newspapers and reports of the day, Manchuria was said to have a currency system of "boundless confusion" (*bunran kiwamareri naki*).[142]

---

140. Yasutomi, *Manshūkoku no kin'yū*, 50–53. Interestingly, a spokesperson for the branch office of YSB in Dairen therefore explains YSB silver notes as a managed currency *avant la lettre*. Compare "Shōhyō no hontai wa nanika / Manshū keizai sōdan" 鈔票の本体は何か／満洲経済相談 (What is the nature of the silver notes? / A discussion of the Manchurian economy), MNP 1935.9.6, KUDA-ID 00499834, especially: "The YSB silver notes have standoffishly not followed the traditional form of the world's currency systems. Rather, the currencies of the world have come to follow the functions that the YSB silver notes have exercised since long ago, and the YSB silver notes have [simply] retained their raison d'être. In other words, whereas currencies used to be linked to gold or silver (mostly gold), they exhibited the characteristics of a [monetary] standard, nowadays one attempts so called managed currencies. The YSB notes were originally a private currency issued by the Yokohama Specie Bank and should be regarded as [. . .] a managed currency, the value of which was determined by the credibility of [this institution], and upheld by the adjustment of its issue through this bank's open market operations."

141. For statistics, compare Yasutomi, *Manshūkoku no kin'yū*, 13 (appendix).

142. See also, in another formulation, "Manshūkoku no kahei seido / ranmyaku o kiwameta sono heisei / keizai jiji kaisetsu" 満洲国の貨幣制度／乱脈を極めたその幣制／経済時事解説 (The currency system of Manchukuo / currency in a state of utmost confusion: an explanation of economic affairs), TNN 1932.5.19–1932.5.23,

Banknotes were to be converted according to the "Kyū kahei seiri benpō" (Regulations governing the adjustment of the old currency),[143] and were allowed to circulate for another two years, with the process of currency readjustment to be completed by the end of June 1935.

The region was also awash with notes issued by yet other institutions, which were inconvertible. There were the "Ma big money notes" (*Ma dayang piao*) of the rebellious Ma Zhanshan,[144] the Jehol notes of the former Jehol Industrial Bank, and the private notes of the different prefectural governments; and, as we have seen, some highly idiosyncratic and mostly local currencies were in circulation, such as the transfer *tael* (in Yingkou) and the Zhenping Yin (or Andong *tael*), of which Nangō prepared several studies as his diary again testifies. They were all to be converted on yet other terms[145]—sometimes without accompanying legislation—and with varying degrees of difficulty. As far as I am aware, there are no official reports documenting social unrest related to the

---

KUDA-ID 00817736. This point is highlighted by: Yasutomi, *Manshūkoku no kin'yū*, 48ff.

143. For the full text of these regulations, see "Kyū kahei seiri benpō" 旧貨幣整理弁法 (Regulations with regard to the adjustment of the old currency), JACAR Ref. B02130936600; or "Manshū kyū kahei seiri benpō zenbun / shikō no hi yori issai ryūtsū kinshi / 2-nengo ni kōryoku o ushinau" 満洲旧貨幣整理弁法全文／施行の日より一切流通禁止／二年後に効力を失う (Full text of the regulations with regard to the adjustment of the old currency / complete prohibition of circulation from date of enforcement / after two years validity will be lost), KSB 1932.7.6, KUDA-ID 00474576.

144. Ma initially resisted the Japanese army at the time of the invasion of Manchuria, later defecting to the new Manchukuo Imperial Army; as his new status as Governor of Heilongjiang Province did not give Ma the power or wealth he had anticipated, he decided to rebel once more, thereby using Japanese money to raise a volunteer force. His changes of allegiance earned him the name of "traitor." The "Ma big money notes" date from this second period of revolt. It was said that these notes were adjusted within one month's time at the conversion rate of 1:4.

145. A very detailed overview is provided by Shibata, *Senryōchi tsūka kin'yū seisaku no tenkai*, 56–58. Contemporary newspapers also provided an account of their adjustment; see the following entries in KUDA: 00464249; 00464564; 00818174; 00076300 (formerly 00159809); 00076369 (formerly 00159878); 00076371 (formerly 00159880); 00076373 (formerly 00159882); 00474659; 00474661; 00474662; 00076374 (formerly 00159883); 00076375 (formerly 00159884); 00076376 (formerly 00159885); 00076386 (formerly 00159895).

process of adjustment. But, as we can also conclude from conversion percentages, the operation was surprisingly successful.

Foreign observers too applauded the Japanese reformers for their efforts at monetary unification, as we understand from the following comment by Edgar Snow in 1934: "Thus far the chief benefit of Japanese rule, the new banking system, has abolished fiat currency which the peasants formerly were forced to accept by avaricious warlords. As remarked earlier, they issued crisp but soon worthless paper [. . .] in exchange for the great soya-bean crop [. . .] and for other cereals, which they then sold for hard money. [. . .] The Central Bank of Manchukuo [. . .] converted most of the more reputable old notes. It succeeded in stabilizing the Manchukuo *yuan* [. . .] at a par with the China dollar. The *yuan* is now worth more than the Japanese yen—a condition not unfavorable to Japanese exporters."[146]

Effects of the Great Depression

In the end, however, it was not China's monetary disorder, but sharp swings in the international silver price that would necessitate the reorientation of Japan's monetary position in Manchuria. In order to understand these events, it is instructive to go back in time a little bit. The story begins with the outbreak of the Great Depression in the United States in October 1929, and its consequential effect on the economies of almost all countries of the globe. There were some remarkable special cases, notably China, especially in the first two or three years of the worldwide economic downturn. As the largest silver-standard economy in the world, it was destined to see and feel the Great Depression in a radically different manner.

---

146. Snow, *Far Eastern Front* (London 1934), 271–72. A similar appreciation can be found in a later account: Jones, *Manchuria Since 1931* (London, 1949), 126–27: "At the inception of this monetary reform there was considerable skepticism expressed about its chances of success. [. . .] However, the currency reform proved more successful than had been expected, the ratio of currency reserve to note issues was kept at an adequate rate, and sufficient popular confidence was engendered to ensure that the new *yuan* came into general use and that the old money was not hoarded. [. . .] This provision of a sound and simplified currency was an important and much-needed reform, and one which did something to mitigate the hostility of the Chinese in Manchuria to the new régime."

There are many interesting and competing accounts of what exactly happened to China at the time, and to what degree geopolitical events, especially decisions made by the Roosevelt administration in the mid-1930s, affected China's fate—not only with regard to the second Sino-Japanese War, but also with regard to the rise of the communists in the early postwar period. Some, particularly earlier, accounts assume that falls in commodity prices effectively shook the economic bases of many Asian countries; some authors still argue that these drops had a devastating impact on certain social groups, especially the rural poor. In a study of Jiangnan's rural economy, David Faure states that the Great Depression ultimately "affected all prices" and "spelled misery for most farmers."[147] Ramon Myers has argued that the Great Depression caused "intolerable rural suffering" and has furthermore assumed that rural distress spilled over into and intensified the effect on the urban commercial and industrial classes.[148]

More recent analyses, largely relying on newly available data and documents, challenge these assertions and present a revisionist view. In this interpretation, the Great Depression did indeed have an impact, but its width and depth have been overstated. Thomas Rawski, for instance, argues that new data "leave very little doubt that contemporary and retrospective accounts of the early 1930s as years of desperate crisis for China's economy contain large elements of exaggeration."[149] In another paper he adds that "the world depression caused no significant or protracted decline in China's real output," not even after the initiation of Roosevelt's silver purchase program.[150] Although the last word about this extremely complicated period has yet to be spoken, not least in view of the difficulty of determining the degree to which different regions, and different classes within those regions, were directly or indirectly affected, it seems that the Great Depression should thus, at least in real terms, be redefined as only one factor in China's multiple crises at the time.

----

147. Faure, "The Plight of the Farmers," 30–31.
148. Myers, *The Chinese Peasant Economy*, 14.
149. Rawski, *Economic Growth in Prewar China*, 177.
150. Rawski, "Milton Friedman, Silver, and China," 757. Another study supporting a similar interpretation is Brandt and Sargent, "Interpreting New Evidence About China and U.S. Silver Purchases."

Yet other authors have argued that climatic factors and politico-military disruptions—especially the occupation of Manchurian territory by Japan—are of far greater significance for grasping the sources of economic turmoil in China in the early 1930s.[151] Their analyses bring us to an important characteristic of the Chinese economic and political system at the time that has thus far been neglected: its regional differentiation and, by consequence, the need to distinguish among regions—particularly to examine how differences in economic structure among regions translated into differences in the way those regions were affected.

The world economic crisis did, of course, make a difference: economic policy makers in Manchuria developed specific perceptions of certain decisions and events during the Great Depression, and they reacted to what they perceived to be happening. And insofar as the attempts of the Nationalist Government to gain control over the currency and the 1935 currency reform were inspired by rising silver prices, the impact of the Depression was considerable indeed. If looked at from this perspective, it makes sense, as Tomoko Shiroyama has very recently pointed out, to consider the Great Depression a "watershed," indeed precisely because of its strong semantic appeal. It provided a pretext for the implementation of reforms, and is thus crucial to our understanding of modern China.[152] In what follows, we trace the impact of the world depression on Manchuria, and how several events paved the last roads toward the yen bloc.[153]

---

151. This also seems to be the conviction of Ramon Myers ("The World Depression and the Chinese Economy," 274): "When we refer to the historical record of the period, then, we do not observe signs of depression such as massive unemployment in the cities or in many parts of the countryside. Where information indicates that misery occurred, we can usually find specific reasons for it: harvests, banditry or warlordism. China simply did not experience any national economic depression as the world depression deepened." This perceived importance of climatic factors led Tim Wright to develop case studies of several Chinese regions in the Great Depression: "The Manchurian Economy and the 1930s World Depression" and "Distant Thunder"

152. Shiroyama, *China During the Great Depression.*

153. For a very thorough account of Manchurian economic history, see Yamamoto, *Manshūkoku no keizaishi kenkyū.*

The Depression in Manchuria

All accounts unequivocally identify the years 1929–31 as a period during which the Chinese economy was relatively secured against the worst effects of the global economic downturn. The explanation for this protection is simple enough: as the price of silver and silver currencies automatically fell against gold, the effect was mostly slightly inflationary. Because China was on a silver standard, it had the equivalent of a floating exchange rate. Chinese producers and merchants actually experienced price stability or even price increases.[154] For exporters, devaluation gave them a chance to cut prices and thereby maintain their favorable position in overseas markets, while limiting its effect on domestic income. On the macro-level, as could be expected, this nevertheless translated into a shrinkage of external trade volume, mainly in response to deteriorating international economic conditions.

This protective mechanism also worked in Manchuria—at least partially. Because the Manchurian economy used both silver and gold currencies, the Depression's impact on Manchuria must be a more complicated one. As demonstrated by Tim Wright, Japanese enterprises (which were mostly active at the upper or infrastructural level of the Manchurian economy and used gold currency) were hit relatively hard. Both Fushun Coal and its parent company, the powerful South Manchurian Railway Company, mainly plagued by higher freight rates, saw their positions decline both internally and externally.[155] So did importers. The decrease in purchasing power by the silver-owning Chinese forced consumers to turn to cheaper domestic surrogates and consequently produced a steady decline in the demand for foreign goods.

As the world depression deepened, the troubles of the trade sector inevitably affected the whole of Manchuria, "north as well as south, smaller rural centers as well as the larger cities."[156] The downturn was worse in Dairen and the SMRC zone, that is to say, where gold currency (and Japanese enterprise) was most prominent; but only months later, the crisis also spread to the regions of Kirin and Heilongjiang.

---

154. Shiroyama, *China During the Great Depression.*
155. T. Wright, "The Manchurian Economy and the 1930s World Depression," 1083.
156. Ibid., 1084.

Around this time the Depression exposed the Achilles' heel of the Manchurian soybean economy: that it was largely monocultural (especially in the north) and dependent on exports.[157] Wright estimates that by 1934 the value added by soybeans declined by 35 percent and their share in the economy by 25 percent. The exports of processed bean products fell particularly sharply.[158] In the Chinese market, boycotts of Manchurian goods were a serious blow to beancake exporters; Germany, originally a major importer of bean oil, first shifted to importing beans for pressing its own oil, then imposed a quota on such imports in the framework of its policy for autarky. Table 4.1 shows that exports recovered briefly in 1931 but then dropped precipitously, especially after 1933. Crop failures in and after 1932 exacerbated the crisis (see column four). Whether these failures led to outbreaks of famine is still a topic of contention among specialists, but it appears nonetheless that their consequences were severe.[159]

Gyrations of the Manchurian Yuan

Of more importance to our discussion than macroeconomic events are a series of monetary decisions that compounded the crisis and that were closely monitored by Manchurian financial authorities. Already mentioned is Finance Minister Takahashi Korekiyo's decision to take Japan off gold and devalue the yen in December 1931, only a month before the meeting of the Commission for Monetary and Financial Affairs in the Mukden Yamato Hotel. Although of crucial importance to save Japan proper from the most dramatic effects of the Great Depression, the consequences of this decision for the Japanese-occupied territory of Manchuria were substantial. Between July 1932 and late 1934, the Manchurian *yuan* rose above 1.10 Japanese yen, from the original level of 0.73 (shortly thereafter, it would rise even further; see Table 4.2). Silver-using Manchurian merchants, like their counterparts in the rest of China, had earlier experienced a similar appreciation of their currency

---

157. For a very fine macroeconomic analysis, see Yamamoto, *Manshūkoku no keizai-shi kenkyū*, 89ff.

158. T. Wright, "The Manchurian Economy and the 1930s World Depression," 1085.

159. Ibid., 1098.

Table 4.1: Manchurian soybean production and trade, 1927–1936 (index: 1929 = 100)

Year	Soybean exports, volume	Soybean and beancake exports, value	Soybean production
1927	66.9	84.7	99.3
1928	88.1	96.3	99.9
1929	100.0	100.0	100.0
1930	81.3	81.1	109.3
1931	102.8	107.5	107.8
1932	92.9	92.0	88.0
1933	85.7	61.6	94.9
1934	90.5	57.3	70.1
1935	64.0	50.7	79.5
1936	71.3	71.6	85.3

SOURCE: T. Wright, "The Manchurian Economy and the 1930s World Depression," 1087.

Table 4.2: Value of the Manchurian *yuan*, July 1932–December 1935

Year	Month	Market price (yen)	Index	Year	Month	Market price (yen)	Index
1932	July	73.19	100.0	1934	April	109.61	149.8
	August	85.58	116.9		May	105.27	143.8
	September	91.79	125.4		June	107.26	146.6
	October	92.96	127.0		July	108.89	148.8
	November	105.21	143.8		August	111.57	152.4
	December	96.82	132.3		September	112.98	154.4
1933	January	97.57	133.3		October	115.38	157.6
	February	98.11	134.0		November	112.17	153.3
	March	96.00	131.2		December	109.70	149.9
	April	96.10	131.3	1935	January	109.40	149.5
	May	98.59	134.7		February	111.34	152.1
	June	99.37	135.8		March	111.36	152.1
	July	99.83	136.4		April	109.74	149.9
	August	100.80	137.7		May	106.60	145.6
	September	106.60	145.6		June	104.33	142.5
	October	105.52	144.2		July	103.60	141.5
	November	108.17	147.8		August	100.91	137.9
	December	109.39	149.5		September	100.00	136.6
1934	January	111.78	152.7		October	100.00	136.6
	February	112.70	154.0		November	100.00	136.6
	March	112.68	154.0		December	100.00	136.6

NOTE: Base year = July 1932.
SOURCE: Manshū chūō ginkō, *Manshū chūō ginkō 10-nenshi*, 325–26; a similar table can be found in Kobayashi, *Dai tōa kyōeiken no keisei to hōkai*, 61; a chart visualizing the same data can be found in Yasutomi, *Manshūkoku no kin'yū* (appendix), 13.

relative to Great Britain's and India's, and they did so again relative to the United States currency in 1933, when that country went off gold. By then, the original protection offered by the silver standard was effectively offset or wiped out. China's balance of payments deteriorated sharply, and from around 1932, the country exported gold and silver to pay for its excess of imports over exports.

Proposals for the harmonization and unification of the Manchurian and Japanese monetary systems appeared as early as the spring of 1933. In March, the First Council of the Special Service Agency (Tokumubu daiichi iinkai) published its "Outline for the realization of Japan-Manchuria monetary unification" (Nichiman heisei tōitsu no jitsugen ni kansuru yōkōan). It proposed, among other things, the elimination of the section on the silver content of the Manchurian *yuan* from the Manchuria Currency Law and its replacement with a clause stipulating that the value of the *yuan* was to be identical to the value of the Japanese yen; it also foresaw the exchange of Manchurian paper money for Japanese money.[160] The rationale offered is the current sluggish foreign (Japanese) investment, when it was very much needed for the "urgent task of the exploitation of Manchuria's and Mongolia's natural resources." Fluctuations in the price of silver and gold deterred Japanese investors, the *Outline* explained; the harmonization of these countries' currency systems would alleviate their fears and allow for stronger connections between both economies. There was nothing revolutionary about this plan, as the gold standard had been envisaged since the earliest days of the conception of Manchukuo; now the time was ripe to realize that vision. After discussion of this report, and heavy criticism from the influential Hoshino Naoki of the country's Department of Financial Affairs, it was shelved.

It resurfaced in June 1933, when Kwantung Army Chief of Staff Koiso Kuniaki convened another meeting, this time without representatives

---

160. The plan and a critique of it can be found in Kobayashi, Nangō, and Katō, *Mantetsu keizai chōsakai to Nangō Tatsune*, 307–11, as "'Nichiman heisei tōitsu no jitsugen ni kansuru yōkōan' ni taisuru Suzuki komon no setsumei yōryō narabi hihan" 「日満幣制統一の実現に関する要項案」に対する鈴木顧問の説明要領並批判 (Advisor Suzuki's main points of explanation and critique of the "Outline for the realization of Japan-Manchuria monetary unification"). The advisor mentioned here is Suzuki Kiyoshi, at that time vice-president of BOC and special adviser to the Kwantung Army.

of the state of Manchuria, whose criticisms had been especially strong. At that time, the Kwantung Army planners foresaw passage of the original proposal "with some amendments and extra conditions."[161] This second attempt too came to naught. Under enormous pressure from both the Bank of Japan and the Ministry of Finance—allegedly even Finance Minister Takahashi intervened—the plan was rejected; newspapers were explicitly ordered not to publish any reference to these discussions, in order not to upset the Manchurian market.[162]

Roosevelt's Silver Purchase Program

It would be another year and a half before the prospect of currency unification was once more discussed. Then, the reason for the discussion was not a policy scheme of one or more ambitious bureaucrats, but an event quite beyond the control of both Japanese and Manchurian policy makers: the decision of the Roosevelt Administration to embark on a controversial silver purchase program to reverse the chronic tendency toward silver depreciation—in the parlance of the day, to "do something" for silver.[163] Preparations began in late 1933 and the formalization of this program through a Silver Purchase Act occurred in early 1934.[164] The Roosevelt administration's silver policies and their impact on economic and political events in China are even more contentious subjects among scholars of Chinese economic history than the effect of the Great Depression.

Milton Friedman, in an article that employs a thesis developed by himself and Anna Schwartz, blasts the silver purchase program as a mere "subsidy to producers of silver" and a "disaster for the Chinese republic ruled by Chiang Kai-shek."[165] Acknowledging that proponents of the program listed benefits to China (through enhanced purchasing power

---

161. Kobayashi, Nangō, and Katō, *Mantetsu keizai chōsakai to Nangō Tatsune*, 19–20.

162. Ibid., 311–12: "Nichiman heisei tōitsu mondai ni tsuite" 日満幣制統一問題 に就いて (On the problem of the monetary unification of Japan and Manchuria).

163. Compare "Johnson Makes Threats: Tells Republicans They Must "Do Something" for Silver." *New York Times*, February 7, 1896.

164. For an intricate political history of these events, see Bratter, "The Silver Episode."

165. Friedman, "Franklin D. Roosevelt, and China," 63. The original argument can be found in Friedman and Schwartz, *A Monetary History of the United States, 1867–1960*.

for the silver-holding Chinese) as one of the program's advantages, Friedman goes on to explain how the program actually produced the opposite effect. The prospect of increased purchasing power was a flawed argument, because silver was not a mere commodity, but China's standard, its money.[166] The effect of the silver purchase program was a maelstrom of deflation, rather than a chance for the Chinese to sell their stocks of silver on favorable terms, in particular because the United States itself had left the gold standard in 1933. Indeed, Chinese commodity prices in terms of dollars, pounds sterling, and other currencies were rising, thus offsetting some of the relative appreciation of the Chinese silver dollar. Yet, the U.S. price of silver rose more sharply than the prices of Chinese products. Consequently, the appreciation of Chinese currency was only partially offset. Instead, imports declined, Chinese exports fell further, and the low level of activity in the economy severely slowed industrial production, with unemployment as a natural outcome; what was worse, plummeting prices for agricultural products ultimately translated into a fall in income, decreasing purchasing power instead of increasing it.[167] Friedman quotes Arthur Young, who functioned as economic adviser to China from 1929 to 1947, describing the period as one in which "China passed from moderate prosperity to deep depression."[168]

Other scholars have offered alternative interpretations. Loren Brandt and Thomas Sargent argue that Friedman (and Schwartz) overestimated the real effects of nominal deflation,[169] and Thomas Rawski charges them with neglecting the effects of an increase in banknotes and deposits as a result of exported specie.[170] In Rawski's view, the increased use of banknotes more than offset the decline in specie so that the quantity of money in the economy rose, thereby producing inflation rather than the opposite: "if anything, Chinese domestic prices increased

---

166. Friedman, "Franklin D. Roosevelt, and China," 73.

167. For statistics, compare Yamamoto, *"Manshūkoku" keizaishi kenkyū*, esp. 98–99.

168. A. N. Young, *China's Nation-Building Effort*, 209; Friedman, "Franklin D. Roosevelt, and China," 73.

169. Brandt and Sargent, "Interpreting New Evidence About China and U.S. Silver Purchases."

170. Rawski, *Economic Growth in Prewar China*, and idem, "Milton Friedman, Silver, and China."

after the implementation of the U.S. silver purchase policy."[171] Recent findings, however, cast serious doubt upon this interpretation. Richard Burdekin, drawing attention to the exodus of silver from the interior of the country to Shanghai, stresses the impact of tightening credit conditions, especially on the countryside (whereas Shanghai was temporarily insulated from the effects of an outflow of silver); he also explains that positive money growth as documented by Rawski could occur because of the sudden increase in silver stock in Shanghai, but was "unambiguously insufficient to avoid deflation."[172] In short, his conclusions tend to endorse Friedman's earlier findings.

Although methodologically very interesting—Burdekin couples an intricate quantitative methodology with a reiteration of contemporary observations—even these conclusions fail to be helpful in the context of a complete discussion of economic events in China. Probably, attention has been concentrated too narrowly on the validity of the official economic legitimation of the silver purchase program at the time (the argument about Chinese purchasing power). It may be more fruitful to interpret American policy from a geopolitical viewpoint, that is to say, in the context of deteriorating U.S.-Japan relations in 1934 and later, especially with regard to these countries' attitudes toward China.

Constantly under strain after the Manchurian Incident, U.S.-Japanese diplomatic relations had been further damaged by several Japanese provocations after 1933. In February of that year, Japan elected international isolation by withdrawing from the League of Nations.[173] Approximately one year later, in March 1934, it endorsed that decision by unilaterally defining its "special relationship" with China, and its "mission" in East Asia. This foreign policy, which came to be known as the Amau Doctrine (*Amō seimei*), after Amō Eiji, a spokesperson of the Ministry of Foreign Affairs, sharply criticized the efforts of several powers to gain influence with Chiang Kai-shek's nationalist government under the pretext of financial or technical aid.[174] At the same time, it signaled the deter-

---

171. Rawski, "Milton Friedman, Silver, and China," 756.

172. Burdekin, "U.S. Pressure on China's Currency."

173. Compare Nish, *Japan's Struggle with Internationalism.*

174. Amō's statement is reproduced in United States Department of State, *Papers Relating to the Foreign Relations of the United States, Japan,* vol. 1, 224–29. The full text is accessible online at http://digital.library.wisc.edu/1711.dl/FRUS.FRUS193141v01.

mination of the Japanese government not to aid China either, as "history shows that these can be attained through no other means than the awakening and the voluntary efforts of China herself,"[175] probably indicating Japan's own inability to do so, as it had not yet recovered from the economic slump of the Shōwa financial crisis in 1927 and the subsequent world depression.

In any case, the Amau Doctrine, more than anything else, figured in American decision making related to China (and Manchukuo). Roosevelt rejected suggestions for a unilateral or a collective loan to the Nanking government, as either would bring the United States into direct conflict with the Amau Doctrine. At the same time, he remained determined to spite Tokyo for its own unilateral policies. The silver purchase program was a more subtle, if equally powerful way to do so. Robert Dallek's diplomatic history of the period makes it clear that, amid Roosevelt's efforts to maneuver between the opposing policy views of the Department of State and the Department of the Treasury, the program was in the final analysis also directed against Japan, even in view of its deleterious consequences for China's own political and economic situation,[176] of which Roosevelt had been informed:

In February 1935 [. . .], when he had received reports of a Japanese proposition to help China fight America's silver policy, the president declared himself "convinced . . . that somehow our silver policy is hurting Japan. I have told this to Henry [Morgenthau] and other people, but nobody seems to know why it would hurt Japan, but I maintain that it does." Finally, when the Governor of the New York Federal Reserve Bank told him in July 1935 that American silver purchases were breaking down China's banks and "throwing the business of the people . . . into chaos," Roosevelt replied that "silver is not the problem of the Chinese past, nor the Chinese present, nor the Chinese future. [. . .]

[B]y November, the Chinese found themselves compelled to abandon the silver standard, sell their bullion, and acquire foreign exchange to support their new currency. To help make this system work, Nanking asked Washington to buy 200 million ounces of silver. [. . .] [B]ecause the State Department believed

---

175. United States Department of State, *Papers Relating to the Foreign Relations of the United States, Japan*, vol. 1, 224.

176. See, for instance, United States Department of State, *Foreign Relations of the United States: Diplomatic Papers, 1934: Vol. III—The Far East.*

it would not offend the Japanese, Morgenthau was able to purchase 175 million ounces of Chinese silver during the next fifteen months.[177]

The Final Reform Effort

The degree to which American action hastened currency reform in China proper has been documented by Shiroyama.[178] Less well known is that America's silver-buying policy was also closely scrutinized by the Manchurian authorities. Although this was apparently unknown to officials in the U.S. Department of the Treasury, what bothered the Japanese was their earlier decision to link the Manchurian *yuan* to the Shanghai silver *tael* through YSB exchange operations. Silver appreciation reversed many earlier presuppositions about Manchukuo's balance-of-payments situation and, hence, which monetary standard to adopt.[179]

As Chinese silver holdings were now massively exported to the United States, it became increasingly difficult to maintain a more-or-less stable exchange rate between the Manchurian *yuan*, the Japanese yen (de facto BOC gold notes), and the Shanghai silver *tael*. After rising to the already alarming level of ¥1.09 in December 1933, the *yuan*'s market value reached an absolute peak of ¥1.15 yen in October 1934, after which it fell again, but still remained much higher than it had been before 1933. As a result, Manchurian silver holders risked being caught in the deflationary spiral that faced their counterparts in China proper.

Worse, however, was that at the same time increasing Japanese investments in Manchuria were tending to drive up the amounts of Bank of Chosen gold notes. As the *Mainichi nippō* of November 9, 1934, reported:

The number of "gold notes" [i.e., BOC gold notes, representative of the gold yen] in circulation within the country has shown a dramatic increase. In July 1932, at the time of the establishment of the Central Bank of Manchukuo, the

---

177. Dallek, *Franklin D. Roosevelt and American Foreign Policy*, 94. Supporting evidence can be found in the work of Dorothy Borg, to which Dallek also refers: Borg, *The United States and the Far Eastern Crisis of 1933–1938*, esp. 46–99 ("The Challenge of the Amau Doctrine").

178. See, for instance, Shiroyama, *China During the Great Depression*; Chi, "China's Monetary Reform in Perspective."

179. Compare, for instance, "Manchoukuo Shows Large Unfavorable Trade Balance for 1934."

issued amount of BOC notes did not exceed ¥70 million, in contrast to the ¥139 million of national currency [*kokuhei*];[180] in September last year, however, the amount rose to ¥116 million, in contrast to ¥180 million of *kokuhei*. At the present time, the amount even surpasses the amount of *kokuhei*. Obviously, this also includes the amount [of BOC notes] circulating within Chō-sen proper, but the recent increase in the amount of BOC notes in circulation [. . .] is due to an increase of notes circulating in Manchukuo.[181]

This circulation of notes was not necessarily problematic, provided that the authorities managed to maintain some par between the *kokuhei* and BOC notes. Yet this very objective was becoming increasingly difficult because of the further shrinkage of the Shanghai silver market; the danger of an economy on a double monetary standard was becoming increasingly apparent. As Kobayashi also remarked, speculative arbitrage exacerbated the "dissociation" (*kairi*) of BOC notes and *kokuhei*, seriously disturbing the market.[182] Soon, therefore, Manchurian newspapers spoke of the "return of Manchukuo's monetary problems," and wondered whether this would necessitate another reform effort, and whether coupling *kokuhei* to the Japanese yen would not rather invite runaway inflation.[183] Or was another reform effort simply too complicated to im-

---

180. The term *kokuhei* was used to differentiate Manchurian currency from the currency in China proper, known as *hōhei* or *fabi*.

181. "Kinpyō no ryūtsūkō tsui ni kokuhei o ryōga su / kokuhei seido tōitsu mondai chūshi no mato e" 金票の流通高遂に国幣を凌駕す／国幣制度統一問題注視の的へ (Amount of gold notes in circulation already surpassing [amount of] *kokuhei* / toward attention for unification with *kokuhei*), MNP 1934.11.7, KUDA-ID 00499166; for another account, see "Manshū Chūgin kahei no hakkōdaka shinkiroku / heisei mondai e no anji" 満洲中銀貨幣の発行高新記録／幣制問題への暗示」 (Record-high issue by the Central Bank of Manchou / hint to the currency problem), MNP 1934.12.4, KUDA-ID 00499250; an estimate of the relationship between *kokuhei* and BOC notes circulating within Manchuria can be found in the appendix to Yasutomi, *Manshūkoku no kin'yū*, 12.

182. Kobayashi, *Dai tōa kyōeiken no keisei to hōkai*, 62.

183. "Futatabi tōjō shite kita Manshūkoku tsūka mondai / hon'i henkō ka, infure ka?" 再び登場して来た満洲国通貨問題／本位変更か、インフレか (Manchurian currency problem reemerges / change the standard, or inflation?), MNP 1934.11.9–1934.11.13, KUDA-ID 00499174; "Ronsō wa tsuzuku / Nichiman tsūka tōsei mondai / kokuhei tōitsu natte saiginmi no koe" 論争はつづく／日満通貨統制問題／国幣統一成って再吟味の声 (Discussion rages on/problem of unifying Japanese and Manchurian currency / calls for reevaluation once *kokuhei* unified), CSS 1934.12.22–1934.12.26, KUDA-ID 00499305; "Manshūkoku heisei mondai / yosan iinkai no ronsō"

plement at this point in time, as the central bank's vice president Yamanari Kyōroku maintained?[184]

Manchurian monetary authorities realized they were caught between Scylla and Charybdis. In Nangō's (only partially preserved) diaries from 1934–35, we find recurrent expressions of his frustration with Manchukuo's monetary situation and increasingly explicit hints at the pressing need for a new wave of reform and the difficulties it would face. Whereas, in September 1934, Nangō still spoke of Manchukuo's balance-of-payment problems and the difficulties of using the Shanghai market in managing them (in entries for Sept. 21 and Sept. 27, 1933), the entries for 1935 increasingly refer to monetary conditions that reinforce the likeliness of monetary reform: "the state of the *kokuhei*" (*kokuhei jijō*) on May 1, "a plan for stabilizing the *kokuhei*/gold note rate" (*kokuhei tai kinpyō sōba ryaku antei su*) on May 5, "the future of the *kokuhei*" (*kokuhei no shōrai*) on May 7, "a plan for an investigation of Manchurian monetary policy" (*Manshūkoku tsūka taisaku ni kan suru chōsa ritsuan*) on July 18, "an urgent inquiry in Manchuria's monetary problems" (*Manshūkoku heisei mondai kinkyū chōsa*) on August 3, and finally "a plan for the reform of the currency of Manchukuo" (*Manshūkoku tsūka kaikaku yōkōan*) on August 4. Nangō had come to realize that the course adopted by himself and his peers in 1932 would have to be reversed.

In September 1935, when the *kokuhei* reached par with BOC gold notes, another large reform effort was unavoidable. The authorities agreed to couple the Manchurian *yuan* to the yen, in other words, to have the economy of Japan proper subsume the Manchurian economy

---

満洲国幣制問題 / 予算委員会の論戦 (The problem of the currency of Manchukuo/debate of the budget council) MNP 1935.2.5–1935.2.7, KUDA-ID 00499405.

184. "Nichiman tsūka tōsei kyūgeki niwa ikanu / mazu kokunai no heisei tōitsu ni zenryoku o / Yamanari Chūgin fukusōsai dan" 日満通貨統制急激にはいかぬ / 先ず国内の幣制統一に全力を / 山成中銀副総裁談 (Japanese-Manchurian monetary unification should not be rushed: first concentrate all energy on the domestic unification of the currency), MNP 1935.1.22, KUDA-ID 00499346; "Manshūkokuhei shutsuran no homare hōka yori heikin ichiwaridaka / 'Nichiman tsūka tōsei' ni wa Manshūkoku gawa ni nanshoku" 満洲国幣出藍の誉れ邦貨より平均一割高 / 「日満通貨統制」には満洲国側に難色 (Manchukuo currency excels its master / on average valued 10 percent higher than the currency of Japan proper / "unification of Japanese and Manchurian currencies" posing difficulties to the side of Manchukuo), KYN 1934.10.26, KUDA-ID 00499143.

(*naichika*).[185] Approximately three months later, on November 30, the Manchurian government promulgated the "Ordinance Regarding the Management of Foreign Exchange" (Kawase kanri rei) together with the "Items of the Directive Based upon the Law Regarding the Management of Foreign Exchange" (Kawase kanri hō ni motozuku meirei no ken), and the "Procedures with Respect to the Law Regarding the Management of Foreign Exchange" (Kawase kanri hō ni kansuru shikō tetsuzuki).[186] This ordinance effectively prohibited the speculative buying and selling of *kokuhei*, stipulated the protection of the country's gold and silver holdings, and fixed the rules of the *kokuhei*'s circulation and diffusion. At the same time, the government prepared a large fiscal stimulus package for Manchurian economic recovery, later developed in the famous Five Year Plan for Manchurian Industrial Development.[187] Roosevelt's controversial silver purchase program had further buttressed Japan's choice for autarky.

Ironically, this episode witnessed, for the last time, the eruption of a longstanding schism within Japan's imperialist constitution. The BOC, originally in favor of a gold standard for Manchukuo, would until the very end contest the decision to couple *kokuhei* to the Japanese yen. The reason for its resistance could hardly be called ideological. As Hoshino Naoki stressed in his memoir, Japan-Manchuria monetary unification had to be achieved at the expense of BOC gold notes for practical reasons.[188] Not only would the notes' continued circulation hamper efforts to manage the exchange stability of the *kokuhei*; officials also feared that the advantages of scale the yen possessed as the currency of Japan

---

185. Yamamoto, *"Manshūkoku" keizaishi kenkyū*, 178.

186. For an explanation of these regulations by Hoshino Naoki, then managing director of Manchukuo's Bureau for Financial Affairs, see "Manshūkoku kawase kanri hō iyoiyo 30-nichi kōfu / naiyō wa Nihon to hobo dōyō daga Nichiman kankei o kōryo" 満洲国為替管理法愈よ三十日公布／内容は日本とほぼ同様だが特に日満関係を考慮 (Law regarding the management of foreign exchange finally promulgated on the 30th / contents roughly identical to [the law] at home, but with consideration of Japanese-Manchurian relations), MNNS 1935.11.30, KUDA-ID 10000540; for related Western commentaries, see Stewart, "Manchoukuo Yuan Linked with Japanese Yen"; Shiman, "North China in a Japanese Economic Bloc."

187. Tim Wright speaks of a "Keynesian recovery" in "The Manchurian Economy and the 1930s World Depression," 1100ff.

188. Hoshino, *Mihatenu yume*, 125–26; see also Yasutomi, *Manshūkoku no kin'yū*, 57.

proper would effectively debilitate Manchukuo currency even within the country's own borders. After difficult consultations between the Central Bank of Manchukuo and BOC, the latter finally agreed to surrender its monetary presence in Manchukuo, close its branches (with the exception of those in Kwantung Province), and cooperate with the authorities to redeem its gold notes.[189] In exchange for these concessions, it was allowed to play an important role in the establishment of the Industrial Bank of Manchou (Manshū kōgyō ginkō) on December 3, 1935, and thus in the country's economic buildup. And what remained of YSB? As a bank with a record of distinguished service to an independent Manchurian currency, it was allowed to remain in Manchukuo and to continue its activities as an exchange bank. The YSB-BOC controversy had thus come full circle. By this time, a highly foreign-exchange-dependent Tokyo had opted for impossible isolation within what it still desperately described as the self-sufficient yen bloc.[190]

---

189. "Kokuhei tai kin'en pā iji / eizoku ikan wa michisū / Senginken kaishū mo shōrai no mondai / sengin wa okusetsu o yūryo" 国弊対金円パー維持／永続如何は未知数／鮮銀券回収も将来の問題／鮮銀は臆説を憂慮 (Kokuhei maintains par with Japanese gold yen / uncertainty as to how long this will last / redemption of Bank of Chosen notes future problem / Bank of Chosen wary of hypothesis), KJN 1935.10.25, KUDA-ID 00474910; "Manshūkoku heisei tōitsu 23-nichi yori jisshi / tsūka un'yō wa Chūgin, Sengin ga kyōryoku / Sengin kongo no taido o seimei" 満州国幣制統一二十三日より実施／通貨運用は中銀、鮮銀が協力／鮮銀今後の態度を声明 (Unification of the currency of Manchukuo to take effect from the 23rd / Central Bank and Bank of Chosen to cooperate with respect to currency management / Bank of Chosen to express its future attitude), MNNS 1935.12.24, KUDA-ID 00818232.

190. Boody, "Manchoukuo, The Key to Japan's Foreign Exchange Problem" and "Politics and the Yen."

Epilogue

In the summer of 1937, I had the honor of accompanying Prince Chichibu to a tea given by the Governor of the Bank of England. While we were sitting round the table, and taking tea, I said to the Governor, "Mr. Norman, I told His Highness that if all the countries of the world continue to expand their budgets for armaments at the present ratio, there will be war, bankruptcy or social revolution. Will you endorse that?" He at once turned to the Prince, and said "Certainly, Your Highness I shall endorse Mr. Kano's words. It is not war *or* bankruptcy *or* social revolution. But it is war *and* bankruptcy *and* social revolution."
—Kanō Hisaakira, *My London Records*

Toward the Pacific War

Around the very time that Nangō and his colleagues were completing Manchuria's monetary reform, Japan's activities throughout Northeast Asia were increasingly coming under the scrutiny of international public opinion and Western policy makers. Such attention had not always been the case. The more cynical Western policy makers and financiers, among them Thomas Lamont, had once been convinced that Japan's influence in the region was a fait accompli and that, therefore, denying loans to Tokyo for the financing of the region's development would be mere legalism.[1] Yet in the late 1930s, the establishment of the Manchurian puppet state, the Amau affair, and other indications of mount-

---

EPIGRAPH. Kano, *My London Records*, 46

1. E. Lamont, *Ambassador from Wall Street*, 158. Compare Mark Metzler, *Lever of Empire*, 126–27.

ing anti-Western and anti-internationalist sentiment in Japan's politics could not possibly be overlooked.

Neither could the reports of Western journalists and intellectuals who visited the region be brushed aside.[2] Freda Utley, an English political activist and widely read author, was an especially vocal critic of the Tokyo regime and of Japan's attacks on China. In 1936, she published *Japan's Feet of Clay*, which was a bestseller in both Great Britain and the United States, but was banned from publication in Japan. It dealt several devastating blows to Japan's image as an international power. Utley, at the time still inspired by socialist and Marxist thought,[3] indicated the imminence of internal upheaval, a recurrent theme in her later anti-Japanese publications.[4] She described the Japanese authorities as paranoid leaders who, wary of uprisings, were prepared to silence the populace forcefully. At the root of the problem were Japan's "social maladjustment" and its "peculiar political system," which, as Utley later asserted, made it "the most aggressive of the powers and the permanent disturber of peace in the Far East."[5]

Yet, as the title suggests, Japan did not pose a formidable threat. Its precarious societal situation made it very vulnerable, and its people's morale was low. And it was not to be considered an economic or technological giant, despite its "big bluff":

Here is a country which claims to be the Britain of the East, whose iron production is half that of Belgium, whose maximum coal production is 1/7 and consumption 1/5 of Britain's. A country which has [. . .] a large navy and mercantile marine, but whose supplies of oil have all to be imported and whose supplies of coal are very scanty. [. . .] Here is an Imperialist Power which produces capital goods—iron, steel, and machinery—in such small quantities that far from being able to export them she cannot even supply her own needs, much less those of the colonies which her armies are conquering."[6]

---

2. See Sugihara, "Economic Motivations Behind Japanese Aggression in the Late 1930s."

3. Later, after living in the Soviet Union for several years, she became an outspoken critic of communism and its related ideologies.

4. Utley, *China at War* and *Japan's Gamble in China*.

5. Utley, *Japan's Gamble in China*, 1.

6. Utley, *Japan's Feet of Clay*, 9.

Borrowing from Marxist methodology, *Japan's Feet of Clay* develops into a larger political-economic assessment and social critique. Utley describes the sorry state of Japan's economic development in the fields of both industry and agriculture;[7] she addresses the consequent problems of labor and the "diseased" structure of the national economy, and arrives at a prophecy of revolution. Current assessments of the state of the Japanese economy in the 1930s are more accurate and less tendentious assessments—but it is nevertheless important to note Utley's allusions to the role of financial matters, as well as their growing prominence in later publications.

In the preface to the second edition published in 1938, for instance, she notes that "Japan has never faced a real war without financial assistance from the West." Shortly after the outbreak of the second Sino-Japanese War, she condemned Western leaders who believed Japan had adopted a policy of the "peaceful penetration" of China because of "Japan's lack of capital," hence its eagerness to obtain financial assistance from Great Britain. China, on the other hand, "had been showing herself strong enough to secure foreign loans and credits without accepting foreign financial control."[8] Japan's situation was bound to deteriorate because the "great advantage she has derived from low labor costs and depreciated exchange since 1932 has been greatly diminished by the sharp rise in raw-material prices on the world market and the even higher price level in Japan."[9] The lack of a large investing middle class, Utley argues, made Japan unable to finance a large war effort through domestic taxation; it would be able to afford warfare only "if assured of foreign credits on a very large scale," something that was practically impossible in the unfavorable international situation that Japan had created for itself. In a conclusion that Utley shared with almost every foreign commentator at the time, war "cannot be successful, cannot but lead quickly to financial catastrophe and the breakdown of the whole process of production."[10]

---

7. Her studies at the London School of Economics in the 1920s had led to the publication of *Lancashire and the Far East* (1931), a study of the British textile industry and its Japanese competition.

8. Utley, *Japan's Feet of Clay*, 3.

9. Ibid., 386.

10. Ibid., 378.

The Greater East-Asia Co-Prosperity Sphere

It is not the historian's task to highlight flaws in Utley's reasoning, but rather to indicate how financial notions, including the prediction of Japan's bankruptcy, dominated the debate not only in the West but even in Japan itself. As was to be expected, finance had also been high on the agenda of the Japanese authorities and their military envoys, albeit not in terms of "surplus capital" ready to venture into China. Instead, later Japanese money doctors projected a "Greater East-Asia Financial Sphere" (*dai tōa kin'yūken*).[11] Although much research into the formation of this ideology remains to be done, its objective was very much like the Nazi scheme to establish a German mark-based *Groß-raumwirtschaft*.[12] The Japanese ideology resembled the German in its visions of creating a self-sufficient bloc-economy (in Japanese called *jikyū jisoku keizaiken*) and of resisting and replacing a world order in which Anglo-American finance occupied the center and in which Japan was confined to the periphery—hence the tendency to include the prefix "new," as in "New Order" (German, *Neuordnung*; Japanese, *shinchitsujo*), the "Konoe new system," and so on.

Like Hjalmar Schacht's "new monetary order" for the German Reich, the Japanese war machine had a strong component of monetary imperialism, and it employed equally familiar instruments: foreign trade and exchange controls,[13] strict price and credit controls,[14] wartime financial laws such as the Emergency Capital Allocation Law (Rinji shikin chōsei hō), and clearing agreements, among others.[15] Newly subjugated terri-

---

11. See Shimazaki, "'Dai tōa kin'yūken' no keisei katei," 1–4; Yamamoto, "'Dai tōa kin'yūken' ron."

12. Studies of Nazi monetary policy are also rather scarce. For older discussions, see Wolfe, "The Development of Nazi Monetary Policy"; Heller, "The Role of Fiscal-Monetary Policy in German Economic Recovery"; Neal, "The Economics and Finance of Bilateral Clearing Agreements: Germany, 1934–8." A more general and recent work is Tooze, *The Wages of Destruction*.

13. See a series of publications by Shibata Yoshimasa: "Nicchū sensō ki gaikoku kawase wariate seisaku no ichi kōsatsu"; "Banki senji Nihon teikoku no tainichi kessai"; "Senji kigyō seibi to sono shikin socchi"; "Ajia Taiheiyō sensō ki Taiwan no taigai kawase kessai"; and "Kotei sōba seido en burokku keisei go no 'Manshūkoku' no taigai kessai."

14. Shibata, *Senji Nihon no kabushiki shijo tōsei*.

15. Shibata, "Nicchū sensō ki Nihon no shihon wariate: 'Rinji shikin chōsei hō' to 'Ginkō nado shikin un'yō rei' no shikō." For the full text of this law, see "Rinji shikin

tory was immediately incorporated into the yen bloc.[16] Within the bloc's boundaries, the (at the time inconvertible) yen did not have the monopoly of legal tender, yet it was nevertheless the measure of everything relating to political economy. It was the standard against which the value of other currencies within the bloc was to be fixed; the "reserve currency" to be held in order to determine the amount of note issue; the currency to be used for settling balance-of-payments accounts within the yen bloc; and the currency to be used for balance-of-payments accounts of countries within the yen bloc to countries outside the bloc—after vetting by Tokyo.[17] The yen thus became the one fixed point in the financial system. Parallels with the gold standard were clear. This was a "yen standard" indeed, established with the express aim of correcting the inefficiencies and fallacies innate to the gold standard and the "wasteful ideologies" of free trade and internationalism. The effect on the occupied territories was immediate. Japanese control over the national economies of regions falling under its jurisdiction was total and totalitarian.

Contrary to wartime propaganda, Tokyo perpetuated the distinction between monetary center and periphery and imported it into the yen bloc. Such an order did not square with the objective of "eternal peace and prosperity" for Asia and meant that some countries in the yen bloc were more equal than others. In geometrical terms, the Greater East-Asian Financial Sphere consisted of concentric circles, whose power varied according to proximity to the center. Regions and peoples at the outer rings constituted an utterly powerless periphery, more or less

---

chōseihō" 臨時資金調整法 (Temporary funds adjustment law), JACAR Ref. A03022078300. For an account of monetary and financial regulations, see Shibata, *Senji Nihon no tokubetsu kaikei.*

16. For very thorough case studies, see Shibata, *Senryōchi tsūka kin'yū seisaku no tenkai* and *Mōkyō ni okeru tsūka kin'yū seisaku no tenkai.*

17. The ideas behind the establishment of a Greater East-Asian Financial Sphere can be found in several official documents: *Kihon kokusaku yōkō* 基本国策要綱 (Outline of the basic policy of the country), JACAR Ref. A06033004700; *Kihon kokusaku yōkō ni motozuku gutai mondai shori yōkō* 基本国策要綱に基く具体問題処理要綱 (Outline of dealing with concrete problems related to the outline of the basic policy of the country), JACAR Ref. B02030525500; *Nichi-Man-Shi keizai kensetsu yōkō ni kansuru ken* 日満支経済建設要綱に関する件 (Issues related to the outline for the establishment of Japanese-Manchurian-Chinese economic cooperation), JACAR Ref. C01004839600; *Dai tōa keizai kensetsujō no kihon hōsaku* 大東亜経済建設上ノ基本方策 (Basic policy with regard to the establishment of the greater East-Asian economy), JACAR Ref. A06030127000.

passive subjects of the dictates and needs formulated at the core. Put in the terminology of this book, the new generation of Japanese money doctors became the financial counterparts of the infamous Nazi death-camp doctors, distorting and perverting the relationship with their "patients." As Metzler has argued earlier, these "money creation schemes were a more extreme version of the gold-exchange standards preceding them: a lever of power and exploitation, allowing the Japanese occupiers to squeeze capital out of capital-poor societies." A few years before, Takahashi Korekiyo had attempted to prevent just such depredations. His overriding of the Manchurian gold faction in 1932 and his threat to revoke the money-creation power of the Bank of Chosen and the Bank of Taiwan in 1935 were efforts to deny the militarists the power to create at will virtual equivalents of Bank of Japan paper money. His gruesome death on the morning of February 26, 1936, removed one of the last pragmatist obstacles to the subservience of all aspects of society to the military. In the colonies, military dominance led to a dangerous experiment with "inflation capital": freshly created (and inconvertible) yen that were used to buy what the Japanese military wanted, and that denied the captive regions and countries the foreign exchange that might have been used for their own growth and industrialization.

That there were always individuals and even whole classes of people who profited from the imperialist exploitation of their regions is self-evident. We know that economic collaboration occurred and that Japan's military authorities welcomed it (if only to avoid the costs of intervention by force).[18] But such collaboration should not obscure that exploitation was pervasive and ultimately enforceable by military means. Paraphrasing Martin Wolfe, one may say that, in terms of efficiency, even the Soviet milking of countries in the East Bloc could not offer anything comparable: "Unlike communism, [German and Japanese] fascism was not for export, and the collaboration and the sensibilities of the conquered peoples were of relatively little concern" to the conquerors.[19] What this meant for countries and territories occupied by Japan we

---

18. See, for instance, My-Van, "Japan and Vietnam's Caodaists"; Kwartanada, "Competition, Patriotism and Collaboration"; Barrett and Shyu, eds., *Chinese Collaboration with Japan, 1932–1945*; Coble, *Chinese Capitalists in Japan's New Order.*

19. Wolfe, "The Development of Nazi Monetary Policy," 400.

know from their rates of inflation: "From the beginning of the Pacific War to the end of the War, the amount of currency issued in the several regions [of the Greater East-Asian Financial Sphere] increased, and the price index [of these regions] shows an identical pattern. Yet, one should not lose sight of the fact that this increase took the form of a rising wave, originating in the center and growing toward the periphery [. . .]. Comparing the outset of the war with its end, prices in Tokyo rose by a factor of one-and-a-half, whereas they rose extraordinarily [elsewhere], i.e., by a factor of 350 in Singapore, and by a factor of 1,850 in Rangoon."[20]

The Great Financial Freeze

Monetary and financial control within the bloc should, however, not be confused with real power and leverage in the world economy. It was rather a symptom of the yen's weakness as a hard currency. Kanō Hisaakira, at the time head of the London branch of the YSB, saw disaster looming, as the epigraph to this chapter shows. Yet even a man as well placed as he was did not realize the extent to which finance was his country's Achilles' heel. In his view, Freda Utley and other "so-called Far-Eastern experts" in Great Britain were "the mouthpiece of Chunking propaganda" and had a poor understanding of Japan's real industrial and financial strength.[21] Yet his attempts to convince British authorities not to follow the American course of action with regard to Japan were of no avail.

In any case, these attempts came too late. Several years before, in 1937, the bombing and sinking of the gunboat U.S.S. *Panay* by Japanese naval aircraft had prompted the Roosevelt administration to investigate the possibility of financial sanctions against Japan.[22] The idea of launching economic warfare to combat Japanese imperialist designs had originated much earlier, after the Russo-Japanese War.[23] Yet after 1937, Roosevelt and his loyal Secretary of the Treasury Henry Morgenthau, Jr., became convinced that the key to stemming Japanese expansionism was to be found in the money markets. Such a conviction fitted perfectly

---

20. Yamamoto, "'Dai tōa kin'yūken' ron," 19; compare statistical tables on p. 20.

21. Kano, *My London Records*, 5.

22. For visual material about the *Panay* incident, see http://www.usspanay.org (accessed April 16, 2009).

23. See Miller, *Bankrupting the Enemy*; for the "siege plan," see Miller, *War Plan Orange*.

with the American perception of Japan's geopolitical situation and vulnerabilities. After the invasion of China in 1937, the Treasury Department, the Federal Reserve, and several other officials of the Roosevelt administration were unanimous (and correct) in their assessment: the war with China would cause Japan's trade balance outside the yen bloc to plunge into deficit because of the diversion from civilian to military production, along with Japan's complicated credit situation. The Americans went on to assert that this would lead to the total depletion of foreign exchange reserves and soon exhaust Japan financially. This predicttion of Japan's imminent bankruptcy (shared by all departments of the administration) prevented the U.S. government from inquiring further into the possibility of a financial freeze. Instead, it embarked on the well-known strategy of an embargo, denying Tokyo access to war materiel.

This policy abruptly changed in August 1940, when officials of the Federal Reserve Bank of New York discovered irregularities in the bookkeeping of the New York branch office of the Yokohama Specie Bank (YSBNY). After further inquiry and talks with the head agent of YSBNY, they came to the conclusion that the bank had shrewdly misled U.S. officials about its movements of international capital. What Japan—through the New York office of this semi-governmental bank—had been trying to conceal was a sophisticated plot to hide a giant war chest of dollars under the noses of the American watchdogs. The former assertions of "imminent bankruptcy" had to be revised, as the fraudulently hidden foreign exchange reserve amounted to more than $100 million in cash and U.S. Treasury securities. Contrary to earlier assumptions, the Japanese war machine was far from exhausted. If its ambitions were not checked, Japan "could go on almost indefinitely."[24]

Only very recently (many of the relevant documents were declassified only in 1996) has Edward S. Miller managed to trace how the Roosevelt administration swiftly awakened the slumbering policy of financial pressure.[25] Within a few months of discovering the YSBNY fraud, administration officials evaluated the size of the cache, drew up reports on the vulnerability of Japanese exports to and imports from the United States, and established the bureaucratic parameters for a financial siege.

---

24. Miller, *Bankrupting the Enemy*, 106.
25. Ibid.

On August 25, 1941, one decision in Washington made the (already inconvertible) yen illiquid, that is not acceptable for payments outside the yen bloc, thereby effectively choking the country's highly import-dependent economy. Wary of an asset freeze, Tokyo had scrambled to get the money out of the United States, but by then it was already too late. Perceiving the asset freeze as a lethal threat,[26] Japan chose the unfortunate path of an extremely costly war against a much more powerful enemy. Of Kanō's apocalyptic predictions, only social revolution did not materialize.

Striving for Economic Independence

How do these events add to our understanding of prewar Japanese money doctoring and, in a wider perspective, Japan's (pre- and postwar) visions of its financial status? What was the driving force undergirding the temporary and regionally disparate experiments with currency imperialism? Much has already been written about the country's "dependent imperialism"—that Japan, while establishing its spheres of influence and building its empire in East Asia, was heavily dependent on foreign capital. As a historical paradigm, dependent imperialism has been employed to set Japan apart from traditional, Marxist explanations of imperialism: there was no surplus capital here that was naturally driven to conquer new markets. But it is easy to lose sight of how utterly improbable Japan's path of expansionism actually was.

Financial issues in particular highlight its precarious and paradoxical nature. Tactics such as borrowing from the Western powers in order to lend to Asian countries or regions Tokyo perceived as important to its political and economic security (which also appeared inconsistent to Japanese policy makers at the time) developed into a pattern. In the cases of Korea, China, and especially Manchuria, such policies employed in different phases of the country's prewar history often functioned as a prelude to more heavy-handed political or military intervention. Yet

---

26. Compare Kanō's remarks (*My London Records*, 13 and 20): "When the U.S.A. and Britain decided to freeze Japan's assets, I told many visitors—chiefly City friends and reporters of the press—at my office, 'this is war.' [. . .] Economic warfare was interpreted by Britain as a more humane measure than actual war. But to a country like Japan, whose industries must rely on the raw materials of the Anglo-American countries, and whose shipping business extends all over the world, this measure is as cruel as the bombing."

this pattern should not deter us from distinguishing among phases in Japan's attempts to combat the problems arising from its difficult financial position. Its experiments with yen diplomacy yielded quite varied outcomes. And these experiments were formulated by diverse political constituencies—including personalities as different as the aristocratic Megata, the quixotic Nishihara, and the technocratic Nangō.

Only a broader ideological frame of reference, an encompassing and self-maintaining set of geopolitical perceptions held by Japanese policy makers, can explain why financial imperialism was adopted by a wide range of political factions and administrations and why it provided tactics that could be resorted to at different phases of Japanese expansionism. This underlying ideological thread was probably not anticommunism. Although it was certainly generic to consecutive administrations and beyond doubt a factor in designing domestic policies, resistance to communism does not offer sufficient explanation for such actions as the monetary occupation of Korea. At no time do the reports of the First Bank or of Megata's aides hint at the need to establish a capitalist bastion against Marxist revolutionaries; neither were such concerns voiced by reformers in Northern China. Pan-Asianism, too, is highly improbable as the central ideology driving these decisions. Pan-Asianist ideas captured only a limited part of the political spectrum, and many economic policy makers (the best example being Takahashi Korekiyo) actively opposed them because of their irrational presuppositions and objectives.

Instead, the recurrent theme across all administrations in this period was Japan's strategic vulnerability and the relative rise of the United States as a formidable power with a potentially self-sufficient economy. These global developments posed a dilemma for the Japanese authorities. Would they be able to adopt Washington's outlook on geopolitical events and employ its universalist rhetoric, thereby denying Japan's disadvantageous strategic position? Or should they combat the rise of American hegemony and try to reverse the expansion of American influence in Asia? This dilemma resulted in an overarching preoccupation with the limits of Japanese autonomy. Indeed, the ideological fixation of Japan's leaders with balancing on the fine line between autonomy and dependence produced an unavoidable paradox: a certain degree of dependence had to be accepted in order to create a certain degree of relative autonomy. As long as Tokyo accepted that the world's monetary geography was dominated by an Anglo-American center, it could carve out a space in which Japan could function as the point of orientation for a political and economic "sub-bloc." But if it resorted to unilateralist decision making and acted solely on its impulse toward autonomy, the carefully balanced house of cards tumbled down. Opting for autonomy created *more* dependence rather than less: international isolation literally discredited Japan's intentions, by lowering the country's political and financial good standing with other countries, or, as in the case of the second Sino-Japanese War, causing its credit to evaporate altogether.

Aftermath

In retrospect, the attempt to build a "new order" after the example of Nazi Germany was doomed to fail. World War II was not just the failure of Japan's political system; it also represented the defeat of "bloc-ism" as a monetary and financial ideology. Incapable of going against the course of world events, Japan and the yen had come full circle. In the words of Fukuzawa Yukichi, Japan was first determined to "leave Asia"; then withdrew into its own sphere, only to experience national humiliation; then it left Asia again, as a linchpin for the dollar standard.[27]

This leaves the crucial question of how to understand the relationship between wartime and postwar realities. Does the postwar situation represent a linear development or a break with the past? Although American-led reform in the occupation years effectively rid Japan of militarist and fascist institutions, there were significant continuities as well. Kobayashi Hideo has famously argued that there are striking similarities in institutional setup and even personnel between the research bureau of the SMRC and the team of bureaucrats responsible for the economic growth spurt in the early fifties.[28] Less provocative but equally illuminating is the view, now shared by most historians, that the mindset behind Japan's spectacular economic growth and technological development continues to be informed by anxiety about the country's strategic vulnerability.[29]

---

27. Metzler, "The Road to the Dollar Standard."
28. Kobayashi, *Manshū to Jimintō.*
29. See, for instance, Samuels, *"Rich Country, Strong Army."*

Monetary matters are much less straightforward and have certainly received far less attention from historians. At first sight, it is easy to conclude that the American military victory translated into the monetary subordination of the yen to the U.S. dollar. To a certain degree (and for a certain period of time), this is a valid assessment. This currency dominance also was what the occupation authorities seemed to have in mind. After the war, Japan's overseas trade was severely constrained, and a complex and often arbitrary system of multiple exchange rates (administratively managed for various kinds of import and export products) came into being. In the very early occupation, the U.S. dollar even functioned as the only currency for foreign exchange—a clear symbol of American dominance in all parts of Japan's social fabric. Only in 1948 did a Federal Reserve Mission recommend abolishing the system of multiple exchange rates and establishing a monetary arrangement that looked very much like a gold-exchange standard. The Bretton Woods agreement, concluded in 1944, made the dollar the only currency convertible into gold, and then only at the request of foreign monetary authorities.[30] Negotiations were now underway with the aim of linking the yen to the dollar at a rate in the neighborhood of ¥300 = $1. American money doctoring on Japanese shores did not end there. Only months after the Federal Reserve Mission visited Tokyo, the Detroit banker Joseph Dodge carried out his Economic Stabilization Plan (ESP), with the objective of wringing inflation out of the Japanese economy. Arguably successful, the Dodge line, as it was called, was nevertheless one of the most draconian stabilization programs ever to be effected in the postwar period. Such a program could have been implemented only under the authoritarian semi-military oversight of the occupation authorities.[31]

The relationship between the U.S. dollar and the Japanese yen was unambiguously asymmetric only until 1952. After that, the yen remained linked to the dollar (at the rate of ¥360 = $1),[32] but Japan's government regained much of its monetary and financial autonomy relative to its American peer. Yet once Japan's spectacular postwar economic growth started to gain steam, the yen-dollar relationship became muddled and

---

30. Thus it makes more sense to refer to a dollar standard than a gold-exchange standard.

31. See Takemae et al., *The Allied Occupation of Japan*, esp. 469ff.

32. See Itō, *Sengo Nihon no taigai kin'yū*.

fraught with paradox.[33] The reason for this confusion lay in the very syntax of the Bretton Woods agreement. Long before Japan's trade surpluses exploded, the Belgian economist Robert Triffin had pointed out that making a national currency into the reserve currency of the world was actually self-contradictory.[34] The key to understanding this is the balance of payments of the country supplying the world's currency. It is a classic example of a policy dilemma (and indeed, it is known as the Triffin dilemma): On the one hand, if such a country (in this case, the United States) rules out the possibility of balance-of-payments deficits, the international community would lose its largest source of additions to reserves. The resulting shortage of liquidity (an extremely strong dollar) could pull the world economy into a contractionary spiral, leading to instability. On the other hand, if such a country chooses to run deficits, a steady stream of its currency would continue to fuel world economic growth. Yet there would be an expensive price tag: excessive deficits (a "dollar glut") would erode confidence in the value of its currency, which would be considered to be overvalued. Then it would no longer be accepted as the world's reserve currency. The fixed exchange-rate system could break down, also leading to instability.

To put this into practice: dollars must both overall flow *out* of the United States and flow *into* the United States, but both cannot happen at once. John Maynard Keynes, the main architect of the Bretton Woods agreement, had foreseen this problem, and had therefore resisted the idea of using U.S. dollars as the world's reserve currency. Instead, he proposed *bancor*, a world currency unit the value of which was to be determined on the basis of 30 commodities, only one of which was gold. American negotiators rejected this proposal, foreseeing a world in which the United States would continue to run balance-of-payments surpluses. However, Keynes's idea still stands. In the wake of the "second great contraction," which started with the 2007 subprime crisis, Governor of the Bank of China Zhao Xiaochuan suggested the adoption of IMF Special Drawing Rights (SDRs) as a global reserve currency in

---

33. This is the topic of many of the writings by Taggart Murphy. See his *The Weight of the Yen* and Mikuni, Murphy, and Armacost, *Japan's Policy Trap*.

34. A similar understanding is echoed by former U.S. Secretary of the Treasury Henry H. Fowler: "Providing reserves and exchanges for the whole world is too much for one country and one currency to bear."

response to the financial crisis.[35] For any national currency attempting to function as the world's currency, tension will arise between achieving domestic monetary policy goals and meeting other countries' demand for reserve currency.

Tokyo's postwar monetary policy making in the era of mounting U.S. trade deficits was very peculiar and its implications are, even today, not fully understood. Japan's trade surplus, which accounted for the lion's share of the U.S deficit, actually promoted the yen to a currency of global prominence. Yet Tokyo, accustomed to doing business and making money under U.S. hegemony and extremely anxious about seeing its currency play a stabilizing role in the world economy—which presupposed the free availability of the yen in world financial markets, and hence, uncontrollability of its exchange rate—opted to step back from assuming this role. In the words of one commentator, "this was not a country ready to run the planet."[36] Using mechanisms such as exchange rate manipulation, Japan continued to prop up the dollar until the "Nixon shocks" ended the convertibility of the dollar into gold; then, a panoply of other financial technologies was used to intervene in foreign-exchange rates. Consecutive administrations in Washington have kept their part of the deal, running up a trade deficit that, in 2009, reached a historic $1.75 trillion. Although the dollar nowadays has all the characteristics of a currency in decline, there is still no alternative in sight to its role as the "world's currency."[37]

Economists have speculated about why Tokyo has maintained this extraordinary and ultimately paradoxical policy course. Lack of leadership is part of the explanation: playing the role of a hegemon requires more than just pumping out yen, as for instance the First Gulf War made clear. Being a leader of nations also implies something less tangible, a self-confidence that one's way of doing things is right and provides an example worth emulating. Of course, Japan's policy is also about yen. To become a leader would mean giving up efforts to control exchange rates and to be, in monetary terms, "in and of the world." But Japan's economic policy is also shaped by historical memory, and this may be where the tensions between the pre- and postwar periods

35. Zhou Xiaochuan, "Reform the International Monetary System."
36. Murphy, *The Weight of the Yen*, 225.
37. See Eichengreen, *Global Imbalances and the Lessons from Bretton Woods*.

are most sharply articulated. In the whole of East Asia, memories of World War II still stand in the way of realizing a stronger regional function for the yen. Tokyo has shown some willingness to play a stronger role in the region, only to find that, whereas its yen was welcome, even the slightest hint of a Pax Nipponica was not.

Although statues of the likes of Megata have long disappeared from East Asian cityscapes, the ghosts of the prewar Japanese money doctors continue to haunt the scenario of an international financial order with a stronger monetary financial role for Japan—and this at a time when such a development is not only possible but also desirable. Exorcizing these ghosts would help turn the page to begin a new story.

Reference Matter

Works Cited

Alacevich, Michele, and Pier Francesco Asso. "Money Doctoring After World War II: Arthur I. Bloomfield and the Federal Reserve Missions to South Korea." *History of Political Economy* 41:2 (2009): 249–70.

Allen, George Cyril. *Japan's Economic Policy.* New York: Holmes and Meier, 1980.

Amess, Kevin, and Panicos Demetriades. "Financial Liberalisation and the South Korean Financial Crisis: Some Qualitative Evidence." Discussion Papers in Economics 01/3. Department of Economics, University of Leicester, 2001.

Amyx, Jennifer. "Moving Beyond Bilateralism? Japan and the Asian Monetary Fund." Governance Working Papers 379. East Asian Bureau of Economic Research, 2002.

Anderton, Douglas L., and Richard E. Barrett. "Demographic Seasonality and Development: The Effects of Agricultural Colonialism in Taiwan, 1906–1942." *Demography* 27:3 (1990): 397–411.

Andrew, A. Piatt. "The End of the Mexican Dollar." *Quarterly Journal of Economics* 18:3 (1904): 321–56.

Bank of Chosen. *Economic History of Chosen.* Seoul: Bank of Chosen, 1920.

———. *Economic History of Manchuria.* Seoul: Bank of Chosen, 1921.

———. *Pictorial Chosen and Manchuria.* Seoul: Bank of Chosen, 1919.

Barrett, David, and Larry Shyu, eds. *Chinese Collaboration with Japan, 1932–1945: The Limits of Accommodation.* Stanford, CA: Stanford University Press, 2001.

Barro, R., and J.-W. Lee. "IMF Programs: Who Is Chosen and What Are the Effects?" NBER Working Paper 9851, May 2002.

Bau, Mingchien Joshua. *The Open Door Doctrine in Relation to China.* New York: Macmillan, 1923.

Beasley, William Gerald. *Japanese Imperialism 1894–1945.* Oxford, UK: Clarendon Press, 1992.

Berger, Gordon Mark. *Parties Out of Power in Japan, 1931–1941.* Princeton, NJ: Princeton University Press, 1977.

Bernanke, Ben. *Essays on the Great Depression.* Princeton, NJ: Princeton University Press, 2004.

Bix, Herbert P. "Japanese Imperialism and the Manchurian Economy, 1900–31." *China Quarterly* 51 (1972): 425–43.

Bloch, Kurt. "Warlordism: A Transitory Stage in Chinese Government." *American Journal of Sociology* 43:5 (March 1938): 691–703.

Boody, Elizabeth. "Manchoukuo, the Key to Japan's Foreign Exchange Problem." *Far Eastern Survey* 6:10 (May 12, 1937): 107–12.

———. "Politics and the Yen." *Far Eastern Survey* 6:11 (May 26, 1937): 117–22.

Borg, Dorothy. *The United States and the Far Eastern Crisis of 1933–1938: From the Manchurian Incident Through the Initial Stage of the Undeclared Sino-Japanese War.* Cambridge, MA: Harvard University Press, 1964.

Braisted, William R. "China, the United States Navy, and the Bethlehem Steel Company, 1909–1929." *Business History Review* 42:1 (Spring 1968): 50–66.

Brandt, Loren, and Thomas Sargent. "Interpreting New Evidence About China and U.S. Silver Purchases." *Journal of Monetary Economics* 23:1 (January 1989): 31–51.

Bratter, Herbert M. "The Role of Subsidies in Japan's Economic Development." *Pacific Affairs* 4:5 (May, 1931): 377–93.

———. "The Silver Episode." *Journal of Political Economy* 46:5 (1938), 609–52

Brown, Sidney Devere and Akiko Hirota, trans. *Diary of Kido Takayoshi 1868–1871.* Tokyo: University of Tokyo Press, 1983.

Burdekin, Richard K. "U.S. Pressure on China's Currency: Milton Friedman and the Silver Episode Revisited." Claremont Institute of Economic Policy Studies. Available online at http://www.claremontmckenna.edu/econ/papers/2005-07.pdf (accessed May 17 2010).

Burkman, Thomas W. *Japan and the League of Nations: Empire and World Order, 1914–1938.* Honolulu, HI: University of Hawai'i Press, 2007.

Byas, Hugh. *Government by Assassination.* New York: Afred A. Knopf, 1942.

Campbell, Charles S., Jr. *Special Business Interests and the Open Door Policy.* New Haven, CT: Yale University Press, 1951.

Campbell, Colin D., and Chung Shick Ahn. "Kyes and Mujins: Financial Intermediaries in South Korea." *Economic Development and Cultural Change* 11:1 (October 1962): 55–68.

Central Bank of Manchou. *The Central Bank of Manchou and Appendix of Laws Pertaining Thereto.* Hsinking: Central Bank of Manchou, 1935.

Cha, Myung Soo. "Imperial Policy or World Price Shocks? Explaining Interwar Korean Consumption Trend." *Journal of Economic History* 58:3 (September 1998): 731–54.

Chaïkin, Nathan. *The Sino-Japanese War, 1894–1895: The Noted Basil Chamberlain Collection and a Private Collection.* Venthône: privately published, 1983.

Chan, K. C. "British Policy in the Reorganization Loan to China 1912–1913." *Modern Asian Studies* 5:4 (November 1964): 355–72.

Chi, Ch'ao-ting. "China's Monetary Reform in Perspective." *Far Eastern Survey* 6:17 (Augustus 18, 1937): 189–96.

Chien, Frederick Foo. *The Opening of Korea: A Study of Chinese Diplomacy, 1876–1885.* Hamden, CT: Shoestring Press, 1967.

Ching, Leo T. S. *Becoming Japanese: Colonial Taiwan and the Politics of Identity Formation.* Berkeley, CA: University of California Press, 2001.

———. "Savage Construction and Civility Making: Japanese Colonialism and Taiwanese Aboriginal Representation." *Positions: East Asia Cultures Critique* 8:3 (Winter 2000): 795–818.

Cho Ki-jun 趙璣濬. *Kindai Kankoku keizaishi* 近代韓国経済史 (An economic history of modern Korea). Tokyo: Kōrai shorin, 1981.

Cho, Yoon Je. "The Role of Poorly Phased Financial Liberalization in Korea's Financial Crisis." In *Financial Liberalization: How Far, How Fast?*, ed. Gerard Caprio, Patrick Honohan, and Joseph E. Stiglitz, 159–87. Cambridge and New York: Cambridge University Press, 2001.

Chōsen sōtokufu 朝鮮総督府. *Chōsen tetsudōshi* 朝鮮鉄道史 (A history of railways in Korea). Seoul: Chōsen tetsudōkyoku, 1915.

Chung, Duck-Koo, and Barry Eichengreen. *The Korean Economy Beyond the Crisis.* Cheltenham, UK: Edward Elgar, 2004.

Chung, Young-Iob. *Korea Under Siege, 1876–1945: Capital Formation and Economic Transformation.* New York: Oxford University Press, 2006.

Coble, Parks M. *Chinese Capitalists in Japan's New Order: The Occupied Lower Yangzi, 1937–1945.* Berkeley, CA: University of California Press, 2003.

Commission on International Exchange. *Report on the Introduction of the Gold-Exchange Standard into China, the Philippine Islands, Panama, and Other Silver-Using Countries.* Washington, DC: G.P.O., 1904.

Conant, Charles. "The Economic Basis of Imperialism." *North American Review* 167: 502 (September 1898): 326–41.

———. "The Gold Exchange Standard in the Light of Experience." *Economic Journal*, 19:74 (June 1909): 190–200.

———. *A History of Banks of Issue.* New York and London: G. P. Putnam, 1915 [1896].

Conroy, Hilary. *The Japanese Seizure of Korea, 1868–1910: A Study of Realism and Idealism in International Relations.* Philadelphia, PA: University of Pennsylvania Press, 1960.

Cook, Harold Francis. *Korea's 1884 Incident: Its Background and Kim Okkyun's Elusive Dream.* Seoul: Royal Asiatic Society, 1972.

Crist, David S. "Russia's Far Eastern Policy in the Making." *Journal of Modern History* 14:3 (September 1942): 317–41.

Daiichi ginkō 第一銀行. "Kabushiki gaisha Daiichi ginkō Kankoku kakuten shutchōsho kaigyō irai eigyō jōkyō" 株式会社第一銀行韓国各店出張所開業以来営業状況 (The state of the First Bank after the establishment of branches and agencies on the Korean peninsula). Yonsan, no date.

———. *Kankoku kahei seiri hōkokusho* 韓国貨幣整理報告書 (Report on the adjustment of Korean currency). Yonsan, 1909.

Daiichi ginkō 80-nenshi hensanshitsu 第一銀行８０年史編纂室, ed. *Daiichi ginkōshi* 第一銀行史 (The history of the Bank of Chosen). Tokyo: Daiichi ginkō, 1957–58.

Dallek, Robert. *Franklin D. Roosevelt and American Foreign Policy, 1932–1945.* Oxford, UK: Oxford University Press, 1979.

Davis, Clarence B. "Limits of Effacement: Britain and the Problem of American Cooperation and Competition in China, 1915–1917." *Pacific Historical Review* 48:1 (February 1979): 47–63.

Demetriades, Panicos, Bassam Fattouh, and Kalvinder Shields. "Financial Liberalization and the Evolution of Banking and Financial Risks: The Case of South Korea." Department of Economics, University of Leicester, Discussion Papers in Economics 01/1 (2001).

Dennett, Tyler. "The Lytton Report." *American Political Science Review* 26:6 (December 1932): 1148–51.

———. "The Open Door Policy as Intervention." *Annals of the American Academy of Political and Social Science* 168 (July 1933): 78–83.

Deuchler, Martina. *Confucian Gentlemen and Barbarian Envoys: The Opening of Korea, 1875–1885.* Seattle, WA: University of Washington Press, 1977.

Dickinson, Frederick R. *War and National Reinvention: Japan in the Great War, 1914–1919.* Cambridge, MA: Harvard University Asia Center, 1999.

Dower, John. "Peace and Democracy in Two Systems: External Policy and Internal Conflict." In *Postwar Japan as History*, ed. Andrew Gordon, 3–33. Berkeley, CA: University of California Press, 1993.

Drake, Paul. *Money Doctors, Foreign Debts, and Economic Reforms in Latin America from the 1890s to the Present.* Wilmington: SR Books, 1993.

Dull, Paul S. "The Assassination of Chang Tso-lin." *Far Eastern Quarterly* 11:4 (August 1952): 453–63.

———. "Count Kato Komei and the Twenty-One Demands." *Pacific Historical Review* 19:2 (May 1950): 151–61.

Duus, Peter. *The Abacus and the Sword: The Japanese Penetration of Korea, 1895–1910.* Berkeley, CA: University of California Press, 1995.

―――. "Economic Dimensions of Meiji Imperialism: The Case of Korea." In *Japanese Colonial Empire*, ed. Ramon Myers and Mark Peattie, 128–71. Princeton, NJ: Princeton University Press, 1984.

Duus, Peter, Ramon H. Myers, and Mark R. Peattie, eds. *The Japanese Informal Empire in China, 1895–1937*. Princeton, NJ: Princeton University Press, 1989.

Earl of Lytton. "The Problem of Manchuria." *International Affairs* (Royal Institute of International Affairs 1931–1939) 11:6 (November 1932): 737–56.

Eckert, Carter. *Offspring of Empire: The Koch'ang Kims and the Colonial Origins of Korean Capitalism*. Seattle, WA: University of Washington Press, 1991.

Eckstein, Alexander, Kang Chao, and John Chang. "The Economic Development of Manchuria: The Rise of a Frontier Economy." *Journal of Economic History* 34:1 (March 1974): 239–64.

Edwards, E. W. *British Diplomacy and Finance in China*. Cambridge, MA: Harvard University Press, 1987.

Eichengreen, Barry. *Global Imbalances and the Lessons from Bretton Woods*. Cambridge, MA: MIT Press, 2010.

―――. *Golden Fetters: The Gold Standard and the Great Depression, 1919–1939*. Oxford, UK: Oxford University Press, 1996.

―――. "House Calls of the Money Doctor: The Kemmerer Missions to Latin America, 1917–1931." In *Money Doctors, Foreign Debts, and Economic Reforms in Latin America from the 1890s to the Present*, ed. Paul Drake, 110–32. Wilmington, DE: SR BOOKS, 1993.

Einaudi, Luca. "The Theory of Imaginary Money from Charlemagne to the French Revolution." Trans. Giorgio Tagliacozzo. In *Enterprise and Secular Change*, ed. Frederic C. Lane and Jelle C. Riemersma, 229–61. London: Allen and Unwin, 1953.

Elliott, Charles Burke. "The Shantung Question." *American Journal of International Law* 13:4 (October 1919): 687–737.

Ericson, Steven. *The Sound of the Whistle: Railroads and the State in Meiji Japan*. Cambridge, MA: Council on East Asian Studies, Harvard University, 1996.

Esthus, Raymond A. "The Changing Concept of the Open Door, 1899–1910." *Mississippi Valley Historical Review* 46:3 (December 1959): 435–54.

Fan Yuan-Lien. "Eastern Trends in the New Sciences: The China Foundation for the Promotion of Education and Culture." *News Bulletin* (Institute of Pacific Relations) (December 1927): 17–20.

Faure, David. "The Plight of the Farmers: A Study of the Rural Economy of Jiangnan and the Pearl River Delta, 1870–1937." *Modern China* 11:1 (January 1985): 3–37.

Ferber, Katalin. "'Run the State Like a Business': The Origin of the Deposit Fund in Meiji Japan." *Japanese Studies* 22:2 (September 2002): 131–51.

Ferrell, Robert. "The Mukden Incident: September 18–19, 1931." *Journal of Modern History* 27:1 (March 1955): 66–72.

Fetter, Frank Whitson. "Lenin, Keynes and Inflation." *Economica New Series* 44 (February 1977): 77–80.

Field, Frederick V. *American Participation in the China Consortiums*. Chicago, IL: University of Chicago Press, 1931.

Finch, George A. "Remission of the Chinese Indemnity." *American Journal of International Law* 18:3 (July 1924): 544–48.

Flandreau, Marc. *Money Doctors: The Experience of Financial Advising, 1850–2000*. London and New York: Routledge, 2003.

Friedman, Milton. "Franklin D. Roosevelt, and China." *Journal of Political Economy* 100:1 (February 1992): 62–83.

Friedman, Milton, and Anna Jacobson Schwartz. *A Monetary History of the United States, 1867–1960*. Princeton, NJ: Princeton University Press, 1963.

Fung, Edmund S. K. "The Chinese Nationalists and the Unequal Treaties 1924–1931." *Modern Asian Studies* 21:4 (1987): 793–819.

Gaimushō 外務省. *Nihon gaikō bunsho* 日本外交文書 (Japanese diplomatic documents) (multiple volumes).

Gaimushō tsūshōkyoku 外務省通商局. "Keijō ryōjikan hōkoku" 京城領事館報告 (Report of the imperial Japanese consulate in Seoul). *Tsūshō isan* 通商彙纂, no. 60 (September 21, 1905): 14–17.

Gallagher, John, and Ronald Robinson. "The Imperialism of Free Trade." *Economic History Review*, New Series 6:1 (1953): 1–15.

Garnett, Porter. "The History of the Trade Dollar." *American Economic Review* 7:1 (March 1917): 91–97.

Gay, Suzanne. *The Moneylenders of Late Medieval Kyoto*. Honolulu, HI: University of Hawai'i Press, 2001.

Gerson, Jack J. *Horatio Nelson Lay and Sino-British Relations, 1854–1864*. Cambridge, MA: East Asia Research Center, Harvard University, 1972.

Graggert, Edwin H. *Landownership Under Colonial Rule: Korea's Japanese Experience, 1900–1935*. Honolulu, HI: University of Hawai'i Press, 1994.

Grajdanzev, A. J. "Formosa (Taiwan) Under Japanese Rule." *Pacific Affairs* 15:3 (September 1942): 311–24.

Green, Elizabeth. "Crisis in Manchuria." *Pacific Affairs* 4:11 (November 1931): 1005–13.

Griffith, Elliott. *Corea, the Hermit Nation*. New York: Charles Scribner's Sons, 1882.

———. "Corea, the Hermit Nation." *Journal of the American Geographical Society of New York* 13 (1881): 125–32.

Hagiwara Hikozō 萩原彦三. *Kankoku zaisei no seiri kaikaku -zaisei komon Megata Tanetarō no gyōseki* 韓国財政の整理改革：財政顧問目賀田種太郎の業績

(The reform plan of Korean finance: the works of financial adviser Megata Tanetarō). Tokyo: Yūhō kyōkai, 1966.

Hanna, Hugh H., Charles A. Conant, and Jeremiah W. Jenks. *Gold Standard in International Trade: Report on the Introduction of the Gold-Exchange Standard into China, the Philippine Islands, Panama, and Other Silver-Using Countries and on the Stability of Exchange.* Washington: G.P.O, 1904.

"The Harvard Debt Doctor's Controversial Cure." *Time,* November 6, 1989, 66.

Hatano Yoshihiro 波多野善大. *Chūgoku kindai gunbatsu no kenkyū* 中国近代軍閥の研究 (An inquiry into modern China's military cliques). Tokyo: Kawade shobō shinsha, 1973.

Hatori Yoshihiko 羽鳥敬彦. *Chōsen ni okeru shokuminchi heisei no seiritsu* 朝鮮に於ける植民地幣制の成立 (The formation of a colonial currency system in Korea). Tokyo: Miraisha, 1986.

Hayashi Gonsuke 林権助. *Waga 70-nen o kataru* わが七十年を語る (Telling 70 years of my life). Tokyo: Daiichi shobō, 1935.

Hekiyōkai 碧榕会, ed. *Yagyū tōdori no hen'ei* 柳生頭取の片影 (Glimpses of director Yagyū). Tokyo: Hekiyōkai, 1917.

Helleiner, Eric. *The Making of National Money: Territorial Currencies in Historical Perspective.* Ithaca, NY: Cornell University Press, 2002.

Heller, Walter W. "The Role of Fiscal-Monetary Policy in German Economic Recovery." *American Economic Review* 40:2 (Papers and Proceedings of the Sixty-Second Annual Meeting of the American Economic Association) (May 1950): 531–47.

Higuchi Hiroshi 樋口弘. *Nihon no tai-Shi tōshi kenkyū* 日本の対支投資研究 (An inquiry into Japanese investments in China). Tokyo: Seikatsusha, 1939.

Hijikata Susumu 土方晋. *Yokohama shōkin ginkō* 横浜正金銀行 (The Yokohama Specie Bank). Tokyo: Kyōikusha, 1980.

H. I. J. M. (His Imperial Japanese Majesty's) Residency General. *Annual Report for 1907 on Reforms and Progress in Korea.* Seoul: Government-General of Chosen, 1908.

———. *The Second Annual Report on Reforms and Progress in Korea (1908–1909).* Seoul: Government-General of Chosen, 1909.

Hitch, Margaret A. "The Port of Tientsin and Its Problems." *Geographical Review* 25:3 (July 1935): 367–81.

Ho, Samuel Pao-San. "Agricultural Transformation Under Colonialism: The Case of Taiwan." *Journal of Economic History* 28:3 (September 1968): 313–40.

Ho, Y. M. *Agricultural Development of Taiwan 1903–1960.* Nashville, TN: Vanderbilt University Press, 1966.

Hollander, J.H. "The Finances of Porto Rico." *Political Science Quarterly* 16:6 (December 1901): 553–81.

Hori Kazuo 堀和生. "East Asia Between the Two World Wars: Industrialization of Japan and Its Ex-Colonies." *Kyoto University Economic Review* 137 (1994): 1–22.

———. "Nihon teikokushugi no Chōsen shokuminchika katei ni okeru zaisei henkaku" 日本帝国主義の朝鮮植民地化過程における財政変革 (Financial reforms in the process of colonizing Korea under Japanese imperial rule). *Nihonshi kenkyū* 日本史研究 217 (September 1980): 1–38.

Hoshino Naoki 星野直樹. *Mihatenu yume* 見果てぬ夢 (Dreaming an impossible dream). Tokyo: Daiyamondosha, 1963.

Hotta, Eri. *Pan-Asianism and Japan's War, 1931–1945*. New York: Palgrave Macmillan, 2007.

Hunsberger, Warren S. "The Yen Bloc in Japan's Expansion Program." *Far Eastern Survey* VII: 22 (November 9, 1938): 251–58.

Hunt, Michael H. "The American Remission of the Boxer Indemnity: A Reappraisal." *Journal of Asian Studies* 31:3 (May 1972): 539–59.

———. "Americans in the China Market: Economic Opportunities and Economic Nationalism, 1890s–1931." *Business History Review* 51:3 (Autumn 1977): 277–307.

Hunter, Janet. "Japanese Government Policy, Business Opinion and the Seoul–Pusan Railway, 1894–1906." *Modern Asian Studies* 11:4 (1977): 573–99.

Ichibangase Yasuko 一番ヶ瀬康子. "Kome sōdō to Nihon shakai jigyō" 米騒動と日本社会事業 (The rice riots and Japanese social work). *Nihon joshi daigaku kiyō* 日本女子大学紀要 20 (1970): 35–47.

Ichikawa Masaaki 市川正明. *Nisshin sensō* 日清戦争(The Sino-Japanese War). Tokyo: Hara shobō, 1979.

Iklé, Frank W. "The Triple Intervention: Japan's Lesson in the Diplomacy of Imperialism." *Monumenta Nipponica* 22:1–2 (1967): 122–30.

Imada Noriya 今田治弥. "Taiwan ginkō no ichidanmen: Suzuki shōten to no kankei" 台湾銀行の一断面：鈴木商店との関係 (A cross-section of the Bank of Taiwan: its relationship with the Suzuki Trading Company). *Kin'yū keizai* 金融経済 (December 1966): 131–43.

Inoue Junnosuke. *Problems of the Japanese Exchange, 1914–1926*. London: Macmillan, 1931.

Inoue Kaoru kō denki hensankai 井上馨侯伝記編纂会, ed. *Segai Inoue Kō den* 世外井上公傳 (The life of the exalted Duke Inoue). 5 vols. Tokyo: Naigai shoseki, 1933.

Iriye, Akira. "Chang Hsüeh-Liang and the Japanese." *Journal of Asian Studies* 20:1 (November 1960): 33–43.

Ishida Kōhei 石田興平. "Eikō ni okeru karogin no kichō to sono suii" 営口における過爐銀の基調とその推移 (The basic situation and changes of transfer money in Yingkou). *Hikone ronsō* 彦根論叢 88 (1962): 1–18.

———. "Eikō ni okeru karogin seido no seiritsu to kikō" 営口における過爐銀制度の成立と機構 (The formation and mechanism of transfer money in Yingkou). *Hikone ronsō* 彦根論叢 86 (1962): 1–12.

Ishida Takehiko 石田武彦. "Chūgoku tōhoku ni okeru ryōsan no dōkō: Manshū jihen mae ni okeru" 中国東北における糧桟の動向：満洲事変前における (Trends of the *liangzhan* in Northeast China: before the Manchurian incident). *Keizaigaku kenkyū* 経済学研究 24:1 (March 1974): 141–94.

Ishikawa Ryōta 石川亮太. "1910 nendai Manshū ni okeru Chōsenginkōken no ryūtsū to chiiki keizai" 1910 年代満州における朝鮮銀行券の流通と地域経済 (The circulation of Bank of Chosen paper money in Manchuria in the 1910s and the local economy). *Shakai keizai shigaku* 社會經濟史學 68:2 (July 2002): 127–44.

Israel, Jerry. "'For God, for China and for Yale': The Open Door in Action." *American Historical Review* 75:3 (February 1970): 796–807.

Itani Zen'ichi 猪谷善一. "Chōsen ni okeru kei no kenkyū" 朝鮮に於ける契の研究 (A study of the *kye* in Korea). In *Kindai Nihon kin'yūshi bunken shiryō shūsei* 近代日本金融史文献資料集成, ed. Takashima Masaaki 高嶋雅明 and Namikata Shōichi 波形昭一, vol. 38, 455–90. Tokyo: Nihon tosho, 2005.

Itō Masanao 伊藤正直. *Nihon no taigai kin'yū to kin'yū seisaku* 日本の対外金融と金融政策, 1914–1936 (Japan's international finance and financial policies, 1914–1936). Nagoya: Nagoya daigaku shuppankai, 1989.

———. *Sengo Nihon no taigai kin'yū: 360 en rēto no seiritsu to shūen* 戦後日本の対外金融：360 円レートの成立と終焉 (Japan's postwar international finance: the birth and demise of the 360 yen rate). Nagoya: Nagoya daigaku shuppankai, 2009.

Jansen, Marius B. "Yawata, Hanyehping, and the Twenty-One Demands." *Pacific Historical Review* 23:1 (February 1954): 31–48.

Japan. Special finance and economic commission to the United States, 1917–1918. *The Imperial Japanese Government's Special Finance and Economic Commission to the United States, headed by Baron Tanetaro Megata* (September 1917-April 1918). Tokyo: Tokyo Printing Company, 1918.

Jones, F. C. *Manchuria Since 1931.* London: Royal Institute of International Affairs, 1949.

Kaida Ikuo 戒田郁夫. *Meiji zenki ni okeru Nihon no kokusai hakkō to kokusaishisō* 明治前期における日本の国債発行と国債思想 (The floating of Japanese bonds in the early Meiji period and national loan ideology). Osaka: Kansai daigaku shuppanbu, 2003.

Kajima Morinosuke. *The Diplomacy of Japan 1894–1922, vol. 1: Sino-Japanese War and Triple Intervention.* Tokyo: Kajima Institute of International Peace, 1976.

Kamakura Takao 鎌倉孝夫. *Nihon teikoku shugi to shihon yushutsu* 日本帝国主義 と資本輸出 (Japanese imperialism and capital exports). Tokyo: Gendai hyōronsha, 1976.

Kaneko Fumio 金子文夫. "Dai ichiji taisenki ni okeru shokuminchi ginkō taikei no saihensei: Chōsen ginkō no "Manshū" shinshutsu o chūshin ni" 第 一次大戦期における植民地銀行体系の再編成：朝鮮銀行の「満 州」進出を中心に (The restructuring of the system of colonial banks during the First World War: with a focus on the Bank of Chosen's move into Manchuria). *Tochi seido shigaku* 土地制度史学 21: 2 (1979/01): 1–21.

―――. *Kindai Nihon ni okeru tai-Manshū tōshi no kenkyū* 近代日本における対 満州投資の研究 (An inquiry into modern Japanese investments in Manchuria). Tokyo: Kondō shuppansha, 1991.

―――. "Nichiro sengo no 'Manshū keiei' to Yokohama shōkin ginkō" 日露戦 後の「満州経営」と横浜正金銀行 (The "administration of Manchuria" after the Russo-Japanese War and the Yokohama Specie Bank). *Tochi seido shigaku* 土地制度史学 19:2 (1977/01): 28–52.

Kang, Chul Wong. "An Analysis of Japanese Policy and Economic Change in Korea." In *Korea Under Japanese Colonial Rule*, ed. Andrew Nahm, 77–88. Kalamazoo, MI: Western Michigan University, 1974.

Kang Tŏk-sang 姜徳相. "Chōsenkahei seiri jigyō ni kan suru kenkyū nōto"朝 鮮貨幣整理事業に関する研究ノート (A research note with respect to the adjustment of Korean currency). *Tsurugadai shigaku* 駿台史学 17 (September 1965): 119–27.

Kankoku seifu zaisei komonbu 韓国政府財政顧問部. *Kankoku zaisei seiri hōkoku* 韓国財政整理報告 (A report on the adjustment of Korean finance). Osaka: Kankoku seifu zaisei komonbu, 1905–1907.

Kano, Hisaakira. *My London Records*. Tokyo: Privately published, 1956.

Katada, Saori N. "Japan and Asian Monetary Regularisation: Cultivating a New Regional Leadership After the Asian Financial Crisis." *Geopolitics* 7:1 (Summer 2002): 85–112.

Kawashima Tomimaru 川島富丸. *Manshūkoku tsūka mondai no kenkyū narabi ni shiryō* 満洲国通貨問題の研究並に資料 (A study of Manchukuo's currency problem and related materials). Vol. 42 of *Kindai Nihon kin'yūshi bunken shiryō shūsei* 近代日本金融史文献資料集成, ed. Takashima Masaaki 高嶋 雅明 and Namikata Shōichi 波形昭一. Tokyo: Nihon tosho, 2005.

Kemmerer, Edwin W. "Economic Advisory Work for Governments." *American Economic Review* XVII:1 (March 1927): 1–12.

―――. "The Establishment of the Gold Exchange Standard in the Philippines." *Quarterly Journal of Economics* 19:4 (August 1905): 585–609.

―――. "A Gold Standard for the Straits Settlements." *Political Science Quarterly* 19:4 (December 1904): 636–49.

———. "A Gold Standard for the Straits Settlements II." *Political Science Quarterly* 21:4 (December 1906): 663–98.

———. "A Proposal for Pan-American Monetary Unity." *Political Science Quarterly* 31:1 (March 1916): 66–80.

———. "Review: Keynes' *Indian Currency and Finance*." *Quarterly Journal of Economics* 28:2 (February 1914): 373–77.

Kerr, George H. "Formosa: Colonial Laboratory." *Far Eastern Survey* 11:4 (February 23, 1942): 50–55.

Keynes, John Maynard. *The Economic Consequences of the Peace*. London: Macmillan, 1919.

———. *Indian Currency and Finance*. Vol. 1 of *The Collected Writings of John Maynard Keynes*. London: Macmillan, 1971 [1913].

Kim Chŏng Myŏng 金正明. *Nikkan gaikō shiryō shūsei* 日韓外交資料集成 (A collection of materials related to Japanese-Korean relations). Tokyo: Hekinandō shoten, 1962–1967.

Kim, Hong-Bum, and Chung H. Lee. "Post-Crisis Financial Reform in Korea: A Critical Appraisal." University of Hawai'i at Mānoa, Department of Economics, Working Papers 200410 (2004).

Kimitada Miwa. "Japanese Opinions on Woodrow Wilson in War and Peace." *Monumenta Nipponica* 22:3/4 (1967): 368–89.

Kimura, Mitsuhiko. "The Economics of Japanese Imperialism in Korea, 1910–1939." *Economic History Review* 48:3 (August 1995): 555–74.

———. "Financial Aspects of Korea's Economic Growth Under Japanese Rule." *Modern Asian Studies* 20, no. 4 (1986): 793–820.

———. "Standards of Living in Colonial Korea: Did the Masses Become Worse Off or Better Off Under Japanese Rule?." *Journal of Economic History* 53:3 (September 1993): 629–52.

Kin'yū kenkyūkai 金融研究会. *Manshū kokuheisei to kin'yū* 満洲国幣制と金融 (The currency system and finance of Manchukuo). Vol. 42 of *Kindai Nihon kin'yūshi bunken shiryō shūsei* 近代日本金融史文献資料集成, ed. Takashima Masaaki 高嶋雅明 and Namikata Shōichi 波形昭一. Tokyo: Nihon tosho, 2005.

Ko Sakatani shishaku kinen jigyōkai 故阪谷子爵記念事業会. *Sakatani Yoshio den* 阪谷芳郎伝 (The biography of Sakatani Yoshirō). Tokyo: Ko Sakatani shishaku kinen jigyōkai, 1951.

Kobata Atsushi 小葉田淳. *Kahei to kōzan* 貨幣と鉱山 (Money and mining). Tokyo: Shibunkaku shuppan, 1999.

Kobayashi Hideo 小林英夫. *Dai tōa kyōeiken no keisei to hōkai* 大東亜共栄圏の形成と崩壊 (The formation and demise of the Greater East-Asian Co-Prosperity Sphere). Tokyo: Ochanomizu shobō, 2006 [1975].

———. *Mantetsu "chi no shūdan" no tanjō to shi* 満鉄「知の集団」の誕生と死 (The birth and death of the South Manchurian Railway "Knowledge Group"). Tokyo: Yoshikawa kōbunkan, 1996.

———. *Mantetsu chōsabu "ganso shinkutanku" no tanjō to hōkai* 満鉄調査部「元祖シンクタンク」の誕生と崩壊 (The birth and demise of the South Manchurian Railway "arch-thinktank"). Tokyo: Heibonsha, 2005.

———. *Mantetsu chōsabu no kiseki: 1907–1945* 満鉄調査部の軌跡：1907–1945 (The locus of the research bureau of the South Manchurian Railway Company). Tokyo: Fujiwara shobō, 2006.

———. *Manshū to Jimintō* 満州と自民党 (Manchuria and the Liberal Democratic Party). Tokyo: Shinchō shinsho, 2005.

Kobayashi Hideo 小林英夫, Nangō Midori 南郷みどり, and Katō Kiyofumi 加藤聖文. *Mantetsu chōsakai to Nangō Tatsune: Manshūkoku tsūka kin'yū seisaku shiryō* 満鉄経済調査会と南郷龍音：満州国通貨金融政策史料 (The research bureau of the South Manchurian Railway Company and Nangō Tatsune: historical materials related to the currency and finance of Manchukuo). Tokyo: Shakai hyōronsha, 2004.

Koh Sung Jae 高承済. *Shokuminchi kin'yū seisaku no shiteki bunseki* 植民地金融政策の史的分析 (A historical analysis of financial policies in the colonies). Tokyo: Ochanomizu shobō, 1972.

Kohli, Atul. *State-Directed Development: Political Power and Industrialization in the Global Periphery.* Cambridge, UK: Cambridge University Press, 2004.

———. "Where Do High Growth Political Economies Come From? The Japanese Lineage of Korea's 'Development State.'" *World Development* 22:9 (1994): 1269–93.

Kojima Hitoshi 小島仁. *Nihon no kinhon'isei jidai (1897–1917)* 日本の金本位制時代 (1897–1917) (Japan's gold-standard era (1897–1917)). Tokyo: Nihon keizai hyōronsha, 1981.

Kokka shihon yushutsu kenkyūkai 国家資本輸出研究会. *Nihon no shihon yushutsu: tai-Chūgoku shakkan no kenkyū* 日本の資本輸出：対中国借款の研究 (The export of state capital: a study of loans to China). Tokyo: Taga shuppan, 1986.

Komine Kazuo 小峰和夫. "Nisshin sensōgo no Nichiman bōeki no seichō: Nichiman bōeki seiritsu no haikei to kōzō" 日清戦争後の日満貿易の成長：日満貿易成立の背景と構造 (The growth of Japanese-Manchurian trade after the Sino-Japanese war: the background and structure of the origin of Japanese-Manchurian trade). *Nihon daigaku nōjūi gakubu ippan kyōshoku kenkyū kiyō* 日本大學農獣医学部一般教養研究紀要 24 (1988): 1–17.

———. "Reimeiki no Nichiman bōeki: Nisshin sensō izen no jōkyō" 黎明期の日満貿易：日清戦争以前の状況 (The dawn of Japanese-Manchurian trade: the situation before the Sino-Japanese War). *Nihon daigaku nōjūi gakubu ippan kyōshoku kenkyū kiyō* 日本大学農獣医学部一般教養研究紀要 20 (1984): 3–22.

Konishi Shirō 小西四郎. *Nisshin sensō* 日清戦争 (The Sino-Japanese War). Tokyo: Kōdansha, 1977.

Kublin, Hyman. "The Evolution of Japanese Colonialism." *Comparative Studies in Society and History* 2:1 (October 1959): 67–84.

Kuhn, Arthur K. "The Lytton Report on the Manchurian Crisis." *American Journal of International Law* 27:1 (Jan., 1933): 96–100.

Kuroda, Akinobu. "Concurrent but Non-Integrable Currency Circuits: Complementary Relationships Among Monies in China and Other Regions." *Financial History Review* 15:1 (April 2008): 17–36.

———. "What Is the Complementarity Among Monies? An Introductory Note." *Financial History Review* 15:1 (April 2008): 7–15.

Kwartanada, Didi. "Competition, Patriotism and Collaboration: The Chinese Businessmen of Yogyakarta between the 1930s and 1945." *Journal of Southeast Asian Studies* 33:2 (June 2002): 257–77.

Kyū sanbō honbu 旧参謀本部, ed. *Nisshin sensō* 日清戦争 (The Sino-Japanese War). Nihon no senshi 日本の戦史. Tokyo: Tokuma shoten, 1995.

Lamont, Edward M. *Ambassador from Wall Street: The Story of Thomas W. Lamont, J. P. Morgan's Chief Executive.* Lanham, MD: Madison Books, 1993.

Langdon, Frank C. "Japan's Failure to Establish Friendly Relations with China in 1917–1918." *Pacific Historical Review* 26:3 (August 1957): 245–58.

Laughlin, Laurence. "The Gold-Exchange Standard." *Quarterly Journal of Economics*, 41:4 (Aug., 1927): 644–63.

———. *A New Exposition of Money, Credit, and Prices.* 2 vols. Chicago, IL: University of Chicago Press, 1931.

Lee, Yur-Bok. *West Goes East: Paul Georg von Möllendorf and Great Power Imperialism in Late Yi Korea.* Honolulu, HI: University of Hawai'i Press, 1988.

Lewis, Michael. *Rioters and Citizens: Mass Protest in Imperial Japan.* Berkeley, CA: University of California Press, 1990.

Li Jia Hong 季家弘 and Shimomura Yoshitoshi 下村良敏. *Dairen o chūshin to suru Shanhai Nihon kan kawase sankakkei* 大連を中心とする上海日本間為替三角形 (The Shanghai-Japan exchange triangle with its focus on Dairen). Vol. 4 of *Shina keizai kenkyū* 支那経済研究, ed. Tsuchiya Keizō 土屋計左右. Shanghai: Uchiyama shoten, 1927.

Li Shih-hui 李世暉. "Jūkyū seiki no tōa ginkaken to Taiwan no heisei kaikaku" 十九世紀の東亜銀貨圏と台湾の幣制改革 (The East Asian silver bloc in the nineteenth century and the monetary system reform of Taiwan). *Keizai ronsō* 経済論叢 177:2 (February 2006): 141–63.

Luhmann, Niklas. *Social Systems.* Stanford, CA: Stanford University Press, 1995.

Luo, Zhitian. "National Humiliation and National Assertion: The Chinese Response to the Twenty-One Demands." *Modern Asian Studies* 27:2 (May 1993): 297–319.

Lynn, Leonard H., and Hayagreeva Rao. "Failures of Intermediate Forms: A Study of the Suzuki 'Zaibatsu.'" *Organization Studies* 16:1 (1995): 55–80.

MacDonagh, Oliver. "The Anti-Imperialism of Free Trade." *Economic History Review*, New Series 14:3 (1962): 489–501.

MacMurray, John V. A., ed. *Treaties and Agreements with and Concerning China, 1894–1919.* 2 vols. New York: Oxford University Press, 1921.

Malone, Carroll B. "The First Remission of the Boxer Indemnity." *American Historical Review* 32:1 (October 1926): 64–68.

Malozemoff, Andrew. *Russian Far Eastern Policy, 1881–1904: With Special Emphasis on the Causes of the Russo-Japanese War.* Berkeley, CA: University of California Press, 1958.

Mamiya Kunio 間宮国夫. "Nihon shihon shugi to keizai dantai: Nisshin ginkō setsuritsu keikaku o megutte" 日本資本主義と経済団体：日清銀行設立計画をめぐって (Japan's capitalism and economic groups: about the plan for a Sino-Japanese bank). *Shakai kagaku tōkyū* 社会科学討究 15:3 (March 1970): 193–213.

———. "Nihon shihon shugi to Nisshin ginkō setsuritsu keikaku" 日本資本主義と日清銀行設立計画 (Japanese capitalism and the plan for a Sino-Japanese bank). *Keizaishigaku* 経済史学 13 (March 1969): 16–24.

"Manchoukuo Shows Large Unfavorable Trade Balance for 1934." *Far Eastern Survey* 4:8 (1935): 61–62.

Manshū chūō ginkō 満州中央銀行. *Manshū chūō ginkō 10-nenshi* 満州中央銀行10年史 (10 years of the Central Bank of Manchou). Hsinking: Manshū chūō ginkō, 1942.

Matsukata Masayoshi. *Report on the Adoption of the Gold Standard in Japan.* Tokyo: H.I.J.M. Minister of Finance, 1899.

———. *Report on the Post-Bellum Administration of Japan.* Tokyo: H.I.J.M. Minister of Finance, 1900.

Matsuno Shūji 松野周治. "Dai niji sekai taisen mae Chūgoku tōhokubu ni okeru Nihon no kin'yū shokatsudō ni tsuite" 第二次世界大戦前中国東北部における日本の金融諸活動について (About various Japanese financial activities in Northeastern China before World War Two). *Keizaigaku ronshū* 経済学論集 21 (March 1983): 111–31.

———. "Teikoku shugi kakuritsuki Nihon no tai-Manshū tsūka kin'yū seisaku" 帝国主義確立期日本の対満州通貨金融政策 (Japanese monetary and financial policies toward Manchuria in the era of the consolidation of Japanese imperialism). *Keizai ronsō* 経済論叢 120:1–2 (August 1977): 53–70.

Matsuoka Kōji 松岡孝児. "The Expansion and Consolidation of the Japanese Gold Exchange Standard." *Kyoto University Economic Review* XII (1937): 56–62.

———. *Kin kawase hon'isei no kenkyū* 金爲替本位制の研究 (An inquiry into the gold exchange standard). Tokyo: Nihon hyōronsha, 1936.

Matsusaka, Yoshihisa Tak. *The Making of Japanese Manchuria, 1904–1932.* Cambridge, MA: Harvard University Asia Center, 2001.

Maxey, Edwin. "The Reconstruction of Korea." *Political Science Quarterly* 25:4 (1910): 673–87.

Mayo, Marlene J. "The Korean Crisis of 1873 and Early Meiji Foreign Policy." *Journal of Asian Studies* 31:4 (August 1972): 793–819.

Mazuzan, George T. "'Our New Gold Goes Adventuring': The American International Corporation in China." *Pacific Historical Review* 43:2 (May 1974): 212–32.

McCormick, Frederick. "The Open Door." *Annals of the American Academy of Political and Social Science* 39 (January 1912): 56–61.

McCormick, Thomas. *China Market: America's Quest for Informal Empire, 1893–1901.* Chicago, IL: Quadrangle Books, 1967.

McNamara, Dennis. *The Colonial Origins of Korean Enterprise, 1910–1945.* New York: Cambridge University Press, 1990.

Megata Tanetarō 目賀田種太郎. "Kankoku kigyō no mokuteki" 韓国企業の目的 (The objectives of Korean enterprises). *Taiyō* 太陽 12:8 (August 1906): 54–56.

Memorandum (Institute of Pacific Relations, American Council). "Memorandum on the Report of the Lytton Commission." *Memorandum* 1:19 (October 7, 1932): 1–6.

Metzler, Mark. "The Cosmopolitanism of National Economics: Friedrich List in a Japanese Mirror." In *Global History: Interactions Between the Universal and the Local,* ed. A. G. Hopkins, 98–130. Basingstoke, UK: Palgrave Macmillan, 2006.

———. *Lever of Empire: The International Gold Standard and the Crisis of Liberalism in Prewar Japan.* Berkeley, CA: University of California Press, 2006.

———. "Policy Space, Polarities, and Regimes." In *Economic Thought in Early Modern Japan,* ed. Bettina Gramlich-Oka and Gregory J. Smits, 217–50. Leiden: Brill, 2010.

———. "The Road to the Dollar Standard: Monetary Hegemony and Japan's Place in the International Order." *Japanese Economy* 30:3 (May–June 2002): 46–81.

Mikuni Akio, R. Taggart Murphy, and Michael H. Armacost. *Japan's Policy Trap: Dollars, Deflation, and the Crisis of Japanese Finance.* Washington, DC: Brookings Institution Press, 2002.

Miller, Edward S. *Bankrupting the Enemy: The U.S. Financial Siege of Japan Before Pearl Harbor.* Annapolis: U.S. Naval Institute, 2007.

———. *War Plan Orange: The U.S. Strategy to Defeat Japan, 1897–1945.* Annapolis: U.S. Naval Institute, 1991.

Minami Manshū tetsudō kabushiki gaisha, ed. "Shanhai shijō no engawase to Manshū no tsūka" 上海市場の円為替と満州の通貨 (Yen exchanges in the Shanghai market and Manchurian currency). In *Shanhai Mantetsu chōsa shiryō* 上海満鉄調査資料, vol. 4. Shanghai: Mantetsu Shanhai jimusho kenkyūshitsu, 1927.

Minami Manshū tetsudō keizai chōsakai 南満洲鉄道経済調査会. *Manshūkoku tsūka kin'yū seido tōitsu ryakushi* 満洲国通貨金融制度統一略史 (A concise history of the unification of Manchukuo's currency and finance). Vol. 42 of *Kindai Nihon kin'yūshi bunken shiryō shūsei* 近代日本金融史文献資料集成, ed. Takashima Masaaki 高嶋雅明 and Namikata Shōichi 波形昭一. Tokyo: Nihon tosho, 2005.

———, ed. *Manshū ni okeru ryōsan* 満州に於ける糧桟 (The *liangzhan* in Manchuria). Dairen: Minami Manshū tetsudō, 1930 [1933].

Miyoshi, Masao. *As We Saw Them: The First Japanese Embassy to the United States* (1860). Berkeley, CA: University of California Press, 1979.

Mizoguchi, Toshiyuki. "The Changing Pattern of Sino-Japanese Trade, 1884–1937." In *The Japanese Informal Empire in China, 1895–1937*, ed. Peter Duus, Ramon H. Myers, and Mark R. Peattie, 10–30. Princeton, NJ: Princeton University Press, 1989.

Mizoguchi Toshiyuki 溝口敏行, and Umemura Mataji 梅村又次. *Kyū Nihon shokuminchi keizai tōkei: suikei to bunseki* 旧日本植民地経済統計：推計と分析 (Economic statistics of Japan's former colonies: estimates and analysis). Tokyo: Tōyō keizai shinpōsha, 1988.

Mizuta Naomasa 水田直昌. *Sōtokufu jidai no zaisei: Chōsen kindai zaisei no kakuritsu* 総督府時代の財政：朝鮮近代財政の確立 (National finance under the rule of the government-general: the consolidation of modern Korean finance). Tokyo: Yūhōkyōkai, 1974.

Mlynarski, Feliks. *Gold and Central Banks.* New York: Macmillan, 1929.

Morikawa Masanori 森川正則. "Terauchi naikaku-ki ni okeru Nishihara Kamezō no tai-Chūgoku 'enjo' seisaku kōsō" 寺内内閣期における西原亀三の対中国「援助」政策構想 (Nishihara Kamezō's thinking of "aid" for China at the time of the Terauchi administration). *Handai hōgaku* 阪大法学 50:5 (January 2001): 809–38.

Moriyama Shigenori 森山茂徳. "Kōgo kaikaku ni okeru shakkan mondai: Inoue Kaoru no kanyo shita dainiji kaikaku to Chōsen shidōshasō taiō o chūshin to shite" 甲午改革に於ける借款問題：井上馨の関与した第二次改革と朝鮮指導者層対応を中心として (The loan problem in the

Gabo reforms: with a special focus on Inoue Kaoru's involvement in the second reform and the reactions of Korea's leaders). *Tōyō gakuhō* 東洋学報 56:2–4, (March 1975): 249–77.

Morris, Andrew. "The Taiwan Republic of 1895 and the Failure of the Qing Modernizing Project." In *Memories of the Future: National Identity Issues and the Search for a New Taiwan*, ed. Stephane Corcuff, 3–24. Armonk, NY: M.E. Sharpe, 2002.

Moulton, Harold G. *Japan: An Economic and Financial Appraisal*. Washington: The Brookings Institution, 1931.

Murakami Katsuhiko 村上勝彦. "Shokuminchi kin kyūshū to Nihon sangyō kakumei" 植民地金吸収と日本産業革命 (The absorption of gold in the colonies and Japan's industrial revolution). *Tōkyō daigaku keizaigaku kenkyū* 東京大学経済学研究 16 (1973): 40-53.

Murphy, R. Taggart. *The Weight of the Yen: How Denial Imperils America's Future and Ruins an Alliance*. New York: W. W. Norton, 1996.

My-Van, Tran. "Japan and Vietnam's Caodaists: A Wartime Relationship (1939–45)." *Journal of Southeast Asian Studies* 27:1 (The Japanese Occupation in Southeast Asia) (March 1996): 179–93.

Myers, Ramon H. *The Chinese Peasant Economy: Agricultural Development in Hopei and Shantung, 1890–1949*. Cambridge, MA: Harvard University Press.

———. "The World Depression and the Chinese Economy, 1930–36." In *The Economies of Africa and Asia in the Inter-War Depression*, ed. Ian Brown, 253–73. London and New York: Routledge, 1989.

Nagaoka Shinkichi 長岡新吉. "Nisshin sensō go no kyōkō to menshihō seki-gyō: sangyō shihon kakuritsuki ni kansuru ichi kōsatsu" 日清戦後の恐慌と綿糸紡績業：産業資本確立期に関する一考察 (The depression after the Sino-Japanese War and the spinning industry: a perspective on the period of consolidation of industrial capital). *Hokkaidō daigaku keizaigaku kenkyū* 北海道大學經濟學研究 16:2 (1966): 67–131; 16:4 (1966): 25–116.

Nakayama Takeo 中山武夫. *Komura Jutarō Den* 小村寿太郎伝 (The biography of Komura Jutarō). Tokyo: Shinkōasha, 1940.

Namikata Shōichi 波形昭一. *Nihon shokuminchi kin'yū seisakushi no kenkyū* 日本植民地金融政策史の研究 (A study of the history of financial policies towards Japan's colonies). Tokyo: Waseda daigaku shuppanbu, 1985.

———. "Nisshin ginkō, Manshū ginkō setsuritsu undō no tenkai katei: Meijiki ni gentei shite" 日清銀行・満州銀行設立運動の展開過程：明治期に限定して (The development process of the movements for the establishment of a Sino-Japanese Bank and a Bank of Manchuria: limited to the Meiji period). *Kin'yū kenkyū* 金融経済 137 (December 1972): 25–65.

———. "Taiwan ginkō no setsuritsu to heiseikaikaku" 台湾銀行の設立と幣制改革 (The establishment of the Bank of Formosa and currency reform).

Dokkyō daigaku keizaigaku kenkyū 独協大学経済学研究 14 (June 1974): 35–64.

Neal, Larry. "The Economics and Finance of Bilateral Clearing Agreements: Germany, 1934–38." *Economic History Review* 32:3 (1979): 391–404.

Nihon ginkō chōsakyoku 日本銀行調査局, ed. *Nihon kin'yūshi shiryō: Meiji Taishō hen* 日本金融史資料：明治大正編. 25 vols. Tokyo: Ōkurashō insatsu-kyoku, 1955–61.

Nihon ginkō 100-nenshi iinkai 日本銀行百年史委員会. *Nihon ginkō 100-nenshi* 日本銀行百年史 (The hundred year history of the Bank of Japan). Tokyo: Nihon ginkō, 1983.

Nihon ginkō tōkeikyoku, ed. *Meiji ikō honpō shuyō keizai tōkei* 明治以降本邦主要経済統計 (Major statistics of the Japanese economy since the Meiji period). Tokyo: Nihon ginkō, 1966.

"Nikkan bōekiron hoi" 日韓貿易論補遺 (Appendix to the theory of Japan-Korea trade). *Tōkyō keizai zasshi* 東京経済雑誌 769 (March 1895).

Nish, Ian. *Japanese Foreign Policy in the Interwar Period.* Westport, CT: Praeger, 2002.

Nishihara Kamezō 西原亀三. *Nishihara Kamezō nikki* 西原亀三日記 (The diary of Nishihara Kamezō). Ed. Yamamoto Shirō 山本四郎. Kyoto: Kyōto joshi daigaku, 1983.

———. *Yume no 70 yonen: Nishihara Kamezō jiden* 夢の七十余年：西原亀三自伝 (A dream of more than 70 years: the autobiography of Nishihara Kamezō). Tokyo: Tōyō bunko, 1965.

Nishikawa Jun. "Nishihara Kamezo and His Age—The Formation of an Expansionist Idea in Japan: A Bibliography." *Waseda seiji keizaigaku zasshi* 早稲田政治經濟學雜誌 290 (1987): 80–108.

Nishikawa Yūichi 西川裕一. "Edo-ki sanka seido" 江戸期三貨制度 (The trimetallic system of the Edo-period). *Kin'yū kenkyū* 金融研究 17:3 (1998): 95-112.

———. "Edo-ki sanka seido no hōga: chūsei kara kinsei e no kaheikeizai no renzokusei" 江戸期三貨制度の萌芽：中世から近世への貨幣経済の連続性 (The sprouts of the trimetallic system of the Edo-period: continuity of the money economy from the middle ages to early modernity). *Kin'yū kenkyū* 金融研究 18:4 (1999): 95–112.

Nishimura Shizuya 西村閑也. "Zai-Shanhai gaikoku ginkō to genchi ginkō, 1890–1913: choppu rōn no mekanizumu" 在上海外国銀行と現地銀行（銭荘）, 1890–1913：チョップ・ローンのメカニズム (Shanghai-based foreign banks and the indigenous banking institutions, 1890–1913: the mechanism of chop-loans). *Keiei shirin* 経営志林 35: 3 (1998): 1–19.

Nochi Kiyoshi 能地清. "Nisshin, Nichiro sengo keiei to taigai zaisei 1896–1913: zaigai seifu shikin o chūshin ni" 日清・日露戦後経営と対外財政 1896–1913：在外政府資金を中心に (Political and economic policies after the Sino- and Russo-Japanese Wars and foreign public finance, 1896–1913: an inquiry into the overseas government funds). *Tochi seido shigaku* 土地制度史学 23:4 (July 1981): 19–40.

North, S. N. D. "The Negotiations Between Japan and China in 1915." *American Journal of International Law* 10:2. (April 1916): 222–37.

Oguma Eiji. *A Genealogy of "Japanese" Self-Images*. Melbourne: Trans Pacific Press, 2002.

Oh, Doo-Hwan. "Currency Readjustment and Colonial Monetary System of 1905 in Korea." *Journal of Social Sciences and Humanities* 65 (1987): 53–86.

Ōhashi Akio 大橋昭夫. *Gotō Shōjirō to kindai Nihon* 後藤象二郎と近代日本 (Gotō Shōjirō and modern Japan). Tokyo: San'ichi shobō, 1993.

Okamoto Shumpei. "A Phase of Meiji Japan's Attitude Toward China: The Case of Komura Jutaro." *Modern Asian Studies* 13:3 (1979): 431–57.

Okazaki Hisahiko 岡崎久彦. *Komura Jutarō to sono jidai* 小村寿太郎とその時代 (Komura Jutarō and his times). Tokyo: PHP kenkyūsho, 1998.

Okazaki Tetsuji and Sawada Michiru. "Effects of a Bank Consolidation Promotion Policy: Evaluating the 1927 Bank Law in Japan." *Financial History Review* 14:1 (2007): 29–61.

Ōkurashō. *Meiji Taishō zaiseishi* 明治大正財政史 (Fiscal history of the Meiji and Taishō periods). Multiple volumes. Tokyo: Ōkurashō, multiple years.

Ōkurashō zaiseishi kin'yū kenkyūsho zaiseishi shitsu 大蔵省財政金融研究所財政史室. *Ōkurashōshi: Meiji/Taishō/Shōwa* 大蔵省史：明治・大正・昭和 (History of the Ministry of Finance: Meiji, Taishō, Shōwa). 4 vols. Tokyo: Ōkurashō, 1998.

Ōmori Tokuko 大森とく子. "Nishihara shakkan ni tsuite: tetsu to kin'en o chūshin ni" 西原借款について：鉄と金円を中心に (On the Nishihara loans: with a special focus on iron and gold yen). *Rekishigaku kenkyū* 歴史学研究 419 (April 1975): 36–51.

Ono, Giichi. *War and Armament Expenditures of Japan*. New York: Oxford University Press, 1922.

Ono Kazuichirō 小野一一郎. *Kindai Nihon heisei to higashi Ajia ginkaken: en to Mekishiko doru* 近代日本幣制と東アジア銀貨圏：円とメキシコドル (Japan's modern currency system and the East-Asian silver sphere: the yen and the Mexican dollar). Kyoto: Minerva shobō, 2000.

Osterhammel, Jürgen. "Imperialism in Transition: British Business and the Chinese Authorities, 1931–37." *China Quarterly* 98 (June 1984): 260–86.

———. "Semi-Colonialism and Informal Empire in Twentieth Century China: Toward a Framework of Analysis." In *Imperialism and After: Continuities and Discontinuities*, ed. Wolfgang J. Mommsen and Jürgen Osterhammel, 290–314. London: Allen and Unwin, 1986.

Overlach, Theodore William. *Foreign Financial Control in China.* New York: Macmillan, 1919.

Papers Relating to the Foreign Relations of the United States, 1899. Washington, DC: G.P.O., 1899.

Patrikeeff, Felix and Harry Shukman. *Railways and the Russo-Japanese War: Transporting War.* London: Taylor and Francis, 2007.

Pauly, Louis W. *Who Elected the Bankers? Surveillance and Control in the World Economy.* Ithaca, NY: Cornell University Press, 1997.

Peng Zizhou 彭沢周. *Meiji shoki Nichi-Kan-Shin kankei no kenkyū* 明治初期日韓清関係の研究 (An inquiry into Japan-Korea-China relations in the early Meiji period). Tokyo: Hanawa shobō, 1969.

Penslar, Derek Jonathan. "Zionism, Colonialism and Technocracy: Otto Warburg and the Commission for the Exploration of Palestine." *Journal of Contemporary History* 25 (1990): 143–60.

Pond, Shepard. "The Spanish Dollar: The World's Most Famous Silver Coin." *Bulletin of the Business Historical Society* 15:1 (February 1941): 12–16.

Presseisen, Ernst L. "Roots of Japanese Imperialism: A Memorandum of General LeGendre." *Journal of Modern History* 29 (1957): 108–11.

Prichard, Earl H. "The Origins of the Most-Favored-Nation and the Open Door Policies in China." *The Far Eastern Quarterly* 1:2 (February 1942): 161–72.

Pugach, Noel. "Making the Open Door Work: Paul S. Reinsch in China, 1913–1919." *Pacific Historical Review* 38:2 (May 1969): 157–75.

Pyle, Kenneth. *Japan Rising: The Resurgence of Japanese Power And Purpose.* New York: Public Affairs, 2007.

Quested, Rosemary. *The Russo-Chinese Bank: A Multi-National Financial Base of Tsarism in China.* Birmingham: University of Birmingham, 1977.

Quo, F. Q. "British Diplomacy and the Cession of Formosa, 1894–95." *Modern Asian Studies* 2:2 (1968): 141–54.

Ravina, Mark. *The Last Samurai: The Life and Battles of Saigo Takamori.* Hoboken, NJ: John Wiley and Sons, 2004.

Rawski, Thomas G. *Economic Growth in Prewar China.* Berkeley, CA: University of California Press, 1989.

———. "Milton Friedman, Silver, and China." *Journal of Political Economy* 101:4 (August 1993): 755–58.

Remer, Charles Frederick. *Foreign Investments in China.* New York: Macmillan, 1933.

Rosenbaum, Arthur. "Railway Enterprise and Economic Development: The Case of the Imperial Railways of North China, 1900–1911." *Modern China* 2:2 (April 1976): 227–72.

Rosenberg, Emily S. *Financial Missionaries to the World: The Politics and Culture of Dollar Diplomacy*. Durham and London: Duke University Press, 2003.

The Russo-Japanese War: A Photographic and Descriptive Review of the Great Conflict in the Far East, Gathered from the Reports, Records, Cable Despatches, Photographs, Etc., Etc., of Collier's War Correspondents. New York: P.F. Collier and Son, 1905.

Saaler, Sven, and J. Victor Koschman, eds. *Pan-Asianism in Modern Japanese History: Colonialism, Regionalism and Borders*. London and New York: Routledge, 2007.

Safford, Jeffrey J. "Experiment in Containment: The United States Steel Embargo and Japan, 1917–1918." *Pacific Historical Review* 39: 4. (November 1970): 439–51.

Sakamoto Masako 坂本雅子. *Zaibatsu to teikoku shugi: Mitsui bussan to Chūgoku* 財閥と帝国主義：三井物産と中国 (*Zaibatsu* and imperialism: Mitsui bussan and China). Kyoto: Minerva shobō, 2003.

Samuels, Richard J. *"Rich Nation, Strong Army": National Security and the Technological Transformation of Japan*. Ithaca, NY: Cornell University Press, 1994.

Sargent, Thomas J., and Francois R. Velde. *The Big Problem of Small Change*. Princeton, NJ: Princeton University Press, 2003.

Scheiber, Harry N. "World War I as Entrepreneurial Opportunity: Willard Straight and the American International Corporation." *Political Science Quarterly* 84:3 (September 1969): 486–511.

Schiltz, Michael. "Money on the Road to Empire: Japan's Choice for Gold Monometallism, 1873–1897." *Economic History Review* (2011).

Schmid, Andre. "Colonialism and the 'Korea Problem' in the Historiography of Modern Japan: A Review Article." *Journal of Asian Studies* 59:4 (2000): 951–76.

Schuker, Stephen. "Money Doctors Between the Wars: The Competition Between Central Banks, Private Financial Advisers, and Multilateral Agencies, 1919–1939." In *Money Doctors: The Experience of Financial Advising, 1850–2000*, ed. Marc Flandreau, 49–77. New York: Routledge, 2003.

Scott, R. P. "The Boxer Indemnity in Its Relation to Chinese Education." *Journal of the British Institute of International Affairs* 2:4 (July 1923): 149–67.

Sheehan, Brett. *Trust in Troubled Times: Money, Banks and State-Society Relations in Republican Tianjin*. Cambridge, MA: Harvard University Press, 2003.

Shibata Yoshimasa 柴田善雅. "Ajia taiheiyō sensō ki Taiwan no taigai kawase kessai" アジア太平洋戦争期台湾の対外為替決済 (Taiwan's foreign exchange settlements at the time of the Pacific War). *Tōyō kenkyū* 東洋研究 134 (December 1999): 15–43.

———. "Banki senji Nihon teikoku no tainichi kessai" 晩期戦時日本帝国の対日決済 (Foreign exchange settlements with Japan in the latter days of the Japanese wartime empire). *Daitō bunka daigaku kiyō* 大東文化大学紀要 45 (2007): A75-A91.

———. "Kotei sōba seido en burokku keisei go no 'Manshūkoku' no taigai kessai" 固定相場制円ブロック形成後の「満州国」の対外決済 (The foreign exchange settlements of "Manchukuo" after the formation of the yen bloc with a fixed exchange rate system). *Chūgoku kenkyū geppō* 中国研究月報 431 (January 1984): 1–23.

———. "'Mōkyō' ni okeru tsūka kin'yū seisaku no tenkai" 「蒙彊」における通貨金融政策の展開 (The development of monetary and financial policies in "Mengjiang"). *Ajia keizai* アジア経済 34:6 (June 1993): 54–79.

———. "Nicchū sensō ki gaikoku kawase wariate seisaku no ichi kōsatsu" 日中戦争期外国為替割当政策の一考察 (An analysis of the foreign exchange allocation control policy during the second Sino-Japanese War). *Tōyō kenkyū* 東洋研究 170 (December 2008): 13–51.

———. "Nicchū sensōki Nihon no shihon wariate: 'Rinji shikin chōseihō' to 'Ginkō nado shikin un'yōrei' no shikō" 日中戦争期日本の資金割当：「臨時資金調整法」と「銀行等資金運用令」の施行 (Japanese fund allocation control during the second Sino-Japanese War: the implementation of the "emergency capital allocation law" and the "imperial ordinance regarding the regulation of bank loans"). *Daitō bunka daigaku kiyō* 大東文化大学紀要, 46 (2008): 123–41.

———. "Nihon no tai-'Manshū' tsūka kin'yū seisaku no keisei to sono kinō no jittai: dai ichiji taisen kara 20-nendai nakagoro ni kakete" 日本の対「満州」通貨金融政策の形成とその機能の実態：第一次大戦から二〇年代中頃にかけて (The formation of Japan's monetary and financial policies towards Manchuria and the nature of its functions: from the First World War to the mid-1920s). *Shakai keizai shigaku* 社會經濟史學 43:2 (1977): 145–73.

———. "Senji kigyō seibi to sono shikin sochi" 戦時企業整備とその資金措置 (Wartime business restructuring and financial measures). *Daitō bunka daigaku kiyō* 大東文化大学紀要 41 (March 2003): 17–50.

———. "Senji Nihon no kabushiki shijō tōsei" 戦時日本の株式市場統制 (Stock market control in wartime Japan). *Tōyō kenkyū* 東洋研究 166 (December 2007): 27–59.

———. *Senji Nihon no tokubetsu kaikei* 戦時日本の特別会計 (Special accounts in wartime Japan). Tokyo: Nihon keizai hyōronsha, 2002.

———. *Senryōchi tsūka kin'yū seisaku no tenkai* 占領地通貨金融政策の展開 (The development of financial policies in the occupied territories). Tokyo: Nihon keizai hyōronsha, 1999.

Shibusawa Eiichi kinen zaidan 渋沢栄一記念財団. *Shibusawa Eiichi denki shiryō* 渋沢栄一伝記資料 (multiple volumes).

Shiman, Russell G. "North China in a Japanese Economic Bloc." *Far Eastern Survey* 4:25 (December 18, 1935): 198–205.

Shimazaki Kyūya 島崎久彌. *En no shinryakushi: engawase hon'isei no keisei katei* 円の侵略史：円為替本位制度の形成過程 (A history of the invasion of the yen: the process of the development of the yen-exchange standard system). Tokyo: Nihon keizai hyōronsha, 1989.

———. "'Dai tōa kin'yūken' no keisei katei" 「大東亜金融圏」の形成過程 (The process of the formation of the "Greater East-Asian Financial Sphere"). 5 parts. *Keizaikei* 経済系 153 (October 1987): 1–40; 154 (January 1988): 19–49; 155 (April 1988): 74–108; 156 (July 1988): 30–75; 157 (October 1988): 1–50.

Shinobu Seizaburō 信夫清三郎. *Nisshin sensō: sono seijiteki-gaikōteki kansatsu* 日清戦争：その政治的・外交的観察 (The Sino-Japanese War: political and diplomatic observations). Tokyo: Fukuda shobō, 1934.

Shinozaki Yoshirō 篠崎嘉郎. *Manshū kin'yū oyobi zaikai no genjō* 満州金融及財界の現状 (The current state of affairs of Manchuria's finance and business world). Dairen: Osaka yagō shoten, 1927–1928.

Shiroyama, Tomoko. *China During the Great Depression: Market, State and the World Economy, 1929–1937*. Cambridge, MA: Harvard University Asia Center, 2008.

Shizuta Hitoshi 静田均. *Chōsen ni okeru kin'yū kumiai no hattatsu* 朝鮮における金融組合の発達 (The development of the financial cooperatives in Korea). Vol. 39 of *Kindai Nihon kin'yūshi bunken shiryō shūsei* 近代日本金融史文献資料集成, ed. Takashima Masaaki 高嶋雅明 and Namikata Shōichi 波形昭一. Tokyo: Nihon tosho, 2005.

Shōda Kazue 勝田主計. *Shinkan man'yū yoreki* 清韓漫遊余歴 (Report on wanderings through China and Korea). Tokyo: privately published, 1910.

Shōda Tatsuo 勝田龍夫. *Chūgoku shakkan to Shōda Kazue* 中国借款と勝田主計 (The China loans and Shōda Kazue). Tokyo: Daiyamondo-sha, 1972.

Slattery, Peter. *Reporting the Russo-Japanese War, 1904–5: Lionel James's First Wireless Transmissions to* The Times. Folkestone: Global Oriental, 2004.

Smethurst, Richard J. *From Foot Soldier to Finance Minister: Takahashi Korekiyo, Japan's Keynes*. Cambridge, MA: Harvard University Asia Center, 2007.

Smith, Sara R. *The Manchurian Crisis, 1931–32: A Tragedy in International Relations*. New York: Columbia University Press, 1948.

Smith, Thomas C. *Political Change and Industrial Development in Japan: Government Enterprise, 1868–1880*. Stanford, CA: Stanford University Press, 1955.

Snow, Edgar. *Far Eastern Front*. London: Jarrolds, 1934.

Soyeda Juichi. "Letter from Japan." *Economic Journal* 9:35 (September 1899): 469–77.

Spencer-Brown, George. *Laws of Form*. London: Allen and Unwin, 1969.

Spidle, Jake W. Jr. "Colonial Studies in Imperial Germany." *History of Education Quarterly* 13:3 (1973): 231–47.

Steinberg, John W. et al. , eds. *The Russo-Japanese War in Global Perspective: World War Zero*, 2 vols. Leiden: Brill Publishers, 2005–2007.

Stewart, John R. "Manchoukuo Yuan Linked with Japanese Yen." *Far Eastern Survey* 5:2 (January 15, 1936): 14–15.

Stiglitz, Joseph. *Globalization and Its Discontents*. London and New York: W.W. Norton and Company, 2002.

Sugihara, Kaoru. "Economic Motivations Behind Japanese Aggression in the Late 1930s: Perspectives of Freda Utley and Nawa Toichi." *Journal of Contemporary History* 32:2 (April 1997): 259–80.

Suleski, Ronald. "The Rise and Fall of the Fengtien Dollar, 1917–1928: Currency Reform in Warlord China." *Modern Asian Studies* 13:4 (1979): 643–60.

Suzuki Ichirō 鈴木一郎. "Gotō Shinpei to Okamatsu Santarō ni yoru kyūkan chōsa: Taiwan no baai" 後藤新平と岡松参太郎による旧慣調査：台湾の場合 (Surveys of old habits by Gotō Shinpei and Okamoto Santarō: the case of Taiwan.) *Tōhoku gakuin daigaku hōgaku seijigaku kenkyūjo kiyō* 東北学院大学法学政治学研究所紀要 8 (February 2002): 41–71.

Suzuki Kōichi 鈴木孝一, ed. *Nisshin sensō, Minbi ansatsu, kyōaku satsujin no jidai* 日清戦争・閔妃暗殺・凶悪殺人の時代 (The Sino-Japanese War, the murder of Queen Min, the era of brutal murders). Nyūsu de ou Meiji Nihon hakkutsu 5. Tokyo: Kawade shobō shinsha, 1995.

Suzuki Takeo 鈴木武雄, ed. *Nishihara shakkan shiryō kenkyū* 西原借款資料研究 (A study of materials related to the Nishihara loans). Tokyo: Tōkyō daigaku shuppankai, 1972.

Suzuki Toshio. *Japanese Government Loan Issues on the London Capital Market, 1870–1913*. London and Atlantic Highlands, NJ: Athlone Press, 1994.

Synn, Seung Kwon. *The Russo-Japanese Rivalry Over Korea, 1876–1904*. Seoul: Yuk Phub Sa, 1981.

Taguchi Ukichi 田口卯吉. "Chōsen no shin kahei chūzō jigyō" 朝鮮の新貨幣鋳造事業 (The task of minting Korea's new coinage). *Tōkyō keizai zasshi* 東京経済雑誌 670 (April 1893).

Tai, Eika. "Kokugo and Colonial Education in Taiwan." *positions: east asia cultures critique* 7:2 (1999): 503–40.

Taira Tomoyuki 平智之. "Dai ichiji taisen izen no tai-Chūgoku shakkan to tōshi shutai" 第一次大戦以前の対中国借款と投資主体 (Loans to China before World War One and the subject of investments). In *Nihon no shihon yushutsu: tai-Chūgoku shakkan no kenkyū* 日本の資本輸出・対中国借款の研究 (Japan's capital exports: an investigation of the China loans), ed. Kokka shihon yushutsu kenkyūkai 国家資本輸出研究会. Tokyo: Taga shuppan, 1986, 13–49.

Taiwan ginkō 台湾銀行, ed. *Taiwan ginkō 20-nenshi* 台湾銀行二十年誌 (Twenty years of the Bank of Taiwan). Taipei: Taiwan ginkō, 1910.

Taiwan ginkōshi hensanshitsu 台湾銀行史編纂室, ed. *Taiwan ginkōshi* 台湾銀行史 (History of the Bank of Taiwan). Tokyo: Taiwan ginkōshi hensanshitsu, 1964.

Takagi, Yasaka. "World Peace Machinery and the Asia Monroe Doctrine." *Pacific Affairs* 5:11 (November 1932): 941–53.

Takahashi Korekiyo 高橋是清. *Takahashi Korekiyo jiden* 高橋是清自伝 (The autobiography of Takahashi Korekiyo). Tokyo: Chikura shobō, 1936.

Takashima Masaaki 高嶋雅明. *Chōsen ni okeru shokuminchi kin'yūshi no kenkyū* 朝鮮における植民地金融史の研究 (A study of colonial financial history in Korea). Tokyo: Ōhara shinseisha, 1978.

Takeda Haruhito 武田晴人. "Furukawa shōji to 'Dairen jiken'" 古河商事と「大連事件」 (Furukawa commerce and the "Dairen affair"). *Shakai kagaku kenkyū* 社會科學研究 32:2 (1980): 1–61.

Takemae, Eiji, Robert Ricketts, Sebastian Swann, and John W. Dower. *The Allied Occupation of Japan*. London and New York: Continuum, 2003.

Tankha, Brij. *Okakura Tenshin and Pan-Asianism: Shadows of the Past*. Honolulu, HI: University of Hawai'i Press, 2008.

T'ang, L. L. (Thung Liang Lee), and M. S. Miller. "The Political Aspect of International Finance in Russia and China." *Economica* 13 (March 1925): 69–88.

Tatai Yoshio 多田井喜生. *Chōsen ginkō: aru en-tsūkaken no kōbō* 朝鮮銀行：ある円通貨圏の興亡 (The Bank of Chosen: the rise and demise of a yen-based currency bloc). Tokyo: PHP kenkyūsho, 2002.

Tatewaki Kazuo 立脇和夫. *Zainichi gaikoku ginkōshi: bakumatsu kaikō kara jōyaku kaisei made* 在日外国銀行史：幕末開港から条約改正まで (A history of foreign banks in Japan: from the opening of the ports to the revision of the treaties). Tokyo: Nihon keizai hyōronsha, 1987.

Thomson, Sandra Caruthers. "Filibustering to Formosa: General Charles LeGendre and the Japanese." *Pacific Historical Review* 40:4 (November 1971): 442–56.

Tokutomi Soho 徳富蘇峰. *Kōshaku Matsukata Masayoshi den* 公爵松方正義伝 (The biography of Prince Matsukata Masayoshi). Tokyo: Kōshaku Matsukata Masayoshi denki hakkōsho, 1935.

Tomimas, Shutaro. *The Open-Door Policy and the Territorial Integrity of China*. New York: University Publishers of America, 1919.

Tooze, Adam. *Statistics and the German State, 1900–1945: The Making of Modern Economic Knowledge*. Cambridge, UK: Cambridge University Press, 2001.

———. *The Wages of Destruction: The Making and Breaking of the Nazi Economy*. New York: Viking, 2006.

Treat, Payson Jackson. *The Far East: A Political and Diplomatic History*. New York and London: Harper and Brothers, 1935.

Tsunoda Fusako 角田房子. *Minbi ansatsu: Chōsen ōchō makki no kokubo* 閔妃暗殺：朝鮮王朝末期の国母 (The murder of Queen Min: the empress of the latter days of the Korean dynasty). Tokyo: Shinchōsha, 1993.

Tsurumi Masayoshi 鶴見誠良. "En burokku no keisei: engawaseken kara enkei tsūkaken he" 円ブロックの形成:円為替圏から円系通貨圏へ (The formation of the yen-bloc: from yen-exchange standard sphere to yen-sphere). *Ajia kenkyū* アジア研究 20:4 (January 1974): 29–55.

Tsurumi, E. Patricia. "Education and Assimilation in Taiwan Under Japanese Rule, 1895–1945." *Modern Asian Studies* 13:4 (1979): 617–41.

———. "Colonial Education in Korea and Taiwan." In *The Japanese Colonial Empire, 1895–1945*, ed. Ramon H. Myers and Mark R. Peattie, 275–311. Princeton, NJ: Princeton University Press, 1984.

Tsurumi Yūsuke. "The Difficulties and Hopes of Japan." *Foreign Affairs* 3:2 (December 15, 1924): 253–65.

———. *Taiwan jidai: 1898–1906-nen* 台湾時代 (Taiwan period: 1898–1906). Vol. 3 of *Seiden Gotō Shinpei* 正伝・後藤新平. Tokyo: Fujiwara shobō, 2005.

Tsutsumi Kazuyuki 堤和幸. "Shinmatsu Taiwan ni okeru hosen no ryūtsū to beikoku torihiki" 清末台湾における呆銭の流通と米穀取引 (The circulation of aiqian in Taiwan of the late Qing and the rice exchange). *Gendai Taiwan kenkyū* 現代台湾研究 30/31 double-issue (November 2006): 56–75.

Twu Jaw-Yann 涂照彦. *Nihon teikoku shugi ka no Taiwan* 日本帝国主義下の台湾 (Taiwan under imperial Japanese rule). Tokyo: Tōkyō daigaku shuppankai, 1975.

Ueda Mitsuo 上田光雄. *Kankoku ni okeru kahei to kin'yū* 韓国ニ於ケル貨幣ト金融 (Money and finance in Korea). Vol. 38 of *Kindai Nihon kin'yūshi bunken shiryō shūsei* 近代日本金融史文献資料集成, ed. Takashima Masaaki 高嶋雅明 and Namikata Shōichi 波形昭一. Tokyo: Nihon tosho, 2005.

United States Department of State. *Foreign Relations of the United States: Diplomatic Papers, 1934, vol. 3, The Far East*. Washington, DC: G.P.O., 1942.

———. *Papers Relating to the Foreign Relations of the United States, Japan: 1931–1941*. Vol. 1. Washington, DC: U. S. Government Printing Office, 1931–41.

Utley, Freda. *Lancashire and the Far East*. London: Allen and Unwin, 1931.

———. *Japan's Feet of Clay*. New York: W.W. Norton and Company, 1936.

———. *China at War*. London: Faber and Faber, 1938.

———. *Japan's Gamble in China*. London: Secker and Warburg, 1938.

Utsunomiya Kiyohito. "Economic Fluctuations in Japan During the Interwar Period: Re-estimation of the LTES Personal Consumption Expenditures" (Bank of Japan discussion paper series 2008-E-6), available online at http://www.imes.boj.or.jp/english/publication/edps/2008/08-E-06.pdf (accessed May 17 2010).

Varg, Paul A. "William Woodville Rockhill and the Open Door Notes." *Journal of Modern History* 24:4 (December 1952): 375–80.

Vissering, Gerard. *The Netherlands East Indies and the Gold-Exchange Standard.* The Hague: Nijhoff, 1916.

Wehler, Hans-Ulrich. "Industrial Growth and Early German Imperialism." In *Studies in the Theory of Imperialism,* ed. Roger Owen and R. B. Sutcliffe, 72–90. London: Longman, 1972.

Weland, James. "Misguided Intelligence: Japanese Military Intelligence Officers in the Manchurian Incident, September 1931." *Journal of Military History* 58:3 (July 1994): 445–60.

White, Trumbull. *Silver and Gold or Both Sides of the Shield: The Doctrines of Free Silver, Mono-Metalism and Bi-Metalism.* Philadelphia, PA: Publisher's Union, 1895 [2001].

———. *The War in the East: Japan, China and Corea.* Philadelphia, PA: Schiffer Books, 1895.

Wilgus, Mary H. *Sir Claude MacDonald, the Open Door, and British Informal Empire in China, 1895–1900.* New York: Garland Publishing, 1987.

Wilkins, Mira. "Japanese Multinational Enterprise Before 1914." *Business History Review* 60:2 (Summer 1986): 199–231.

Winston, A. P. "Chinese Finance Under the Republic." *Quarterly Journal of Economics* 30:4 (August 1916): 738–39.

Wolfe, Martin. "The Development of Nazi Monetary Policy." *Journal of Economic History* 15:4 (December 1955): 392–402.

Woo, Jung-en. *Race to the Swift: State and Finance in Korean Industrialization.* New York: Columbia University Press, 1991.

Wray, William D. "Japan's Big-Three Service Enterprises in China, 1896–1936." In *The Japanese Informal Empire in China, 1895–1937,* ed. Peter Duus, Ramon H. Myers, and Mark R. Peattie, 31–64. Princeton, NJ: Princeton University Press, 1989.

Wright, Mary C. "The Adaptability of Ch'ing Diplomacy: The Case of Korea." *Journal of Asian Studies* 17:3 (May 1958): 363–81.

Wright, Quincy. "The Manchurian Crisis." *American Political Science Review* 26:1 (February 1932): 45–76.

Wright, Tim. "The Manchurian Economy and the 1930s World Depression." *Modern Asian Studies* 41:5 (2007): 1073–1112.

———. "Distant Thunder: The Regional Economies of Southwest China and the Impact of the Great Depression." *Modern Asian Studies* 34:3 (July 2000): 697–738.

Yamamoto Yūzō 山本有造. "'Dai tōa kin'yūken' ron" 「大東亜金融圏」 論 (The debate about the "Greater East-Asian Finance Sphere"). *Jinbun gakuhō* 人文學報 79 (March 1997): 1–26.

———. *"Manshūkoku" keizaishi kenkyū* 「満洲国」経済史研究 (A study of the economic history of "Manchukuo"). Nagoya: Nagoya daigaku shuppankai, 2003.

———. "Shokuminchi tōji ni okeru 'dōkashugi' no kōzō: Yamanaka moderu no hihanteki kentō" 植民地統治における「同化主義」の構造：山中モデルの批判的検討 (The structure of "assimilationism" in colonial rule: a critical inquiry of the Yamanaka model). *Jinbun gakuhō* 人文學報 83 (2000): 57–73.

Yamazaki Genjirō 山崎源二郎. *Yagyū Kazuyoshi* 柳生一義. Tokyo: privately published, 1922.

Yasutomi Ayumu 安冨歩. *"Manshūkoku" no kin'yū* 「満州国」の金融 (The finance of "Manchukuo"). Tokyo: Sōbunsha, 1997.

———. "Finance in 'Manchukuo,' 1932–1945." LSE STICERD Discussion Paper No IS/98/345, January 1998.

Yi Sŏng-nyun 季碩崙. *Kankoku kahei kin'yūshi (1910 izen)* 韓国貨幣金融史 (1910 以前) (The monetary and financial history of Korea [before 1910]). Ed. Suzuki Yoshinori 鈴木芳徳, trans. Fujita Yukio 藤田幸雄. Tokyo: Hakutō shobō, 2000.

Yokohama shōkin ginkō 横浜正金銀行, ed. *Yokohama shōkin ginkōshi* 横浜正金銀行史 (The history of the Yokohama Specie Bank). Tokyo: Yokohama shōkin ginkō, 1920.

Yokoi Kaori 横井香織. "Yagyū Kazuyoshi to Taiwan ginkō no 'nanshi nanyō' chōsa" 柳生一義と台湾銀行の「南支南洋」調査 (Yagyū Kazuyoshi and the Bank of Taiwan's "southern expansion" survey). *Tōyō shihō* 東洋史訪 11 (March 2005): 35–47.

Yoshimura Michio 吉村道男 , ed. *Danshaku Megata Tanetarō* 男爵目賀田種太郎 (Biography of Baron Megata Tanetarō). Vol. 1. Tokyo: Ko Megata danshaku denki hensankai, 1938.

Young, Arthur N. *China's Nation-Building Effort, 1927–1937: The Financial and Economic Record.* Stanford, CA: Hoover Institution Press, 1971.

Young, Carl Walter. *Japan's Special Position in Manchuria.* Baltimore, MD: Johns Hopkins Press, 1931.

Young, Louise. *Japan's Total Empire: Manchuria and the Culture of Wartime Imperialism.* Berkeley, CA: University of California Press, 1998.

Zhou Xiaochuan. "Reform the International Monetary System." Online: http://www.pbc.gov.cn/english/detail.asp?col=6500&id=178 (accessed: May 26, 2010).

Glossary

Aiqian 呆錢
Amō Eiji 天羽英二
Amō seimei 天羽声明
Amur Provincial Bank 黑龍江省
　官銀号
Andong 安東
Andong *tael* 安東銀
Arai Kentarō 荒井賢太郎
Arai Seiichirō 荒井誠一郎
Atō tshūshō ginkō 亜東通商銀行
Azukari shōken 預かり証券

Banjin 蕃人
Bōeki gin 貿易銀
Bunsōteki bubi 文装的武備

Canton 広東
Cao Rulin 曹汝霖
Chabang 茶幇
Ch'ainbae 差人輩
Changchun 長春
Chiao 角
Chihō kin'yū kumiai 地方金融組合
Chongno 鐘路
Chŏnhwan'guk 典圜局
Ch'ŏnil Bank 天一銀行
Chōsen ginkō 朝鮮銀行

Chūka kaigyō ginkō 中華匯業銀行

Dai Chōsenkoku kahei jōrei 大朝鮮
　国貨幣条例
Dai tōa kin'yūken 大東亜金融圏
Dai tōa kyōeiken 大東亜共栄圏
Daiichi kokuritsu ginkō 第一国立
　銀行
Daiichiji kōtsūginkō shakkan 第一次
　交通銀行借款
Daikan ginkō 大韓銀行
Dainiji Kōtsū ginkō shakkan 第二次
　交通銀行借款
Dai niji zengo shakkan 第二次善後借
　款
Daiqian 夃錢
Dairen 大連
Dairen chūshin shugi 大連中心
　主義
Daizu keizai 大豆経済
Dayang 大洋
Dōbun dōshu 同文同種
Duan Qirui 段祺瑞

Eiseikyoku 衛生局
Engawase ken 円為替圏
Enkei tsūkaken 円系通貨圏

Esaki Masumi 江崎真澄
Eulmi Incident 乙未事変
Eum 於音 (魚驗)

Fabi 法幣
Fenghuang Iron and Steel Company 鳳凰山鉄鋼
Fengtianpiao 奉天票
Frontier Bank 邊業銀行
Fujiadian 傅家甸
Fujiwara Masafumi 藤原正文
Furyō saiken 不良債権
Fushun Coal 撫順炭鉱

Gi Manshūkoku 偽満州国
Gindate 銀建て
Gin gensōten 銀現送点
Gin kawase kanri tsūka 銀為替管理通貨
Ginkō tsūshinroku 銀行通信録
Ginkōza 銀口座
Gokuin tsuki ginka 極印付銀貨
Guantie 官帖
Guanyinhao 官銀号
Gunju kōgyō dōin hō 軍需工業動員法
Guoluyin 過爐銀
Gotō Shinpei 後藤新平
Gotō Shōjirō 後藤象二郎
Gunpyō 軍票

Hansŏng Bank 漢城銀行
Hansŏng kyōdō sōko 漢城共同倉庫
Hanyeping 漢治萍
Harbin 哈爾濱
Hayashi Gonsuke 林権助
Heilongjiang 黒龍江
Heisei oyobi kin'yū shimon iinkai 幣制および金融諮問委員会
Hikyakuya 飛脚屋

Hishida Seiji 菱田静治
Honjō gunshireikan kyakka ni teishutsu seru manshū no heisei narabi ni kin'yū ni kan suru ikensho 本庄軍司令官閣下ニ提出セル満州ノ幣制並ニ金融ニ関スル意見書
Hoshino Naoki 星野直樹
Huiduiguan 匯兌館
Hui-dui-p'iao 匯兌票

Ichihara Morihiro 市原盛宏
Ichiran barai tegata 一覧払い手形
Igarashi Yasushi 五十嵐保司
Inch'ŏn 仁川
Inoue Junnosuke 井上準之助
Inoue Kaoru 井上馨
Ippan kaikei 一般会計
Irobe Mitsugi 色部貢
Itaku hanbai 委託販売
Itō Bunkichi 伊藤文吉
Iwasaki Yanosuke 岩崎弥之助
Iwasaki Yatarō 岩崎弥太郎

Jehol notes 熱河票
Jiangsu 江蘇
Jiaozhou 膠州灣
Jigen 時言
Jiji shinpo 時事新報
Jijkyoku ni ōzuru tai-shi keizaiteki shisetsu no yōkō 時局に応ずる対支経済的施設の要綱
Jikyū jisoku keizaiken 自給自足経済圏
Jilin (Kirin) 吉林

Kahei kaigi 貨幣会議
Kaigai ginkō 海外銀行
Kaigai tokuha zaisei keizai iinkai 海外特派財政経済委員会

Kaikoku 開国

Kairai kokka 傀儡国家

Kaiyuan 開原

Kan'ei tsūhō 寛永通宝

Kanghwa treaty 江華島条約

Kankoku heisei kaikaku ni kansuru jōgansho 韓国幣制改革に関する情願書

Kankoku ginkō 韓国銀行

Kanmon 貫文

Kankoku nōkō ginkō 韓国農工銀行

Kanō Hisaakira 加納久朗

Kansen daiyō shōken 韓銭代用証券

Kansen tegata 韓銭手形

Kantōgun tōchibu 関東軍統治部

Kido Kōin (Kido Takayoshi) 木戸孝允

Kiga yushutsu 飢餓輸出

Kikkai tetsudō shakkan maekashikin 吉会鉄道借款前貸金

Kindate 金建て

Kinka hon'i 金貨本位

Kinken 金券

Kirin Yong Heng Provincial Bank 吉林永衡官銀号

Kodama Gentarō 児玉源太郎

Kōgyō Nihon / nōgyō Taiwan 工業日本／農業台湾

Koike Chōzō 小池張造

Koiso Kuniaki 小磯國昭

Kōkansho 交換所

Kokka yūkitai setsu 国家有機体説

Kokko ginkō 国庫銀行

Kokugin 黒銀

Kokusai shūshi mondai 国際収支問題

Kōmu gonen kahei jōrei 光武五年貨幣条例

Komura Jutarō 小村寿太郎

Koteikashi 固定貸

Kōtsū ginkō 交通銀行

Kuei-yuan tael 規銀元

Kuping tael 庫平両

Kye 契 (稧)

Kyŏlse 結税

Kyū kahei seiri benpō 旧貨幣整理弁法

Li Hongzhang 李鴻章

Liang Qichao 梁啓超

Liangzhan 糧桟

Liao river 遼河

Liaoning 遼寧省

Longjing 龍井村

Lüshun (Port Arthur) 旅順

Ma dayang piao 馬大洋票

Ma ti yin 馬蹄銀

Ma Zhanshan 馬占山

Mankan kōkan 満韓交換

Manmō shinkokka no heisei ni tsuite 満蒙新国家の幣制に就て

Manshū ni okeru tsūka tōitsu to Nissenman bōeki hattensaku 満州に於ける通貨統一と日鮮満貿易発展策

Manshū kōgyō ginkō 満州興業銀行

Manshūkoku 満州国 (Manchukuo/Manchoukuo)

Mantetsu 満鉄

Mantetsu keizai chōsakai 満鉄経済調査会

Masuda Nobuyuki 増田信之

Masuda Takashi 益田孝

Matsukata Masayoshi 松方正義

Matsumoto Kenjirō 松本健次郎

Matsumoto Osamu 松本修

Matsusaki Hisashi 松崎寿

Mazhenguan 媽振館

Megata Tanetarō 目賀田種太郎

Mitsui bussan 三井物産

Miura Gorō 三浦梧楼

Mizumachi Kesaroku 水町袈裟六

Motono Ichirō 本野一郎

Mugai tsūyō 無碍通用

Mukden (Fengtian) 奉天

Mukden (Fengtian) Provincial Bank
　奉天官銀号

Mukizu ichien ginka
　無傷一円銀貨

Museigen hōka 無制限法貨

Mutsu Munemitsu 陸奥宗光

Naichi 内地

Naichika 内地化

Namigawase 並為替

Nangō Tatsune 南郷龍音

Nicchō shūkōjōki 日朝修好条規

Nichigin dakanken 日銀兌換券

Nichiman heisei tōitsu no jitsugen ni
　kan suru yōkōan 日満幣制統一
　の実現に関する要綱案

Nigawase 荷為替

Nihon kōgyō ginkō
　日本興業銀行

Nijū keizai 二重経済

Nikka kyōdō bōteki gunji kyōtei
　日華共同防的軍事協定

Nishihara Kamezō 西原亀三

Nisshi keizai teikei 日支経済提携

Nisshin ginkō 日清銀行

Niuzhuang 牛荘

Oeibeg 外劃

Ōhashi Hanshichirō 大橋半七郎

Okakura Tenshin 岡倉天心

Ōkubo Toshimichi 大久保利通

Ōkuma Shigenobu 大隈重信

Ōkura Kihachirō 大蔵喜八郎

Ōmiwa Chōbei 大三輪長兵衛

Ōsaka seidō kaisha
　大阪製銅会社

Paekt'ong 白銅貨

Provincial Bank of the Eastern
　Three Provinces 東三省官銀号

Pusan 釜山

Qianzhuang 銭荘

Rinji gunjihi tokubetsu kaikei 臨時軍事
　費特別会計

Rinji shikin chōsei hō 臨時資金
　調整法

Rinji Taiwan kyūkan chōsakai 臨時
　台湾旧慣調査会

Saigō Takamori 西郷隆盛

Sakaguchi Takenosuke 坂口竹之助

Sakatani Yoshirō (Yoshio) 阪谷
　芳郎

Sangp'yŏng t'ongbo 常平通宝

Seikanron 征韓論

Seikan suiriku bōeki shōtei 清韓
　水陸貿易章程

Senji keizai dōin keikaku shigi 戦時
　経済動員計画私儀

Senman ittaika 鮮満一体化

Shandong 山東

Shantou 汕頭

Shenhui 申匯

Shibusawa Eiichi 渋沢栄一

Shidehara Kijūrō 幣原喜重郎

Shimosaka Fujitarō 下坂藤太郎

Shina kanzei mondai to Nihon 支那
　関税問題と日本

Shinchitsujo 新秩序

Shinkoku seifu yūdenbu 清国政府
　郵伝部

Shinozaki Yoshirō 篠崎嘉郎

Shinshiki kahei hakkō shōtei 新式
　貨幣発行章程

Shōda Kazue 勝田主計

Shōhyō 鈔票

Shōken 証券

Shutō Masatoshi 首藤正寿

Sipingjieh 四平街

Sitie 私帖

Sō 宗

Sōdanyaku 相談役

Sogin 粗銀

Sōritsu iinkai 創立委員会

Suzuki Kiyoshi 鈴木穆

Sycee 銀錠

Taipei shōkō danwakai 台北商工
談話会

Tai-Shi seisaku no yōtei 対支政策
の要諦

Taiwan heisei kaikaku ni kansuru
iken 台湾幣制改革に関する
意見

Taiwan sōtokufu tokubetsu kaikei hō
台湾総督府特別会計法

Takahashi Korekiyo 高橋是清

Tegata kumiai 手形組合

Ten'yū 天祐

Terauchi Masatake 寺内正毅

Tianjin 天津

Tianjin treaty 天津条約

Tiao 吊

Tie yingtzu 帖(銀)子

Tiehling 鐵嶺

Tōa meishu ron 東亞盟主論

Tokubetsu kashitsuke 特別貸付

Tokumubu daiichi iinkai 特務部
第一委員会

Tokushu ginkō 特殊銀行

Tōkyō keizai zasshi
東京経済雑誌

Tomita Tetsunosuke
富田鉄之助

Tōyō eien no heiwasaku 東洋永遠
の平和策

Tōyō jikyūken 東洋自給圏

Tōyō keizai shinpō
東洋経済新報

Tōyō kōro kakuchō oyobi
Nisshinkan kin'yū kikan ni
kansuru ikensho
東洋航路拡張及び日清間金融
機関に関する意見書

Tōyō takushoku gaisha 東洋拓殖
会社

Tsushima 対馬

Uchibu 打歩

Ŭijŏngbu 議政部

Un'yō 雲揚

Wang dao 王道

Wonsan 元山

Xiamen 廈門 (Amoy)

Xinji 信局

Yagyū Kazuyoshi 柳生一義

Yalu river 鴨緑江

Yamanari Kyōroku
山成喬六

Yamashita Yoshitarō
山下芳太郎

Yangban 兩斑

Yangqian 洋錢

Yasuda Zenjirō 安田善次郎

Yasumatsu Morinosuke
安松盛之助

Yingkou 営口

Yōgin 洋銀

Yokinbu 預金部

Yoneyama Umekichi
米山梅吉

Yŏpchŏn 葉錢

Yuan Shikai 袁世凱

Yūsen denshin shakkan 有線電信
借款

Zaisei komonbu
　財政顧問部
Zeikan tegata 税関手形
Zeimukanbu 税務監部
Zhang Xueliang 張学良
Zhang Zhuolin 張作霖

Zhao Xiaochuan 周小川
Zheng Chenggong (Koxinga)
　鄭成功
Zhenping Yin 鎮平銀
Zhili 直隸
zōhei ekikin 造幣益金

Index

Harvard East Asian Monographs
(*out-of-print)

Harvard East Asian Monographs

Harvard East Asian Monographs

Harvard East Asian Monographs

Harvard East Asian Monographs